Tony Butcher

D0862679

SAMS
Teach Yourself
MySQL
in 21 Days

SECOND EDITION

SAMS

201 West 103rd St., Indianapolis, Indiana, 46290 USA

Sams Teach Yourself MySQL in 21 Days, Second Edition

Copyright © 2003 by Sams Publishing

International Standard Book Number: 0-672-32392-3

Library of Congress Catalog Card Number: 2002104733

Printed in the United States of America

First Printing: December 2002

05 04 03 02   4 3 2 1

Trademarks

All terms mentioned in this book that are known to be trademarks or service marks have been appropriately capitalized. Sams Publishing cannot attest to the accuracy of this information. Use of a term in this book should not be regarded as affecting the validity of any trademark or service mark.

Warning and Disclaimer

Every effort has been made to make this book as complete and as accurate as possible, but no warranty or fitness is implied. The information provided is on an "as is" basis. The authors and the publisher shall have neither liability nor responsibility to any person or entity with respect to any loss or damages arising from the information contained in this book.

ACQUISITIONS EDITOR
Shelley Johnston

DEVELOPMENT EDITOR
Damon Jordan

MANAGING EDITOR
Charlotte Clapp

PROJECT EDITOR
Matthew Purcell

COPY EDITOR
Geneil Breeze

INDEXER
Erika Millen

PROOFREADER
Leslie Joseph

TECHNICAL EDITOR
Chris Newman

TEAM COORDINATOR
Amy Patton

MULTIMEDIA DEVELOPER
Dan Scherf

INTERIOR DESIGNER
Gary Adair

COVER DESIGNER
Aren Howell

PAGE LAYOUT
Ayanna Lacey

GRAPHICS
Steve Adams
Tammy Graham
Oliver Jackson
Laura Robbins

Contents at a Glance

Contents

About the Author

Tony Butcher is a consultant for Tribal Internet. The company develops database-driven Web sites using MySQL, with PHP and other languages. He also takes on specialist MySQL consulting work and has installed, developed, repaired and tuned MySQL systems for over five years.

Having first encountered MySQL in 1997, he quickly recognised it as a powerful tool for enterprise-level systems. Since then has he used it in several mission-critical, heavy-load online databases.

Tony is an occasional contributor to newspapers and trade magazines, writing on various topics relating to computing and the Internet. He also co-authored the first edition of this book.

Dedication

Foe Clarisse and Jasper

Acknowledgments

I would like to thank my wife Dorte, who made this book possible in many ways. Several years ago she gave me confidence to do what I wanted to do: to write. Without that spark, this book wouldn't have been written. In the course of writing these chapters, she encouraged, supported and tolerated me, and all this while bearing us a son. My thanks go to my young children for putting up with my absence, because "Daddy's working."

I'd like to thank my team at Tribal Internet for their support while I have been distracted from my day-job. They've shown commitment and dedication while I wasn't around to help.

To my parents and my friends, I have to say Thanks for being there for me (even though I haven't been there for them for too long).

I would like to thank the folks at MySQL AB, who apart from producing an excellent product have helped me make sure the content of this book is accurate.

Finally, I'd like to thank Shelley Johnston and the team at Sams Publishing for their guidance and for making the writing of this book enjoyable.

We Want to Hear from You!

As the reader of this book, *you* are our most important critic and commentator. We value your opinion and want to know what we're doing right, what we could do better, what areas you'd like to see us publish in, and any other words of wisdom you're willing to pass our way.

You can email or write me directly to let me know what you did or didn't like about this book—as well as what we can do to make our books stronger.

Please note that I cannot help you with technical problems related to the topic of this book, and that due to the high volume of mail I receive, I might not be able to reply to every message.

When you write, please be sure to include this book's title and author as well as your name and phone or email address. I will carefully review your comments and share them with the author and editors who worked on the book.

Email: outsource@samspublishing.com

Mail: Mark Taber
           Associate Publisher
           Sams Publishing
           201 West 103rd Street
           Indianapolis, IN 46290 USA

Reader Services

For more information about this book or others from Sams Publishing, visit our Web site at www.samspublishing.com. Type the ISBN (excluding hyphens) or the title of the book in the Search box to find the book you're looking for.

Introduction

Since the idea of a relational database management system (RDBMS) was conceived in the early 1970s, databases have evolved from being ways to store data electronically to cornerstones of many business operations.

Whether an RDBMS is used as a data warehouse or as a means of accessing key information rapidly, so useful are these systems that they are now integrated into the workflow of almost every organization. In many cases, an RDBMS is an organization's most valuable intangible asset.

The proliferation of Internet usage by organizations and individuals has made databases more important—and powerful—than ever before. When a database is accessible over the Internet or a company intranet, things become possible that never were before.

Any Web site of at least moderate complexity—whether it has an online store, a searchable directory, a discussion forum, or a content management system—employs a database. On the World Wide Web, data constantly flows from databases in response to user queries and activities, and those same databases log activity, purchases, and visitor information.

Online databases are seldom treated as stale repositories. They are more like living entities whose veins pulse with information. They are always connected, always being used, and never turned off.

Over the years, the architecture of computing has changed. After the dumb-terminal and large-mainframe era of the 1970s and early 1980s, PCs appeared. Being inexpensive, PCs proliferated, and mainframes became obsolete in most applications. With them databases were transformed from centralized systems to small databases on every desktop. But from an information standpoint, this was not entirely a good thing.

The affordability of PCs brought the power of a relational database to millions of desktops. But the ease of creating databases meant that in many organizations "information islands" were created. Just as one user created a standalone database—easily, and with an attractive front-end, using a tool such as Access or FileMaker—so another user in the same organization created a similar database to hold the same information.

The duplication of effort and of information is not difficult to see. Little surprise then, that as the Internet and other localized networks extend their tendrils into every corner of every organization, the paradigm is now shifting again. The wisdom of the centralized model is shifting data back toward centralized storage, but now with far more adaptability than before.

One benefit of this is that network-enabled organizations no longer need to keep information solely for the eyes of trusted employees; they can make selected information—product brochures, airline timetables, price lists—available to customers who remain anonymous, and who are anywhere on the planet.

Big databases have been expensive things. Some of the richest companies in the world were created out of the database business. What's more, people expect them to be costly. But this book is about a database that can you can get for free.

How can it be *free*?

The answer is that it's *open source*. The open source phenomenon means that this database, and thousands of other software products, are available for download and use without charge.

The philosophy behind open source software is fundamentally different from closed-source commercial software. Whereas most paid-for software relies on the secrecy of its source code and the value of intellectual capital invested in it, open source products can be downloaded and used for free, and thus enjoy rapid deployment and use by many users.

The "free" concept needs some explanation: Open source software is normally made available under the GNU Public License (GPL), and this means that the programs can be downloaded and used for free, provided that the terms of the license are adhered to. In simple terms, the GPL enables open source software to be used without charge, for any purpose, but restricts a developer's right to redistribute the open source code in another application that is a closed-source package. The GPL lets you use the open source product, but prevents you from trying to sell your own product that makes use of it, unless you either comply with the GPL or pay for a non-GPL commercial license.

There's often a profit-making business behind an open source product. Such companies just have a different business model from software vendors that rely on their code staying secret. An open source business has to earn its income in ways other than selling software. Their revenue comes from support and professional services for their products, from selling enhancements to the basic product, from selling licenses for onward distribution, and by facilitating the sales of hardware or other products or services.

Can open source software be trusted? A common assumption is that anything that's free can't be very good, so is it wise to rely on open source software for mission-critical applications?

The transparency of being able to read source code means that bugs, enhancements, and other issues are discussed publicly on mailing lists and Web discussion boards. If a product is buggy, it will quickly be uncovered as such. Under scrutiny like this, a product that continues to be used, discussed, fixed, and enhanced can quickly evolve to have exceptionally high qualities—of reliability, stability, security, and performance.

Linux, Apache, Perl, PHP, gcc (the GNU C compiler), to name but a few, are all open source products that have had enormous success. Despite commercial competition, Apache is the most widely used Web server on the Internet, and Linux continues to rise in popularity as a rock-solid server platform. To uncover many more, you only need to visit Web sites such as Sourceforge (http://www.sourceforge.net/) or Freshmeat (http://www.freshmeat.net/). And of course, another such open source product is MySQL.

MySQL

Back in the 1990s when the Swedish consultancy TcX had a business problem that they couldn't solve with other databases in existence at the time, they created their own and called it MySQL.

TcX made MySQL freely downloadable, and because of this and because the product worked well, MySQL rose in popularity. It gained a reputation among database developers for its speed, compactness, simplicity, and reliability. Several years later, MySQL is the world's most popular open source RDBMS, with as many as 27,000 downloads reported per day, and an estimated four million installations around the world.

The MySQL product is now owned by MySQL AB, a company formed in 2001 to take over the product from TcX. Although still fully behind the open source principle, MySQL AB's business model is now aligned behind consultancy, support, and the sales of licenses. Paid-for licensing (as opposed to GPL) applies when MySQL is compiled and distributed within other applications.

This is a noteworthy business model: It demonstrates that developing high-quality open source software and allowing it to be used for free can create a renowned and profitable business.

At a technical level, MySQL is a full-fledged relational database management system, ideally suited to run as a server in a high-volume, mission-critical environment. MySQL's developers claim it is the fastest database you can currently get—equal to or better than any database that you have to pay for—and independent tests have backed up this claim. A number of MySQL AB's own benchmark comparisons are available at http://www.mysql.com/information/benchmarks.html, and the same Web site also has links to third-party independent tests.

MySQL is easy to install, small in disk usage, and easy to administer. It uses ANSI-standard SQL92 (American National Standards Institute Structured Query Language), making it compatible with other mainstream database systems.

The server runs *multithreaded*; this means that it allows connections from multiple clients at once. It also has a full suite of security features that allow careful and precise allocation of user privileges.

Perhaps most important of all, it runs on just about any operating system that exists. Although developed initially on the Linux platform, it runs happily on all types of Windows operating systems as well as on Mac OS X and commercial varieties of Unix.

MySQL is supported in many ways. This book will show you how to do this yourself: You'll see how to perform its installation, run queries, administer and repair databases, connect to MySQL from other applications, even add to its function library and embed a copy of the database server in new pieces of software you might write. But if you need extra support—and most commercial users will demand that commercial support be available—you can purchase this from MySQL AB and its support partners around the world. More informally, MySQL is supported via discussion forums on the Internet and via the detailed MySQL Technical Reference manual, which is distributed in electronic form from the MySQL Web site as a free download.

For these reasons, MySQL can hold its own in both technical and commercial terms when compared with big-name products such as Oracle, Microsoft SQL Server, IBM DB2, Sybase, and others. When you consider that MySQL can be used for free, the argument is too compelling to ignore.

It's therefore little wonder that MySQL has emerged from the relatively obscure world of developers and software-dabblers into the spotlight of mainstream organizations around the world. All kinds of end-user companies are studying it, testing it, and talking about it, and many are already using it in earnest in situations critical to their business.

How This Book Is Organized

In this book, you will learn how to use MySQL in 21 days. Over the course of three weeks, with one lesson each day, you will gradually increase your knowledge of MySQL to an advanced standard.

In the first week you will look at the basic principles of what MySQL is, how to install it and start using it, how to create a database, and how to define tables and get data into them:

- Day 1, "Introduction to MySQL," explains the background of MySQL and the open source movement from which it comes, briefly covers the principles of licensing, and looks at MySQL's main features.
- Day 2, "Installing MySQL," shows you how to install MySQL on the most common platforms.
- Day 3, "Getting Started with Database Design," describes ways of analyzing real-world business problems and designing relational databases to solve them.
- Day 4, "Getting Hands-On with MySQL," is designed to give you a feel for MySQL and to make you comfortable running simple SQL queries and commands.
- Day 5, "MySQL Data Types," describes how data is represented in MySQL and the column types available for storing information.
- Day 6, "Manipulating a Database," deals with how to perform actions at a database and table level, such as creating and modifying databases and tables.
- Day 7, "Inserting and Updating Data," shows you how to insert data into tables, and how to update data after it is already in them.

The second week shows how to query a MySQL database, explains how to use MySQL with a number of APIs, and goes into the details of the MySQL security system:

- Day 8, "Querying Data," explains how to run queries that extract data from a database.
- Day 9, "Joins and Indexes," follows on from Day 8 and shows you how to run queries that extract data from several tables at once using joins. It also shows you how to apply indexes to impose constraints on data, and to improve the performance of queries.
- Day 10, "Operators and Functions in MySQL," gives you a sample of the many operators and functions you can use to do arithmetic and string operations, to process date and time information, and to perform queries that aggregate data.
- Day 11, "Using PHP," gives you a quick tutorial on PHP, a popular scripting language for dynamic Web sites, and shows you how to use it to run queries on MySQL databases.
- Day 12, "Using the Perl DBI," shows you how to use Perl, a powerful language found on almost all Unix-type systems, to interface with MySQL.
- Day 13, "Using the C API," is for C programmers and shows how to use this language to interface with MySQL.
- Day 14, "Security," explains MySQL's security systems, including its powerful user permissions system.

The final seven days get progressively more advanced, showing you how to administer MySQL and then dealing with a range of topics relevant for those running mission-critical systems and software developers:

- Day 15, "Administration," deals with a wide range of administrative tools, such as utilities for controlling the MySQL server's operation and performing database backups.

- Day 16, "Repair and Maintenance," shows you how to deal with a corrupted database and how to perform checking and optimization tasks.

- Day 17, "Transactions and Table Locking," shows you how to perform transaction-safe operations in MySQL, first by using locks and then by using InnoDB, the transaction-safe table handler that has recently been implemented in MySQL.

- Day 18, "Optimizing Performance," describes a number of techniques for making your database run faster. It illustrates how the use of indexes and table and query design can improve performance, and shows some techniques for measuring performance and determining the effectiveness of a database design.

- Day 19, "Replication," explains how MySQL can be used as the basis of mission-critical or load-balanced systems. It shows you how to set up a master-slave replicating pair so that you can set up your own replicating system.

- Day 20, "Embedding the MySQL Server," shows you how to embed a MySQL database server in another software application, thus allowing you to deliver a MySQL-powered application in a single binary. It also explains the GPL and commercial license system, and when each type of license applies.

- Day 21, "Extending MySQL's Function Library," explains how to add to MySQL's already-extensive function library, by writing your own functions.

Who Should Read This Book

This book is aimed at the developer who has at least some knowledge of relational databases and SQL. If you're familiar with a database such as Access, but you're not familiar with SQL, you should still be able to benefit; however, you may find it helpful to pick up a text on SQL to read as an accompaniment to this book.

You should know at least one programming language, although it doesn't have to be one of those covered here, namely C, PHP, and Perl. This book's coverage of PHP is "from the ground up," so as long as you know the principles of coding, you should be able to use PHP and its API. However, the greatest benefit will be had by those who already have experience in at least one of these languages and by developers who are comfortable running SQL queries and administering a database server.

This book tries to find a low common denominator among its readers. It even explains a few fundamental principles of databases, although it deals with most elementary teachings as succinctly as possible to avoid the boredom of a reader who already knows these things.

This book is aimed unashamedly at the Linux user. Admittedly, there are a considerable number of Windows-based MySQL users. However, MySQL was developed first for the open source platform, and this is arguably the environment in which it works best and is most adaptable. Therefore most examples are shown on a Linux platform, but where there are differences for the Windows platform, these will be explained so that Windows users are not left behind.

Conventions Used in This Book

When a new term is introduced, it will be named in *italics*. A description or explanation will then follow.

When the name of a command, a program, a file, or a directory is given, it will be given in a `monospaced` font. Examples of this will be SQL commands such as `SELECT` or programs such as `mysqladmin`.

The definition of a piece of syntax will be given like this:

```
SELECT column1, column2 FROM table
```

In syntax such as this, words such as `SELECT` are presented in monospaced font so that you can see the actual words that comprise the command. However, words such as `column1` represent placeholders, which will be replaced by a word specific to your system when you use the command. So in this example, `column1` might be replaced by, say, `customer_name` when you apply the `SELECT` command in practice.

When defining syntax, brackets `[ ]` will be used to denote an optional section of code. The pipe, or bar, symbol | will be used to show you where one piece of code or another can be used, with the relevant section enclosed by brackets `[ ]` if it is optional, or braces `{}` if one of the choices is mandatory.

So you may see this sort of thing:

```
command  and_a_placeholder {either_this | or_this} [maybe_this | maybe_that]
```

You may see things like `command` given in lowercase or UPPERCASE; you'll generally see SQL commands written in UPPERCASE, and other things, such as program names, written in lowercase. If you're allowed to use upper- or lowercase in a given situation, it will be noted that you can, but otherwise follow the case shown in the syntax to ensure correct operation.

Where an interaction is being described, the part that is typed by you will be given in **bold**. So an interaction may look like this:

```
mysql> SELECT * FROM mytable;
```

In this example, `mysql>` is the prompt you will see on the screen, whereas the words starting with `SELECT` until the end of the words in bold are what you must type.

You will encounter the Unix prompt for the `root` user, looking like this:

```
#
```

and the prompt for non-`root` users looking like this:

```
$
```

In either case, it indicates that you can type something after the prompt, the words you see in bold:

```
$ type this
```

After a line such as this, you will normally see some lines that are non-bold; this is output representative of what you should expect, like this:

```
This is the output.
```

The text will be interspersed with information that is helpful at the time.

Note

A Note includes useful, interesting, or important information that relates to the surrounding text.

Caution

A Caution is used to highlight a potential danger, or is a note that stresses something you must do with extreme care to avoid problems.

Tip

A Tip includes a piece of advice on how to do something in an easier way.

Finally, every lesson (except for Day 1) will be concluded with a Q&A section with answers to common questions, a Quiz of short questions to test your knowledge, and Exercises for you to do. By reading these things and tackling the Quiz and Exercises, you will confirm what you have learned before moving on to the next lesson.

Week 1

At a Glance

Day

1

2

3

4

5

6

7

WEEK 1

DAY 1

Introduction to MySQL

Today you will take a quick tour of MySQL, gaining an overview of the product, the philosophy, and the company behind it.

You will learn:

- What MySQL is
- The key features of MySQL
- The commercial aspects of MySQL

What Is MySQL?

MySQL is the world's most popular open source relational database management system (RDBMS). It has every quality to be an RDBMS for business but, unlike its rivals, can be used for free under the GNU General Public License (GPL).

MySQL—pronounced "my-ess-queue-ell"—takes its name from SQL, the language for database querying developed by IBM. The "My" is said to come from the name of the daughter, My, of MySQL's Finnish designer, Michael "Monty" Widenius.

MySQL has a history stretching back over 10 years. It was conceived when Monty and TcX, the Swedish consultancy for which he worked, were looking for a database system to solve particular business problems for TCX's customers. They tried using a similar database product called mSQL, but found it couldn't quite do the job. So they created a new system and called it MySQL.

MySQL had some similarities with mSQL and retains some of them today, though these are mostly for compatibility. Apart from that, MySQL has a heritage all its own.

Although MySQL was written by the developers of TcX to provide solutions for their customers, it was made available as open source software. It evolved rapidly and gained a reputation among the developer community for its robustness, speed, and ease of use. Because MySQL was open source, developers enjoyed the ease with which they could apply it and adapt it to all sorts of database uses, and without having to pay for it.

More recently, things have stepped up a gear. The company MySQL AB was formed (*AB* being the Swedish form of "incorporated" or "limited company"). Privately owned, MySQL AB owns the source code and the MySQL trademark. In 2001, the company received venture capital backing, appointed a CEO, and watched its employees grow in numbers, in several countries. MySQL as a product emerged from the relative obscurity of the open source world and stepped into the broader commercial limelight.

The product now boasts an estimated four million installations worldwide, with around 27,000 downloads from the MySQL Web site per day. MySQL is the *de facto* open source database leader and is quickly becoming the database behind many high-volume, business-critical applications. Major corporations such as Yahoo!, Motorola, NASA, Silicon Graphics, Hewlett Packard, Xerox, and Cisco rely on it because of its high speed and high reliability.

MySQL as a Relational Database Management System

What do we mean by *relational database management system*, or even *database* for that matter?

A *database* is a suite of structured files on a computer that are organized in such a way that information can be accessed in a structured manner. It's difficult to go to the bank, shop at a store, or surf the World Wide Web without encountering a database. Databases are efficient storage houses of information that can make information available in just about any way imaginable.

The particular kind of database we're interested in here is a *relational database*, though there are other kinds. The relational database model was developed by E. F. Codd in the early 1970s. Although databases at the time were typically just hierarchical file systems—highly inefficient and difficult to manage—the relational model changed the way information was structured.

Relational databases comprise one or more *tables*, which themselves are two-dimensional matrices consisting of *rows* and *columns*. A row of data is often called a *record*, and where that row intersects with a column, there is a *field*.

What makes a database *relational* is the capability to cross-reference between data in one table and data in another. Access to the tables and their data, whether to a single table or several, is made possible by *queries*. Queries are executed by the relational database management system.

A database *management system* is a different thing from a database. It's the system that makes a database appear out of what's essentially just a bunch of files on a computer disk. It creates a "window" through which you can look, making those files look like structured information. It runs queries on the tables, putting data in and getting data out.

But more than that, such a system *manages* a database, or indeed several databases. This means more than just processing queries: It implies a system doing many more tasks, such as controlling access to databases, performing administration tasks, logging activity, and managing runtime resources such as memory and disk usage.

Fundamental Features of MySQL

MySQL has all the features of a relational database management system. Let's look a little closer at what it can do.

MySQL is a database *server* (though it does come with a number of simple client programs). It is typically used in *thin client* environments. In other words, it is used in client-server systems where the bulk of the processing and storage takes place on the server, and the client is little more than a dumb terminal. Although dumb terminals were the norm in the 1970s and 80s, they drifted out of popularity with the advent of the personal computer. However, they are again in vogue, with Web browsers such as Netscape and Microsoft Internet Explorer being the ubiquitous faces of thin clients at the beginning of the 21st century.

Importantly, MySQL performs multithreaded processing, which means that it allows multiple clients to connect to it and run queries simultaneously. This makes it extremely fast and well suited to client-server environments such as Web sites and other environments that process numerous transactions for multiple users.

MySQL features a user permissions system, with which it can control users' access to any number of its databases. So sophisticated is the system that few competing RDBMSs can match its levels of security and the granularity to which user permissions can be set.

Recent developments have also added the capability for MySQL to handle encrypted connections, and SSL (Secure Sockets Layer) and X509 certification can be used to protect data in transit as it passes between server and client.

MySQL competes with other products such as Oracle, Sybase, DB2, and Microsoft SQL Server. They are all relational database servers. However, products such as Microsoft Access and Filemaker are quite different. They are still databases but concentrate their processing on the client front-end; although they come in shareable versions, they lack the management systems that are a key part of a true RDBMS, such as the control of user access and multithreaded processing capability.

The Benefit of Being Open Source

Although MySQL is developed by a commercial operation, it is freely downloadable and usable as open source software.

Open source doesn't simply mean "free"—we'll look at MySQL from a commercial perspective in a moment—there's more to the philosophy than that. By being open source, MySQL has an inherent degree of transparency and adaptability not present in closed-source products.

A few people—particularly among those who are used to buying software from a large commercial vendor—think that open source products let hackers find the holes in the system and exploit them. They assume that because of this, open source products are less secure.

The first part of this understanding is absolutely true, but the assumption is wrong. It's true to say that security holes can become apparent far earlier in the life of a product when it's open source; this is because its source code can be read and analyzed, and vulnerabilities easily spotted. But precisely because of this transparency, any weakness quickly gets fed back to the developers who can react to eliminate the problem.

The Web is busy with people installing, applying, and testing open source products, and those same people feed their questions and experiences into public newsgroups and discussion forums. Any weakness in an open source product quickly becomes known—and when it does, it gets talked about in a big way, and the developers notice. Some users even fix the problem themselves and in turn make the code available for integration with the original product.

There's just no chance of covering up a minor problem, let alone a security flaw! The developer of the product has no choice but to incorporate a fix as quickly as possible. Contrast this with products where the source code—sometimes even the specifications of file format or functionality—is unavailable to outsiders. Only a small band of in-house developers have access to this information, yet they would be in the best position to identify problems. Bugs can therefore take longer to come to light and be fixed, and when a security flaw affects many users, the effect can be catastrophic.

Tip

For more information on the philosophy behind open source software, read the seminal book *The Cathedral and the Bazaar* by Eric S. Raymond.

You may find the Free Software Foundation's definition of *free software* interesting reading. The Foundation's Web site can be found at `http://www.fsf.org/`, and its description of the term *free software* is at `http://www.fsf.org/philosophy/free-sw.html`.

A Solution for Business

Business problems usually require solutions that are upgradable to cope with changing needs. A rip-and-replace product is largely unsatisfactory, even if the product that replaces the obsolete system is from the same vendor. MySQL responds to these demands by having adaptability in many ways.

MySQL is highly scalable. It can be run on a single-user desktop machine, or it can be run on a server for access by millions of clients.

And it doesn't stop there: Newer versions of MySQL support *replication*. This means that a whole suite of servers can run in concert, with client requests being shared among them and the servers working together to feed each other data. By doing this, MySQL satisfies the needs of high-volume transaction processing environments, such as ISPs, banks, and retailers.

Replication also provides a further benefit: high availability for mission-critical applications. Distributing user queries across multiple servers not only balances server load, but also builds more robustness into the system. With geographical dispersal of servers connected via the Internet, it is possible to build a system that is virtually unbreakable.

MySQL can also adapt to unusual and specialist demands. Any developer can add to MySQL's function library without difficulty; this extendibility is a key part of the MySQL philosophy. MySQL's code can also be changed at a more fundamental level to suit particular requirements. Contrast this with closed-source products, where such adaptability is out of the question, and only the vendor can add a new core feature to its software.

MySQL can be run on just about any platform that exists. It runs on all types of Unix, including Solaris, IBM-AIX, Irix, and HP-UX to name but a few; on all flavors of Linux and BSD; on Windows 95, 98, Me, NT, 2000, and XP; on Mac OS X; and on Amiga. You can therefore run it on just about anything from a simple Windows desktop PC to multiprocessor server hardware running Unix or Linux.

What if there's a platform you want to use that's not listed here, such as an old operating system, a mobile device, or an embedded system? Quite possibly MySQL will run: The answer is, try it! Where a precompiled MySQL binary isn't available, you can simply compile the source code for your platform.

Application-level interfaces to MySQL are many and varied. Connecting from a Unix-type system is easy, with languages such as C and PHP having connectivity built-in, and Perl and Java needing only the addition of an API. If your application can't connect directly, you can use ODBC to connect from products such as Filemaker and Access, and from programs made using development tools such as Visual Basic.

What about interoperability? If you start to use MySQL, can you still use other databases alongside it? MySQL doesn't force you to be MySQL-only. You can run MySQL along-side databases from other vendors, and this is true both in terms of the applications you run and data storage.

MySQL uses an SQL language that complies with the ANSI-92 standard for SQL (with a few minor omissions and some small extensions), so you should be able to pick up your application code and switch its SQL queries from your old database to MySQL with minimal changes.

 Note

> The ANSI is the American National Standards Institute. The correct term for the SQL standard is ANSI SQL92, which was agreed on in 1992 and defines a standard for SQL (Structured Query Language). This is the baseline standard for the language used by all major RDBMSs.
>
> There is also an ANSI SQL99 standard (from 1999), which the developers of MySQL are working toward.

But changing to MySQL is not a one-way street: You can pick up code written for MySQL and run it on something else, again with minimal change. Although MySQL uses its own formats for data storage, you can import and export with ease, with MySQL recognizing a wide range of data formats.

> **Tip**
>
> If you want to know the differences in functionality between MySQL and your existing database system, you can use the Crash-Me comparison Web page, at `http://www.mysql.com/information/crash-me.php`. This lets you compare two database systems and gives detailed information about what one product lacks or has in addition, compared with the other.

Are there things missing from MySQL? Yes, a few features of other databases are missing at the time of writing (the version described in this book is 4.0.2).

Most notably, subselects (the capability to run a SELECT query on the resultset of another SELECT query, in a single SQL statement) are not yet available, though probably will be by the time you read this.

Views, stored procedures, and triggers are also not available at the time of writing, but features such as these are specialist requirements rather than ordinary database needs. There's hardly an application that cannot be written without them, and they are generally demanded by large-system people who want to port a system to MySQL without any change in their application code.

MySQL as a realistic business offering is developing fast. Transaction-safe tables, perceived as an important omission for many business systems, have been incorporated into MySQL using the InnoDB table type, and replication is now fully implemented for the demands of load-balanced or high-availability systems, with even more functionality due in the forthcoming releases.

Another new dimension that has been opened up recently is the capability for MySQL to be compiled into another piece of software; it can be used as an "embedded server" and therefore lets you compile an entire MySQL database server into another system. You could distribute the software, perhaps an application that you install on a Windows PC and double-click to start, without the end user ever needing to know that at its heart is a MySQL database.

As you can see, things that even one or two years ago were minor omissions have now been made standard features, or are due to be incorporated in the near future.

The Commercial View of MySQL

MySQL is an open source product and is available under the GNU Public License (GPL). Because of this, you can download MySQL and immediately start using it for free.

Under the GPL, can use MySQL for free on anything from your own desktop PC to a Web server with millions of visitors. Even if you're an ISP offering MySQL as a tool for Web site developers, you don't have to pay anything for it.

However, there are scenarios in which MySQL must be paid for. If you compile any part of the MySQL software into another application and distribute it, you must purchase a commercial license. A recent development is the capability to compile MySQL into an application as an embedded server; to distribute such a MySQL-powered application, you must pay a license fee per copy distributed.

Note
> For information about the GNU Public License, visit http://www.gnu.org/licenses/gpl.html. You will also learn about the details of GPL and commercial licensing in Day 20, "Embedding the MySQL Server," and you can read more about it on the MySQL Web site at http://www.mysql.com/support/arrangements.html.

The embedded server concept is a key thing in two ways: From a technological perspective, it means that we may encounter MySQL in anything from Windows applications to telephones, or even smart fridges that keep a note of their contents! But in commercial terms, it means that MySQL AB can align itself behind MySQL as a commercial product that generates revenue from licensing.

This is good for us, as users or developers. Although MySQL will still be free for many purposes, software authors who integrate MySQL into their own software and make it available for sale will, quite fairly, pay for each copy they're distributing. And by having a revenue stream feeding back to MySQL AB, it means that MySQL will be alive, well, and getting even better for a long time to come.

So for companies thinking of using MySQL—this brilliant, free product—why else would they hold back? A fundamental worry for them is support. It's easy for developers to tinker with new products without fear of commercial risk, but any corporation investing millions in a new computer system will want to make sure that it's going to get backup when needed, and not find itself landed with technology whose development has ceased and nobody wants to support.

Companies used to buying software from big-ticket software vendors are the ones with the greatest fear of this, when taking their first steps into open source. They need to know that the people who produce their systems will be there to back them up, fix bugs in the product, and keep enhancing it. Although a lot of open source software relies on rather informal networks of people to support and maintain the software, MySQL AB is making sure that support is available to a corporate standard, including 24*7 telephone support, training, and consultancy services. MySQL AB is also developing a network of partners around the world who offer the same services.

For these reasons, MySQL is not just a technologist's product; it is a viable product for business with strong arguments in its favor. Apart from equaling or even surpassing big-name database products in technical merit, MySQL is fast acquiring the commercial respectability needed to persuade mainstream business that it is an outstanding solution for the enterprise.

Summary

Today you were introduced to MySQL: what it is, where it came from, and what its principal features are.

You've learned the principles of how it runs—an open source, multithreaded, business-quality relational database management system. Although it can be used for free under the GNU Public License, it is a product that holds its own against the databases of big-name software vendors.

Q&A

Q If MySQL is free, how can the company that makes it exist?

A MySQL is open source; it's not quite the same thing as "free." There's more to the business model, which is important to understand.

MySQL can be used without charge under the GNU Public License. This freedom of use benefits both users and the product itself because it becomes widely used and accepted, as well as becoming thoroughly tested in a wide range of environments. MySQL's easy availability has led to there being thousands of people around the world who participate, directly or indirectly, in the continual improvement of the software.

The availability of MySQL under a commercial non-GPL license means that there is a revenue stream to MySQL AB from developers who are embedding and distributing the product in their applications. You will learn more about the principles of licensing in Day 20.

MySQL AB also has other revenue streams, including consultancy, support, and training.

Q How much does it actually cost to license MySQL?

A If you're distributing the embedded server, you must pay per copy you distribute. You will find commercial details on the MySQL Web site at `http://www.mysql.com/`.

DAY 2

Installing MySQL

Today you will learn how to install MySQL. This lesson covers installation on Linux and Unix, Windows, and Mac OS X.

In the course of today's lesson, you will encounter several new programs, notably the `mysql` console program and the `mysqladmin` administration program. The instructions require you to use these programs to get started, but these are powerful programs that need deeper coverage. You'll therefore learn about them more thoroughly in later lessons.

Today, you will learn:

- How to install MySQL on Linux, Windows, and Mac OS X
- How to stop and start the MySQL server
- How to start the MySQL server automatically at system boot time

Installation Overview

You will first need to download the appropriate distribution of MySQL, and this is explained in the next section. You should then study whichever section is appropriate for your operating system to install MySQL.

Downloading MySQL

To download MySQL, go to the official Web site at `http://www.mysql.com/` and follow the link to `Downloads`. You may want to follow the link to `Mirrors` to find a mirror site near you: this reduces Internet traffic and can speed up download time.

Along with the MySQL software, you may also want to download the MySQL Technical Reference. This highly detailed document covers the intricacies of installation and possible problems you may encounter, as well as the use of MySQL. The MySQL developers do a good job of keeping this up-to-date with the software releases, so you should find that any recent patches or new features are covered in it.

You'll need to decide which version of MySQL to download. If you're planning to use MySQL in a production environment, you'll want a stable release. If you're feeling more adventurous and want to experiment with the latest features, you could download the latest Beta or even Alpha code. These versions have been tested by the MySQL developers but have undergone much less testing in the wider world.

Working with source code ensures that you have the full suite of software for MySQL and allows you to look at the code that the developers have written. C programmers especially may be interested in looking under the hood at how MySQL works. Another benefit is that you can determine how MySQL is compiled (optimizing performance in certain ways), whereas a precompiled binary will have its parameters already set by the compilation performed by the developers. However, compiling from source does require you to have a C compiler (usually not a problem for Linux users where gcc should already be present), and you may need a little more patience, especially if installation doesn't go smoothly. Nevertheless, help is at hand. Today's lesson provides assistance on the compilation process, so don't be afraid to give it a try.

Caution

MySQL binary distributions are the most rigorously tested by users in the wider world; source distributions, because you compile them yourself, produce binaries that are less well tested. For example, a problem can be introduced by a particular version of a compiler, which will take longer to come to light. If you're not using the same compiler version MySQL AB use to produce their binaries, your binary will not have been so thoroughly tested.

Therefore if you are installing MySQL for a production system, and especially if you are using a newer compiler (such as gcc version 3.0 series), it is advisable to look out for warnings about such issues, which will normally be posted on the `Downloads` page at `http://www.mysql.com/`.

Because this book is aimed principally at MySQL version 4, the examples are shown using version 4. Although 4.0.1 is shown in today's installation routines, you should just replace this version number with the version number you're working with. The principles are also the same for earlier versions of MySQL, but where something applies differently for such versions, it will be noted as such.

Installing on Linux

2

For installation on Linux or Unix, we'll consider binary, source, and RPM methods of installation. You will need to have root access to your machine to perform these installations.

Binary Installation on Linux

The binary installation method can be the easiest and quickest. Download the binary to disk. The downloaded file will be called something like mysql-4.0.1-pc-linux-gnu-i686.tar.gz (or similar, according to MySQL product, version, your system hardware, and operating system).

Note

> Since early versions of MySQL 4, there has been a choice of MySQL "products." All the binaries have been compiled by MySQL from the same source version, but they differ in the optional components that have been included in the compilation.
>
> The MySQL products are as follows:
>
> - MySQL Classic—The basic software for MySQL, including server and client utilities
> - MySQL Pro—The MySQL software bundled with the InnoDB table handler, for transaction-safe processing (described in Day 17, "Transactions and Table Locking")
> - MySQL Max—The MySQL software bundled with many extras, such as the InnoDB and BDB table handlers, RAID disk support, and other new features
>
> You should study the details on http://www.mysql.com/ for detailed and up-to-date information of the contents of each product.
>
> For the purposes of this book, if you decide to use a binary distribution, it is recommended that you download the MySQL Pro version.

While the software is downloading, you may want to prepare your system for MySQL. The MySQL server needs a Linux user and group to run, both called mysql. You can create these as follows (as root):

```
# groupadd mysql
# useradd mysql -g mysql
```

If you get a response that the useradd command could not be found, such as the following (using the bash shell):

```
bash: useradd: command not found
```

you may need to specify the full path to the groupadd and useradd programs—for example, /usr/sbin/useradd. If you get a message after the second command saying

```
useradd: user mysql exists
```

it may be because MySQL has previously been installed on your system. (You can check by viewing your /etc/passwd and /etc/group files.) You can modify the mysql user to give it the group mysql as follows, using usermod (again you may need to precede it with the full path to usermod):

```
# usermod mysql -g mysql
```

You're now ready to install the binary.

We recommend that you move the downloaded .tar.gz file into /usr/local because this is a good place to install. It's where well assume that you will be installing both MySQL and possibly other server software, such as Apache and PHP.

Change to that directory, unzip, and untar the file:

```
# cd /usr/local
# gunzip mysql-4.0.1-pc-linux-gnu-i686.tar.gz
# tar -xvf mysql-4.0.1-pc-linux-gnu-i686.tar
```

Then, still in /usr/local, check (using ls) whether a subdirectory called /usr/local/mysql already exists (it might, if MySQL has previously been installed). Provided that it does not exist, you should make a symbolic link to the directory you just created, like this:

```
# ln -s mysql-4.0.1-pc-linux-gnu-i686 mysql
```

This makes it convenient to refer to the MySQL directory as simply /usr/local/mysql.

Occasionally, people have difficulties installing the binary on their system. Problems can arise, among other things, from a missing library or include on your system. To get around this, you could try a source installation.

Should you encounter problems, consult the "Q&A" section at the end of this lesson and the MySQL installation notes in the file INSTALL-BINARY, which you will find in the installation directory.

Source Installation on Linux

Installing MySQL from the source distribution takes a little longer than the other methods but has the advantage of allowing you to tailor the installation to your system. For example, you can set compile-time options to optimize MySQL for speed, to enable BDB and InnoDB tables, and to allow user-defined functions to be created. A source installation is a good idea if you want to follow all the examples in this book because some of the more advanced lessons require you to recompile MySQL to enable special options.

As with the binary installation, the MySQL server needs a user and group to run, both called mysql:

```
# groupadd mysql
# useradd mysql -g mysql
```

 Note   See the advice under the instructions in the previous section "Binary Installation on Linux" if these commands do not run smoothly.

Download the source file to disk and save it somewhere such as under /usr/local/src. The source file will be called something like mysql-4.0.1.tar.gz. Change to the right directory, unzip, and untar:

```
# cd /usr/local/src/
# gunzip mysql-4.0.1.tar.gz
# tar -xvf mysql-4.0.1.tar
```

You will need to do a configure, then a make, then a make install. We recommend that you try configure with simple options to start with—just one, --prefix=/usr/local/mysql, which tells the compiler to do the installation in a target directory called /usr/local/mysql. (The file INSTALL-SOURCE in the MySQL source directory contains details of many more configure options.) Run it as follows:

```
# ./configure --prefix=/usr/local/mysql
```

Then use make to compile with gcc:

```
# make
```

Then install into the target directory that you specified just now:

```
# make install
```

The preceding simple routine should work on most Linux and Unix installations. Should you encounter compiler errors, consult the "Q&A" section at the end of this lesson and the MySQL installation notes in the file INSTALL-SOURCE. You can also check the latest online documentation for recent changes and known problems of particular configurations, as well as discussion archives online.

Tip

> Each time you run make, it creates some files. To remove these, type
>
> `# make clean`
>
> or for a more comprehensive cleanup:
>
> `# make distclean`
>
> Remember also that each time you run configure, you must run make again afterward.

RPM Installation on Linux

MySQL recommends RPM (for Red Hat Package Manager) as the preferred method of installing on Linux. Although the RPMs you download have been prepared on a Red Hat system, you should be able to install them on any Linux system that supports rpm and uses glibc.

You will need a number of the following separately downloadable RPMs:

- MySQL-4.0.1-2.i386.rpm, the server
- MySQL-client-4.0.1-2.i386.rpm, the client programs
- MySQL-bench-4.0.1-2.i386.rpm, benchmark and test suites (requires Perl and msql-mysql-modules)
- MySQL-devel-4.0.1-2.i386.rpm, libraries and includes used for building other programs
- MySQL-shared-4.0.1-2.i386.rpm, client shared libraries
- MySQL-embedded-4.0.1-2.i386.rpm, the embedded server

You will need the server and client programs, the first two RPMs in the preceding list. However, you may also want to download the other RPMs and install them too.

To install an RPM (as root), type the following (this example shows just the server being installed):

`# rpm -i MySQL-4.0.1-2.i386.rpm`

To install several RPMs at a time, you can place many .rpm files on the same line separated by spaces.

To check whether a particular RPM is installed, use -q:

`# rpm -q MySQL-4.0.1-2.i386.rpm`

Note

If you install from RPMs, the files and data will be stored in a different location from what is recommended elsewhere in this lesson. Binaries will be placed in /usr/bin and data in /var/lib/mysql.

You can see which files an RPM contains and where they will be installed like this:

```
# rpm -qpl MySQL-4.0.1-2.i386.rpm
```

Unlike other installation methods, you should not need to set file permissions explicitly, and you should even find that after installing the server RPM, MySQL is alive and ready for use. Furthermore, the RPM installs entries in /etc/rc.d, which starts MySQL automatically at system boot time.

Initializing the Data Directory and File Permissions

If you did a binary or source installation on your Linux system, you now need to create the directory in which data is to be stored and ensure that file permissions are set correctly.

A script called mysql_install_db creates the directory and basic contents for you. This installs the base files that contain the grant tables for user permissions. First change to the installation directory (the precise name depends on how you installed it); then run the install script.

If you did a binary install:

```
# cd /usr/local/mysql
# ./scripts/mysql_install_db
```

If you did a source install:

```
# cd /usr/local/src/mysql-4.0.1
# ./scripts/mysql_install_db
```

Running mysql_install_db should not overwrite data files that exist already.

Note

If you suspect that something's wrong with the default databases that MySQL sets up with this script, you may need to rerun mysql_install_db.

However, this script will *not* overwrite existing grant tables. If you're performing a fresh installation (that is, you're sure that there are no "real" MySQL users), you should delete these tables. Simply delete the directory (/usr/local/mysql/data/mysql or /usr/local/mysql/var/mysql, according to the type of install you did) and the three files it contains.

Then run the mysql_install_db script again to re-create the grant tables in their default state.

One last task before starting the server is to set the file permissions correctly in the `mysql` directory. The `-R` switch in the following commands specifies descending into each directory recursively:

```
# chown -R root /usr/local/mysql
# chown -R mysql /usr/local/mysql/var
# chgrp -R mysql /usr/local/mysql
```

Note

> If you installed from binary, you may have to specify the full directory name (such as /usr/local/mysql-4.0.1-pc-linux-gnu-i686) rather than the directory symlink (/usr/local/mysql), because the recursive switch may fail to follow the symlinks to the files beneath it. You may want to check that chown and chgrp did their job by doing ls -l in each directory.
>
> Also, in binary distributions, the data directory will be called data rather than var as in a source distribution. So in the second of the preceding three steps, you will need the following:
>
> ```
> # chown -R mysql /usr/local/mysql/data
> ```

An optional step is to set up a `my.cnf` file, by copying it from a standard one that is provided:

```
# cp support-files/my-medium.cnf /etc/my.cnf
```

(For a "medium sized" system, copy `my-medium.cnf`. There are other sample `my.cnf` files, the idea being that you choose one according to how much RAM you have. But this choice is not critical unless you're tuning MySQL for a production system.)

The `my.cnf` file is not essential, but it's a good idea to install it now because you'll need it for some of the more advanced topics in this book. `my.cnf` is used to set MySQL options, such as to enable transaction-safe tables, or to set system variables. You will learn more about this file in Day 15, "Administration."

Starting the MySQL Server

The MySQL server runs as a *daemon* called `mysqld`. (The "d" at the end stands for daemon!) A daemon is a process that you'll only know is running when you try to communicate with it, or when you use the `ps` command to show what Unix processes are running (for example, `ps -aux` for an extensive report).

A daemon sits quietly listening for a client that wants to connect to it. If a request comes, the daemon acts on the request, and when it's finished, the daemon disappears into the background again. The other programs included with the distribution, such as `mysql` and `mysqladmin`, are not daemons but client programs that run in the foreground.

The MySQL daemon, `mysqld`, can be started directly, but the recommended method is via a shell script called `mysqld_safe`. (Prior to MySQL 4.0 it was called `safe_mysqld`, which worked in the same way.) This starts `mysqld` and keeps an eye on it to ensure that it keeps running if an error occurs. It also does some logging of the server condition, saving this into the data directory.

You should now start the MySQL server. Use the `mysqld_safe` script as shown here, an interaction showing a correct startup of the `mysqld` daemon:

```
# /usr/local/mysql/bin/mysqld_safe --user=mysql &
[1] 10661
Starting mysqld daemon with databases from /usr/local/mysql/var
```

In this example, we specified the Linux user `mysql`, under which the daemon should run. The & specifies that it should run as a background process.

If you see error messages at this point telling you that MySQL could not start (for example, `daemon ended`), you will need to try to diagnose the problem. In most cases, a failure to start occurs because the file ownerships and permissions have not been set properly, so you should go back to the earlier steps and verify that the changes were made correctly. Alternatively, startup may fail because you already have another `mysqld` running. You can look in the log file called *hostname*`.err` in your data directory for more details on errors that occurred (where *hostname* is the fully qualified domain name of your host). For example:

```
# cd /usr/local/mysql/var
# tail linux.somedomain.com.err
```

If no domain has been set for your machine, you may just need to do this:

```
# tail linux.err
```

`tail` is the Linux program that prints the last few lines of the given file, such as `linux.err`.

You can stop the MySQL server using the `mysqladmin` client program, with the option `shutdown`. You can run `mysqladmin` by changing to the directory where MySQL is installed and running this:

```
# cd /usr/local/mysql
# bin/mysqladmin shutdown
```

You should be able to do the same from anywhere on your system, including the full path to mysqladmin, like this (assuming that you installed MySQL in /usr/local/mysql as suggested):

```
# /usr/local/mysql/bin/mysqladmin shutdown
```

The preceding line assumes that you are the Unix root user and there's no MySQL root password set (which will be the case if you just installed MySQL). If you're not the Unix root user, or there's a password set for the MySQL root user, you may have to specify the MySQL user and password, like this:

```
$ /usr/local/mysql/bin/mysqladmin shutdown -u root -p
Enter password:
```

You can test whether the server is running by typing this:

```
$ /usr/local/mysql/bin/mysqladmin ping -u root -p
Enter password:
mysqld is alive
```

This is just one simple way of using the mysqladmin program. You'll learn much more about its many capabilities in Day 15.

Setting the root Password

MySQL has a comprehensive set of rules for granting access rights to users. These rules are held in a set of tables called the *grant tables*. You can use these for fine control over what your database's users may do, down to database, table, and even column level. You'll learn more about this in Day 14, "Security."

MySQL has a root user by default, who has the greatest control over the server and its databases. In Day 4, "Getting Hands-on with MySQL," you'll set up individual user accounts, but for now we'll just make the root account secure. With the MySQL server running, set the root password as follows:

```
$ /usr/local/mysql/bin/mysqladmin -u root password newpass
```

You don't have to be the Linux root user to run this because the command you're typing specifies the MySQL user to be root (-u root).

If you change the password again, you will have to enter the current password for the root user. You'll need to type it when prompted:

```
$ /usr/local/mysql/bin/mysqladmin -u root -p password anotherpass
Enter password:
```

Starting the MySQL Server at Boot Time

You'll probably want the MySQL server to start up automatically whenever you boot the operating system. This is done automatically if you installed from RPM, but for binary and source installation, you will need to make a few minor changes.

Under the directory that contains your MySQL source or binary files, go into the support-files directory and locate the file called mysql.server. This script invokes mysqld_safe. Copy this script into your Linux startup directory, which will typically be /etc/rc.d or /etc/init.d. Study your Linux documentation to determine the correct location.

Here's an example, which works on SuSE Linux. First change directory (using cd) to the MySQL source or binary directory (depending on how you installed); then do this:

```
# cp support-files/mysql.server /etc/init.d
# chmod +x /etc/init.d/mysql.server
```

Then make symbolic links from it as follows:

```
# ln -s /etc/init.d/mysql.server /etc/rc.d/rc3.d/S99mysql
# ln -s /etc/init.d/mysql.server /etc/rc.d/rc5.d/S99mysql
# ln -s /etc/init.d/mysql.server /etc/rc.d/rc0.d/S01mysql
```

This causes MySQL to be started automatically when the server is started (in runlevels 3 and 5) and shut down when the server is shut down (the final line, for runlevel 0).

Making Access More Convenient

You probably won't want to keep typing the full path to MySQL's various client utilities. You'll start using these a lot sooner (starting with mysql in Day 6, "Manipulating a Database"). You will find it much more convenient to just type the program's name.

For more convenient access to the mysql console program, mysqladmin, and other utilities such as mysqlshow and mysqldump, make a symbolic link from each program to a directory in your Linux PATH.

The most appropriate directory to put them in is /usr/bin. The following interaction shows how to display your PATH and create the links:

```
# echo $PATH
/usr/sbin:/bin:/usr/bin:/sbin:/usr/X11R6/bin
# cd /usr/bin
# ln -s /usr/local/mysql/bin/mysql .
# ln -s /usr/local/mysql/bin/mysqladmin .
# ln -s /usr/local/mysql/bin/mysqlshow .
# ln -s /usr/local/mysql/bin/mysqldump .
# ln -s /usr/local/mysql/bin/myisamchk .
```

Installing on OS X

Apple's OS X ("OS Ten") is a combination of a graphical front-end with a core operating system based on BSD. The ease-of-use of a Macintosh front-end is welded to a reliable Unix-based core.

The BSD core means that MySQL, PHP, Apache, and other applications that run on Linux, can normally be run on OS X.

You will need to have Administrator privilege to perform this installation. On OS X, this doesn't mean becoming root; it just requires that you log on as a user with Administrator privilege.

Download the binary file called something like mysql-4.0.1-alpha-apple-darwin5.1-powerpc.tar.gz (the filename depends on the MySQL version) from the MySQL Web site. When the download is finished, double-click the icon, and it should unpack into a folder called mysql-4.0.1-alpha-apple-darwin5. (The folder's name may be slightly different on your system, so in the next instructions you may need to modify them to suit your system.)

Then move the folder to /usr/local directory using the following commands. Start up Terminal and type this:

```
$ cd Desktop
$ sudo mv mysql-4.0.1-alpha-apple-darwin5 /usr/local
```

This first changes to the Desktop directory (where you downloaded the compressed file to) and moves the new folder to the /usr/local directory. You need sudo before mv because superuser permissions are required to place anything in the /usr/local directory, and you will be asked to enter your OS X Administrator password (not the root password).

You'll need to create the MySQL user, so start up System Preferences, select Users, and click on the New User button. Specify Name as MySQL User, specify short name mysql, and create a password of your choice.

Then change to the new directory, run the script to initialize the data directory, change file ownerships to mysql, and start the server:

```
$ cd /usr/local/mysql-4*
$ sudo ./scripts/mysql_install_db
$ sudo chown -R mysql /usr/local/mysql-4*/*
$ sudo ./bin/mysqld_safe --user=mysql &
```

To verify that things have gone well, make sure that MySQL is running as it should be. Still in Terminal, start the `mysql` console by typing the following:

```
$ /usr/local/mysql-4*/bin/mysql -u root
```

This brings up the `mysql` monitor, logging in as the MySQL `root` user as specified after the `-u`. You can experiment further if you want (as we'll do soon), or simply type

```
mysql> exit
```

to end the session.

After you complete the installation, set the `root` password. This can be done as follows:

```
$ /usr/local/mysql-4*/bin/mysqladmin -u root password newpass
```

Subsequent password changes will need you to provide the existing one by adding a `-p`; so for future changes, you would use

```
$ /usr/local/mysql-4*/bin/mysqladmin -u root -p password newpass
```

After a password has been set, you will also need the `-p` option when using the `mysql` program, as well as the `-u` option to specify the MySQL user to log in as. (We'll go into starting and using `mysql` more thoroughly in Day 6, "Manipulating a Database.") To start `mysql` with a username and password specified, you would use

```
$ /usr/local/mysql-4*/bin/mysql -u root -p
```

This completes a basic installation for MySQL on OS X. It is possible to make the client scripts more convenient to use, without typing the full path (as we did in the Linux installation), and you can also have the MySQL server start up automatically when you start OS X. We omitted these steps from this lesson to keep things simple. You will find more notes on these things on the accompanying Web site, or at `http://www.entropy.ch/software/macosx/mysql/`, which has a good deal of information and downloadable packages.

Installing on Windows

To install on Windows, download the Windows binary from the MySQL Web site. This should be a `.zip` file. After the download finishes, use a program such as WinZip to unzip the file and install.

You can use Windows Explorer to find the directory where MySQL was installed on your `C:` drive. You can start the server by double-clicking on the `mysqld.exe` executable in your `\mysql\bin` directory.

On Windows, MySQL runs as a server program, which means that it is a background process that sits quietly and waits for client connections. You can shut down the server by going to a DOS prompt, changing the MySQL directory, and running `mysqladmin shutdown`. You can also shut down the server via the Task Manager (press Ctrl+Alt+Delete to see this), but this is a drastic way of shutting down and is not recommended.

On Windows 95/98, if you want the MySQL server to start up automatically when you start the machine, place the `mysqld.exe` file (or a shortcut to it) in your Windows Startup directory. On Windows NT or 2000, go to the Control Panel and then Services, where you should find `mysqld`. Check the item to make it start automatically.

Summary

In this lesson, you saw the various ways of installing the MySQL server and client utilities. We covered the most popular operating systems, so you should have found a routine that works successfully on your platform.

As well as basic installation, you learned how to make the MySQL server start up automatically on system startup.

In upcoming lessons, we will cover the steps to prepare MySQL for real use, such as setting up users and creating databases.

Q&A

Q I have forgotten the `root` password. What should I do?

A If you forget the `root` password, you'll need to change it to something you know. Shut down `mysqld`. On Linux you may need to run

```
# ps -ax | grep mysql
```

to find out the process ID of the `mysqld_safe` process. You should see something like this:

```
221  ??  S      0:00.09 sh /usr/local/bin/mysqld_safe
501  ??  S      0:00.30 /usr/local/libexec/mysqld
512 std  R+     0:00.01 grep mysql
```

The processes to kill in this example are first 221 (`mysqld_safe`) and 501 (`mysqld`); there may be one or more instances of `mysqld`, although only one is shown here. You will probably have to do the somewhat drastic -9 kill, so make sure that no other database users are on the system. (Having open tables at this time can cause data corruption.) Then type the following:

```
# kill -9 221
# kill -9 501
```

The -9 specifies a nonignorable kill, and the last number in each case is the number of the process, derived from the result of listing the processes as shown previously.

Now restart the MySQL daemon, telling MySQL to ignore the grant tables. Change to the installation directory and do as follows:

```
# cd /usr/local/mysql
# bin/mysql_safe --skip-grant-tables --user=mysql &
```

Go into the mysql console:

```
#  mysql
```

(you won't need to specify -p) and change the root password, by typing the following:

```
mysql> USE mysql;
mysql> UPDATE user SET password=PASSWORD('newpass')
WHERE user='root';
```

Then exit:

```
mysql> exit
```

Back at the command line, flush privileges:

```
# /usr/local/bin/mysqladmin flush-privileges
```

You now have changed the root password and got mysqld running again with the grant tables reread and privileges back in place.

Q What options are there when building the server from source?

A If you are compiling MySQL from source, you can compile with a range of optional parameters that will customize your installation.

We'll look at the options in a moment, but in all cases, if you have compiled already, you will first need to clean up from the previous compilation.

First, cd to the source directory. Then type the following line:

```
# make distclean
```

Then run ./configure with options set (more on this in a moment). Afterward, you will recompile with the following:

```
# make
# make install
# scripts/mysql_install_db
```

Now let's have a look at some of the options you might want to use.

If you want to use the BDB and InnoDB table types (InnoDB is compiled by default, but BDB must be specified: see Day 7 for more on transaction-based processing), you may want to recompile MySQL using the following procedure:

```
# ./configure \
> --prefix=/usr/local/mysql \
> --with-bdb
```

You will need to create and edit the /etc/my.cnf file to enable InnoDB tables to be created, removing the # (indicating a comment) from all lines to do with InnoDB. See the MySQL Technical Reference for more details on this.

For optimal performance, you may want to give configure two more switches that tell it to use assembler code wherever it can and to create a static linked program, thus speeding up the final compiled program. (This is also known to get around some problems with Red Hat distributions.)

```
# ./configure \
> --prefix=/usr/local/mysql \
> --enable-assembler \
> --with-mysqld-ldflags=-all-static
```

Note that you can combine these switches with the ones described previously.

Workshop

The quiz and exercises are provided to help you solidify your understanding of the material covered today. Try to understand the quiz and exercise answers before continuing to tomorrow's lesson.

Quiz

1. What does the following line do?

   ```
   $ mysqladmin ping -u root -p
   ```

2. True or False: The MySQL server runs as a daemon.

3. True or False: The mysql client program runs as a daemon.

Quiz Answers

1. It tests whether the MySQL daemon is running.

2. True.

3. False.

Exercise

1. Install MySQL for your operating system. Start the MySQL server and check that it's running with a mysqladmin ping.

DAY 3

Getting Started with Database Design

Today's lesson is about the process whereby a business need can be modeled and therefore translated into the definition for a database system. What you'll learn today is central to the design of all relational databases.

In particular, you will learn:

- How to analyze business needs in terms of business processes, business rules, and business objects
- How to identify transactions and relationships
- How to define an outline database design and specify application requirements that fulfill the business needs
- How to normalize your data structure

After you have studied today's lesson, you should be able to take a business scenario and represent it in database form.

The Need for Business Analysis

Business analysis and top-down database design are often neglected, or shortcuts are taken, especially when the developer is eager to "get his hands dirty" and start building a system. But rushing into system development is like building a house without an architect: you're lacking the overall, but detailed, picture of what you're trying to achieve.

This lesson is about standing back from the keyboard and monitor, and thinking about what need your database will fulfill. Most databases are built with a business need in mind, and the satisfactory delivery of that need—perhaps the satisfaction of your client— is the primary goal.

If you build a system that's either inadequate or too sophisticated, the client is unlikely to thank you. Either it will fail to solve his problem or it will be too expensive to build. By better analysis of the requirement and careful design, you should be able to get the system to precisely fit the need.

Analyzing Business Needs

The business need has to be studied to tease out certain characteristics. These are roughly summarized as follows:

- The *business process*, or what actually goes on in the business
- The *business rules*, or what is allowed to happen, and what isn't
- The *business objects*, the actual things that exist in the business

Put together, these things describe the goings-on within the business and in the business function you're trying to model. Some organizations have these things written down as formal procedures, whereas in other scenarios people just get on and do things; the procedures only existing in people's knowledge.

Whichever is the case, start by studying the information that's there by asking questions and forming a picture of what goes on.

 Tip

In some cases, a database is commissioned so as to simplify or even completely change an existing process. You will need to distill out what *needs* to be done versus what *is* done.

You will often encounter a good deal of superfluous information. You'll need to take note of it, but distill it out of your model if it's not relevant.

Business Processes

Identifying business processes is often a good time for drawing a process flow of what you think is going on:

- It helps you form a picture in your own mind of what's going on.

- You can show it to other people who know the process and talk it through, reconfirming it to make sure that you have it right.

- It may uncover missing links in your understanding, or even failings in the process as it's been described.

- It provides a reference point to look back on as the project moves forward. By compiling notes and process diagrams as things develop, you have an audit trail of the development of your ideas and understandings.

A process diagram can be as formal as you want, created with special software, or can be a pencil-and-paper sketch. Figure 3.1 shows a simple process diagram.

FIGURE 3.1

A simple business process diagram.

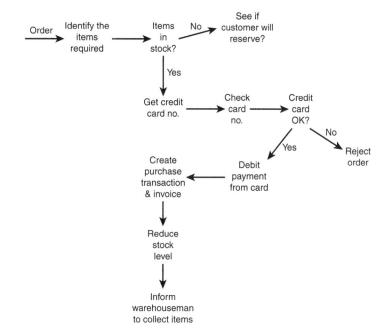

Inherent in the language used to describe events in the process is the concept of *transactions*. A transaction is an essential part of the business process where a definable event occurs.

A business transaction may itself be comprised of smaller transactions. However, it may be important to carry out a transaction completely, or not at all.

For example, the system for an online store may dispatch the goods ordered and update the stock level, but not just dispatch the goods. In your process diagram, you will normally have such smaller events described, but it should be clear which of them are grouped together into transactions that must not be divided.

Because most electronic business systems and the Internet operate on a transaction basis, it is important to understand your business process as a sequence of transactions rather than any kind of real-time continuum.

Business Rules

When it comes to business rules, some things will be defined clearly, whereas many rules will be common sense. Rules declared by the business may come about because of business strategy, they may arise from local management decisions, or they may be in place because of legislation or other causes. Declared rules are the most easy to spot.

There are also "common sense" rules, which are present in an implied sense. With any kind of rule, never ignore the need to ask questions of the obvious, and look for clarification in what is obscure or complex. With implied rules, the need to ask questions is most important.

For example, the rule "customers' payments must be non-negative and greater than zero" might sound like a common sense rule for an ordering process.

But the statement must be questioned. If the answer is not clear, you need to understand the rule a little more, and perhaps ask some "What if?" questions.

For example, what would a negative payment mean, when applying the preceding rule? A negative payment from the customer would effectively be a refund, so to fully understand the scenario you need to find out how refunds are implemented.

And what of zero payments? Perhaps there's a "Buy one, get one free" policy, which under certain circumstances might mean that a zero payment would be allowed. Again, you must ask the question.

As with the mapping out of business processes, a paper and pencil (or even a suitable software package) is of great benefit for defining the business rules, whether they be declared or implied.

Business Objects

Business objects are the "nouns" or "things" of the system you're trying to model.

For example, a store with a product ordering system might have objects like these:

- Products
- Product categories
- Customers
- Purchases
- Invoices
- Credit card
- Bank

Establishing the business objects is generally a little easier than establishing processes and rules, but make sure that you look out for both tangible things (such as products) and intangibles (such as purchases).

3

After you identify the objects, you need to study the characteristics of each. For example, an invoice might have the following characteristics:

- Invoice number
- Date of issue
- Value excluding sales tax
- Customer name and address
- Value of sales tax
- Value including sales tax

Putting the Picture Together

After you identify the business objects and understand the rules and processes that bind them together, a picture begins to emerge. With this picture, you can start to define the database application required to fulfill the need.

There's not a clear path for translating objects, processes, and rules into an electronic system, but business objects often translate roughly into database tables.

After all, relational databases were conceived to model business entities: each table often represents a business object, each column represents a characteristic of that object, and each row of data represents an instance of that object.

The business process you've described will to a large extent be implemented by the application software you specify. It will dictate what you have on each screen of the electronic system and what information flows between which objects.

For example, "check the customer's credit card details" will typically be some form of query sent to the bank, and the outcome will be a screen telling the customer whether his card appears to be okay. Likewise the acceptance of the order may generate an email to the warehouseman to collect some products from the physical store.

The business rules will manifest themselves in several ways: they may influence the data types allowed in the tables (for example, a customer's name will be a text field, not a number), but will also dictate what's allowed by the application (for example, the application may check that a credit card number is a number, and not text).

Looking at the rules in relationship terms, they will dictate where there are one-to-one, one-to-many, and many-to-many relationships between business objects—and thus between tables. For example, there may be many invoices for a given customer (but each invoice has only a single customer), so in this sense the business rules look likely to govern our use of indexes in the tables representing these objects (namely, invoices and customers).

Relationship Modeling

In this book, we're not dealing on the entire application development process but concentrating on how to create a database design that models business needs.

As you've just seen, the business objects in particular dictate the database's tables. But the database also is influenced heavily by business rules because they govern things such as data types, allowable values, and relationships between tables.

Relationships are probably the single greatest challenge for the system architect: not only are relationships the most complex things to design, but if you define them wrongly, it can be even more difficult to sort out things later.

Apart from making sure that the business need is suitably represented, the designer needs to think about things such as normalization of data. This can mean tables looking a little different in their final form than in the initial pencil sketch. We'll look at how to implement normalization later today.

Because much of this book is about how to design tables bearing in mind technical and performance limitations, we won't go into these considerations here. Today, let's concentrate on the types of relationships you'll encounter, and how to represent them in your database design.

One-to-One Relationships

One-to-one relationships are generally the easiest to model. In the store example, when a customer buys something, it creates one purchase transaction and one invoice.

This would typically mean a one-to-one relationship between a `purchases` table and an `invoices` table.

In some cases, you might combine items in a one-to-one relationship into a single table—after all, why have two tables?

You may prefer having two tables so that you can record unsuccessful purchases (perhaps the customer's credit card payment failed) without having an empty invoice part on that record. Or you may want to attach different security levels to the two tables (which personnel can access the tables, and what they can do).

There may also be technical reasons for breaking things into two or more tables, where they logically belong in the same table. For example, if you're trying to develop an electronic library, to model books in a real library, it might seem logical that one of your business objects is a book. Therefore you would expect to have a table of books, perhaps with the one single table containing the title, author, and complete contents of each book. However, storage and performance limitations are likely to mean that this is a bad idea. You'll learn more about how data is stored in Day 5, "MySQL Data Types."

If you do have two tables in a one-to-one relationship, you will need an *index*, or a *key* field, to relate them together. Often you'll want a key to be a *primary key*—this means that it is unique and must always contain some data.

Figure 3.2 illustrates how tables of `purchases` and `invoices` might be represented, being related by purchase ID.

FIGURE 3.2

A one-to-one relationship.

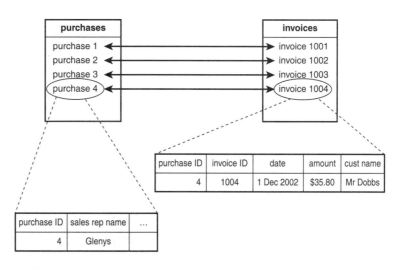

Tip

> Don't worry about the technicalities of indexes or keys—you'll learn about these in Day 9, "Joins and Indexes." For now, if you've not encountered indexes before, it's sufficient to think of them as unique numbers or identifiers that identify something.
>
> A *relationship* is formed where one object's identifier exists in a table representing some other object.

One-to-Many Relationships

One-to-many relationships are perhaps the most common kind of relationships that a database designer has to deal with.

In our store example, you would find that many relationships are one-to-many, such as many purchases to one customer, or many products to one product category, as shown in Figure 3.3.

FIGURE 3.3

A one-to-many relationship.

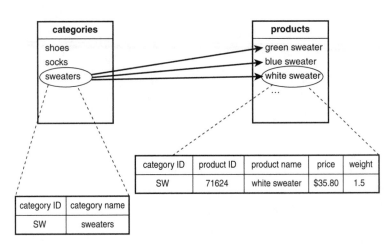

As you will see from Figure 3.3, keys are used again. On the product categories object (which will become a table called, say, `categories`) there is a primary key for the product category ID. No two categories can have the same ID, and every category must have an ID.

On the products object (which in the database will be a table called `products`), each item has a category ID to indicate which category it belongs to. Because the relationship is one-to-many, several products will have the same category ID. Therefore the category ID is a multiple key in this table, and because it really belongs to a different table, it's often referred to as a *foreign key*.

The products table's primary key is the product ID, to uniquely identify each product. This is essential when you're creating further relationships between products and other objects.

Many-to-Many Relationships

The relationships you've seen so far have been fairly easy to forge, just by having a key in one table whose values correspond with key values in another table. But with a many-to-many relationship—several instances of one object are related to several instances of another object—this structure is inadequate.

A many-to-many relationship might occur in our store if we relate products with purchases. For example, several different products usually exist in a single purchase, and any one product can be bought in several purchases (that is, by many customers).

This can not be represented by a one-to-many relationship because it would be too restrictive, and the two-table approach just doesn't let us model the true picture. So a third table is required—a *linking table*—to represent the many-to-many relationship (see Figure 3.4).

3

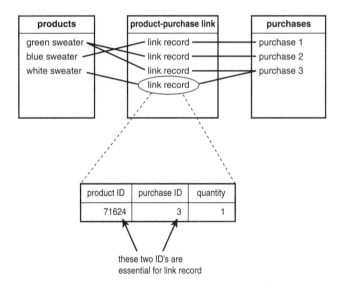

FIGURE 3.4

A many-to-many relationship.

Figure 3.4 shows how a many-to-many relationship might be represented between products and purchases. The middle table, the product-purchase link table, has one entry (one row) for each incidence of a product being purchased.

Each linking table row can be simple: it necessarily has to store the primary key from each of the tables it links. In this example, it means the product ID (the primary key of the products table) and the purchase ID (the primary key of the purchases table). In Figure 3.4, this table is also used to store additional information, the quantity of items in the order.

Figure 3.4 shows purchase 1 being for a blue sweater, purchase 2 being for a green sweater, and purchase 3 being for a green sweater and a white sweater.

Normalization

After your data is modeled into tables, you need to ensure that the tables are truly relational. Far from being just good practice, making your data relational is essential for efficient processing of transactions, good use of storage, and ease of data management. Making a data structure relational is achieved by the process of *normalization.*

Normalization is probably the most important tool for database designers. It is central to relational database theory and is the key process that translates data models from flat-files to efficient, relational formats.

There are nine rules for normalization, which arise from numerous theories of data modeling. However, in this lesson we'll keep things simple and explain the first three normal forms. These are really all you need for the majority of modeling exercises.

First Normal Form

First Normal Form, put in simple language, states that any columns that occur multiple times in a table should be removed and placed in a different table.

For example, imagine that you have a (non-normalized) purchases table like that shown in Figure 3.5.

As you can see, there are multiple columns for both product name and product quantity, both of which are repeated three times. This is not only wasteful of storage space for small orders (where only one product is ordered) but also allows only three different products to be ordered at a time.

First Normal Form means removing these multiple columns (product name and quantity) from the table (purchases) to another table (in this case products_ordered). After this is done, the tables will be normalized to First Normal Form. However, note that a key will be needed on the new table (products_ordered) to relate each product back to the relevant purchase in the first table.

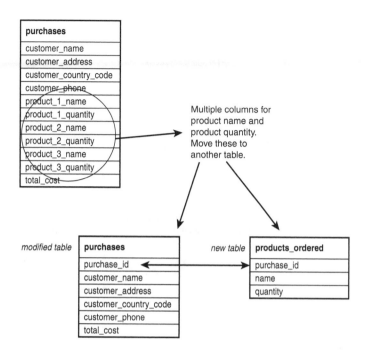

FIGURE 3.5

Applying normalization to First Normal Form.

Second Normal Form

The rule of *Second Normal Form* states that, in addition to the design complying with First Normal Form, all data not relying on a table key to uniquely identify it should be removed and placed in a different table.

Imagine that you have a table describing products available in the store. Each record includes information about the individual product (its name, price, and so on) and also a category description (such as "sweater," "shoes," and so on).

Because several products will be in any given category, the category name would have to be repeated several times within the table.

Not only would this representation be wasteful of space, because descriptions of the categories are being included repeatedly, but also it's difficult to change something. For example, if you initially had a category, "sweaters," and then introduced a new category, "polar neck sweaters," you would risk creating ambiguities in the table if you updated some of the descriptions. You would not be managing your data efficiently and reliably.

Figure 3.6 shows a sample `products` table, in which the `category_name` column is removed according to the Second Rule, and this category information is moved off to another table.

FIGURE 3.6

*Applying normaliza-
tion to Second Normal
Form.*

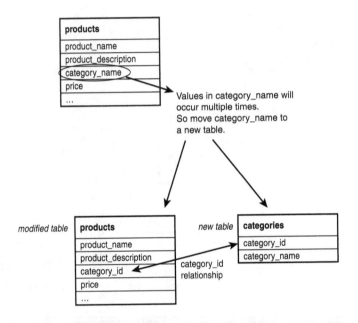

Going to Second Normal Form means that the category data would be removed and exist in a categories table its own right. To keep the relationship, a non-unique key would need to be added to both the categories and products tables to relate products to their categories (refer to Figure 3.3).

Third Normal Form

Third Normal Form is all about eliminating dependencies within a table. It states that, in addition to the design complying with Second Normal Form, all non-key data that is dependent on other non-key data in the same table should be placed in a different table.

Imagine that the table customers includes every customer's address, the name of the country in which the customer lives, and the ISO abbreviation for that country, as shown in Figure 3.7. The ISO country code and the country name are dependent because a given country will always have the same ISO code.

To comply with Third Normal Form, you must remove the country name from the customers table and place it in a new table, countries. So countries will have both iso_country_code (a key to relate the country back to the customers table) and country_name.

customers can keep the iso_country_code column because this is key data (and therefore smaller). By removing country_name, the non-key, dependent data is removed.

FIGURE 3.7

Applying normaliza-
tion to Third Normal
Form.

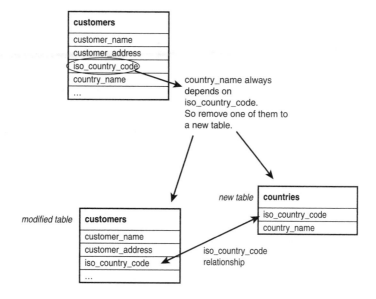

Other Considerations When Designing Tables

It is possible to perform several other forms of normalization, but it's beyond the scope of all but the most specialized database design texts to cover these.

In some circumstances, there may also be reasons for not normalizing every table to Third Normal Form, or not even normalizing at all. For simple databases, it may not be worth the increased complexity of a multitable architecture, with keys having to be added as part of the normalization process. Data in normalized tables is normally more difficult to manage because applications have to be more complex to display data and to insert, update, and delete records. This is because such operations normally require SQL which references several tables rather than just one.

Another reason for not normalizing is that when actual database performance is considered, doing cross-referencing between tables (performing *joins*) may slow down the live system.

These considerations are discussed more in Day 9, and techniques for improving performance are looked at in Day 18, "Optimizing Performance."

Apart from normalizing your database, you need to specify data types for the columns in your table: you need to progress your table specifications from the concepts of text or number, to the concepts of fixed- or variable-length text columns, integer or floating-point number columns, and so on. The column types implemented in MySQL are considered in Day 5.

Summary

In today's lesson, you learned how to start creating a new database by looking at the design process.

You saw the importance of analyzing the business needs in terms of business processes, business objects, and the rules that bind them together. Taken together, these things form an outline of your database design in terms of tables and applications.

We paid particular attention to database table design, and you learned about normalizing data to make it truly relational.

This has been a relatively non-MySQL specific lesson, but in the days that follow, you will see how these fundamental principles are implemented in a MySQL environment.

Q&A

Q When should I normalize a database?

A The best time to normalize is immediately after you have worked out what tables you need to model the business need.

It's possible to normalize the database later in the process, after application development has started and even after the system is functioning. However, doing changes later in the development process, especially when there's live data in your tables, requires more effort because you will then have to modify application code and migrate data, which will be far more complicated.

Nevertheless, the normalized model you achieve at this stage will often be refined, especially if you pay careful consideration to performance, which can lead to you denormalizing data or using other tactics to improve speed (or minimize storage) in a production system.

Q The outline here seems rather brief. Is it really so simple?

A The purpose of this book is to teach you primarily about MySQL. Tutorials on modeling business needs and designing databases can fill entire books, even study courses!

Q Is there a limit on how many business objects, processes, and rules I can define?

A If you're trying to model a complex business activity, there will be many processes, objects, and rules. The rules, in particular, can be extensive, ranging from rules that are clearly stated to those that are common sense. It's up to you to establish those that are salient and matter to the business model, and to separate out those that have no influence.

Workshop

The quiz and exercises are provided to help you solidify your understanding of the material covered today. Try to understand the quiz and exercise answers before continuing to tomorrow's lesson.

Quiz

1. True or False: You must normalize a database so that it can be built.

2. True or False: There are more than three normal forms of a database.

Quiz Answers

1. False. However, a database that is not normalized will not usually work efficiently, and the data will not be easy to manage.

2. True. There are many more (in fact nine), though only the most important three are covered in this lesson.

Exercises

1. A collection of music CDs is to be represented by a table `cds`, and the table contains information that models the artist's name, the title of the CD, and the tracks on the CD. Imagine that the table currently has the columns `artist`, `title`, `name_track1`, `name_track2`, and so on up to `name_track20`. Which column or columns would you move to another table to normalize to First Normal Form?

2. In the preceding example, which column would you move to another table to normalize to Second Normal Form?

3. In the preceding example, which column would you move to another table to normalize to Third Normal Form?

Answers to Exercises

1. To achieve First Normal Form, you would move `name_track1`, `name_track2`, and so on up to `name_track20` to another table. These are multiple instances of effectively the same column.

2. To achieve Second Normal Form, you would move `artist` to another table. Because (typically) an artist will record several albums, it would appear multiple times.

3. The table is already in Third Normal Form because no columns in the table depend on other columns.

DAY **4**

Getting Hands-On with MySQL

Today you will take a quick tour of MySQL. You will get an overview of the following topics:

- The essential programs and files that make up the MySQL package
- How to start and stop the `mysql` client program
- How to create a MySQL user and set the user's password
- An introduction to ODBC

Most of the things covered today will be explained in more detail in later lessons; today's lesson gives you just enough general knowledge to follow the practical examples in this book. After today, you should feel comfortable navigating through the various programs and files that make up the MySQL database system.

The Essential Programs and Files of MySQL

From the installation process in Day 2, "Installing MySQL," you will have noticed that the MySQL package is made up of many programs, files, and subdirectories. There's no need to get confused by these; for most purposes you can get by using only a few of them.

If you installed MySQL from source in Day 2, you will have two directories: a source directory (called mysql-VERSION) and an installation directory (mysql).

If you installed from the binary package on either Linux or Windows, or you installed the RPM, you will just have an installation directory, mysql.

Let's have a look at what's in the installation directory. Here's a sample listing of what you'll see if you install MySQL from source:

```
# ls -l /usr/local/mysql
total 48
drwxr-xr-x   12 root      mysql      4096 Aug 12 11:43 .
drwxr-xr-x   36 root      root       4096 Aug 18 14:40 ..
drwxr-xr-x    2 root      mysql      4096 Aug 18 14:41 bin
drwxr-xr-x    3 root      mysql      4096 Aug 12 09:31 include
drwxr-xr-x    2 root      mysql      4096 Aug 18 14:41 info
drwxr-xr-x    3 root      mysql      4096 Aug 12 09:32 lib
drwxr-xr-x    2 root      mysql      4096 Aug 18 14:41 libexec
drwxr-xr-x    3 root      mysql      4096 Aug 12 09:32 man
drwxr-xr-x    6 root      mysql      4096 Aug 18 14:41 mysql-test
drwxr-xr-x    3 root      mysql      4096 Aug 12 09:32 share
drwxr-xr-x    7 root      mysql      4096 Aug 18 14:41 sql-bench
drwx------    9 mysql     mysql      4096 Sep 15 14:33 var
```

Here's what the listing looks like when you install a precompiled MySQL binary package:

```
# ls -l /usr/local/mysql
total 4780
drwxrwxr-x   13 505       mysql         4096 Feb 27  2002 ./
drwxr-xr-x   36 root      root          4096 Aug 18 14:40 ../
-rw-rw-r--    1 505       mysql        19106 Oct 11  2001 COPYING
-rw-rw-r--    1 505       mysql        47577 Oct 11  2001 COPYING.LIB
-rw-rw-r--    1 505       mysql       122323 Oct 11  2001 ChangeLog
-rw-rw-r--    1 505       mysql       148255 Oct 11  2001 INSTALL-BINARY
-rw-rw-r--    1 505       mysql         1976 Oct 11  2001 README
drwxrwxr-x    2 505       mysql         4096 Oct 12  2001 bin/
-rwxrwxr-x    1 505       mysql          773 Oct 12  2001 configure*
drwxrwx---    4 505       mysql         4096 Oct 12  2001 data/
drwxrwxr-x    2 505       mysql         4096 Oct 12  2001 include/
drwxrwxr-x    2 505       mysql         4096 Oct 12  2001 lib/
drwxrwxr-x    2 505       mysql         4096 Oct 12  2001 man/
-rw-rw-r--    1 505       mysql      2344144 Oct 11  2001 manual.html
```

```
-rw-rw-r--    1 505      mysql      2029500 Oct 11   2001 manual.txt
-rw-rw-r--    1 505      mysql        86599 Oct 11   2001 manual_toc.html
drwxrwxr-x    6 505      mysql         4096 Oct 12   2001 mysql-test/
drwxrwxr-x    2 505      mysql         4096 Oct 12   2001 scripts/
drwxrwxr-x    3 505      mysql         4096 Oct 12   2001 share/
drwxrwxr-x    7 505      mysql         4096 Oct 12   2001 sql-bench/
drwxrwxr-x    2 505      mysql         4096 Oct 12   2001 support-files/
drwxrwxr-x    2 505      mysql         4096 Oct 12   2001 tests/
```

The two preceding code examples are nearly the same. The main difference is that the binary listing has some additional files (such as INSTALL-BINARY and README) that are documentation files. If you install from source, these files are left in the source directory.

You might find that these subdirectories and files look bewildering. For simple database use, you only need to know about two of the subdirectories:

- The executables directory, called bin, where MySQL's programs reside.
- The data directory, called var when you install from source or data when you install from binary; this is where data and log files reside.

The other subdirectories have various purposes, such as lib and include, which include system libraries, and scripts, which contains scripts (including the mysql_install_db script, which you used in Day 2 to install the default databases).

For you to run simple practical exercises, it's not essential to know the MySQL directory tree in any more detail than this. However, in more advanced lessons, you'll look at most of these directories and files in more detail, particularly in Day 15, "Administration."

The Executables Directory

All the executable programs reside in the bin directory. These programs include

- mysqld, the MySQL daemon itself
- mysqld_safe (which was called safe_mysqld prior to version 4), a script that runs mysqld for you
- client utility programs, including mysql, mysqladmin, mysqldump, mysqlshow, myisamchk, and others

The mysqld_safe script, which you met in Day 2, is used to startup and run mysqld, the MySQL daemon. It monitors its status and logs activity. Both programs run in the background, with mysqld listening for requests from clients.

Requests to connect to the database, or actual queries sent to mysqld, can come from anywhere. You can use any one of the client programs to do so (such as the mysql client utility), an API (such as PHP, Perl, or ASP with an Apache Web server), or some other program that you have installed on the server.

In most of this book, we will use the client program called mysql, a versatile console utility. It has a simple command-line interface. In Day 2, you saw briefly how to invoke it. An interaction with mysql looks like this:

```
# mysql
Welcome to the MySQL monitor.  Commands end with ; or \g.
Your MySQL connection id is 8 to server version: 4.0.2-alpha-log

Type 'help;' or '\h' for help. Type '\c' to clear the buffer.

mysql>
```

The final prompt is where you can issue a command or an SQL query.

Tip

If you didn't follow the suggestions in Day 2 to make a symbolic link from this program to one of the directories in your PATH (or change your PATH to include the MySQL bin directory), you will need to specify the full pathname each time. For example:

```
# /usr/local/mysql/bin/mysql
```

If you're not logged in to your server as the root user, you will need to tell MySQL that you want to connect as root, by adding -u root:

```
$ /usr/local/mysql/bin/mysql -u root
```

(Note that the Linux root user is not the same thing as the MySQL root user. It's just for convenience that the names are the same, because root is the user with maximum privileges in each case. Furthermore, if a Linux user john exists, there won't necessarily be a MySQL user called john, and vice versa.)

If you have already set a password for the MySQL root user, you will need to add -p to tell mysql you want to supply a password when you try to connect:

```
$ /usr/local/mysql/bin/mysql -u root -p
Enter password:
```

While you're in the mysql console, you might want to try running some simple SQL. For example, it will be useful to create a database called store, in which you can run some of the example queries later in this book:

```
mysql> CREATE DATABASE store;
Query OK, 1 row affected (0.09 sec)
```

To list the databases that exist on this server, do this:

```
mysql> SHOW DATABASES;
+----------+
| Database |
+----------+
| test     |
| mysql    |
| store    |
+----------+
3 rows in set (0.03 sec)
```

Remember to end each line with a ; (semicolon). It's not part of the SQL query but tells mysql that you've finished your statement.

When you're finished with the console, just give it an exit command:

```
mysql> exit
Bye
```

In Day 6, "Manipulating a Database," you will have a more thorough tour of mysql. For now, it's sufficient that you know how to start it, run a simple query, and exit.

Of the other client programs you will find in MySQL's bin directory, the most versatile is mysqladmin. It can undertake a wide range of administration tasks, from giving information about the status of the MySQL server, to shutting it down. This program is invoked from the operating system command line and is passed one or more parameters that specify what it should do.

For example, to show the current status of the MySQL server, you could run it with status:

```
# mysqladmin -p status
Uptime: 782512  Threads: 1  Questions: 53  Slow queries: 1  Opens: 14
 Flush tables: 1  Open tables: 2  Queries per second avg: 0.000
```

While we're looking at mysqladmin, make sure that you are comfortable restarting the MySQL server. Shut it down like this:

```
# mysqladmin -p shutdown
Enter password:
```

and start it up again using mysqld_safe, like this:

```
# /usr/local/mysql/bin/mysqld_safe &
[1] 27097
linux:/usr/local/mysql # Starting mysqld daemon with databases from
 /usr/local/mysql/var
```

4

The response shown includes the unique Linux process ID number (also called a `pid`), in this case `27097`, though it will be different on your system.

When starting up, remember to add the `&` (ampersand) on Linux or Unix systems, to tell it to run in the background.

If either of these operations didn't go to plan (especially the startup), go back to Day 2 and make sure that you configured everything properly.

You will learn more about `mysqladmin` in Day 6 and study it in further detail in Day 15.

Other notable client programs to be found in the executables directory include `mysqldump` for exporting databases, and `myisamchk` for doing repairs and maintenance. You will encounter these and other programs in Day 15, as well as in other relevant places throughout this book.

The Data Directory

The data directory (called `var` or `data`) contains the actual databases that belong to MySQL. Here's an example:

```
# cd /usr/local/mysql/var/
# ls -l
...
drwx------    2 mysql    mysql        4096 Oct 12  2001 mysql/
drwx------    2 mysql    mysql        4096 Sep 24 16:07 store/
drwx------    2 mysql    mysql        4096 Oct 12  2001 test/
```

Inside the data directory you will find subdirectories such as those shown previously (in this example `mysql`, `store`, and `test`). Each of these contains one database. The subdirectory contains numerous files, incorporating table definition files, files of actual data, and files holding indexes.

(You may have noticed another "mysql" here; there is a database called `mysql`, which is used to control user access to the MySQL server. It stores data about user accounts and privileges. You'll see how to use this to control user access in a moment.)

There may be other files in your data directory. There will be a file called *hostname*`.err`, which is the MySQL error log (where *hostname* is the fully qualified domain name of your host, or just the name of the host if you have no domain set for your machine). You may also see files with names beginning in `ib`, which are for storing `InnoDB` table information, and files called *hostname*`-bin.00n`, which are logs of queries that have been run on your server.

You will study the content of the data directory more closely in Day 15.

Configuration Files

MySQL can optionally use a global configuration file, called `my.cnf` (it may be called `my.ini` in Windows), and user configuration files, called `.my.cnf`.

On Unix systems, the global configuration file resides in `/etc`, with `.my.cnf` files residing in users' home directories.

Because the configuration files are optional, you won't need to install or edit them for the examples in the early parts of this book. However, you will look at them in detail in Day 15.

MySQL Users

When anything tries to connect to MySQL, we call it a *client*, whereas MySQL is the database *server*. To manage who, how, and for what purpose clients can connect, MySQL has a sophisticated user privilege system. Its settings are stored in *grant* tables in the database called `mysql`.

In Day 2, you saw how to connect to MySQL as the its `root` user. `root` can do anything on a MySQL database, but for any kind of database development work this is simply too much power to grant to ordinary users, whether they be real people or software applications.

MySQL's privilege system enables you to create users and assign them privileges. You can let users do things on a global level, or just within a given database, or you can exercise precise control at more granular levels.

Not only can you control *what* users have access to but *how* they can access it; for example, the privilege system lets you specify whether a user can just read from a database, or whether he can make changes to it.

Here's how to create a user called `tony` who can connect from `localhost` using password `mypass`. He will have access to the database you created previously in this lesson, called `store`.

```
mysql> GRANT ALL ON store.* TO tony@localhost IDENTIFIED BY 'mypass';
Query OK, 0 rows affected (0.14 sec)
```

In the preceding line, `ALL` means "all privileges": the user is permitted to take any action, such as reading or deleting data, or even modifying tables, but only on tables in the `store` database. He cannot access any other database.

This user can now connect to the MySQL database and select the `store` database like this, all in one line:

```
# mysql -u tony -p store
Enter password:
```

That's all you need to know about the privilege system for now. However, you will learn about it in more detail in Day 14, "Security."

Should you want to change a user's password, you can do this most easily from the command line:

```
# mysqladmin -u tony -p password newpass
Enter password:
```

This sets the password to newpass, although you will need to enter the existing password (which you previously set to mypass) at the prompt.

Installing ODBC

In many situations, clients connect to MySQL through TCP/IP. This is what happens when you connect to MySQL through one of its client utilities, or when using an API such as that in PHP or Perl.

However, if you write a program using a development environment such as Visual Basic, Visual C++, and Java, or you have a program such as Access connecting to MySQL, you will need to use a different connection method: ODBC.

ODBC stands for Open Database Connectivity. It is a standard protocol that has been made an integral part of many Microsoft development environments, as well as other vendors' products. ODBC enables an application to talk to any database in a standardized way.

An ODBC driver must be installed wherever ODBC is to be used, and the client must be configured using DSN (Data Source Name) information about the server it's connecting to. The driver forms an abstraction layer, so that database-specific communications are translated into the ODBC standard language for passing between client and server.

To use ODBC with MySQL you will need to install MyODBC, the MySQL driver for ODBC. On the server, this allows programs such as Visual Basic applications to connect. On the client machine (if it's a different machine from the server), you will also need to install MyODBC so as to tell your application about MySQL.

You can download the appropriate driver from the Downloads section of the MySQL Web site at http://www.mysql.com/Downloads/. The file will be called myodbc-VERSION-win95.zip for Windows 95, 98, and Me; myodbc-VERSION-nt.zip for Windows NT, XP, and 2000; MyODBC-VERSION-1.i386.rpm for the Linux RPM; or MyODBC-VERSION.tar.gz for the Linux-archived source.

If you want to connect a Windows client machine to a Linux server, you will need to download both the Windows MyODBC and the Linux ODBC drivers, installing the appropriate one on each machine.

On Windows, unzip your distribution, and run the setup program. Follow the instructions, which are simple and self-explanatory. With the software successfully installed, you will need to go to the Control Panels and run the ODBC Data Source Administrator. While on the User DSN tab, click the Add button to add a new data source.

You will see a window with the list of available data source drivers. Click on the MySQL driver; then click the Finish button. This brings up a window with the configuration parameters of that data source. You're telling ODBC the parameters with which to connect to MySQL.

You need to fill in the first five fields, including

- A DSN (data source name), which is typically the database name, such as store
- The hostname (for example, an IP address), such as 192.168.1.100
- The database name, in this example, store
- The username, such as tony
- The user's password, such as mypass

To install on Linux or Unix, you will need to install MyODBC and either iODBC or unixODBC.

Download the required files from your closest mirror and place them in a suitable directory. Then unpack them, like this (with this example showing unixODBC):

```
# gunzip MyODBC-2.50.39.tar.gz
# tar -xf MyODBC-2.50.39.tar
# gunzip unixODBC-2.2.3.tar.gz
# tar -xf unixODBC-2.2.3.tar
```

Change to the unixODBC (or iODBC) directory:

```
# cd unixODBC-2.2.3
```

Read the instructions in INSTALL using your favorite editor. Then compile as follows:

```
# ./configure
# make
# make install
```

Note

If you encounter problems in either step of the compilation, read the INSTALL instructions carefully again (you may need to apply options to configure), or study resources on the Web for assistance.

4

Now do the same with MyODBC itself. Change to the `MyODBC` directory:

```
# cd ../MyODBC-2.50.39
```

Read the `INSTALL` file. Then compile—for example, like this:

```
# ./configure --prefix=/usr/local/odbc --with-unixODBC=/usr/local \
> --with-mysql-libs=/usr/local/mysql/lib/mysql \
> --with-mysql-includes=/usr/local/mysql/include/mysql
# make
# make install
```

If you are using this machine as an ODBC client, you will also need to set up the DSN details. Remember to read the instructions in the `INSTALL` file, which contains important information on how to do this on your system.

After you have successfully compiled and installed both packages, restart the MySQL daemon. Your MySQL server should now be ready to receive connections via ODBC.

You can find out more about iODBC at `http://www.openlinksw.com/` and unixODBC at `http://www.unixodbc.org/`.

Summary

Today has mostly been an overview of MySQL: a quick look at its directories, programs, and other files. You have seen some examples of its client utility programs, such as `mysql` and `mysqladmin`.

You should now be comfortable starting up the `mysql` console (even if you've not covered it in much detail yet). You should be able to run a simple command to create a database and to create a user. The exercises you completed are designed to make sure that you're able to follow the coming days in a hands-on manner.

Finally, today you learned about ODBC, which is necessary for applications in which you're not connecting to MySQL through TCP/IP, such as from an application like Access. You saw how to install the relevant drivers on both Windows and Linux platforms.

Q&A

Q Do I really need just a few of the many components in MySQL?

A There are many components, but yes, you can do basic things with MySQL with just one or two utilities (`mysql` and `mysqladmin`) and knowledge of how to start the MySQL daemon (`mysqld_safe`).

There's much to learn besides these: the other programs, details of the data directory, how to use the MySQL configuration file—you haven't seen these things yet. But we will cover these in the course of this book.

Q Is the directory structure shown the only one that is possible?

A Certainly not. In Day 2, it was suggested that you install MySQL in a particular directory, namely /usr/local/mysql. One reason for this is so that you can look in this directory and see all relevant files together, without them being mixed in with other things on your server.

However, you can install MySQL in many other ways. You can install just under /usr/local (the default on some Linux systems that have MySQL installed by default) in which case you would still have the same directories (such as bin for executables), but each directory might contain other non-MySQL things. Another common configuration is to have the data directory under /var.

Q So many things are called "mysql"—Can you summarize what is what?

A The things called "mysql" are as follows:

- MySQL is the name of the overall product.

- mysql is the name of the directory in which MySQL's components reside.

- mysql as found in MySQL's bin directory is the client console program.

- There is also a database called mysql, which contains the *grant tables*, the definitions of database users and their privileges.

- mysqld is the MySQL daemon, the executable that runs, listening, in the background, and processes requests when they come to it.

Q Do I need to learn about ODBC?

A If you're connecting to MySQL from any of the included client programs, such as mysql, then no. You also don't need it if you want to run queries via Perl, or by using PHP or ASP within an Apache Web server.

However, if you're using a product such as Access as a front-end to MySQL, or if you're connecting from an application that you've written using Visual Basic or some other development environment, you will need to connect to MySQL via ODBC.

ODBC puts an abstraction layer in place, and programs such as Access communicate through the abstraction layer (in the case of MySQL, using MyODBC).

Workshop

The quiz and exercises are provided to help you solidify your understanding of the material covered today. Try to understand the quiz and exercise answers before continuing to tomorrow's lesson.

Quiz

1. True or False: The executable that is the main MySQL database program is called `mysqld`.

2. True or False: In MySQL, the actual databases reside elsewhere, outside the normal file structure.

Quiz Answers

1. True. The "d" at the end of `mysqld` stands for daemon, because MySQL runs in the background listening for connections.

2. False. Databases are really just files; MySQL, like other relational database management systems, makes these ordinary files look like something special, like tables and data.

Exercises

1. List the command(s) for restarting the MySQL server.

2. State the command for starting the `mysql` console program, assuming that a link to it is in one of your PATH directories. Invoke it as user `david` and indicate that you want to be prompted for a password.

Answers to Exercises

1. The command to stop the server is

```
# mysqladmin -p shutdown
Enter password:
```

and the command to start it up again is

```
# /usr/local/mysql/bin/mysqld_safe &
```

2. You would use

```
# mysql -u david -p
```

DAY 5

MySQL Data Types

MySQL has the capability to store, represent, and manipulate data in many ways. In today's lesson, you will learn about MySQL's various data and column types.

In particular, today you will learn:

- The numeric data types, including `INT`, `FLOAT`, and `DECIMAL`
- The textual and binary data types, including `CHAR`, `VARCHAR`, `TEXT`, and `BLOB`
- Data types for handling sets of data values, `ENUM` and `SET`
- Special column attributes, such as `AUTO_INCREMENT` and `BINARY`
- How MySQL represents date and time

A good grasp of MySQL's column types is essential for later lessons in which you will create tables with columns of the types you learn here. Today's lesson gives you a clear understanding of behaviors and storage characteristics of the various column types, and, in some cases, the impact they can have on one another and on the table design as a whole.

Overview of Data and Column Types

Strictly speaking, *data* types are slightly different from *column* types: the term *data types* refers to how MySQL interprets and handles that data; *column types* refers to the declaration of the column in the table. For a given column type, there will be peculiarities in the manner of inserting and returning the data; there will be certain storage requirements and limitations on the values that can be represented.

MySQL can handle the following data types:

- Numeric values
- String values
- Date and time values
- The NULL value

For each data type (numeric, string, temporal), several column types usually are available. Most of this lesson explores these column types.

Examples of declaring column types will normally be in the context of creating a table. We will use the following syntax to create a table and declare one or more columns:

```
CREATE TABLE table_name (
 column_name column_type [attributes],
 ...
)
```

Day 6, "Manipulating a Database," looks more closely at how to use CREATE TABLE. But for now it's important that you concentrate on MySQL's column types so that you understand how they behave and what kinds of data they can hold, before putting things into practice.

In the CREATE TABLE syntax shown previously, it's sufficient for now that you notice that after we declare *table_name*, there is a set of parentheses containing a list of column declarations, separated by commas if there's more than one. Each column declaration has a column name, a column type, and optionally some extra attributes.

Attributes usually contain either the NULL or the NOT NULL specifier. This can be applied to any column type and declares whether the column can ever take the value NULL. The NULL value can be thought of as meaning "without value," although it is not the same thing as 0, which is clearly "zero." If you try to perform arithmetic on a NULL value, the result will always be NULL.

A further attribute can also set a DEFAULT value to which a value in that column will be set if a row is inserted with that column not declared. So you might have a column declared as follows, which does not permit a NULL to exist in my_column, but in an insert operation sets its value to 1 unless otherwise defined:

```
my_column INT NOT NULL DEFAULT 1
```

There may also be type-specific attributes, such as AUTO_INCREMENT for an integer column, or BINARY with a VARCHAR column. Each of these attributes along with the column type to which it relates is in today's lesson.

Numeric Column Types

MySQL can represent both integers (numbers with no fractional part) and floating-point numbers (those with a fractional part).

Table 5.1 shows the numeric column types.

TABLE 5.1   Numeric Display Formats

Type Name	Range	Storage Required
TINYINT	signed: -128 to 127	
	unsigned: 0 to 255	1 byte
SMALLINT	signed: -32768 to 32767	
	unsigned: 0 to 65535	2 bytes
MEDIUMINT	signed: -8388604 to 8388607	
	unsigned: 0 to 16777215	3 bytes
INT	signed: -2147483648 to 2147483647 (-2^{31} to $2^{31}-1$)	
	unsigned: 0 to 4294967295 (0 to $2^{32}-1$)	4 bytes
BIGINT	signed: -2^{63} to $2^{63}-1$	
	unsigned: 0 to $2^{64}-1$	8 bytes
FLOAT	minimum non-zero: ±1.175494351E-38	
	maximum: ±3.402823466E+38	4 bytes
DOUBLE	minimum non-zero: ±2.2250738585072014E-308	
	maximum: ±1.7976931348623157E+308	8 bytes
DECIMAL(M,D)	depends on M and D	M+2 bytes

5

You might use an integer (one of the family of INT types) to represent the number of products in a shopping basket, the number of people on a mailing list, and so on. You might use a floating-point type (FLOAT, DOUBLE, DECIMAL) to represent the value of items in a shopping basket, the probability of an event occurring, or the precise distance between two points.

Suppose that you're creating a table to hold a list of products in a shopping basket. You could create a table with the following declaration:

```
CREATE TABLE shopping_basket (
  cust_num INT UNSIGNED,
  item_num INT UNSIGNED,
  num_items SMALLINT,
  unit_cost DECIMAL(6,2))
```

This example creates a table called shopping_basket with four columns. The first column

```
  cust_num INT UNSIGNED,
```

declares cust_num as a column of type INT, an integer of length 4 bytes.

It has the additional declaration of being UNSIGNED, which means that it can never hold a negative number. Instead, you make best use of its positive range, which Table 5.1 tells you may be from 0 to 4294967295. If you attempt to store a number outside this range, it will be clipped at whichever end of this range it tries to exceed.

The column num_items is of type SMALLINT. It is signed (because it's not declared UNSIGNED) and according to Table 5.1 can hold positive or negative values from -32768 to 32767 (including 0).

A column called unit_cost is declared in the example as DECIMAL(6,2). DECIMAL columns have a display size as set by the two parameters in parentheses (M,D). Such columns can store a total of $M+2$ characters, including the digits themselves, the decimal point and the minus sign for negative numbers. For positive numbers, the space reserved for the minus sign can be used by a digit, thus extending the range of possible positive numbers. D decimal places will be stored after the decimal point.

Therefore in the example here, DECIMAL(6,2) can store 8-character numbers (because 8 is $M+2$, or 6 plus 2) between -9999.99 and 99999.99. (But note that the length is always 2 more than M, and not $M+D$.) A DECIMAL(9,3) column would be able to store 11-character numbers (because 11 is 9 plus 2), with a range from -999999.999 to 9999999.999.

DECIMAL type columns actually hold data as string values rather than floating-point values, which helps preserve the decimal precision of the values stored.

Floating-point columns of type FLOAT or DOUBLE can hold zero, or a number in a range from a minimum to a maximum as shown in Table 5.1.

Numeric Column Attributes

When declaring a numeric column, not only can the column name and type be specified but also some column attributes. Here again is the syntax for declaring a column, this time with *attributes* expanded into two kinds of attributes:

```
column_name column_type [column_attributes] [general_attributes]
```

Table 5.2 shows the possible *column_attributes* for numeric columns.

TABLE 5.2 Numeric Column Attributes

Specification for column_attributes	Use and Meaning
UNSIGNED	Integer columns; don't allow negative values
ZEROFILL	All numeric column types; pad displayed values with zeros
AUTO_INCREMENT	Integer columns; increment value by 1 each time NULL is inserted

UNSIGNED

You saw in the preceding example of the shopping_basket table how you could declare integer type columns as UNSIGNED. An unsigned integer type allows only non-negative values to be represented but increases the range of possible positive values.

ZEROFILL

The ZEROFILL column attribute can be used with any numeric column type. Whenever displaying a value of a column with ZEROFILL specified, the output will be padded with leading zeros up to the display width of the column.

You might use it together with an explicit declaration of the display length of the column—for example:

```
column_name INT(M) ZEROFILL
```

where M is the display width of an INT column, or like this:

```
column_name FLOAT(M,D) ZEROFILL
```

where M is the display width of a FLOAT column, and D is the number of decimals.

Setting the display width does not limit the maximum value a column can hold; it merely sets the minimum length that will be displayed when used with ZEROFILL to pad out unused digits with zeros.

5

With an integer column, unused space to the left will be padded out with zeros. With a floating-point column, unused space to the right of the least significant decimal will be padded out with zeros.

For example, you could create a simple table with two fields using a statement like this:

```
CREATE TABLE my_table (
 my_int INT(5) ZEROFILL,
 my_float FLOAT(8,6) ZEROFILL
 )
```

You could insert some data using a statement like this:

```
INSERT INTO my_table VALUES (20, 3.1415), (1000, 2436.125), (100000, 2.7)
```

(You'll study INSERT more on Day 7, "Inserting and Updating Data.") If you display what the table now holds, you would see the following:

```
+--------+-------------+
| my_int | my_float    |
+--------+-------------+
|  00020 |    3.141500 |
|  01000 | 2436.125000 |
| 100000 |    2.700000 |
+--------+-------------+
```

Notice how the integer values are padded out with leading 0s, except in the last row where the value is wider than the display width of 5. In the floating-point column, the number of decimals is fixed, as specified, at 6, with zeros filling out toward the right.

AUTO_INCREMENT

You can use the AUTO_INCREMENT attribute to generate a unique, autonumbered identifier. Each time a row is inserted into a table with an AUTO_INCREMENT column, provided that column has NULL written to it, the value placed in the new row will automatically be set to one more than the previous highest value.

AUTO_INCREMENT can be useful. You may have a table of invoices that you want to have numbered uniquely (the same invoice number never being used twice). Each time an invoice is created, you want to issue an invoice number that is next in sequence from the previous one. AUTO_INCREMENT saves you the bother of running a query to find the previous highest-numbered invoice and adding one to it.

For example, you might create the table like this:

```
CREATE TABLE invoices (
 invoice_num INT AUTO_INCREMENT NOT NULL PRIMARY KEY,
 amount DECIMAL(9,2))
```

invoice_num is the AUTO_INCREMENT column, but notice that you have also declared it as NOT NULL and as the PRIMARY KEY.

MySQL permits only one auto-increment column per table and requires that it is also declared as a key (although it could be a UNIQUE key rather than the PRIMARY KEY). You should also declare it as NOT NULL.

Note

You will learn about how to use indexes (also known as keys) in Day 9, "Joins and Indexes."

If you're not already familiar with what an index is, you can envisage it as an extra column of data in a table, which provides a faster route to any row in the table. The index is kept sorted, so that accessing any row in the table is more efficient.

Indexes can also be used to enforce rules on data, such as uniqueness. A UNIQUE or PRIMARY KEY will prevent duplicate values from occurring in a given column, and a PRIMARY KEY will also prevent any NULL values from appearing in that column.

By default, an AUTO_INCREMENT column will have its start-of-sequence value set to 1. In other words, the first time you insert a row of data, the AUTO_INCREMENT value automatically is set to 1. You can override this start-of-sequence number in your table declaration by setting AUTO_INCREMENT = *number*. The following table declaration assumes that you might like your invoices to be numbered starting from 1000000:

```
CREATE TABLE invoices (
 invoice_num INT AUTO_INCREMENT NOT NULL PRIMARY KEY,
 amount DECIMAL(9,2))
 AUTO_INCREMENT = 1000000
```

5

To see what happens when you insert some data, you could run this query:

```
INSERT INTO invoices VALUES (NULL,0.99), (NULL,6.50), (NULL,1.50)
```

Notice how NULL is inserted into the AUTO_INCREMENT field so as to let it be set automatically. Now the contents of the table would look like this:

```
+-------------+--------+
| invoice_num | amount |
+-------------+--------+
|     1000000 |   0.99 |
|     1000001 |   6.50 |
|     1000002 |   1.50 |
+-------------+--------+
```

As you can see, invoice numbers 1000001 and 1000002 have been created automatically. If you were to insert yet another row of data, the number 1000003 would be used.

MySQL keeps track of the maximum value used in an AUTO_INCREMENT column (and therefore it knows the value to use next) until the table is emptied using a statement of the following form:

```
DELETE FROM table_name
```

This clears the initial sequence number and causes subsequent INSERT statements to restart the auto column at 1.

However, if you empty a table using a more complex query, such as this:

```
DELETE FROM table_name WHERE 1
```

the start-of-sequence information will not be cleared, and subsequent INSERT actions will use values where the previous data left off. So in the second example given previously, even though the table has been emptied, the next number to be used will still be 1000003.

Note

Versions of MySQL prior to 3.23 behaved a little differently in that AUTO_INCREMENT caused an INSERT to use a value one greater than the maximum value in the column at that time.

So using an older version of MySQL in the previous example, if you deleted the row with the highest invoice number (1000002) and then performed an INSERT to add a new record, the new row created would have invoice number 1000002.

Because of this potentially undesirable effect, in MySQL 3.23 and later, when using MyISAM and InnoDB table types (but not ISAM and BDB), the previous highest number would not be reused, and the next invoice number (in this case 1000003) would be used instead.

You can set the value of an AUTO_INCREMENT column explicitly if you want, although you should never assign it a negative value. For example:

```
INSERT INTO invoices VALUES (1000003,9.20)
```

Because the value is set explicitly, the auto-increment behavior will not take effect. However, take care when doing this because you might inadvertently try to set a duplicate value for a unique field, causing MySQL to return an error.

String Column Types

MySQL has a range of string column types. Although in name they are intended for storing string or textual data, you can in fact use them to store any kind of data you want, including numbers, images, sounds, and binary data.

Your choice of string column type for a given application largely depends on the length of data you want to store and how you want to work with the data. Table 5.3 shows MySQL's string column types.

TABLE 5.3   String Column Types

Type Name	Maximum Size
CHAR(*M*)	*M* bytes
VARCHAR(*M*)	*M* bytes
TINYBLOB	2^8-1 bytes
BLOB	2^{16}-1 bytes
MEDIUMBLOB	2^{24}-1 bytes
LONGBLOB	2^{32}-1 bytes
TINYTEXT	2^8-1 bytes
TEXT	2^{16}-1 bytes
MEDIUMTEXT	2^{24}-1 bytes
LONGTEXT	2^{32}-1 bytes
ENUM('*value1*','*value2*',...)	65565 values
SET('*value1*','*value2*',...)	64 values

5

In essence, CHAR defines a fixed-length column type, whereas VARCHAR and the TEXT and BLOB types are variable-length types. CHAR and VARCHAR are intended for small strings (up to 255 characters long), whereas the TEXT and BLOB types are intended for longer strings.

ENUM and SET are special string column types that must take values from a list of allowed values.

CHAR and VARCHAR Column Types

The CHAR and VARCHAR column types both take the *M* parameter, which sets the maximum length permissible. *M* must be between 1 and 255. If you try to insert a string longer than *M* into a CHAR or VARCHAR field, it will be truncated.

The main difference between CHAR and VARCHAR types is in the way they use their storage: a CHAR(*M*) type always uses *M* bytes of storage, values being padded out to the right with spaces to the specified length, *M*. When you retrieve a value from a CHAR field, the trailing spaces will be removed.

A VARCHAR, in contrast, takes up just enough storage to hold the value (in fact, 1 byte more, because it also stores the value's length). So if you have a VARCHAR(255) column and insert a 10-character string into it, it takes up 11 bytes of storage.

Consider the following example, which creates a table called people to illustrate the use of CHAR and VARCHAR:

```
CREATE TABLE people (
 initials CHAR(3),
 last_name VARCHAR(100))
```

Now insert some data, using the INSERT statement and a list of value sets:

```
INSERT INTO people VALUES ("Elizabeth", "Downey"), ("G", "Washington")
```

Now see what's stored in the table:

```
+----------+------------+
| initials | last_name  |
+----------+------------+
| Eli      | Downey     |
| G        | Washington |
+----------+------------+
```

As you can see, Elizabeth has been truncated to Eli because it's too long for the three-character column. (Your application would have trapped this attempt to put a name into an initials field, right?) However, the second row has been stored correctly.

How can you check that the spaces will be removed from the CHAR field when you read from it? Use the CONCAT function, which concatenates, or joins, values together. If there's nothing after initials, you know the trailing spaces have been removed.

The following line

```
SELECT CONCAT(initials, last_name) FROM people
```

produces this:

```
+---------------------------+
| CONCAT(initials, last_name) |
+---------------------------+
| EliDowney                 |
| GWashington               |
+---------------------------+
```

Note

> The CONCAT() function is just one of many functions that exist in MySQL's function library.
>
> Although the purpose of this function is to concatenate a number of string values together, MySQL has functions for handling strings, performing arithmetic, working with times and dates, running encryption algorithms, and much more.
>
> You will learn about the function library in Day 10, "Operators and Functions in MySQL."

It worked. The values joined seamlessly together, proving that the trailing spaces in the CHAR field were removed.

Silent Column Changes

It may sound strange, but MySQL is loathe to mix CHAR and VARCHAR column types in the same table. In the preceding example, the table looked like this when we created it:

```
+-----------+--------------+------+-----+---------+-------+
| Field     | Type         | Null | Key | Default | Extra |
+-----------+--------------+------+-----+---------+-------+
| initials  | char(3)      | YES  |     | NULL    |       |
| last_name | varchar(100) | YES  |     | NULL    |       |
+-----------+--------------+------+-----+---------+-------+
```

This is what we expected. But let's add another column, a CHAR(10). We could do this using an ALTER TABLE statement (more on how to alter tables in Day 6):

```
ALTER TABLE people ADD COLUMN title CHAR(10)
```

Now view the description of the table again:

```
+-----------+--------------+------+-----+---------+-------+
| Field     | Type         | Null | Key | Default | Extra |
+-----------+--------------+------+-----+---------+-------+
| initials  | char(3)      | YES  |     | NULL    |       |
| last_name | varchar(100) | YES  |     | NULL    |       |
| title     | varchar(10)  | YES  |     | NULL    |       |
+-----------+--------------+------+-----+---------+-------+
```

Notice what's happened to the title column: MySQL has silently changed it from a CHAR(10) to a VARCHAR(10).

It's more efficient for MySQL to process fixed-length rows of data. In other words, for optimal performance, it prefers the entire table to be defined using fixed-length columns. However, if any column is variable length (VARCHAR, TEXT, or BLOB), it might as well treat the whole thing as variable length.

5

MySQL converts any VARCHAR columns with a length of less than four to type CHAR. But if any column has a variable length, all CHAR columns longer than three characters are converted to VARCHAR.

MySQL performs these changes for efficiency of performance and to make best use of its data storage. However, they should not affect your handling of data.

BINARY Column Attribute

You can specify the BINARY column attribute for CHAR and VARCHAR columns. This causes values in those columns to be treated as binary strings.

You can use it as follows:

```
column_name CHAR(M) BINARY
```

or

```
column_name VARCHAR(M) BINARY
```

Values in those columns will then be handled in a case-sensitive way in comparison and sorting operations.

The BINARY attribute is "sticky": if you use a BINARY column in an expression with other non-BINARY columns, the entire expression will be handled as a binary value. Any comparison will thus be done in a case-sensitive way.

BLOB and TEXT Column Types

BLOB and TEXT are families of column types intended as high-capacity binary and textual storage. You can use them to store all manner of data: text, binary data, images, compressed files, and so on. They are typically used where large-volume storage is required.

The actual column types come in the forms TINYBLOB, TINYTEXT, BLOB, TEXT, MEDIUMBLOB, MEDIUMTEXT, LONGBLOB, and LONGTEXT. As shown previously in Table 5.3, the BLOB and TEXT types themselves can store 2^{16}-1 bytes, which is 65 kilobytes. The LONG forms can store as much as 2^{32}-1 bytes, which is 4 gigabytes of data.

BLOB means *binary large object*, and this family of types is intended for storing binary data (or any kind of data represented in binary form), whereas TEXT types are intended for large amounts of text. However, BLOB and TEXT are essentially the same thing, and the only difference between the two families is that when doing comparison and sorting, BLOB values, being binary, are case sensitive. TEXT values are not, and comparison and sorting are not performed in a case-sensitive way.

A TEXT family column is really just like a large capacity VARCHAR column, and like VARCHAR, its storage requirements are dictated by the length of the stored value in each row. (TEXT types require between 1 and 4 bytes of storage in addition to the length of data stored. These extra bytes record the length of the stored value.)

In comparison, a BLOB family column is really just like a VARCHAR BINARY column. BLOB storage requirements are the same as for the corresponding TEXT type.

ENUM and SET Column Types

The ENUM and SET column types can be used to hold column values chosen from a given set of strings. The possible strings (think of them as "members") are declared at table creation time, and after that only these values may be inserted into the column.

ENUM

You can use the ENUM column type where you want the column to contain exactly one of the allowed members specified at table creation time.

For example, you might create a table with an ENUM column specifying a set of three enumeration members:

```
CREATE TABLE my_table (
 number ENUM("one", "two", "three") NULL)
```

This example declared that the column can be NULL, though you could also have put NOT NULL to not allow null values to exist.

The ENUM column would be allowed to hold any one of the string values: NULL (because we declared it can be NULL), "", "one", "two", and "three".

For each ENUM column, a corresponding index exists, which is a numeric representation of the number of each possible member, starting from 1. In this case, the corresponding indexes would be NULL, 0, 1, 2, and 3, respectively.

Although NULL is a legal value in this case, an index of 0 denotes that an illegal value has been inserted. 1, 2, and 3 correspond with the valid members.

Now see what happens by inserting some rows of data, some of it valid, and some not:

```
INSERT INTO my_table VALUES (NULL), (""), ("one"), ("three"), ("four")
```

Note that the second value "" and the final value "four" are not in the set of valid members. Let's write a simple query to display the contents of the table, showing both the string value of the number column and the corresponding index value, which you get by treating the ENUM column as a number (by adding zero to it, number+0):

```
SELECT number, number+0 FROM my_table
```

5

This gives the following output:

```
+--------+----------+
| number | number+0 |
+--------+----------+
| NULL   |     NULL |
|        |        0 |
| one    |        1 |
| three  |        3 |
|        |        0 |
+--------+----------+
```

As you can see, we retrieved both the string value of the ENUM column and the corresponding index value. The 0 values denote the attempts to enter illegal values.

NULL is a valid value, although if we had declared the column as NOT NULL, the insert would be treated as illegal. Inserting NULL among other valid values would put a 0 into that row, whereas inserting a single row with NULL would cause an error.

If you insert a numeric into an ENUM column, that number will be assumed to be the index of that enumeration member. Thus if we do this:

```
INSERT INTO my_table VALUES (2)
```

it would cause a row with value two to be added because this member has the index value 2.

When sorting on an ENUM column, the sort order is governed by the index of the members (in other words, from the order in the CREATE TABLE declaration) rather than the members' textual representations. Therefore, sorting the data in the simple table here by adding ORDER BY:

```
SELECT number FROM my_table ORDER BY number
```

would produce the following:

```
+--------+
| number |
+--------+
| NULL   |
|        |
|        |
| one    |
| two    |
| three  |
+--------+
```

As you can see, one, two, and three are usefully in the order in which they were declared rather than in string-comparison order.

SET

The SET column type works in much the same way as ENUM. However, although ENUM can hold only one of the enumeration members, SET can hold any number of members, including all of them.

Here's an example that declares the members of a column:

```
CREATE TABLE pizza (
 topping SET ("pepperoni", "prawns", "anchovies", "tuna", "cheese") NULL)
```

To insert data into the rows, you can now specify the SET column to have no value, a single value from the valid members, or many values:

```
INSERT INTO pizza VALUES (""), ("pepperoni"), ("anchovies,tuna")
```

Notice how when we inserted data for the third row (in the third set of parentheses), we specified two valid members separated by a comma. Here's what the table now holds:

```
+----------------+
| topping        |
+----------------+
|                |
| pepperoni      |
| anchovies,tuna |
+----------------+
```

The first item was nothing (""), which leaves nothing in the table at the first row. Now let's try inserting two more rows, one with an invalid member, and one with a NULL:

```
INSERT INTO pizza VALUES ("chicken"), (NULL)
```

This adds two more rows, one containing no value, and one containing NULL:

```
+----------------+
| topping        |
+----------------+
|                |
| pepperoni      |
| anchovies,tuna |
|                |
| NULL           |
+----------------+
```

Because we declared that the column could contain NULL when we created the table, inserting a NULL results in a NULL in the data. However, if we had declared the column as NOT NULL, inserting a NULL would have resulted in an empty value in that row, denoting an attempt to enter an illegal value.

5

As with ENUM, we can display the SET field and the index numbers of its members:

```
SELECT topping, topping+0 FROM pizza
```

produces

```
+----------------+-----------+
| topping        | topping+0 |
+----------------+-----------+
|                |         0 |
| pepperoni      |         1 |
| anchovies,tuna |        12 |
|                |         0 |
| NULL           |      NULL |
+----------------+-----------+
```

The indexes are created in a different way from ENUM and are derived from the combined binary representations of the members present in the value. Study the MySQL Reference Manual if you require more information on how these values are represented.

Date and Time

MySQL has a range of data types for handling date and time information. Time formats have an intuitive order that you're used to in daily life: *hours:minutes:seconds*. Dates, on the other hand, are always output in the format: *year:month:day*. Both conform to ANSI-92 standard format.

All date and time data types have a range of legal values and a "zero" value to which a field will be set if you attempt to put an illegal value into it.

When outputting date and time, you usually have the option to ask MySQL to give you the data in either string or numeric form. The format depends on the context in which it's used in your SQL.

MySQL is flexible when accepting date and time information. For example, the date 2003-05-12 means the same to it as 2003/05/12, or 3+5+12, or even 20030512.

Date and Time Column Types

Table 5.4 shows MySQL's column types for representing date and time information.

TABLE 5.4 Date and Time Column Types

Type Name	Meaning	Zero Value
DATE	Date in format *YYYY-MM-DD*	0000-00-00
TIME	Time in format *hh:mm:ss*	00:00:00
DATETIME	Date and time in format *YYYY-MM-DD hh:mm:ss*	0000-00-00 00:00:00
TIMESTAMP	Autoset date and time, in its longest format *YYYYMMDDhhmmss* (in longest format)	00000000000000
YEAR	Year in format *YYYY*	0000

DATE

The DATE column type records the date of an event without storing time information. MySQL is Year 2000 compliant in its date storage.

DATE values can range from 1000-01-01 to 9999-12-31 and occupy 3 bytes of storage.

You can specify dates as *YYYY-MM-DD*, *YYYY/MM/DD*, or *YYYYMMDD*, or with almost any punctuation separating the components of a date.

TIME

The TIME column type stores the time of an event, independent of any particular date. TIME values occupy 3 bytes of storage.

TIME values can range not just from 00:00:00 to 23:59:59 but also can include negative time—in fact, from -838:59:59 to 838:59:59. This allows you to represent not just time of day but also the elapsed time between two events, or even degrees, minutes, and seconds of longitude and latitude.

As with DATE and other data types, MySQL has a relaxed approach to accepting data, and you can use almost any punctuation marks as delimiters to separate the hours, minutes, and seconds. Thus 08:32:20 could be represented as 08-32-20, or you can do without the leading zeros, as in 8.32.20.

You can even specify time without delimiters, as in 083220 or 83220. But be careful before getting too minimalist: MySQL reads time from the right, expecting seconds to be declared but not necessarily hours. Therefore 8:32 or 0832 will be interpreted as 8 minutes, 32 seconds. It's wise to stick to MySQL's standard format wherever possible to avoid confusion.

5

Caution

> Valid times outside the allowable range will be clipped at the lower and
> upper ceilings of `-832:59:59` and `832:59:59`, but will not be set to `00:00:00`.
> However, invalid times such as where the minutes or seconds exceed 59 will
> be set to `00:00:00`.
>
> Because `00:00:00` is itself a valid time, you would have no way of knowing it
> was set to that value legally or as the result of an invalid time. Therefore,
> you should write your application carefully so that illegal times are trapped
> before being passed to MySQL.

DATETIME

The DATETIME column type holds the entire date and time of an event in a single column.

DATETIME values occupy 8 bytes of storage and can range from `1000-01-01 00:00:00` to `9999-12-31 23:59:59`.

TIMESTAMP

TIMESTAMP is a useful field format whereby a TIMESTAMP column will be set to the current system date and time whenever that row is updated or inserted into the table. It conveniently gives the record a "last updated" timestamp without you having to set it explicitly.

TIMESTAMP can only handle dates from the beginning of 1970 (`19700101000000`) through to some time in the year 2037. It is related to Unix time whose "epoch" started on 1 January 1970. (It was during 1970 that Brian Kernighan suggested the name "Unix.") The upper limit of current 4-byte Unix time falls during the year 2037.

A TIMESTAMP column occupies 4 bytes of storage, and although it can be declared to display between 2 and 14 digits of date and time, it always holds the same data internally. Table 5.5 shows a list of the display formats that TIMESTAMP offers.

TABLE 5.5   TIMESTAMP Display Formats

Column Specification	Display Format
TIMESTAMP(14)	YYYYMMDDhhmmss
TIMESTAMP(12)	YYYYMMDDhhmm
TIMESTAMP(10)	YYYYMMDDhh
TIMESTAMP(8)	YYYYMMDD
TIMESTAMP(6)	YYYYMM
TIMESTAMP(4)	YYYY
TIMESTAMP(2)	YY

Make sure that you understand what the different lengths mean. If an update to a row is made at 9:30:00 on 12 May 2002, any TIMESTAMP column would be set to this time to the nearest second. However, a TIMESTAMP(14) column would output the update date and time as 20020512093000, whereas a TIMESTAMP(8) would output the same date and time as 20020512, displaying the date but not outputting the time at all.

Although the main point of using a TIMESTAMP is that it sets its value automatically, you can set its value explicitly if you prefer. You can set a TIMESTAMP to any date and time within its legal range. If you try to enter an illegal value, the "zero" value for this column type will be used.

When setting a TIMESTAMP field with a value specified as a number, the value should be 14, 12, 8, or 6 digits long. When setting the value as a string, always use at least six characters. This ensures that at least year and month are specified.

Note

You can alter a TIMESTAMP column declaration without losing data. Because it always occupies the same amount of storage, you are simply "revealing" more or less of the stored data. By widening a field, you will find that new data gets displayed. Likewise, if you narrow the column, you will not lose data, but merely hide the less significant digits from display.

YEAR

The YEAR column type records the year of an event and occupies just 1 byte of data.

YEAR values can range from 1901 to 2155. You can set a YEAR in either string or numeric notation.

Transferring Data Between Date and Time Column Types

MySQL lets you transfer data from a column of one type to a column of another type. You can also change the declaration of a column from one type to another.

Why would you want to transfer data between different column types? For example, you may have a DATETIME field that records the precise date and time a customer made a purchase. After a while you may want to archive the data by transferring it to another table, but you're only interested in preserving the date of the transaction.

If you're moving data to a column type that can't hold all the existing data, the part that cannot be represented will be lost. If you're moving data to a column type that can hold more information than the existing data, the unpopulated portion will be set to the "zero" value.

Therefore if you have data from a DATETIME or TIMESTAMP column and want to put it into a DATE column, there will be nowhere to store the time information, and it will be lost.

Conversely, if you have a DATE value and want to write it to a DATETIME or TIMESTAMP column, MySQL will insert 00:00:00 for the time portion.

Because the various column types have different ranges of legal values, the accepting column must be able to represent the data that it is given, or the data will be lost. For example, attempting to place DATE information with a year not in the range 1970 to 2037 into a TIMESTAMP field will cause the data to be "zeroed." Data will not merely be clipped at the upper and lower limits.

Summary

Today, you took a close look at MySQL's data and column types. You looked at integer, floating-point, binary, text, date, and time column types. You examined what they can store and how data is inserted into and retrieved from them. You learned about ENUM and SET, column types that can take values only from a declared valid list.

You also learned about some special kinds of columns, such as AUTO_INCREMENT for creating sequences of integers and TIMESTAMP for automatically inserting the date and time.

Q&A

Q Can I use floating-point numbers for all my numeric storage?

A Strictly speaking, floating-point numbers can represent anything that an integer can represent (and more). However, they are far less efficient to process, and you do not have the benefit of features such as AUTO_INCREMENT. In general, always use an integer type unless you really need to store fractional information.

Q I don't understand the difference between CHAR and VARCHAR; they seem so similar. And I just created a table with a mixture of CHAR and VARCHAR fields, and all my CHAR fields disappeared!

A CHAR column types have a fixed-length storage requirement and consume the full storage regardless of what data is held.

VARCHAR columns only consume as much storage as the value in them requires. They are thus more efficient on storage, even though MySQL in general can perform better with all fixed-width (for example, CHAR) columns in a table. MySQL does silent column changes between CHAR and VARCHAR types to optimize tables. However, this should not affect the storage of your data, nor should it interfere with how you insert or retrieve data.

Q Can I store images in MySQL?

A Yes. The various BLOB data types (TINYBLOB, BLOB, MEDIUMBLOB, LONGBLOB) are intended for storing binary data, and, theoretically at least, this includes images, sounds, and compressed files as well as textual data.

However, in practice you may find it more difficult to get images into and out of MySQL than other kinds of data because you would need to write your application to handle images as binary data. If your application is for a dynamic Web site, it's probably easier for the Web page that holds the HTML tag for the image to link to the image file rather than to a script in which MySQL extracts an image from the database.

So in essence, although it's possible to hold data in a BLOB column, you may well find it easier to store the image in your usual file system and for MySQL to merely store the path to the file.

Q What is the best format for specifying dates and times to MySQL?

A MySQL is relaxed in that it can accept date and time data in a wide range of styles, delimited with punctuation marks or not delimited at all. For the sake of clarity, the best practice may be to submit your data in the same format as MySQL outputs it (*YYYY-MM-DD* for dates and *hh:mm:ss* for times) if data is available in these formats from your application.

Q Can I have a table with two AUTO_INCREMENT columns?

A No. MySQL allows only one such column per table, and it must be declared as a key (index).

Workshop

The quiz and exercises are provided to help you solidify your understanding of the material covered today. Try to understand the quiz and exercise answers before continuing to tomorrow's lesson.

Quiz

1. If you want to represent integer numbers from 0 up to 2,147,483,647, what column type would you use?

2. If you have a column of type SMALLINT with the attribute AUTO_INCREMENT, and existing rows contain the values 1, 4, 5, and 6, what value would be inserted into the column if a new row of data was added?

3. True or False: The maximum value of a TIME column is 23:59:59.

4. True or False: When performing comparisons and sorting operations on data in a column of type VARCHAR BINARY, data will be handled in a case-sensitive way.

Quiz Answers

1. INT (signed or unsigned).

2. 7.

3. False. Values can range from -838:59:59 to 838:59:59.

4. True.

Exercises

1. Write a line of SQL to declare a column called color whose values can be only one of red, green, blue, yellow. The declaration should allow a NULL value to be specified.

2. If you wanted to store the value "red,yellow" in the column described in Exercise 1, what should the column declaration have been?

Exercises Answers

1. color ENUM ("red", "green", "blue", "yellow") NULL

2. color SET ("red", "green", "blue", "yellow") NULL

DAY **6**

Manipulating a Database

Today you will learn how to manipulate a database and its tables in MySQL. In particular, you will learn:

- How to create a database
- How to drop (delete) a database
- How to create tables, declaring the names of columns and their data types
- How to drop (delete) tables
- How to describe a table
- How to alter the columns and indexes of a table

An important tool for doing these tasks is the `mysql` program, which you first saw in Day 2, "Installing MySQL." Before studying how to work with databases and tables, you will learn how to use `mysql` to run SQL queries, both in interactive and batch modes.

You will also see more of the versatile `mysqladmin` program and be introduced to `mysqlshow`.

Note

> In today's lesson, you will see examples of MySQL's client programs being run like this from the operating system command line:
>
> `$ mysql`
>
> We'll assume that you have already made `mysql` and related programs executable from anywhere on your operating system, without prefixing them with the full path to the binary program. (If not, see Day 2 for details on how to do this.)
>
> If the programs are not executable like this, you will need to specify the full path to MySQL's `bin` directory in your installation to run them. For example:
>
> `$ /usr/local/mysql/bin/mysql`

Using the `mysql` Client Program

Before studying the ways of handling databases and tables, it's worthwhile to learn how to use the `mysql` client program. You will see some examples of it being used, but if you don't fully understand the SQL used in the examples, don't worry; we will go through the queries themselves later today.

`mysql` allows you to run SQL queries on a MySQL database. It can be invoked as an interactive monitor or console with a command-line interface, or in batch mode, allowing you to pass it an entire file of SQL.

You can use the following general formats to invoke it, in console mode:

`mysql [options] [database_name]`

or in batch mode:

`mysql [options] [database_name] < filename`

You can usually put the *options* and *database_name* in any order, and within the *options*, you can specify the username and password. You can see the full list of options for `mysql` by running

`$ mysql -help`

The options for `mysql` are many and varied, but they are mostly for more advanced use. We'll just look at passing the username and password options, but you'll see `mysql` operating in both modes.

User Permissions for Client Programs

mysql and the other client programs (mysqladmin, mysqlshow, and others) can be invoked only by a valid MySQL user who has been set up in MySQL's permission, or *grant*, tables. (You'll learn more about the grant tables in Day 14, "Security.") If you run a client program as a MySQL user who has a password set in the grant table, the correct password will have to be provided for the program to run. Without a valid username and password, MySQL refuses the database connection, and the client program terminates.

The principle of giving username and password is the same no matter which client program is used, and in the case of mysql, no matter whether it's run interactively or in batch mode. In the following examples, we'll look at invoking mysql with various ways of specifying username and password, but mysqladmin and other programs need username and password to be specified in the same way, as you will see later today.

Remember that a MySQL user is not the same as a Unix or Windows user. Even the MySQL root user who has the same name as the Unix root user has this name only out of convention. Like the Unix root user, the MySQL root is the most powerful user on the database server; but beyond this convention, there is no necessary connection between them, and this goes for all other users too.

When starting a client program such as mysql, you have the option of specifying the MySQL user using the -u option. If you don't specify -u, MySQL assumes that your MySQL username is the same as your system username and tries to connect to MySQL with this username.

The following example shows the user logging in as the MySQL root user:

```
$ mysql -u root -p
Enter password:
```

At the prompt, you have to type the password, but it won't be displayed. It doesn't matter who the user is logged in as on the operating system. The -u root (or in general, -u *username*) option specifies the username, and the -p option tells the program you want to offer a password.

You could always offer the password on the command line, like this:

```
$ mysql -u root -prootpass
```

where rootpass is the password for that user and follows immediately after the -p without a space. In this case, it's the MySQL root user, but the password is not necessarily the same as the Unix root password (and for good security should be different). If you are already logged in as system root user, you can omit -u to connect to MySQL with that username, thus:

```
# mysql -prootpass
```

6

Another way of doing the same thing is longhand, like this:

```
# mysql --password=rootpass
```

But the following is incorrect because there is a space after `-p`:

```
# mysql -p rootpass
```

Although it may be convenient to offer your password on the command line like this, it's not good practice. It's better that your password (and especially the `root` password) never appears onscreen. In Day 14, you will learn more about the reasons for this and will learn some convenient ways of starting client programs. But for the time being, you're recommended to invoke them as shown here.

Also note that if no password has been set for a given user in the grant table, you don't need to specify `-p` at all (and of course, not type a password). If you're the system `root` user and no MySQL root password has been set, you can start a client program as simply as this:

```
# mysql
```

However, having no password (especially for the MySQL `root` user) is dangerous and should be avoided.

As mentioned previously, you can specify a database name when starting `mysql`. The following example shows the user logging in as the MySQL `root` user, specifying *database_name* on the command line as the database `test`:

```
$ mysql -u root -p test
Enter password:
```

Now that you've seen how to start `mysql`, it's time to look at what you can actually do with it.

Using `mysql` in Console Mode

Here's how to start `mysql` as an interactive monitor. The following example shows a user logging in as the MySQL `root` user `cms` as the database to connect to:

```
$ mysql -u root -p test
Enter password:
Welcome to the MySQL monitor.  Commands end with ; or \g.
Your MySQL connection id is 17 to server version: 4.0.1-alpha-log

Type 'help;' or '\h' for help. Type '\c' to clear the buffer.

mysql>
```

The last line of the server's response is the `mysql` command prompt. It's waiting for you to type a command or query.

Without specifying a database, you would type this instead:

```
$ mysql -u root -p
Enter password:
```

When inside the `mysql` console, to tell `mysql` to use a particular database—say `mysql` (and thus disconnect from any database you're already connected to, for example, `test`)—you can use the `use` command by typing the following:

```
mysql> use mysql
Database changed
```

Inside the `mysql` console, you can give commands to `mysql` itself and issue SQL queries to be run on a database. SQL queries must be terminated with a semicolon. However, in the previous example, you typed a `mysql` command (`use`) rather than a SQL query, so a semicolon (`;`) is optional.

Commands and queries are not case sensitive, although I'll generally show `mysql` commands in lowercase and SQL in uppercase.

Now let's try some simple SQL:

```
mysql> SHOW TABLES;
+-----------------+
| Tables_in_mysql |
+-----------------+
| columns_priv    |
| db              |
| func            |
| host            |
| tables_priv     |
| user            |
+-----------------+
6 rows in set (0.00 sec)
```

In the preceding example, a `SHOW` query is used to list the tables in the `mysql` database that we selected previously.

A query can occupy a single line, as shown previously or can be spread over several lines. This will be useful when queries become long, but for now just try spreading a simple query across several lines.

We'll illustrate this with a `DESCRIBE` query (also abbreviated as `DESC`), which returns the column names and properties of a table:

```
mysql> DESCRIBE
    -> user
    -> ;
```

6

```
+-----------------+-------------------+------+-----+---------+-------+
| Field           | Type              | Null | Key | Default | Extra |
+-----------------+-------------------+------+-----+---------+-------+
| Host            | char(60) binary   |      | PRI |         |       |
| User            | char(16) binary   |      | PRI |         |       |
| Password        | char(16) binary   |      |     |         |       |
| Select_priv     | enum('N','Y')     |      |     | N       |       |
| Insert_priv     | enum('N','Y')     |      |     | N       |       |
| Update_priv     | enum('N','Y')     |      |     | N       |       |
| Delete_priv     | enum('N','Y')     |      |     | N       |       |
| Create_priv     | enum('N','Y')     |      |     | N       |       |
| Drop_priv       | enum('N','Y')     |      |     | N       |       |
| Reload_priv     | enum('N','Y')     |      |     | N       |       |
| Shutdown_priv   | enum('N','Y')     |      |     | N       |       |
| Process_priv    | enum('N','Y')     |      |     | N       |       |
| File_priv       | enum('N','Y')     |      |     | N       |       |
| Grant_priv      | enum('N','Y')     |      |     | N       |       |
| References_priv | enum('N','Y')     |      |     | N       |       |
| Index_priv      | enum('N','Y')     |      |     | N       |       |
| Alter_priv      | enum('N','Y')     |      |     | N       |       |
+-----------------+-------------------+------+-----+---------+-------+
17 rows in set (0.00 sec)
```

(Your output may have more lines than this; this example shows the older, smaller format of the user table.)

Notice that the second line in the preceding example contains a different type of prompt:

```
    ->
```

This prompt keeps appearing on every line until you terminate the query with a semicolon (;).

There are also other types of prompts. The following:

```
    '>
```

and

```
    ">
```

appear when you have typed, but not terminated, a single or double quote, respectively. mysql is reminding you that you opened the quotes but have not yet closed them. Should you want to cancel a query you have started, type \c.

mysql has some convenient ways of helping you reissue queries and commands you have run previously, with or without modification. You can use the up-arrow key (Ctrl+P) to recall the previous line typed and the down-arrow key (Ctrl+N) to go to the next line that has been typed. Use the left and right arrows (Ctrl+B and Ctrl+F) to move left and right within a line, and use the Backspace key to delete the character to the left of the cursor.

Typing should always insert rather than overtype, and if you are in a multiwindow environment, you should also be able to copy text from another application and paste it into the monitor.

Note

The command-line editing facility is available only on systems that have the GNU `readline` library installed and available at compile time.

This is the default on most installations, but if this is missing, you should study the install notes included with your MySQL distribution for more informat ion.

To see a full list of options for the `mysql` client program, type **help**; to exit, type **exit** or **quit**.

Using `mysql` in Batch Mode

You can use the `mysql` client program in batch mode. This means that instead of interacting with the monitor, you can tell `mysql` to go and process a text file containing SQL.

This is a powerful feature. Your text file can detail commands for creating databases, creating tables, and inserting data. Or it may run queries or process updates on existing data.

This facility means that you can import a stream of data from a file, such as when restoring or relocating a database (more on this in Day 15, "Administration"). Or you may have a set of queries that you want to run on a nightly basis from a scheduling program such as Unix's `cron`.

Run `mysql` in batch mode like this:

```
mysql [options] [database_name] < filename
```

For example, if you have a file called `batch.sql` that contains lines of SQL and you want to run its commands against the database `mydb`, you could do this:

```
$ mysql -u root -p mydb < batch.sql
Enter password:
```

The < symbol is a Unix operator to redirect standard input to `mysql`, effectively telling `mysql` to read the file and process its SQL statements. The same can be achieved as shown in the following example, using the Unix `cat` command to print the contents of the file and the | (pipe) symbol to redirect standard output to `mysql`:

```
$ cat batch.sql | mysql -u root -p mydb
Enter password:
```

There's effectively no limit as to what SQL the file can contain, but note that the user who invokes `mysql` must have sufficient privileges to perform the SQL contained within the file. If not, it fails to process.

6

Creating, Dropping, and Selecting a Database

Now that you have seen how to use MySQL's basic client tools, it's time to start putting them to use. You will first use them as you learn how to create a database and then go on to do other kinds of database manipulation.

Creating and dropping a database is something that you may seldom do, except during the design phase of a project, yet the ways of doing these things are important for you to grasp. As you will see, there are often two or more ways to do the same thing, so you will learn both the SQL and the client-driven ways to manipulate databases.

Creating a Database

To create a database from a Unix console, use the `mysqladmin` command with the following format:

```
mysqladmin create database_name -u username -p
```

As you can see, the preceding line runs `mysqladmin` with the keyword `create` to create a database, followed by name of the database, *database_name*. The user authentication options may also be required, as explained previously for the `mysql` client.

In the following example, we create the database `store` and authenticate ourselves as root:

```
$ mysqladmin create store -u root -p
Enter password:
```

Whatever *username* you use, you will have to make sure that that user has sufficient privileges to create a database. (This is unlikely to be a limitation for `root`, but you may find yourself using other usernames that have fewer privileges.) The creation privilege is defined by the `Create_priv` setting for that user in the `mysql` database's `user` grant table. You'll learn more about privileges in Day 14.

Another way to create a database is using the `mysql` program.

Start the `mysql` console without specifying a database name (because you're about to create it). Your session should look like this:

```
$ mysql -u root -p
Enter password:
Welcome to the MySQL monitor.  Commands end with ; or \g.
Your MySQL connection id is 13 to server version: 3.23.46-log

Type 'help;' or '\h' for help. Type '\c' to clear the buffer.

mysql>
```

The SQL statement for creating a database takes the following form:

```
CREATE DATABASE [IF NOT EXISTS] database_name
```

To run this in the `mysql` monitor, you could type your SQL like this:

```
mysql> CREATE DATABASE store;
Query OK, 1 row affected (0.06 sec)
```

The `Query OK` feedback means that your query worked without error, and `1 row affected` means that the database was created.

If you run the preceding SQL and a database with that name exists already, an error results. Alternatively, you can add `IF NOT EXISTS` in your SQL to suppress this error if it should occur. (`IF NOT EXISTS` was added in MySQL 3.23.)

On a Unix system, database names are case sensitive. So in the preceding example, you will be able to refer to the database only as `store`, never as `STORE` or `Store`.

Although the database has been created, it contains no tables yet. The effect of this has been to create a new, empty directory in MySQL's data directory. This directory will eventually hold all the files corresponding to the tables of the database.

There's no technical reason why an application shouldn't create a database. You could have a user-invoked program that runs SQL to do the same as we just did here. However, creating and dropping databases are serious matters; think carefully about whether you want a program, potentially run by someone other than you, to perform such powerful queries on your system.

Listing Databases

To get a list of databases, you can use the `mysqlshow` program; it simply shows what databases exist on the server. When run from the command line, it takes this format:

```
mysqlshow [options] [database_name [table_name [column_name]]]
```

You can use it to show just the list of databases, or information about databases, tables, and columns within them. For now we'll just use it in its simplest mode, passing the minimum options to it. (We'll return to `mysqlshow` in Day 15.)

The *options* may include `-u` and `-p` for specifying username and password (though there are other options), which you can offer in the same way as with `mysql`. So a simple example of running `mysqlshow` could be like this:

```
$ mysqlshow -u root -p
Enter password:
+-----------+
| Databases |
+-----------+
```

6

```
| store    |
| mysql    |
| test     |
+----------+
```

You can do the same thing by running a query from `mysql`. From inside the `mysql` console, you can use the SQL SHOW DATABASES, like this:

```
mysql> SHOW DATABASES;
+----------+
| Database |
+----------+
| store    |
| mysql    |
| test     |
+----------+
3 rows in set (0.00 sec)
```

Dropping a Database

Dropping a database means deleting it, together with all tables and data within it. Using mysqladmin, you can drop a database like this:

```
$ mysqladmin drop store -u root -p
Enter password:
Dropping the database is potentially a very bad thing to do.
Any data stored in the database will be destroyed.

Do you really want to drop the 'store' database [y/N] y
Database "store" dropped
```

As you can see, `mysqladmin` gives a stern warning and asks for confirmation before proceeding.

You can also drop a database using the SQL DROP statement, seen from within the `mysql` monitor:

```
mysql> DROP DATABASE store;
Query OK, 0 rows affected (0.00 sec)
```

This time the effect is instant, and the database disappears! Needless to say, take care when using the DROP statement.

When dropping a database, the corresponding directory under MySQL's data directory will be deleted.

Manipulating Tables

Now that you can use the `mysql` program and run the commands to create a database, you're ready to build on this knowledge and start manipulating tables.

This section will show you how to create a table, drop a table, view a table's description, and alter a table's column declarations.

Creating a Table

You can create a table using the `CREATE TABLE` command, whose syntax is as follows:

```
CREATE [TEMPORARY] TABLE
  [IF NOT EXISTS] table_name
  [(create_definition,...)]
  [table_options] [select_statement]
```

Before looking at the many options for `CREATE TABLE`, let's try a simple example. Say that we want to create a database for a content management system called `cms`, and within it a table called `articles`. We could use the following, first creating the database `cms`, then selecting the same database, and finally creating the table:

```
mysql> CREATE DATABASE cms;
Query OK, 1 row affected (0.06 sec)
mysql> use cms;
Database changed
mysql> CREATE TABLE articles (
    -> article_id INT(9) NOT NULL auto_increment,
    -> headline TEXT NOT NULL,
    -> date_post DATETIME NOT NULL DEFAULT '0000-00-00 00:00:00',
    -> text_body TEXT,
    -> text_summary TEXT,
    -> who_created INT(9) DEFAULT NULL,
    -> email_sent INT(1) NOT NULL DEFAULT '0',
    -> date_email DATETIME DEFAULT NULL,
    -> who_approved INT(9) DEFAULT NULL,
    -> pic VARCHAR(255) DEFAULT NULL,
    -> PRIMARY KEY  (article_id)
    -> );

Query OK, 0 rows affected (0.03 sec)
```

The first line of the `CREATE` statement contains the name of the table we want to create (`articles`). This is followed by the column definitions, one per line. The line containing `PRIMARY KEY` specifies the column (`article_id`), which will be the primary key for the table.

In the `CREATE TABLE` line, we could add `IF NOT EXISTS` to avert an error message if a table with that name exists already. `CREATE TABLE` will not overwrite an existing table.

6

Creating a Temporary Table

You can optionally use the statement to create a temporary table by using the TEMPORARY keyword.

A temporary table exists only for the life of the current database connection. It automatically is deleted when the connection is closed or dies. Two different connections can use the same name for a temporary table without conflicting with each other.

Temporary tables can be useful when queries get complex. For example, you might want to assemble some data from another table and do some processing or updates on it without affecting the main table. Versions of MySQL prior to 4.1 have no subselect capability, and temporary tables are a convenient way of performing the equivalent of a subselect.

 Note

> The TEMPORARY TABLE functionality was added in MySQL version 3.23.
>
> As of MySQL version 4.0.2 a new permission type is required for creating temporary tables. Non-root users need to have the Create_tmp_tables privilege set in the user grant table. See Day 14, if you experience difficulties creating temporary tables.

Here's an example dialogue to create a temporary table called tmp with a single column:

```
mysql> CREATE TEMPORARY TABLE tmp (
    -> name VARCHAR(100) NULL);
Query OK, 0 rows affected (0.00 sec)
```

Creating a Table from a SELECT

A SELECT query produces a resultset of data that has been extracted from another table (you will study it in more detail in Day 8, "Querying Data.") You can use CREATE TABLE to create your new table with this result data from a SELECT in a single statement.

CREATE TABLE...SELECT extracts column declarations and data from the SELECT query's resultset and uses them to both create and populate the new table.

You can create a normal or a temporary table from a SELECT, and the creation of a temporary table is shown in the following example:

```
mysql> CREATE TEMPORARY TABLE tmp
    -> SELECT subscriber_id, name
    -> FROM subscribers
    -> WHERE name LIKE 'John%';
Query OK, 1 row affected (0.01 sec)
Records: 1  Duplicates: 0  Warnings: 0
```

Now let's display the contents of the new table:

```
mysql> SELECT * FROM tmp;
+---------------+------------+
| subscriber_id | name       |
+---------------+------------+
|             2 | John Brown |
+---------------+------------+
1 row in set (0.00 sec)
```

The new table takes its column names and declarations from the SELECT query; there's no way to declare them separately. If you want to make the column names different, you have to use an alias in your SELECT.

You would run the SELECT query like this, using the keyword AS to name the alias of subcriber_id as id:

```
mysql> CREATE TEMPORARY TABLE tmp
    -> SELECT subscriber_id AS id,
    -> name
    -> FROM subscribers
    -> WHERE name LIKE 'John%';
Query OK, 1 row affected (0.00 sec)
Records: 1  Duplicates: 0  Warnings: 0

mysql> SELECT * FROM tmp;
+----+------------+
| id | name       |
+----+------------+
|  2 | John Brown |
+----+------------+
1 row in set (0.00 sec)
```

Notice from the output that the column subscriber_id had its name changed to id in the table we created by the AS id clause.

Note

An *alias* is a way of referring to a column or table by a shorter or more convenient name than its real name. To create an alias on a column, you just need to include a clause like this in your SELECT query:

...*real_column_name* AS *alias_name*

To create an alias on a table, you just need to include a clause like this:

...*real_table_name* AS *alias_name*

Aliases are convenient to use on columns because the alias may refer to a column on which functions or operators are applied, which may be a rather lengthy reference. They're convenient to use on tables when you need to refer to that table several times in your SQL and need a shorter name.

You'll see more examples of aliases in Day 8, "Querying Data," and Day 9, "Joins and Indexes."

6

Specifying Table Types

Through the *table_options* parameter of CREATE TABLE, you can specify the MySQL
table type. You can choose from any of the table types shown in Table 6.1.

TABLE 6.1 MySQL's Table Types

Table Type	Description
ISAM	MySQL's original table handler.
HEAP	The data for this table is only stored in memory.
MyISAM	The binary portable table handler that replaces ISAM.
MERGE	A collection of MyISAM tables used as one table.
BDB	Transaction-safe tables with page locking.
InnoDB	Transaction-safe tables with row locking.

ISAM, HEAP, and MyISAM are available for MySQL versions 3.23.6 or later. MERGE, BDB,
and InnoDB are available only for MySQL versions 4.0 onward, and you will need to
have compiled and configured MySQL with support for the BDB or InnoDB table types if
you want to use them. You'll learn more about these table types in Day 17, "Transactions
and Table Locking."

Use the following syntax for your *table_options*:

TYPE = *table_type*

Therefore, to create a table of the type InnoDB, use

TYPE = InnoDB

If you don't specify TYPE, the MyISAM table type will be used by default.

Listing Tables

You can list the tables of a database using the SQL:

SHOW TABLES

For example, if you are connected to a database within mysql, you can do this:

mysql> **SHOW TABLES;**

Dropping a Table

Dropping a table means deleting the table definition and all data in the table.

You can drop a table using

DROP TABLE *table_name*

For example:

```
DROP TABLE subscribers
```

drops the table subscribers.

Altering a Table

After a table has been created, it's still possible to change the specifications of its columns. You can use the ALTER TABLE statement, which takes the following form:

```
ALTER TABLE table_name action_list
```

You can make multiple changes at a time to the same table. Just specify an action_list of changes separated by commas. An action list can include any number of these actions.

The possible actions for modifying columns are shown in Table 6.2.

TABLE 6.2   Actions Performed by ALTER TABLE (Column-Related)

Action Syntax	Action Performed
ADD [COLUMN] column_declaration [FIRST	AFTER column_name]	Add a column to the table
ALTER [COLUMN] column_name {SET DEFAULT literal	DROP DEFAULT}	Specify new default value for a column or remove old default value
CHANGE [COLUMN] column_name column_declaration	Modify column declaration
MODIFY [COLUMN] column_declaration	Modify column declaration without renaming
DROP [COLUMN] column_name	Drop a column and all data contained within it
RENAME [AS] new_table_name	Rename a table
table_options	Change table options

In Table 6.2, column_name always represents the current name of the column. The column_declaration is the new declaration, in the same format as if it were in a CREATE TABLE statement. This must include the name of the column after the change, even if the name does not change. new_table_name is the name of the table after the table is renamed.

For example, to add a column to the subscribers table—say, date_of_birth—do this:

```
mysql> ALTER TABLE subscribers
    -> ADD COLUMN date_of_birth DATETIME;
Query OK, 4 rows affected (0.00 sec)
Records: 4  Duplicates: 0  Warnings: 0
```

6

```
mysql> DESCRIBE subscribers;
+---------------+--------------+------+-----+---------+----------------+
| Field         | Type         | Null | Key | Default | Extra          |
+---------------+--------------+------+-----+---------+----------------+
| subscriber_id | int(9)       |      | PRI | NULL    | auto_increment |
| name          | varchar(100) | YES  |     | NULL    |                |
| email         | varchar(100) |      |     |         |                |
| date_of_birth | datetime     | YES  |     | NULL    |                |
+---------------+--------------+------+-----+---------+----------------+
4 rows in set (0.00 sec)
```

MySQL adds the column and, because there happen to be four rows in the table already, tells us that four rows were affected.

To drop the column again, do this:

```
mysql> ALTER TABLE subscribers
    -> DROP COLUMN date_of_birth;
```

Now we'll be a little more ambitious. We'll add the date_of_birth column again, but this time put it immediately after the name column, using the AFTER keyword:

```
ADD COLUMN date_of_birth DATETIME AFTER name
```

To make things interesting, we'll also modify the email column to make it 200 characters long rather than 100:

```
MODIFY email VARCHAR(200)
```

Run the combined statement with commas separating the actions, like this:

```
mysql> ALTER TABLE subscribers
    -> ADD COLUMN date_of_birth DATETIME AFTER name,
    -> MODIFY email VARCHAR(200);
Query OK, 4 rows affected (0.00 sec)
Records: 4  Duplicates: 0  Warnings: 0
```

```
mysql> DESCRIBE subscribers;
+---------------+--------------+------+-----+---------+----------------+
| Field         | Type         | Null | Key | Default | Extra          |
+---------------+--------------+------+-----+---------+----------------+
| subscriber_id | int(9)       |      | PRI | NULL    | auto_increment |
| name          | varchar(100) | YES  |     | NULL    |                |
| date_of_birth | datetime     | YES  |     | NULL    |                |
| email         | varchar(200) | YES  |     | NULL    |                |
+---------------+--------------+------+-----+---------+----------------+
4 rows in set (0.00 sec)
```

Notice how we separated the two actions with a comma. We could make all sorts of changes to the table like this.

In this example, the change made to the email field was fairly safe: the field got longer so that no data would be lost. However, if making fields shorter, be aware that in rows where there's too much data for the new field size, the data will be truncated down to the shorter length.

In addition to changing columns, you can alter the table_options you saw just now in the definition of CREATE TABLE. Although there are many possibilities for table_options not documented here, one thing you may want to use it to alter is the table type. For example, you can change the table from a MyISAM table to an InnoDB table:

```
mysql> ALTER TABLE subscribers
    -> TYPE = InnoDB;
Query OK, 4 rows affected (0.11 sec)
Records: 4  Duplicates: 0  Warnings: 0
```

You can use ALTER TABLE to add and drop indexes on tables. If you're not sure about using indexes yet, don't worry; we'll cover that in Day 9. For now, let's just say that there are ways of making your table operations more efficient, and they can enforce rules such as uniqueness of data in a given column. An index (also known as a *key*) behaves like an external column to the table, thus an index can be dropped without affecting any data. Here's how to add an index:

```
ADD INDEX [index_name] (index_columns)
ADD PRIMARY KEY (index_columns)
ADD UNIQUE [index_name] (index_columns)
```

where *index_columns* is the name of the column to index, or a list of column names separated with commas. *index_name* is optional, and, if omitted, the name of the first indexed column will be used as the name of the index.

To drop indexes:

```
DROP INDEX (index_name)
```

which is the same as

```
DROP KEY (index_name)
```

and to drop a primary key:

```
DROP PRIMARY KEY
```

For example, to make name an index, you can do this:

```
mysql> ALTER TABLE subscribers
    -> ADD INDEX name (name);
Query OK, 4 rows affected (0.00 sec)
Records: 4  Duplicates: 0  Warnings: 0
```

6

```
mysql> DESCRIBE subscribers;
+---------------+--------------+------+-----+---------+----------------+
| Field         | Type         | Null | Key | Default | Extra          |
+---------------+--------------+------+-----+---------+----------------+
| subscriber_id | int(9)       |      | PRI | NULL    | auto_increment |
| name          | varchar(100) | YES  | MUL | NULL    |                |
| date_of_birth | datetime     | YES  |     | NULL    |                |
| email         | varchar(15)  | YES  |     | NULL    |                |
+---------------+--------------+------+-----+---------+----------------+
4 rows in set (0.00 sec)
```

The MUL in the Key field against name tells us that it's now a "multiple" key (that is, a non-unique key).

You could also ask MySQL to show the indexes using the SHOW command again. You might like to try this:

```
mysql> SHOW INDEXES FROM subscribers;
```

or

```
mysql> SHOW KEYS FROM subscribers;
```

To drop the index again, do this:

```
mysql> ALTER TABLE subscribers
    -> DROP INDEX name;
```

Remember, this drops only the index, not the original column or its data.

Summary

Today you learned some fundamental and important techniques for building a MySQL database. You learned how to use the mysql client program, in both its interactive and batch modes. You saw how to pass it username and password information for authenticating that user to MySQL, a principle that you can now apply to all of MySQL's client programs.

For manipulating databases, you learned how to create, list, and drop databases, and you saw how to create, list, drop, and alter tables within them.

Finally, you looked at how to add, show, and drop indexes on your tables. You learned the syntax for doing these things within the CREATE TABLE and ALTER TABLE statements, and you saw some examples. In Day 9, you'll learn more about the various kinds of indexes, how they work in detail, and when to apply them.

Q&A

Q **Is there a more graphical way to manipulate databases and tables than the command-line methods like `mysql`?**

A The `mysql`, `mysqladmin`, and other client programs require you to type commands longhand, but they are standard components of the MySQL client distribution and highly versatile, which is why you're advised to learn how to use them. If you prefer a more graphical method, you could try the `phpMyAdmin` program. This provides a convenient Web-based interface for almost all of MySQL's functions with minimal typing. However, to best learn MySQL's functionality and language, we recommend that you stick to the command-line programs while you're studying this book.

Q **How many databases or tables can be supported on a MySQL server?**

A MySQL allows virtually any number of databases, and any number of tables within each database. You're more likely to be limited by the number that you can manage effectively.

Q **How big can a MySQL table be?**

A The size of the largest possible MySQL table depends on the operating system MySQL is running on. With the `MyISAM` table type on MySQL version 3.23 and onward, the maximum table size is 8 terabytes. However, all data in a given table will be stored in a single file, and because of this, your operating system may limit a table size to be smaller than this.

For example, Linux on Intel can be 2GB, 4GB, or more depending on version. Linux on Alpha will probably handle 8TB. Solaris will support 2GB on its version 2.5.1, 4GB on 2.6 and 2.7, and supposedly 8TB on Ultra-Sparc. On a Windows platform, expect a limit of around 2TB. See the MySQL documentation for more information.

Workshop

The quiz and exercises are provided to help you solidify your understanding of the material covered today. Try to understand the quiz and exercise answers before continuing to tomorrow's lesson.

6

Quiz

1. True or False: `mysql` is an interactive program only; you cannot make it read a text file of SQL.

2. When running the following command from the Unix command line, what database (if any) will `mysql` connect to?

   ```
   $ mysql -p password
   ```

3. True or False: After you create a table, it cannot be renamed.

4. True or False: Using `ALTER TABLE`, you can make multiple changes to a table in a single statement.

Quiz Answers

1. False. `mysql` can be used interactively or in batch mode.

2. It will try to connect to a database called `password`.

3. False. Use `ALTER TABLE table_name RENAME AS new_table_name`.

4. True. Your action list can contain many actions, but remember to separate them with commas.

Exercises

Write a series of commands to do the following:

1. Create a database called `contacts` using `mysqladmin`.

2. List your databases without going into the `mysql` monitor.

3. Go into the monitor, selecting the contacts database as you enter.

4. Create a table in your database called `people`, with a 50-character `VARCHAR` field for `name`, a 100-character field for `email`.

5. Alter the table to add a field for `phone`. It should be a `VARCHAR` of 50 characters and be located immediately after `name`.

6. Enlarge the `name` field to 100 characters, add a non-unique key on that field, and change the name of the `email` field to `email_address`.

7. Display the table description.

Answers to Exercises

1. At command prompt:

   ```
   $ mysqladmin create contacts-
   ```

   or with authentication:

   ```
   $ mysqladmin create contacts -u someuser -p
   ```

2. At command prompt:

```
$ mysqlshow -u someuser -p
+------------+
| Databases  |
+------------+
| cms        |
| contacts   |
| mysql      |
| test       |
+------------+
```

3. Going into the mysql monitor:

```
$ mysql -u someuser -p contacts
```

4. Creating the table:

```
mysql> CREATE TABLE people (
    -> name VARCHAR(50),
    -> email VARCHAR(100)
    -> );
```

Note that you could do this in fewer lines.

5. Adding the phone column:

```
mysql> ALTER TABLE people
    -> ADD COLUMN phone VARCHAR(50) AFTER name;
```

6. Doing multiple changes to the table:

```
mysql> ALTER TABLE people
    -> MODIFY name VARCHAR(100),
    -> ADD KEY name (name),
    -> CHANGE email email_address VARCHAR(100);
```

7. Describing the table:

```
mysql> DESCRIBE people;
+---------------+--------------+------+-----+---------+-------+
| Field         | Type         | Null | Key | Default | Extra |
+---------------+--------------+------+-----+---------+-------+
| name          | varchar(100) | YES  | MUL | NULL    |       |
| phone         | varchar(50)  | YES  |     | NULL    |       |
| email_address | varchar(100) | YES  |     | NULL    |       |
+---------------+--------------+------+-----+---------+-------+
3 rows in set (0.01 sec)
```

Note that you could also use the shorter form, DESC.

6

DAY **7**

Inserting and Updating Data

Now that you have learned how to set up and manipulate MySQL databases and tables, today you will learn how to get data into them. In particular, you will learn:

- How to get data into your database (using INSERT and REPLACE)
- How to perform modifications on your data (using UPDATE)
- How to import data from text files, using mysql, mysqlimport, and LOAD DATA INFILE

Inserting Data Using INSERT

The INSERT statement is the primary way of getting data into a database. It takes the following format:

```
INSERT [LOW PRIORITY | DELAYED] [IGNORE]
  [INTO] table_name
  SET column_name1=expression1, column_name2=expression2,...
```

or

```
INSERT [LOW PRIORITY | DELAYED] [IGNORE]
  [INTO] table_name [(column_name,...)]
  VALUES (expression,...),(...)...
```

or

```
INSERT [LOW PRIORITY | DELAYED] [IGNORE]
  [INTO] table_name [(column_name,...)]
  SELECT...
```

The first form is a the most verbose but is in many cases the most convenient because the SET... explicitly names each column and states what value (evaluated from each *expression*) should be put into it.

Here's an example that adds a row of data to the subscribers table of a content management system, which contains the columns subscriber_id, name, and email:

```
mysql> INSERT INTO subscribers
    -> SET name='Carl Jacobs',
    -> email='cj@email.com';
```

After running this, see what the row looks like in the table:

```
mysql> SELECT * FROM subscribers
    -> WHERE name LIKE 'Carl%';
+---------------+-------------+--------------+
| subscriber_id | name        | email        |
+---------------+-------------+--------------+
|             6 | Carl Jacobs | cj@email.com |
+---------------+-------------+--------------+
```

The INSERT statement sets the values of only two columns, and the auto-increment property of the subscriber_id column set its value to 6 automatically.

If other columns were in the table (in general, any columns not named in an INSERT), these would have been set to their default values. This default is normally NULL, but depending on how you define the column, you can set the default to another value when you create the column. See Day 5, "MySQL Data Types," if you do not recall how to do this.

Using the INSERT...VALUES... format requires just a comma-separated list of the data. For each row inserted, each data value must correspond with a column. In other words, the number of values listed must match the number of columns, and the order of the value list must be the same as the columns.

Although this form is more compact, it may not be the best in every instance, such as when you don't want to populate all columns in a new record. A column may, for example, be an auto-incrememt or timestamp column, in which case there's no need to set its value explicitly, or you may simply want to leave it empty for the time being.

To use this form of the INSERT statement but omit specifying a value for the first field, the query would look like this:

```
mysql> INSERT INTO subscribers
    -> VALUES (NULL, 'David Swift', 'dave@mail.net');
```

As you can see, we had to match the three columns of the table with three expressions in the statement. Where we didn't want to insert data (into the subscriber_id field), we had to insert a NULL to allow the auto-increment to behave normally. The same would be required if there were a TIMESTAMP column type, and we didn't want to influence the date.

Be careful when using INSERT in this way: if you ever add a column to your table, any application that performs an INSERT...VALUES... statement will stop working. The statement expects to find the same number of columns as it has expressions, and if they don't match, MySQL returns an error.

A variation on this second form allows you to name the columns you want to populate and supply values for those columns only. You can use it like this:

```
mysql> INSERT INTO subscribers
    -> (name, email)
    -> VALUES ('Susan Jones', 'susan@mymail.org');
```

Here we listed in parentheses the columns we intend to populate. Any column omitted from the list will be set to its default value.

We can also use this second form to insert multiple rows in a single statement. The following examples show how you can rewrite the last two examples into a single statement:

```
mysql> INSERT INTO subscribers
    -> VALUES (NULL, 'David Swift', 'dave@mail.net'),
    -> (NULL, 'Susan Jones', 'susan@mymail.org');
```

Notice how we placed a comma after the first set of values in parentheses. You can have any number of value sets listed like this in the same INSERT statement.

Similarly, you can use the form in which you list the column names. You can use it like this:

```
mysql> INSERT INTO subscribers
    -> (name, email)
    -> VALUES ('David Swift', 'dave@mail.net'),
    -> ('Susan Jones', 'susan@mymail.org');
```

The third form of INSERT can be used to insert data that is a resultset of a SELECT statement. You saw a similar technique to do a CREATE TABLE...SELECT... in Day 6, "Manipulating a Database," when we created a table and selected the data into it. Now we have no need to create the table, merely to select data into it:

```
mysql> INSERT INTO subscribers
    -> SELECT * FROM tmp;
```

7

This selects all rows of data from the `tmp` table and inserts it into `subscribers`. (You could also perform more complex `SELECT` queries here, which you'll learn about in Day 8, "Querying Data.")

Note that when using `INSERT...SELECT`, you cannot have the table that is the target of the `INSERT` mentioned anywhere in the `FROM` clause of the `SELECT`.

Issues When Using INSERT

A number of issues may arise when using `INSERT`. Some actions result in errors, whereas others can cause MySQL to insert data with unexpected results.

When using `INSERT...VALUES` (without naming the column list), and when using `INSERT...SELECT`, the column count must match the number of values specified (or the count of the expressions retrieved from the `SELECT`). If not, you will see an error like this:

```
ERROR 1136: Column count doesn't match value count at row 1
```

In any kind of `INSERT`, make sure that the data types you specify in your list of values are compatible with the column types into which they will be inserted. When doing an `INSERT...SELECT`, the column types from the `SELECT` resultset should match, or at least be compatible with, the column types in the target table of the `INSERT`. If not, you may get unexpected results.

When data is a different type from the column into which it's being inserted, MySQL tries to store the data as best it can. For example, if you try to insert textual data into a numerical column (for example, you selected a `VARCHAR` column in an `INSERT...SELECT`, but the corresponding column in the target table is an `INT`), the leading numerical part of each value will be used (if there is one) or zero if not. Likewise, if you insert data into columns that are too small, the data values will be truncated.

When performing an `INSERT`, there is always a possibility that the statement will try to cause a duplicate of a primary or unique key. You would see an error like this:

```
ERROR 1062: Duplicate entry '2' for key 1
```

The error message here is referring to key `1`, which in the `subscribers` table is the `subscriber_id` field, the primary key. It tell us that a column with a `subscriber_id` of 2 already exists, and the `INSERT` is trying to insert a record with the same value in this field, thus causing an error.

However, it is possible to subdue errors by using the keyword `IGNORE` in the `INSERT` statement. Here's an example that would otherwise cause a duplicate key error:

```
mysql> INSERT IGNORE INTO subscribers
    -> VALUES (2, 'Kylie Johnson', 'kylie@email.com');
Query OK, 0 rows affected (0.00 sec)
```

By using IGNORE, any duplicate rows will simply be ignored. They won't be imported, and the data at the related row of the target table will be left untouched. In your application, you may be wise to check how many rows were affected (imported) whenever using IGNORE because ignoring a record may constitute a failure condition in your application that needs to be handled properly.

LOW PRIORITY and DELAYED Inserts

If you specify INSERT LOW_PRIORITY, the insert waits until all other clients have finished reading from the table before executing.

If you specify INSERT DELAYED, the client performing the query gets an instant acknowledgment that the insert has been performed, although in fact the data will only be inserted when the table is not in use by another thread. This may be useful if you have an application that needs to complete its process in minimum time, or simply where there's no need for it to wait for the effect of an INSERT to take place. This might be the case if you're adding data to a log, or to a table that keeps an audit trail of some database activity.

INSERT DELAYED is a MySQL extension to the ANSI SQL92 standard and works only with tables of ISAM or MyISAM type.

Inserting and Replacing Data Using REPLACE

The REPLACE statement works similarly to INSERT. It always tries to insert the new data, but when it tries to insert a new row with the same primary or unique key as an existing row, it deletes the old data and replaces it with the new.

It takes the following format:

```
REPLACE [LOW PRIORITY | DELAYED]
  [INTO] table_name
  SET column_name1=expression1, column_name2=expression2,...
```

or

```
REPLACE [LOW PRIORITY | DELAYED]
  [INTO] table_name [(column_name,...)]
  VALUES (expression,...),(...)...
```

or

```
REPLACE [LOW PRIORITY | DELAYED]
  [INTO] table_name [(column_name,...)]
  SELECT...
```

7

To illustrate how to use REPLACE, suppose that we have data in the subscribers table that looks like this:

```
+---------------+----------------+------------------------+
| subscriber_id | name           | email                  |
+---------------+----------------+------------------------+
|             1 | Tony Butcher   | tony@internet.com      |
|             2 | John Brown     | john@somewhere.com     |
|             3 | Shelley Griffin| shelley@home.net       |
+---------------+----------------+------------------------+
```

Say that we want to replace the data in the second row, in which the primary (and thus unique) key subscriber_id equals 2. We perform the replace like this:

```
mysql> REPLACE INTO subscribers
    -> VALUES (2, 'John Brown', 'john@elsewhere.com');
```

For contrast, now we'll perform another REPLACE like this, in which the unique key (a subscriber_id of 15) does not already exist:

```
mysql> REPLACE INTO subscribers
    -> VALUES (15, 'Fred Sorrell', 'fred@myco.com');
```

The data in the subscribers table now looks like this:

```
+---------------+----------------+------------------------+
| subscriber_id | name           | email                  |
+---------------+----------------+------------------------+
|             1 | Tony Butcher   | tony@internet.com      |
|             2 | John Brown     | john@elsewhere.com     |
|             3 | Shelley Griffin| shelley@home.net       |
|            15 | Fred Sorrell   | fred@myco.com          |
+---------------+----------------+------------------------+
```

As you can see, the REPLACE statement replaces rows that are related by their unique or primary key, but otherwise inserts new rows of data.

The other formats for REPLACE (using SET and SELECT) work on the same principle, with the new data being declared or received via a resultset from a SELECT query as you saw with INSERT.

Take care when using REPLACE (column_name,...) VALUES.... Any column omitted from the list will be set to its default value (such as NULL). Rows matched by a unique key thus will lose any previous data.

Performing Updates

With the UPDATE command, you can modify the values of existing data in a table. The format for the statement is as follows:

```
UPDATE [LOW PRIORITY] [IGNORE] table_name
  SET column_name1=expression1, column_name2=expression2,...
  [WHERE where_definition]
  [LIMIT num]
```

There are basically two parts to the query: the SET portion, to declare which column to set to what value; and the WHERE portion, which defines which rows are affected.

Let's practice using CREATE and INSERT again to create a temporary table called products and populate it with some data:

```
mysql> CREATE TEMPORARY TABLE products
    -> (product_name VARCHAR(20), price FLOAT(9,2));

mysql> INSERT INTO products
    -> VALUES ('Green sweater', 10.00),
    -> ('Brown jacket', 12.00);
```

If you want to set all prices to 10.00, you could do this:

```
mysql> UPDATE products SET price=10.00;
```

Because there is no WHERE condition, the UPDATE will be applied to every row in the table.

Updates can perform modifications dependent on the original value of the column they affect. For example, to multiply all prices by 1.5, you could do this:

```
mysql> UPDATE products SET price=price*1.5;
```

This statement would look at each price, multiply it by 1.5, and save the result back into the same column.

You can also perform several modifications in turn. For example:

```
mysql> UPDATE products SET price=price*1.5,
    -> price=price+0.50,
    -> product_name=UCASE(product_name);
```

Processing works from left to right through the SQL and in this example would multiply all prices by 1.5, then add 0.50, and then convert all values in the product_name column to uppercase.

If you use a WHERE condition, updates are applied only to rows meeting that condition. For example, to increase prices by 50 percent where the current product price is less than 10.00, you could do this:

```
mysql> UPDATE products SET price=price*1.5
    -> WHERE price < 10.00;
```

7

In general, it's common to have a WHERE condition in an UPDATE; in most cases, you won't want to update all rows of data, and frequently you will want to update only a specific row, perhaps referenced by a key, such as like this:

```
mysql> UPDATE products SET price = 28.00
    -> WHERE id = '103';
```

This example updates the price of the item whose id is 103, to 28.00.

You can add LIMIT *num* to limit the effect of your UPDATE statement. Using this keyword restricts the maximum number of rows affected by the update to *num*.

> **Note**
>
> Don't worry if you're not comfortable using WHERE and LIMIT. In particular, WHERE is a sophisticated clause with many possible ways of zooming in on specific rows of data and is a condition you will use often with SELECT statements. You will learn how to use the WHERE condition and the LIMIT clause in Day 8, but after you have a grasp on using them with SELECT statements, you will be able to apply them with UPDATE statements.

By adding the keyword IGNORE to an UPDATE, the statement keeps processing even if a modification occurs that tries to infringe on a primary or unique key. In normal circumstances (without IGNORE), the statement would abort with an error.

If you specify LOW_PRIORITY, the update waits until all other clients finish reading from the table before executing.

Importing Data

MySQL offers a variety of ways of getting data into a database. You've just seen how to use SQL statements to do this. This section looks at how you can import and process data in bulk.

Batch Import Using `mysql`

Recall from Day 6 that you can import data by using the `mysql` client program in batch mode.

You can write the syntax in two ways. One is like this:

```
mysql [options] databasename < filename
```

The same is possible by changing the order of things on the command line and using the Unix cat program and a | (bar, or pipe) to pipe an entire file to mysql for processing:

```
cat filename | /usr/local/mysql/bin/mysql [options] databasename
```

Provided that your PATH Unix environment variable contains the path to mysql, this shorter form does the same thing:

```
cat filename | mysql [options] databasename
```

Both commands make mysql read the text file specified by filename and process any SQL it finds there. Such a file might include table specifications, data, or both, such as Listing 7.1.

LISTING 7.1   Example of a File to Be Imported

```
 1: #
 2: # Table structure for table `subscribers`
 3: #
 4:
 5: DROP TABLE IF EXISTS subscribers;
 6: CREATE TABLE subscribers (
 7:   subscriber_id int(9) NOT NULL auto_increment,
 8:   name varchar(100) default NULL,
 9:   email varchar(15) default NULL,
10:   PRIMARY KEY  (subscriber_id)
11: ) TYPE=InnoDB;
12:
13: #
14: # Dumping data for table `subscribers`
15: #
16:
17: INSERT INTO subscribers VALUES (1, 'Tony Butcher', 'tony@internet.com');
18: INSERT INTO subscribers VALUES (2, 'Kylie Johnson', 'kylie@email.com');
19: INSERT INTO subscribers VALUES (3, 'Shelley Griffin', 'shelley@home.net');
20: ...
```

Lines 1 through 3 and 13 through 15 are comments because they begin with # and are ignored by mysql, as are the blank lines 4, 12, and 16. The other lines should be familiar SQL. These can include DROP TABLE (line 5), CREATE TABLE (lines 6–11), and INSERT statements (line 17 onward) that establish tables and populate the database. They could also include UPDATE, DELETE, and other statements. Because of this flexibility, it's actually best thought of as a method for general batch processing rather than purely for import.

7

Here's an example of batch processing being used to import SQL from a file called
subscribers.sql into the content management database called cms by the user root:

```
$ mysql -u root -p cms < subscribers.sql
Enter password:
```

and this is the same with cat and |:

```
$ cat subscribers.sql | /usr/local/mysql/bin/mysql -u root -p cms
Enter password:
```

Using mysql to process SQL from a file is convenient when the data has previously been
output from a SQL-based database. However, a SQL file is not the most compact way to
store data, and when data is from an external source, it often comes in a different format.
You need to be able to handle other file formats, such as CSV (comma-separated values)
and tab-delimited, and mysqlimport allows you to handle different file formats.

Importing Data from a File with `mysqlimport`

The mysqlimport utility reads a range of data formats, including comma- and tab-
delimited, and inserts the data into a database. The syntax for mysqlimport is as follows:

```
mysqlimport [options] database_name filename1 filename2 ...
```

You normally invoke it from the command line. For example, for the user root to import
data into the cms database from file subscribers.txt, the syntax would be this:

```
$ mysqlimport -u root -p cms subscribers.txt
cms.subscribers: Records: 4  Deleted: 4  Skipped: 0  Warnings: 0
```

The filenames must correspond with the tables into which their data will be imported. If
a filename contains one or more . (dots), the portion before the first dot will be assumed
to be the name of the table. Hence the subscribers.txt file will always be imported
into a table called subscribers.

mysqlimport can be run with a number of options. Table 7.1 shows a list of options and
what effect they have on the import.

TABLE 7.1 Options for mysqlimport

Option	Action
-r or --replace	Cause imported rows to overwrite existing rows if they have the same unique key value.
-i or --ignore	Ignore rows that have the same unique key value as existing rows.
-f or --force	Force mysqlimport to continue inserting data even if errors are encountered.
-l or --lock-tables	Lock each table before importing (a good option on a busy server).
-d or --delete	Empty the table before inserting.

TABLE 7.1   continued

Option	Action
`--fields-terminated-by='char'`	Specify the separator used between values of the same row, default \t (tab).
`--fields-enclosed-by='char'`	Specify the delimiter that encloses each field; default is none.
`--fields-optionally-enclosed-by='char'`	Same as `--fields-enclosed-by`, but delimiter is used only to enclose string-type columns; default is none.
`--fields-escaped-by='char'`	Specify the escape character placed before special characters; default is \ (backslash, which if specified would be '\\').
`--lines-terminated-by='char'`	Specify the separator used to terminate each row of data; default is \n (newline).
`-u` or `--user`	Specify your username; default is Unix login name.
`-p` or `--password`	Specify your password.
`-h` or `--host`	Import into MySQL on the named host; default is `localhost`.
`-s` or `--silent`	Silent mode; output appears only when errors occur.
`-v` or `--verbose`	Verbose mode, print more commentary.
`-L` or `local`	Name a local file on the client.
`-V` or `--version`	Print program version information and exit.
`-?` or `--help`	Print help message and exit.

Let's run a slightly more complex example. Say that we want to import data from a file called `subscribers.txt` into the `subscribers` table of the `cms` database. We want to replace any old records for subscribers with the new data, using the primary key `subscriber_id` to tie the imported rows to the old. We declare the field and line terminators, and we also want a verbose explanation of what's happening.

The import file (`subscribers.txt`) looks like this:

```
"15";"Fred Sorrell";"fredsorrell@newco.com"
"NULL";"Jane Frankum";"jane@home.net"
```

The first line contains a replacement for subscriber number 15 (which already exists), and the second line contains a new record that should be added. Notice how this line contains NULL for its `subscriber_id`, which causes MySQL to allocate a new unique value for this auto-increment field.

We could type this:

```
$ /usr/local/mysql/bin/mysqlimport -p -vr \
$ --fields-enclosed-by='\"' \
$ --fields-terminated-by=';' \
```

7

```
$ --lines-terminated-by='\n' \
$ cms subscribers.txt
Enter password:
Connecting to localhost
Selecting database cms
Loading data from SERVER file: /home/tonyb/subscribers.txt into subscribers
cms.subscribers: Records: 2  Deleted: 1  Skipped: 0  Warnings: 0
Disconnecting from localhost
```

We added the -v (verbose) option and used the -r option to replace old rows with the new. (Note that -v and -r are combined into -vr for brevity, but you cannot put anything other than a space after -p, or it will be interpreted as a password.) We were explicit about how the fields are enclosed and separated, and we declared which character denotes an end of row.

The response from mysqlimport reports that two records were imported, and one row was deleted. MySQL deletes rows that are to be replaced by a corresponding new row—hence one deletion before the insertion of the new record.

The affected rows in the subscribers table now look like this:

```
+---------------+-----------------+------------------------+
| subscriber_id | name            | email                  |
+---------------+-----------------+------------------------+
|            15 | Fred Sorrell    | fredsorrell@newco.com  |
|            56 | Jane Frankum    | jane@home.net          |
+---------------+-----------------+------------------------+
```

Importing from a File with LOAD DATA INFILE

Like many operations in MySQL, there's more than one way of importing data. What can be done with mysqlimport is possible using the SQL statement LOAD DATA INFILE.

Both techniques accomplish the same thing. If you have access to a Unix or Windows command line and MySQL's client programs, you may prefer mysqlimport. If you have access via a connection to only the MySQL database (but not to the command line), or if you're importing from within an application, you may have to use LOAD DATA INFILE. The latter method has marginally more flexibility (the table name is not governed by the filename), but apart from that it's down to what you feel more comfortable with.

To use LOAD DATA INFILE, you can run the SQL from within the mysql monitor or from within an application. It takes this format:

```
LOAD DATA [LOW_PRIORITY | CONCURRENT] [LOCAL]
  INFILE 'filename'
  [REPLACE | IGNORE]
  INTO TABLE table_name
  [FIELDS [TERMINATED BY 'char']
    [[OPTIONALLY] ENCLOSED BY 'char']
```

```
[ESCAPED BY 'char' ]]
[LINES TERMINATED BY 'char']
[IGNORE num LINES]
[(column_name1,column_name2,...)]
```

Looking at the various keywords and parameters, you will notice that many are nearly the same as for `mysqlimport`. An important difference is that you must specify the file-name as well as the table name, but this means that you don't have to make *filename* (or the portion before any . in its name) correspond to *table_name*.

Make sure that MySQL can correctly find the file you specify: you might need to supply the full path to the file. Without the full path, MySQL locates the home directory for the logged-in MySQL user and starts looking there.

The `REPLACE` and `IGNORE` keywords are used like the `mysqlimport` `-r` and `-i` options, replacing rows with duplicate unique keys or ignoring those in the import file, respectively.

The `FIELDS` keyword can be followed by the `TERMINATED`, `ENCLOSED`, and `ESCAPED` key-words, and like `LINES TERMINATED BY`, these options have the same effect as the corresponding keywords after `mysqlimport`.

By specifying `LOW_PRIORITY`, execution waits until no other clients are reading from the table. By specifying `CONCURRENT` with a `MyISAM` table, other clients will be able to read from the table while `LOAD DATA INFILE` is executing.

The `LOCAL` keyword means that a local file on the client will be used for reading.

The `IGNORE` *num* `LINES` causes the load to ignore *num* lines at the start of the file.

If you want to load only some of a table's columns, you can specify `(column_name1,column_name2,...)`. Columns that are in the file but whose names are not in the list will be ignored.

To run the same import we ran previously with `mysqlimport`, the SQL would now look like this in the `mysql` monitor:

```
mysql> LOAD DATA INFILE '/home/tonyb/subscribers.txt'
    -> REPLACE INTO TABLE subscribers
    -> FIELDS ENCLOSED BY '\"' TERMINATED BY ';'
    -> LINES TERMINATED BY '\n';
Query OK, 3 rows affected (0.00 sec)
Records: 2  Deleted: 1  Skipped: 0  Warnings: 1
```

If the `subscribers.txt` file contained the names of the columns in its first line (a common format for exported data), and perhaps an extra column of data that isn't wanted, it might look like this:

7

```
Some id;Name;Email Address;Extra Data
"15";"Fred Sorrell";"fredsorrell@newco.com";"some address"
"NULL";"Jane Frankum";"jane@home.net";"some address"
```

then your SQL might look like this:

```
mysql> LOAD DATA INFILE '/home/tonyb/subscribers.txt'
    -> REPLACE INTO TABLE subscribers
    -> FIELDS ENCLOSED BY '\"' TERMINATED BY ';'
    -> LINES TERMINATED BY '\n'
    -> IGNORE 1 LINES
    -> (subscriber_id,name,email);
Query OK, 3 rows affected (0.00 sec)
Records: 2  Deleted: 1  Skipped: 0  Warnings: 3
```

Here we added IGNORE 1 LINES to skip the title line in the file, and, in parentheses (), we added the names of the three columns we're interested in so as to ignore the Extra Data column present in the text file.

Summary

Today you learned the various ways of getting data into a MySQL database. You learned about the important INSERT, REPLACE, and UPDATE statements in SQL.

You studied the various utilities that can perform bulk inserts and updates, including mysql for processing SQL from a file in batch mode, and mysqlimport for importing data from a text-delimited file. You also learned how to use the latter's SQL equivalent, LOAD DATA INFILE.

Q&A

Q Can I import an entire database using mysql batch import, mysqlimport, and LOAD DATA INFILE?

A Yes. Any of these methods can be used to process files that create databases, tables, and the data within them. In the simple examples you saw today, we only imported small amounts of data. However, files containing SQL are processed by mysql in batch mode and can be of any size and contain any legal SQL.

Q How do I export data from MySQL?

A We'll cover methods of extracting data and saving it in a text file in Day 8, "Querying Data," and Day 15, "Administration." This includes mysqldump, the counterpart of mysqlimport, and SELECT INTO OUTFILE, the counterpart of LOAD DATA INFILE.

Workshop

The quiz and exercises are provided to help you solidify your understanding of the material covered today. Try to understand the quiz and exercise answers before continuing to tomorrow's lesson.

Quiz

1. True or False: `mysqlimport` does the same thing as `LOAD DATA INFILE`.

2. True or False: `mysqlimport` does the same thing as `mysql` when used in batch mode.

3. Assume that you have a table `products` that looks like this:

```
+------+---------------+-------+
| id   | product_name  | price |
+------+---------------+-------+
|  102 | Brown jacket  | 13.00 |
|  114 | Brown shoes   | 43.99 |
|  122 | Black shoes   | 49.99 |
+------+---------------+-------+
```

   What's wrong with the following SQL:

```
INSERT INTO products
VALUES ('Green sweater', 10.00),
('Brown jacket', 12.00)
```

4. Using the same table as in question 3, what would happen if you issued the following statement:

```
REPLACE INTO products
VALUES (102, 'Light brown jacket', 10.00)
```

Quiz Answers

1. True. `LOAD DATA INFILE` is the SQL version and almost identical in operation to the `mysqlimport` utility.

2. False. `mysqlimport` expects "raw" data in some text-delimited form, whereas `mysql` used in batch mode processes SQL statements read from a text file.

3. The column count does not match the number of values in each line of data, and it produces an error.

4. It would modify the row with `id` of `102`, changing the name to `Light brown jacket` and setting the price to `10.00`.

7

Exercises

1. Run the following SQL to create a `products` table:

```
mysql> CREATE TEMPORARY TABLE products
    -> (id INT(9) auto_increment,
    -> product_name VARCHAR(20),
    -> price FLOAT(9,2),
    -> PRIMARY KEY (id));
mysql> INSERT INTO products
    -> VALUES (101, 'Green sweater', 10.00),
    -> (102, 'Brown jacket', 12.00);
```

   Now write an UPDATE statement using the following form:

```
UPDATE table_name
  SET column_name1=expression1, column_name2=expression2,...
```

   Your statement should update the table with new prices, reducing the prices of all articles by 10 percent.

2. Create a text file called `produpdate.txt` that looks like this:

```
101,NULL,0
102,"Brown jacket",13.00
103,"Leather jacket",26.00
```

   Write a LOAD DATA INFILE statement to load a file containing a new product list. Products may be additions to the catalog or be updates to existing products.

Answers to Exercises

1. You should get this:

```
mysql> UPDATE products
    -> SET price=price*0.9;
Query OK, 2 rows affected (0.00 sec)
Rows matched: 2  Changed: 2  Warnings: 0
```

2. Your SQL should look like this:

```
mysql> LOAD DATA INFILE '/home/tonyb/produpdate.txt'
    -> REPLACE INTO TABLE products
    -> FIELDS OPTIONALLY ENCLOSED BY '\"' TERMINATED BY ','
    -> LINES TERMINATED BY '\n';
```

   and your table should now look like this:

```
+-----+----------------+-------+
| id  | product_name   | price |
+-----+----------------+-------+
| 101 | NULL           |  0.00 |
| 102 | Brown jacket   | 13.00 |
| 103 | Leather jacket | 26.00 |
+-----+----------------+-------+
```

Week 2

At a Glance

DAY **8**

Querying Data

Today's lesson is about two of the most important queries in SQL: SELECT and DELETE.

SELECT is the primary means of getting data out of any SQL database. Today's lesson will teach you:

- The fundamentals of a SELECT query
- How to apply conditions for selection with a WHERE clause
- How to control the output of a SELECT query, using DISTINCT, ORDER BY, GROUP BY, and LIMIT
- How to use operators, functions, and aggregating functions within a SELECT

You will also learn some slightly more advanced techniques:

- How to apply further conditions to a resultset with a HAVING clause
- How to output data from a SELECT query into another table or file
- How to do full-text searching
- How to perform subselects, and how to get by without them

Finally, you will learn how to remove data from a table using DELETE.

The Basics of SELECT Queries

The SELECT query can be run with a range of possible arguments. Its syntax, showing the majority of its options (but not all), looks like this:

```
SELECT
  [DISTINCT]
  select_expression,...
  [INTO {OUTFILE | DUMPFILE} '/path/to/filename' export_options]
  [FROM table_references
  [WHERE where_definition]
  [GROUP BY {column_name | column_alias}
    [ASC | DESC], ...]
  [HAVING where_definition]
  [ORDER BY {column_name | column_alias}
    [ASC | DESC], ...]
  [LIMIT [offset,] num_rows]
```

Some arguments have been omitted for clarity where they are less frequently used. See Appendix B, "SQL Reference," for the full detail.

You will often use just a small part of its syntax; often just this:

```
SELECT
  select_expression,...
  [FROM table_name]
  [WHERE where_definition]
```

Let's consider this simpler form first, before exploring some of the more complex possibilities.

SELECT Queries Made Simple

In simple terms, the SELECT query lets you read data from a table. If you're reading from a table and add a WHERE clause, you can require that the returned table rows match a condition that you specify, denoted in the preceding syntax by where_definition.

You can select from a single table or several tables, and you can write expressions around column names, so that table values are processed in some way before reaching the resultset. You can also have a SELECT query with no tables and purely evaluate expressions. You'll see some examples of these things in a moment.

Let's look at a query that reads every row from a single table, products, which has columns for id, product_name, and price. SELECT reads each row of the table in turn and puts the data into a resultset. The resultset can then be displayed to the user (as we'll do in our examples, in the mysql console), but it could be returned to an application that is querying MySQL through an API.

You can use a wildcard * to retrieve the data in every column of a table. Here's the sample query:

```
mysql> SELECT * FROM products;
```

This is identical to naming all the columns:

```
mysql> SELECT id, product_name, price FROM products;
```

(Remember from Day 4, "Getting Hands-On with MySQL," that the trailing semicolon; after the query is not part of the query itself and just tells the mysql console that you've finished your query.)

The output looks like this:

```
+------+--------------------+-------+
| id   | product_name       | price |
+------+--------------------+-------+
|  102 | Light brown jacket | 10.00 |
|  103 | Leather jacket     | 28.00 |
|  104 | Charcoal trousers  | 39.50 |
|  113 | Dark grey jacket   | 10.00 |
+------+--------------------+-------+
```

The names of the columns in products are returned as column headers in the resultset, with the data for every row in the body of the resultset.

You can restrict the data you retrieve to include just a subset of the columns. For example, to get only the column product_name, you would name just this column, like this:

```
mysql> SELECT product_name FROM products;
+--------------------+
| product_name       |
+--------------------+
| Light brown jacket |
| Leather jacket     |
| Charcoal trousers  |
| Dark grey jacket   |
+--------------------+
```

You can control which rows are retrieved by adding a WHERE condition. For example, to only retrieve products with an id equal to 102, and to display product_name and price, you would do this:

```
mysql> SELECT product_name, price FROM products
    -> WHERE product_id=102;
+--------------------+-------+
| product_name       | price |
+--------------------+-------+
| Light brown jacket | 10.00 |
+--------------------+-------+
```

You can ask SELECT to evaluate expressions for you, without needing to refer to a table. For example:

```
mysql> SELECT 12.50 * 7, 1+2, 'hello world';
+-----------+-----+-------------+
| 12.50 * 7 | 1+2 | hello world |
+-----------+-----+-------------+
|     87.50 |   3 | hello world |
+-----------+-----+-------------+
```

In this example, the query has multiplied two numbers together using the * multiplication operator, added two numbers using +, and returned a constant string.

SELECT can also evaluate functions, of which MySQL has a large library. For example, it can process dates and times, and here's an example of it getting the current time using the function NOW():

```
mysql> SELECT NOW();
+---------------------+
| NOW()               |
+---------------------+
| 2002-09-07 20:05:45 |
+---------------------+
```

Operators and functions are explained more thoroughly in Day 10, "Operators and Functions in MySQL."

SELECT in More Detail

Now that you've seen how SELECT works in its most simple form, it's time to look at more of its possibilities. Take a look at its syntax again:

```
SELECT
  [DISTINCT]
  select_expression,...
  [FROM table_references
  [WHERE where_definition]
  [GROUP BY {column_name | column_alias}
    [ASC | DESC], ...]
  [HAVING where_definition]
  [ORDER BY {column_name | column_alias}
    [ASC | DESC], ...]
  [LIMIT [offset,] num_rows]
```

Let's go through the preceding syntax again, this time a little more thoroughly:

- select_expression specifies a list of things to be retrieved or evaluated: names of columns, constants, or the result of evaluating operators and functions (comma-separated if more than one, and optionally with alias names).

- *table_references* specifies a list of tables in which any named columns reside (comma-separated if more than one table, and optionally with table alias names and/or join specifications).

- *where_definition* specifies the conditions for inclusion of rows.

- DISTINCT specifies that only unique rows should be returned.

- The GROUP BY clause specifies how results should be grouped, by a column given by *column_name* or *column_alias*; can be in either ascending (ASC) or descending (DESC) order.

- The HAVING clause specifies how additional processing should be applied to a resultset, just before being sent to the user.

- The ORDER BY clause specifies how results should be sorted, by a column given by *column_name* or *column_alias*; can be in either ascending (ASC) or descending (DESC) order.

- The LIMIT clause specifies how the resultset should be limited, by allowing only a subset of the total rows it may comprise given by *num_rows*, optionally omitting *offset* rows.

Don't worry about taking all this in at once! We'll spend much of today going through these options one by one.

In the syntax just now, *aliases* were mentioned. You should recall from Day 6, "Manipulating a Database," that an alias is a way of calling a table, a column, or some expression by another name. You use the keyword AS to declare an alias. The meaning of the alias will be the same as the original thing, but the alias is a shorter or more convenient name.

The syntax also mentioned *joins*. What's a join? SELECT can retrieve data from several tables at once, and in doing so can also cross-reference rows in one table with rows in another. You'll learn how to perform joins in Day 9, "Joins and Indexes."

If you use a *where_definition* in a SELECT, it defines what limitations you placed on the rows that are retrieved. You already saw in this lesson how to limit the rows retrieved from the products table by placing a restriction on their names. You can have several conditions in a WHERE clause, including operators, functions, and expressions, which are brought together using AND and OR conditions, among other things.

Here's an example of a more complex SELECT statement, which combines column names, expressions, and a WHERE clause:

```
mysql> SELECT product_name, price, price*(17.5/100)
    -> FROM products
    -> WHERE product_name LIKE 'Leather%'
    -> AND price < 30;
```

```
+----------------+-------+------------------+
| product_name   | price | price*(17.5/100) |
+----------------+-------+------------------+
| Leather jacket | 28.00 |            4.900 |
+----------------+-------+------------------+
```

In this example, the *select_expression* contains not just two column names, but an expression that multiplies price by 17.5/100 (for calculating sales tax, for example).

Rows will only be retrieved where the overall *where_definition* resolves to a logical "true." The *where_definition* contains two conditions, combined with an AND clause. So products must have a name starting with the word Leather *and* have a price of under 20 to be included in the resultset.

When executing the SELECT query, MySQL considers each row of the table products and checks that the *where_definition* evaluates to "true." You could of course write this:

```
mysql> SELECT product_name, price, price*(12.5/100)
    -> FROM products
    -> WHERE 1;
```

It would retrieve every row (as if you had omitted the WHERE clause) because the *where_condition* is 1—a logical true—for every row.

You've seen how to define what will be retrieved by a query, and how to apply a WHERE clause. But what about the other elements of a SELECT? Let's look at those now.

Controlling the Resultset of a SELECT Query

How else can you control what is returned by SELECT? Here are a few other controls that can apply:

- Only retrieve rows that are *distinct*—that is, you want no duplicate rows in your resultset.
- Sort the resultset. You can have the resultset data listed in the order you specify.
- Group the data in the resultset.
- Retrieve only the first *n* rows of the total resultset, or retrieve *n* rows starting from a given row number.

The tools that enable you to control the resultset in these ways are DISTINCT, ORDER BY, GROUP BY, and LIMIT. Let's look at each one in turn.

Selecting with DISTINCT

The keyword DISTINCT tells SELECT to retrieve only unique rows in the resultset. Duplicate rows appear only once in the output.

Look at the sample products table again:

```
mysql> SELECT * FROM products;
+------+--------------------+-------+
| id   | product_name       | price |
+------+--------------------+-------+
|  102 | Light brown jacket | 10.00 |
|  103 | Leather jacket     | 28.00 |
|  104 | Charcoal trousers  | 39.50 |
|  113 | Dark grey jacket   | 10.00 |
+------+--------------------+-------+
```

Suppose that you want to list prices only, but you want each price to appear *only once* in the resultset, regardless of how many products have that price. You would use DISTINCT, like this:

```
mysql> SELECT DISTINCT price FROM products;
+-------+
| price |
+-------+
| 10.00 |
| 28.00 |
| 39.50 |
+-------+
```

Although there's more than one product whose price is 10.00, the number 10.00 is returned only once.

Note, however, that MySQL looks for *entire rows* of the resultset to be distinct. So the following query now returns items with the same price multiple times, because their product_name is different between the rows:

```
mysql> SELECT DISTINCT price, product_name FROM products;
+-------+--------------------+
| price | product_name       |
+-------+--------------------+
| 10.00 | Light brown jacket |
| 28.00 | Leather jacket     |
| 39.50 | Charcoal trousers  |
| 10.00 | Dark grey jacket   |
+-------+--------------------+
```

Sorting the Resultset with ORDER BY

It's common to want to sort the resultset. You can sort rows on numerical or string values, and even sort on several things in a defined order of precedence.

Here's a simple example, listing the products in price order:

```
mysql> SELECT * FROM products ORDER BY price;
+------+--------------------+-------+
| id   | product_name       | price |
+------+--------------------+-------+
```

```
|   102 | Light brown jacket | 10.00 |
|   113 | Dark grey jacket   | 10.00 |
|   103 | Leather jacket     | 28.00 |
|   104 | Charcoal trousers  | 39.50 |
+-------+--------------------+-------+
```

As you can see, the rows are sorted with the lowest price first. They're in ascending order (lowest first).

You can use the keyword ASC if you want to be absolutely clear when declaring the sort order, but it's not necessary because ascending is the default. This does the same thing:

```
mysql> SELECT * FROM products ORDER BY price ASC;
```

To sort in descending order, use DESC, like this:

```
mysql> SELECT * FROM products ORDER BY price DESC;
+-------+--------------------+-------+
| id    | product_name       | price |
+-------+--------------------+-------+
|   104 | Charcoal trousers  | 39.50 |
|   103 | Leather jacket     | 28.00 |
|   102 | Light brown jacket | 10.00 |
|   113 | Dark grey jacket   | 10.00 |
+-------+--------------------+-------+
```

Tip

Don't overuse the * wildcard in SELECT queries when you're writing applications. You should retrieve all columns if you need them, but not otherwise.

Retrieving columns that your application doesn't need just wastes system resources and slows down performance.

You can sort just as easily on a text column, like this, which puts items in alphabetical order:

```
mysql> SELECT * FROM products ORDER BY product_name;
+-------+--------------------+-------+
| id    | product_name       | price |
+-------+--------------------+-------+
|   104 | Charcoal trousers  | 39.50 |
|   113 | Dark grey jacket   | 10.00 |
|   103 | Leather jacket     | 28.00 |
|   102 | Light brown jacket | 10.00 |
+-------+--------------------+-------+
```

> **Note**
>
> Particular rules define the order of sorting.
>
> For example, A always comes before (is less than) B. With nonbinary data types lowercase letters are treated as equal to uppercase letters. But if you use a BLOB type or the BINARY operator when declaring the column, the cases will be treated differently, and lowercase letters will come before uppercase.
>
> The rules for sorting are explained in Day 10.

You can sort on several columns and impose an order of sort precedence by listing several resultset columns in your ORDER BY clause. Put them in order of sort precedence.

For example, to list the items by price first (descending) and product_name second (ascending), you would do this:

```
mysql> SELECT * FROM products ORDER BY price DESC, product_name;
+-------+---------------------+--------+
| id    | product_name        | price  |
+-------+---------------------+--------+
|   104 | Charcoal trousers   | 39.50  |
|   103 | Leather jacket      | 28.00  |
|   113 | Dark grey jacket    | 10.00  |
|   102 | Light brown jacket  | 10.00  |
+-------+---------------------+--------+
```

Grouping the Resultset with GROUP BY

You may want to return your data in groups as well as sorting it. The principal reason for doing this is to apply an *aggregating function*, which provides information about each group rather than about individual rows.

To explain this, consider a new example table called child_products:

```
mysql> SELECT * FROM child_products;
+------+--------------+------+--------+
| id   | name         | age  | price  |
+------+--------------+------+--------+
| 101  | Toy train    | 3-5  | 12.99  |
| 102  | Racing car   | 3-5  | 9.99   |
| 103  | Spinning top | 3-5  | 7.50   |
| 104  | Teddy bear   | 0-2  | 12.50  |
| 105  | Kitchen      | 2-3  | 24.99  |
+------+--------------+------+--------+
```

Each item has a unique id number, a name, the age range of its intended customers, and a price.

You can use a GROUP BY clause to group items by age, like this:

```
mysql> SELECT * FROM child_products GROUP BY age;
+-----+------------+------+-------+
| id  | name       | age  | price |
+-----+------------+------+-------+
| 104 | Teddy bear | 0-2  | 12.50 |
| 105 | Kitchen    | 2-3  | 24.99 |
| 101 | Toy train  | 3-5  | 12.99 |
+-----+------------+------+-------+
```

But this is not very useful! It has made the age column distinct, but the row it chooses to display with each distinct age range has effectively been chosen at random. Using GROUP BY in this way and retrieving several columns is seldom helpful.

Now consider this:

```
mysql> SELECT age FROM child_products GROUP BY age;
+------+
| age  |
+------+
| 0-2  |
| 2-3  |
| 3-5  |
+------+
```

This time products are grouped by age, but only age has been displayed in the result. In other words, the resultset contains only group level data, and not the misleading row-level data from within each group.

But note that this behavior is the same as SELECT DISTINCT, which you saw earlier today. The following query gives the same result:

```
mysql> SELECT DISTINCT age FROM child_products;
```

Note

Notice that GROUP BY is not just grouping but sorting as well. It has the same possibilities as ORDER BY—that is, ASC (the default) and DESC.

So you could do this, to sort the groups in descending order:

```
mysql> SELECT age FROM child_products GROUP BY age DESC;
+------+
| age  |
+------+
| 3-5  |
| 2-3  |
| 0-2  |
+------+
```

However, it's probably clearer to use GROUP BY age ORDER BY age DESC, even though it's a little more verbose.

The most common use of GROUP BY is in conjunction with aggregating functions. These perform some operation on the values retrieved within each group (even though the individual values do not appear in the resultset).

SUM() and COUNT() are commonly used aggregating functions, which add up items by group and count the number of items in each group, respectively.

Here's an example of GROUP BY with SUM(). It adds up the total cost of items in each age range:

```
mysql> SELECT age, SUM(price) FROM child_products GROUP BY age;
+------+------------+
| age  | SUM(price) |
+------+------------+
| 0-2  |      12.50 |
| 2-3  |      24.99 |
| 3-5  |      30.48 |
+------+------------+
```

You can use COUNT() in much the same way, to return a count of items in each group:

```
mysql> SELECT age, COUNT(*) FROM child_products GROUP BY age;
+------+----------+
| age  | COUNT(*) |
+------+----------+
| 0-2  |        1 |
| 2-3  |        1 |
| 3-5  |        3 |
+------+----------+
```

Why is there a * in COUNT(*)? The asterisk (*) tells the query to look for any row that exists and count it. It doesn't care what the row's values are, just that the row is there.

You can name a column, COUNT(price) for example, which would only count items where price is not NULL or empty. * is used here just in case any product has no price; this query would still count it.

As well as SUM() and COUNT(), the expressions that may be used with GROUP BY include the following:

- AVG()—Return the mean, or average, value of data in the group
- MAX()—The maximum value
- MIN()—The minimum value
- STD()—The standard deviation

Caution

> Don't name columns in your GROUP BY clause that are also used by your aggregating function. It defeats the object of grouping!
>
> For example, this is nonsense because nothing gets grouped:
>
> ```
> mysql> SELECT age, SUM(price) FROM child_products GROUP BY price;
> +------+------------+
> | age  | SUM(price) |
> +------+------------+
> | 3-5  |       7.50 |
> | 3-5  |       9.99 |
> | 0-2  |      12.50 |
> | 3-5  |      12.99 |
> | 2-3  |      24.99 |
> +------+------------+
> ```
>
> You would also get a misleading result if there are several products at the same price because a value for age would be returned at random.

Here's a slightly more complex example, combining the averaging function AVG(), GROUP BY, and ORDER BY, and using an alias:

```
mysql> SELECT age, AVG(price) AS avg_p FROM child_products
    -> GROUP BY age
    -> ORDER BY avg_p;
+------+-----------+
| age  | avg_p     |
+------+-----------+
| 3-5  | 10.160000 |
| 0-2  | 12.500000 |
| 2-3  | 24.990000 |
+------+-----------+
```

This query finds the average price of items in each age group and then sorts by the average price (the alias avg_p).

A GROUP BY clause must always be placed before an ORDER BY clause.

Restricting the Resultset Using LIMIT

When you run a SELECT query, you may not want to return the entire resultset to your application.

You may just want the first row, or a small number of rows, and it's more efficient to restrict this in the SELECT than to return a large resultset to your application and discard all but a few rows.

Alternatively, your application may be a kind of search engine, which has a paginated output. You want a handy way of selecting the first 20 rows for display to the user, or perhaps the second 20 rows, and so on.

These kinds of controls are made easy with the LIMIT keyword. You use LIMIT like this:

```
SELECT
  select_expression,...
  ...
  [LIMIT [offset,] num_rows]
```

As you can see, you may pass it just one parameter, an integer *num_rows*; this tells SELECT the maximum number of rows to return.

For example, here's a query that limits the resultset to two rows:

```
mysql> SELECT * FROM child_products LIMIT 2;
+-----+-----------+------+-------+
| id  | name      | age  | price |
+-----+-----------+------+-------+
| 101 | Toy train | 3-5  | 12.99 |
| 102 | Racing car| 3-5  |  9.99 |
+-----+-----------+------+-------+
```

(Note that LIMIT specifies the *maximum* number to return; if the entire resultset has fewer rows than this, you'll only get what's there!)

LIMIT is commonly used with either an ORDER BY or GROUP BY clause. It's not essential, but without something to control the order of the output, you will get a random selection of rows. So this usage is common:

```
mysql> SELECT * FROM child_products ORDER BY id LIMIT 2;
+-----+-----------+------+-------+
| id  | name      | age  | price |
+-----+-----------+------+-------+
| 101 | Toy train | 3-5  | 12.99 |
| 102 | Racing car| 3-5  |  9.99 |
+-----+-----------+------+-------+
```

This time the resultset is ordered by id, and because this has unique values, the query will return the same data every time.

You can also specify an *offset*: in other words, the number of rows to ignore before capturing *num_rows* rows. In the following example, four rows are ignored before looking for two rows to return:

```
mysql> SELECT * FROM child_products ORDER BY id LIMIT 4,2;
+-----+---------+------+-------+
| id  | name    | age  | price |
+-----+---------+------+-------+
| 105 | Kitchen | 2-3  | 24.99 |
+-----+---------+------+-------+
```

This skips four rows and then tries to return two. But because only five rows are in the table, it returns only one. If your *offset* was greater than the number of rows in the table, the query would return an empty resultset.

More Advanced Uses of SELECT

So far today you have seen the fundamental uses of the SELECT query. You'll now see how to use this versatile query in some more sophisticated ways.

Restricting the Resultset with HAVING

On some occasions when you're writing a query, you want to restrict the resultset on the basis of some data in the resultset that has been aggregated.

For example, suppose that you want to find, out of the table of child_products, which age range has products costing less than $10.00.

You want to write this:

```
SELECT age, MIN(price) FROM child_products
  WHERE MIN(price)<10.00
  GROUP BY age
```

This query, if it worked, would group the products by age, use MIN() to find the minimum price in each group, and return results where the minimum price is less than $10.00.

But it doesn't work; the WHERE clause just won't allow it. Even if you use an alias, such as SELECT ... MIN(price) AS mp, it won't work.

The way around the problem is to use a HAVING clause. You can think of it like this: a HAVING clause sits back and lets the rest of the query do its work and create an initial resultset, and then applies a restriction to the resultset.

HAVING is like an extra WHERE clause, applied to the resultset rather than the tables. Its syntax is this:

```
SELECT
  select_expression,...
  ...
  [HAVING where_definition]
  ...
```

HAVING uses a *where_definition* that you can construct in the same way as in a WHERE clause. You must place HAVING after any GROUP BY clause but before any ORDER BY clause.

Here's how you could use it to solve the example problem of finding products whose minimum group price is less than $10.00:

```
mysql> SELECT age, MIN(price) FROM child_products
    -> GROUP BY age
    -> HAVING MIN(price)<10.00;
+------+------------+
| age  | MIN(price) |
+------+------------+
| 3-5  |       7.50 |
+------+------------+
```

As you can see, the query groups the data by age, finds the minimum price in each group, and then applies the HAVING condition to the minimum price.

MySQL also lets you use an alias to do the same thing (although this would not be allowed in the ANSI-92 standard). Here the alias is called lowest:

```
mysql> SELECT age, MIN(price) AS lowest FROM child_products
    -> GROUP BY age
    -> HAVING lowest<10.00;
+------+--------+
| age  | lowest |
+------+--------+
| 3-5  |   7.50 |
+------+--------+
```

Caution

MySQL optimizes the WHERE clause so as to run the SELECT query in the most efficient way. However, the HAVING clause is not optimized.

Therefore, never place a condition in a HAVING clause that could otherwise be placed in a WHERE clause.

Selecting into Another Table or File

Instead of running a query and sending the resultset to the user, the mysql console, or an application program, you may want to use the resultset to populate another table, or even to save it in a file.

You should recall from yesterday's lesson how we did this:

```
mysql> INSERT INTO subscribers
    -> SELECT * FROM tmp;
```

You just have to place an INSERT statement before a SELECT statement, and the resultset from the SELECT is inserted as rows into the table specified by the INSERT.

Remember that the number of columns and their types must correspond between the resultset data and the table you want to populate. Go back and study yesterday's lesson again if you need to recap on this.

Saving your resultset into a file is even simpler. Place the following INTO syntax in your SELECT query:

```
SELECT
  select_expression,...
  [INTO {OUTFILE | DUMPFILE} '/path/to/filename' export_options]
  ...
```

The keywords INTO OUTFILE cause the resultset to be written to a file given by /path/to/filename (which must not exist already).

For example, you could extract the whole child_products table to a file like this:

```
mysql> SELECT * INTO OUTFILE '/tmp/prods.txt'
    -> FROM child_products;
Query OK, 5 rows affected (0.02 sec)
```

The file produced would look like this by default (using the Unix cat program to display it):

```
$ cat prods.txt
101     Toy train       3-5     12.99
102     Racing car      3-5     9.99
103     Spinning top    3-5     7.50
104     Teddy bear      0-2     12.50
105     Kitchen         2-3     24.99
```

You can use export_options to control the field delimiters, end-of-line characters, and other formatting. The options are the same as for LOAD DATA INFILE, which you met in yesterday's lesson. LOAD DATA INFILE is ideally suited for reading a data file that has been created by SELECT INTO OUTFILE.

 Note

SELECT INTO OUTFILE is the SQL equivalent of mysqldump, a useful command-line utility. You will learn how to use mysqldump in Day 15, "Administration."

The INTO DUMPFILE option is a little more specialized. It is for writing a single row of data to a file, without any line terminations or escaping of special characters. You would rarely use this, except if you need to extract BLOB data from a MySQL table and create a file of it.

For example, if you have an image stored as a `BLOB` in a table `pictures`, you might do this:

```
SELECT image INTO DUMPFILE '/path/to/image_filename/'
FROM pictures WHERE id=123
```

Note

The `mysql` user needs write permission to the directory where you want to create the output file, and the user executing the query needs the `File_priv` privilege. See Day 14, "Security," for more about user privileges.

Full-text Searching

You can use MySQL to perform full-text searching. Introduced in version 3.23.23, and improved in version 4.0.1, this feature of MySQL is developing quickly and becoming increasingly powerful.

Full-text searching allows you to create queries that search text columns in a similar way to a search engine on the Web. You can search for rows containing a given string, with the result being weighted according to either natural language rules, or Boolean logic.

Full-text searching has the advantage of not needing such a precise match as = (equals) or `LIKE`, both of which require the entire search string to exist in the table to find a match. With a full-text search, the words of the search pattern are considered individually and not case-sensitively, and only one of the search words needs to match for a row to be retrieved. Results are by default returned in order of match quality, with the best match first.

A full-text search system is ideal for databases with large quantities of textual data, such as a content management system, in which articles have hundreds or thousands of words to be searched.

However, to illustrate things so that you can see what's going on clearly, let's consider a sample scenario of a table of `cities`. You want to be able to give a city name to a `SELECT` query and retrieve cities with similar names. (This might be useful for a "yellow pages" type directory; if the search engine isn't sure exactly what city you mean, it might reply with "Do you mean...?")

To run a full-text search, you have to have a `FULLTEXT` index applied to the column or columns you want to search in. (Don't worry too much about how indexes work right now; you'll cover `FULLTEXT` and other types of index in Day 9, "Joins and Indexes.")

To add a `FULLTEXT` index to a table of `cities`, on the column `city_name`, you would do this:

```
mysql> ALTER TABLE cities ADD FULLTEXT(city_name);
```

If the table is large, this may take a little time because MySQL has to read every word in the given column and create an entry in the index for it.

The full-text search operation itself involves a SELECT with a MATCH...AGAINST operator. The MATCH clause has the following syntax:

```
MATCH (column_name1[, column_name2, ...]) AGAINST ('search_string')
```

Let's say that you want to search the cities table for cities with names like "Palm Springs." You could write a full-text query like this:

```
mysql> SELECT city_name FROM cities
    -> WHERE MATCH (city_name) AGAINST ('Palm Springs');
+-----------------------+
| city_name             |
+-----------------------+
| Palm Springs          |
| Palm Bay              |
| Palm Desert           |
| Palm Coast            |
| Palm Beach            |
| North Palm Beach      |
| Palm Beach Shores     |
| West Palm Beach       |
| Hot Springs           |
...
| West Siloam Springs   |
| White Sulphur Springs |
+-----------------------+
```

This is the simplest type of full-text search. The MATCH...AGAINST was placed in the WHERE clause. The search compares the given words of the search_string with the FULLTEXT index on city_name. The search is efficient and takes a short time to run compared to using LIKE.

The results look sensible: they all contain at least one of the search words, and they're sorted into the order of best match first. The first row of the resultset is a perfect match, later results match only one of the words, and the worst results are those in which the search words occupy a smaller proportion of the row's value. (The row values are longer, so the search terms appear less "relevant.") A kind of fuzzy logic is taking place, and MySQL has been fine-tuned to do this in a way that makes the results appear most meaningful.

8

Caution

MySQL tries to look for *relevant* matches of the search terms in the table rows, but it tries to ignore certain words (in the search string) that appear too common to be worthy of meaning. It won't see any relevance for:

- A search word fewer than four characters long
- Common English words, as defined by its stop-word list
- Words that occur in more than 50% of the table's rows

For example, if you try to search on the word "Key" you'll get no result because the word is just too short:

```
mysql> SELECT city_name FROM cities
    -> WHERE MATCH (city_name) AGAINST ('Key');
Empty set (0.00 sec)
```

You may consider this unsatisfactory. This behavior can be changed by modifying the MySQL variable ft_min_word_len. You can see what this is set to on your system by doing SHOW VARIABLES, like this:

```
mysql> SHOW VARIABLES LIKE 'ft%';
+-------------------------+-----------------+
| Variable_name           | Value           |
+-------------------------+-----------------+
| ft_min_word_len         | 4               |
| ft_max_word_len         | 254             |
| ft_max_word_len_for_sort | 20             |
| ft_boolean_syntax       | + -><()~*:""&|  |
+-------------------------+-----------------+
```

You'll see how to adjust this variable in Day 15. It's also possible to edit the stop-word list, but you can do this only on a source distribution. In the myisam/ directory under the MySQL source directory, you will find a file called ft_static.c. You will need to edit the word list in this file and recompile MySQL to make the change take effect.

To overcome the situation of rows not being returned if the search string occurs in more than 50% of rows, you can perform a full-text search in Boolean mode. You'll see how to do this in a moment.

It's possible to see what level of relevance is being calculated by MySQL when it performs its full-text comparison. You just need to repeat the MATCH...AGAINST expression in the *select_expression*:

```
mysql> SELECT city_name, MATCH (city_name) AGAINST ('Palm Springs') FROM cities
    -> WHERE MATCH (city_name) AGAINST ('Palm Springs');
+--------------------+------------------------------------------+
| city_name          | MATCH (city_name) AGAINST ('Palm Springs') |
+--------------------+------------------------------------------+
| Palm Springs       |                            14.176851272583 |
| Palm Bay           |                             7.9398336410522 |
| Palm Desert        |                             7.8505783081055 |
```

```
| Palm Coast         |                              7.8505783081055 |
| Palm Beach         |                              7.8505783081055 |
| North Palm Beach   |                              7.763307094574 |
| Palm Beach Shores  |                              7.763307094574 |
| West Palm Beach    |                              7.763307094574 |
| Hot Springs        |                              6.3981976509094 |
...
| West Siloam Springs |                             6.2559466362 |
| White Sulphur Springs |                           6.2559466362 |
+---------------------+----------------------------------------------+
```

Because the MATCH...AGAINST expression is the same in both places, the MySQL query
optimizer recognizes this and only runs the full-text code once, so it's not wasteful of
system resources.

As you can see in the preceding output, the right-hand column of the resultset is a non-
negative floating-point number representing a relevance value of the search string compared with each row.

Although the default behavior is to list best matches first (as it has done in the preceding
example), you can override this with other sort criteria if you prefer. You just need to add
an ORDER BY clause.

As well as running full-text searches using the fuzzy matching process, you can run them
in Boolean mode. Boolean, or logic-based full-text searching, is done by placing the
words IN BOOLEAN MODE in the parentheses of the AGAINST clause, like this:

```
mysql> SELECT city_name FROM cities
    -> WHERE MATCH (city_name) AGAINST ('+Palm +Springs' IN BOOLEAN MODE);
+---------------+
| city_name     |
+---------------+
| Palm Springs  |
+---------------+
```

This returned just one result, and a precise match! How did it do this?

The AGAINST clause contains a + (plus sign) before each of the words: the example used
+Palm +Springs.

The + before a word specifies that rows *must contain* that word for the row to be considered a match. If several words are preceded by a +, all words must be present (but in any
order).

You could instead put a - (minus sign) before the word, specifying that rows *must not
contain* that word. For example:

```
mysql> SELECT city_name FROM cities
    -> WHERE MATCH (city_name) AGAINST ('+Palm -Springs' IN BOOLEAN MODE);
```

```
+-------------------+
| city_name         |
+-------------------+
| North Palm Beach  |
| Palm Beach        |
| West Palm Beach   |
| Palm Beach Shores |
| Palm Desert       |
| Palm Bay          |
| Palm Coast        |
+-------------------+
```

This time the search looked for cities containing `Palm`, but without `Springs`.

 Caution
> When performing full-text searching in Boolean mode, MySQL does not ignore matches on words present in more than 50% of rows, but does still consider stop-words and short words (less than four characters by default) irrelevant and returns an empty set if nothing more interesting is given in the search string.

In addition to the + and - modifiers in Boolean mode, several more modifiers can be used to fine-tune the way searching takes place. Table 8.1 lists the modifiers and their meanings.

TABLE 8.1   Modifiers for Full-text Searching in Boolean Mode

Modifier	Meaning
+	Word must be present in all rows returned.
-	Word must not be present in any rows returned.
( )	Used to group words and modifiers.
>	Give this word a greater relevance.
<	Give this word a lesser relevance.
*	Can be added to the end of a search word for wildcard matching.
"	Apply the match on the words between the quotes.

The following query looks for cities containing the word `South`, and either `Fork` or `Kensington`, with `Kensington` being declared as rated higher (using>) than `Fork` (using <). It uses parentheses to process the `Kensington` and `Fork` comparisons together:

```
mysql> SELECT city_name,
    -> MATCH (city_name)
    -> AGAINST ('+South +(>Kensington <Fork)' IN BOOLEAN MODE) AS relevance
    -> FROM cities
    -> WHERE MATCH (city_name)
    -> AGAINST ('+South +(>Kensington <Fork)' IN BOOLEAN MODE)
    -> ORDER BY relevance DESC;
+-------------------+-------------------+
| city_name         | relevance         |
+-------------------+-------------------+
| South Kensington  |              1.25 |
| South Fork        | 0.83333337306976  |
+-------------------+-------------------+
```

The preceding example also deliberately sorted on relevance (notice how the third line created an alias, relevance, and how the query has an ORDER BY...DESC clause). In Boolean mode, results are not sorted by default.

In the following example, the * is added after a word as a wildcard, to match all cities beginning with London:

```
mysql> SELECT city_name FROM cities
    -> WHERE MATCH (city_name) AGAINST ('+London*' IN BOOLEAN MODE);
+---------------+
| city_name     |
+---------------+
| London        |
| London Colney |
| New London    |
| Londonderry   |
+---------------+
```

Note that these are not necessarily in order of relevance because this is not done by default in Boolean mode.

You can use double quotes (") to combine several words, but only look for the precise pattern, like this:

```
mysql> SELECT city_name, MATCH (city_name)
    -> AGAINST ('+"South Fork"' IN BOOLEAN MODE) AS relevance FROM cities
    -> WHERE MATCH (city_name) AGAINST ('+"South Fork"' IN BOOLEAN MODE);
+------------+-----------+
| city_name  | relevance |
+------------+-----------+
| South Fork |         1 |
+------------+-----------+
```

This returns only rows that contain South Fork, with the words in the order given.

How to Perform Subselects

As of version 4.0.2 of MySQL, it is not possible to perform subselects in MySQL. However, by the time you read this, version 4.1 will probably be available. The new version is due to have the facility for subselects.

What is a subselect? A subselect is basically a SELECT within a SELECT. It's a way of nesting one SELECT query within another.

With a subselect, you can do a SELECT from a resultset that itself has just been produced by another SELECT.

Subselects are likely to look like this:

```
SELECT * FROM child_products
  WHERE id IN
    (SELECT id FROM safe_products)
```

This query would first run a SELECT on a table of safe_products (finding products classified as "safe"). Then the SELECT in the first line would be run, selecting data from the child_products table where the id is present in the resultset of the first query.

(This is a simple example and can actually be performed without necessarily needing a subselect. It's written as a subselect so as to show you the format.)

Subselects are an elegant way of writing complex, often multitable, queries in one go. However, you can get by without them because the same subselect query can be implemented in other ways:

- If you're selecting from two or more tables, consider using a join; you'll learn about these in Day 9.

- If that doesn't work, create a temporary table and select the data into it; then, for the final SELECT query, select rows out of the temporary table to get the final resultset.

Any query, no matter how complex, can be implemented without subselects (though not always with the same efficiency or convenience). This is why MySQL has not suffered for not having them so far.

Combining Resultsets with UNION

Introduced in MySQL 4.0.0, UNION is a keyword that can be used to glue two or more SELECT queries together. Each SELECT query is performed independently, but the resultsets are joined together.

The UNION syntax looks like this:

```
SELECT select_query1
  UNION [ALL]
  SELECT select_query2
    [UNION [ALL}
    SELECT select_query3]
```

You can join any number of resultsets together. With this syntax, *select_query1* can be unioned with the result of *select_query2*, which itself may be unioned with *select_query3*, and so on.

For example, imagine that you want to list the cheapest products from the child_ products table, and the cheapest products from the teenage_products table.

Perhaps teenage_products looks like this:

```
mysql> SELECT * FROM teenage_products;
+-----+-------------+-------+--------+
| id  | name        | age   | price  |
+-----+-------------+-------+--------+
| 101 | Bicycle     | 10-15 |  69.00 |
| 102 | Make-up kit | 12-16 |  19.00 |
| 103 | Trampoline  | 12-18 | 120.00 |
+-----+-------------+-------+--------+
```

Now let's write a query that gets the cheapest from each table and unions the resultsets together:

```
mysql> SELECT 'teens',MIN(price) FROM teenage_products
    -> UNION
    -> SELECT 'kids',MIN(price) FROM child_products;
+-------+------------+
| teens | MIN(price) |
+-------+------------+
| teens |      19.00 |
| kids  |       7.50 |
+-------+------------+
```

Because of the UNION, the two SELECT queries are executed and their resultsets combined to produce the output you see here. The data formats from the resultsets must be identical or an error will result. Note also that the column names of the resultset (here, the string constant teens, and the aggregating function MIN(price)) get their names from the first SELECT query.

Normally, each SELECT works as if DISTINCT has been specified, thus yielding unique rows in the resultset. However, UNION can optionally be given the keyword ALL, in which case it returns all rows that have been extracted. For example:

```
mysql> SELECT id FROM teenage_products
    -> UNION ALL
    -> SELECT id FROM child_products;
+-----+
| id  |
+-----+
| 101 |
| 102 |
| 103 |
| 101 |
| 102 |
| 103 |
| 104 |
| 105 |
+-----+
```

This query now selects product ids from both tables. If there are duplicates in the result-set, they will appear.

Deleting Rows with DELETE

The final thing we'll look at today is the DELETE statement. Quite simply, DELETE removes rows of data from a table.

Here is its syntax:

```
DELETE FROM table_name
 [WHERE where_definition]
 [ORDER BY column_list]
 [LIMIT num_rows]
```

You should see immediately several similarities with the SELECT query (which is why we're looking at it now!).

For a start, there's a WHERE clause, which restricts the delete action to just those rows meeting the condition. This works exactly the same as in a SELECT statement.

Occasionally, you may also use a LIMIT clause, and if so, you may also use an ORDER BY clause. (ORDER BY has no effect without LIMIT.) You may choose a limit of 1 for safety (so that you can't delete everything by mistake), or you may find a reason for deleting *num_rows* rows of data.

Here's a simple example:

```
mysql> DELETE FROM child_products WHERE id=105;
Query OK, 1 row affected (0.01 sec)
```

In this example, the product with id 105 is deleted.

Here's another example:

```
mysql> DELETE FROM child_products WHERE name LIKE 'toy%';
Query OK, 1 row affected (0.00 sec)
```

Now all products are deleted if their name starts with the word `toy`.

Finally, to empty a table just do this:

```
mysql> DELETE FROM child_products;
Query OK, 3 rows affected (0.00 sec)
```

In this case, every remaining row is deleted from the table. Take care with `DELETE`!

Summary

In today's lesson, you learned a good deal about writing queries for MySQL.

The central theme was the `SELECT` query, the principal tool for getting data out of your database in the form of a resultset. You learned how to construct a `WHERE` clause, and how to include operators and functions within various parts of the query.

You saw how to sort and group the resultset using `ORDER BY` and `GROUP BY`, and how to limit the number of rows returned using `LIMIT`. All this is fundamental to your SQL skillset, as is the application of the `DELETE` query for deleting data, which uses the `WHERE`, `LIMIT`, and `ORDER BY` clauses just like `SELECT` does.

You also covered some more advanced topics, such as the `HAVING` clause for doing last-minute processing on the resultset, applying further conditions to it (similar to `WHERE`) just before sending it to the user.

You saw how to channel the output of queries into other tables and files, and you studied the principles of full-text searching using MySQL's powerful `MATCH...AGAINST` syntax. Finally, you had a brief look at subselects and how to collect resultsets together using `UNION`.

Q&A

Q How can I select from more than one table at a time?

A If you want to cross-reference rows of one table with those of a second (or indeed a number of tables), you want to perform a join. See tomorrow's lesson for information on how to perform joins.

Alternatively, if you want to select data from one table and combine it to data selected from another, you should consider using `UNION`, as described previously.

Workshop

The quiz and exercises are provided to help you solidify your understanding of the material covered today. Try to understand the quiz and exercise answers before continuing to tomorrow's lesson.

Quiz

1. True or False: SELECT can only get data out of tables.

2. True or False: You can't have ORDER BY and GROUP BY in the same SELECT statement.

3. True or False: A HAVING clause is processed after a WHERE clause.

Quiz Answers

1. False. You can use it like the "equals button" on a calculator. It can evaluate any kind of expression, including comparisons, functions, and constants.

2. False. You can have both, but GROUP BY must precede ORDER BY.

3. True. But don't put anything in a HAVING clause that you could put in a WHERE clause because it won't be optimized by the query optimizer.

Exercises

1. Write a SELECT query that extracts data (all columns) from a table of cities, ordering by city name and showing result numbers 31 through 40.

2. Write a SELECT query that extracts the city name from a table of cities, listing each unique city name only once.

3. Write a SELECT query that does a full-text search for the words "Learn some SQL" in the headline and text_body columns of a table articles in a content management system. It should return the headline of relevant articles.

4. Say why the search in Exercise 3 would be inadequate in the default full-text mode and suggest how you could improve it.

Answers to Exercises

1. You should have this:
   ```
   mysql> SELECT * FROM cities ORDER BY city_name LIMIT 30,10;
   ```

2. You should have this:
   ```
   mysql> SELECT DISTINCT name FROM cities;
   ```

3. You should have this:

```
SELECT headline FROM articles WHERE
MATCH (headline, text_body) AGAINST ("Learn some SQL");
```

For full-text searching in default mode (not Boolean), you will need an index on at least the `headline` and `text_body` columns. You can apply such an index like this:

```
ALTER TABLE articles ADD FULLTEXT(headline,text_body);
```

4. Default full-text mode may be unsatisfactory on the text "Learn some SQL" because:

- "SQL" is less than four letters in length, so it will be ignored in the search string.
- "some" is a common English word and is in the stop-word list, so it will also be ignored.

You can improve the search by doing a full-text search in Boolean mode. For example, the following will return headlines of articles in which all words are present:

```
SELECT headline FROM articles WHERE
MATCH (headline, text_body) AGAINST ("+Learn +some +SQL" IN BOOLEAN MODE);
```

However, you will need to edit the stop-word list and remove "some" and change the `ft_min_word_len` variable to be less than 4.

Joins and Indexes

In yesterday's lesson you saw how to retrieve data using the SELECT statement. Today you will learn how to select data from several tables at once using a join. Joining tables is a fundamental operation of relational databases.

Another key concept you'll learn today is indexes. Indexes can be applied to tables to make retrieving data from them more efficient, especially when performing joins between tables.

Today you will learn:

- How to perform the various kinds of joins in MySQL
- The benefits of using indexes, when to use them, and when not to
- What kinds of indexes are available and how to apply indexes to tables in a database

Joining Tables

Joins are a fundamental aspect of relational databases. They allow you to extract data on entities related by design—represented by related tables—in your database.

A *join* occurs when you retrieve data from tables related by some shared data, often (but not necessarily) a shared reference number or *index*. For example, if you have a table of customers and a table of orders, good design in a relational database will ensure that the two are related together by some common data between the tables, perhaps by storing a customer number on every order record. By performing a join, you can retrieve information in a resultset where each row combines data from both tables: information about each order will be combined with information about the customer who placed it, and the combination will appear as such in the resultset.

As you will see in a moment, there are several kinds of joins. They work by considering a relationship between each row of one table and each row of another table; they differ in the way they allow relationships to be made and therefore in the way they relate tables together.

The Inner Join

The most common type of join is an *inner join*. When you perform an inner join between tables, rows with matching values are put into the resultset, but where values do not match (or a row simply isn't present in one table), they are ignored. Because the join looks for equivalence between the columns it specifies and is considered the default type of join, it is sometimes called an *equi-join* or simply a *join*.

As you'll see in a moment, there are two kinds of syntax for performing an inner join: a newer method that is ANSI-92 compliant, and an older method that isn't.

 Note
> MySQL is compliant to the ANSI-92 standard, and the ANSI-92 syntax is the modern, and slightly more efficient way, to perform a join. However, the older method is fully implemented in MySQL, and many people prefer it because it's easy to read, and it's what they're used to.

The modern ANSI syntax uses the INNER JOIN keywords in the FROM part of a SELECT statement, and this defines which tables will be joined and the relationship between them. The older syntax lists the tables to be joined in the FROM part, but separated by commas, and defines the relationship in the WHERE clause.

You can write a join using INNER JOIN like this:

```
SELECT *
FROM table1
INNER JOIN table2 ON table1.id_column = table2.id_column
```

or using the older form:

```
SELECT *
FROM table1, table2
WHERE table1.id_column = table2.id_column
```

Let's think of a content management system in which we have a table of articles, which holds items of news or features that may be published on the Web site. Here's a SELECT statement run through the mysql console that displays the contents of the table:

```
mysql> SELECT article_id, headline, user_id FROM articles;
+------------+--------------------------------+---------+
| article_id | headline                       | user_id |
+------------+--------------------------------+---------+
|          1 | MySQL to Adopt a Dolphin       |       2 |
|          2 | MySQL 4.1 goes live            |       3 |
|          3 | New Downloads on our Website   |       2 |
+------------+--------------------------------+---------+
```

There's also a table of users (authorized personnel), who may be writers of the articles, or editors who approve them:

```
mysql> SELECT user_id, name, auth_group FROM users;
+---------+----------------+------------+
| user_id | name           | auth_group |
+---------+----------------+------------+
|       2 | Clare Scriven  | writer     |
|       1 | Tony Butcher   | writer     |
|       3 | John Schreiber | writer     |
|       5 | Peter Stamp    | editor     |
+---------+----------------+------------+
```

We're going to perform an inner join between the tables to see who's written which articles.

We will write the join specifying the names of the two tables, users and articles, in the FROM clause, aliasing them for readability (using AS) to u and a, respectively, and relating the tables on the user_id column, which exists in both tables:

```
mysql> SELECT u.name, u.auth_group, a.headline
    -> FROM users AS u
    -> INNER JOIN articles AS a ON u.user_id = a.user_id;
+----------------+------------+------------------------------+
| name           | auth_group | headline                     |
+----------------+------------+------------------------------+
| Clare Scriven  | writer     | MySQL to Adopt a Dolphin     |
| John Schreiber | writer     | MySQL 4.1 goes live         |
| Clare Scriven  | writer     | New Downloads on our Website |
+----------------+------------+------------------------------+
```

See what happened? We matched rows where the user_id on the articles table corresponds with the user_id in the users table. If it's not immediately clear, take a moment to look back at the contents of the two preceding tables and perform the join in your head!

In this example, the `user_id` column has the same name in both tables. When this is the case, you can use the keyword USING rather than ON to simplify your SQL. The keyword USING should be followed in parentheses by the column or columns, separated by commas, which are to be matched across the tables. You could thus write the same query like this:

```
mysql> SELECT u.name, u.auth_group, a.headline
    -> FROM users AS u
    -> INNER JOIN articles AS a USING (user_id);
+----------------+------------+------------------------------+
| name           | auth_group | headline                     |
+----------------+------------+------------------------------+
| Clare Scriven  | writer     | MySQL to Adopt a Dolphin     |
| John Schreiber | writer     | MySQL 4.1 goes live          |
| Clare Scriven  | writer     | New Downloads on our Website |
+----------------+------------+------------------------------+
```

We could write the same query using the older syntax:

```
mysql> SELECT u.name, u.auth_group, a.headline
    -> FROM users AS u, articles AS a
    -> WHERE u.user_id = a.user_id;
+----------------+------------+------------------------------+
| name           | auth_group | headline                     |
+----------------+------------+------------------------------+
| Clare Scriven  | writer     | MySQL to Adopt a Dolphin     |
| John Schreiber | writer     | MySQL 4.1 goes live          |
| Clare Scriven  | writer     | New Downloads on our Website |
+----------------+------------+------------------------------+
```

You can add extra conditions to the WHERE clause; for example, you may want to ensure that you only list people who have their auth_group set to writer:

```
mysql> SELECT u.name, a.headline
    -> FROM users AS u
    -> INNER JOIN articles AS a ON u.user_id = a.user_id
    -> WHERE u.auth_group = 'writer';
```

or with the older syntax:

```
mysql> SELECT u.name, a.headline
    -> FROM users AS u, articles AS a
    -> WHERE u.user_id = a.user_id
    -> AND u.auth_group = 'writer';
```

Both output the following:

```
+----------------+------------------------------+
| name           | headline                     |
+----------------+------------------------------+
| Clare Scriven  | MySQL to Adopt a Dolphin     |
| John Schreiber | MySQL 4.1 goes live          |
| Clare Scriven  | New Downloads on our Website |
+----------------+------------------------------+
```

Note

If you want your code to comply with the ANSI method (for maximum portability), never use the WHERE clause to relate tables together. You should only put conditions here that are limiting criteria that work on one table at a time.

9

In the preceding examples, you may have noticed that we wrote things like this:

```
SELECT u.name, u.auth_group, a.headline...
```

See how we put the alias of each table name before the name of the field? You would be correct to assume that `a.headline`, for example, could also be written as just `headline` because the column `headline` only appears in the `articles` table, so the `a.` is redundant. Although this would be perfectly correct and a little more compact, I prefer to be totally clear in my SQL as to which column comes from which table, and it reduces the risk of my SQL containing an ambiguous column reference.

The Left Join

A *left join* returns all rows from the table referred to in the left-hand side of a JOIN, regardless of whether they match rows in the other table.

For example, we might want to list the people in the `users` table together with the articles they have written. The difference from an inner join is that the people will appear even if they haven't written anything. Where no match occurs, a NULL appears in the resultset rather than matching data.

The syntax is almost the same as the ANSI inner join, but with the words LEFT JOIN instead:

```
mysql> SELECT u.name, u.auth_group, a.headline
    -> FROM users AS u
    -> LEFT JOIN articles AS a ON u.user_id = a.user_id;
+----------------+------------+------------------------------+
| name           | auth_group | headline                     |
+----------------+------------+------------------------------+
| Clare Scriven  | writer     | MySQL to Adopt a Dolphin     |
| Clare Scriven  | writer     | New Downloads on our Website |
| Tony Butcher   | writer     | NULL                         |
| John Schreiber | writer     | MySQL 4.1 goes live          |
| Peter Stamp    | editor     | NULL                         |
+----------------+------------+------------------------------+
```

In this query, the NULLs under `headline` correspond with any user who has no articles associated with him.

A left join can also be useful if you want to write a query to identify rows in a table that have *no* corresponding entry in another table.

For example, let's say that we want to find all users who have failed to contribute an article. We just need to perform a left join and add a WHERE clause to look for NULL in the resultset:

```
mysql> SELECT u.name, u.auth_group
    -> FROM users AS u
    -> LEFT JOIN articles AS a ON u.user_id = a.user_id
    -> WHERE a.headline IS NULL;
+--------------+------------+
| name         | auth_group |
+--------------+------------+
| Tony Butcher | writer     |
| Peter Stamp  | editor     |
+--------------+------------+
```

A LEFT JOIN can also be used with the alternative syntax, LEFT OUTER JOIN, which is synonymous.

The Natural Joins

The *natural join* and *natural left join* are really just shortcuts to what you could achieve using an inner join and a left join, respectively. The shortcut is possible where you have columns in your tables with matching names.

In the preceding examples, we had a column called user_id in both the users and the articles table. Because the column has the same name in each, for our natural join we could write the following:

```
mysql> SELECT u.name, u.auth_group, a.headline
    -> FROM users AS u
    -> NATURAL JOIN articles AS a;
+-----------------+------------+------------------------------+
| name            | auth_group | headline                     |
+-----------------+------------+------------------------------+
| Clare Scriven   | writer     | MySQL to Adopt a Dolphin     |
| John Schreiber  | writer     | MySQL 4.1 goes live          |
| Clare Scriven   | writer     | New Downloads on our Website |
+-----------------+------------+------------------------------+
```

Note that a natural join as performed in the preceding example (really a simplified way of writing an inner join) omits the keyword INNER, and you should just write NATURAL JOIN.

For the natural left join, we would do this:

```
mysql> SELECT u.name, u.auth_group, a.headline
    -> FROM users AS u
```

```
-> NATURAL LEFT JOIN articles AS a;
+----------------+------------+-----------------------------+
| name           | auth_group | headline                    |
+----------------+------------+-----------------------------+
| Clare Scriven  | writer     | MySQL to Adopt a Dolphin    |
| Clare Scriven  | writer     | New Downloads on our Website |
| Tony Butcher   | writer     | NULL                        |
| John Schreiber | writer     | MySQL 4.1 goes live         |
| Peter Stamp    | editor     | NULL                        |
+----------------+------------+-----------------------------+
```

As you can see, a natural join or natural left join does the same things as an inner or left join, just using less SQL. However, you may find that for the tiny savings in code the meaning becomes less clear. Indeed, a natural join relates *all* columns that have matching names, and this may be more than you want! The natural join is used less commonly than the other kinds of joins.

The Cross Join

Users often inadvertently use a *cross join* when trying to construct an inner join in the non-ANSI method, the telltale sign being a huge resultset. A cross join is also known as a *Cartesian join* or a *full join*.

A cross join is performed like this:

```
SELECT *
FROM table1, table2
```

As you can see, there is neither a JOIN keyword nor is there any relationship being defined between the tables in a WHERE clause.

Every row of each table is crossed with every row of every other table, even if there's nothing to match between them. This results in many combinations. For example:

```
mysql> SELECT u.name, u.auth_group, a.headline
    -> FROM users AS u, articles AS a;
+----------------+------------+-----------------------------+
| name           | auth_group | headline                    |
+----------------+------------+-----------------------------+
| Clare Scriven  | writer     | MySQL to Adopt a Dolphin    |
| Tony Butcher   | writer     | MySQL to Adopt a Dolphin    |
| John Schreiber | writer     | MySQL to Adopt a Dolphin    |
| Peter Stamp    | editor     | MySQL to Adopt a Dolphin    |
| Clare Scriven  | writer     | MySQL 4.1 goes live         |
| Tony Butcher   | writer     | MySQL 4.1 goes live         |
| John Schreiber | writer     | MySQL 4.1 goes live         |
| Peter Stamp    | editor     | MySQL 4.1 goes live         |
| Clare Scriven  | writer     | New Downloads on our Website |
| Tony Butcher   | writer     | New Downloads on our Website |
| John Schreiber | writer     | New Downloads on our Website |
| Peter Stamp    | editor     | New Downloads on our Website |
+----------------+------------+-----------------------------+
```

As you can see, the query appears out of control! The cross join is not commonly used, at least not intentionally.

Indexes

An *index*, also known as a *key*, provides a means of rapidly accessing specific rows of data within a table.

Indexes Explained

Suppose that you have a users table that holds details about many people. When you ask MySQL to retrieve all rows matching a given criterion, it reads through the entire table, row by row, retrieving data from all rows that match the criterion. Even if you want to retrieve only a single specific row, it must read every row of the table.

Reading through an entire table like this—an operation known as a *table scan*—does the job but is highly inefficient. That's where an index can help.

Say that we have a query in which we want to retrieve the row referenced by a given user_id in table users. The table might look like this:

```
+---------+----------------+
| user_id | name           |
+---------+----------------+
|       3 | Clare Scriven  |
|       1 | Tony Butcher   |
|       2 | John Schreiber |
|       5 | Peter Stamp    |
+---------+----------------+
```

As you can see, the user_id numbers are not in any particular order, and we've no idea how many rows to retrieve. Our query may look like this:

```
SELECT * FROM users WHERE user_id = '2'
```

Without an index, MySQL has to read every row, looking at the user_id for each person and seeing whether it matches the one we're looking for.

Figure 9.1 illustrates the effect an index has on this table, when applied to the user_id column.

An index is like an additional column on a table that holds the contents of the original column, but sorted into order. Every entry in the index points back to the row from which it is derived, so by identifying which row you want from the index, you can quickly find the corresponding row in the table.

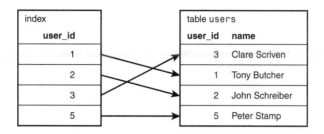

FIGURE 9.1

Using an index on the user_id *column.*

9

Why is this more efficient? Values in the index are kept in order, so if a query tries to retrieve data from a row with a given user_id, MySQL looks in the index for that user_id rather than scan the entire table. A search algorithm within MySQL helps it find that value in the index quickly, helped by the fact that the values are sorted. After MySQL finds the relevant item in the index, it does a seek to the related table row and retrieves the data. MySQL can stop searching the index as soon as it encounters a different value (because the index is sorted!).

If the user_id column is declared as *unique*, this further helps efficiency because MySQL knows there's only one row to retrieve. For this reason, unique indexes generally improve performance more than non-unique indexes.

In the preceding example, you saw what happens in a query when you apply an index to the user_id column. However, in general, tables may have many more columns that are used by queries to find a given row. Such a table might therefore have many indexes, some unique and some non-unique, according to the data they hold. Then, any query that tries to look up data according to the value of an indexed column, will benefit from the index being present.

When and When Not to Use Indexes

You will have realized by now that applying an index—or even several indexes—to a table is generally a good idea. However, let's spend a few moments understanding when they're useful, what goes on to create an index, and why they are not always desirable.

When to Use Indexes

Use an index for all columns referred to in a WHERE clause in a SELECT statement. For example:

```
SELECT name FROM users WHERE user_id = 3
```

indicates that the user_id column in table users should be indexed. Similarly, if your query tries to find the maximum or minimum value of a column, it would run much more quickly with an index on the column named in the MAX() or MIN() function.

Wherever you use ORDER BY or GROUP BY, an index would be an advantage. Because both operations perform a sort on the values in the column they specify, having that column's values presorted as an index is clearly an advantage.

Finally, columns on which you perform a join should be indexed. So if you write this:

```
SELECT u.name, u.auth_group, a.headline FROM users AS u
INNER JOIN articles AS a ON u.user_id = a.user_id;
```

the user_id columns in both tables ought to be indexed. The columns to be indexed are those appearing after ON or USING. The process of matching values across these columns requires multiple comparisons, and an index reduces the workload for MySQL.

Always use a unique index rather than a non-unique index if you can. As well as enforcing uniqueness in a column (which may or may not be a necessity), they speed up read operations because MySQL knows in advance exactly how many rows it expects to retrieve.

Where columns cannot be unique, columns whose values are nearer to being unique are better candidates for an index than columns with frequently occurring values. For example, if you have a table of people who will be looked up by name (such as a phone directory), a "last name" column would be a stronger candidate than a "first initial" column because last names are more diverse than first initials (although in practice you might index both).

When Not to Use Indexes

Indexes are beneficial to database queries that read data, but when a write operation is taking place, they actually create extra work. For example, if you perform an INSERT to create a new row of data in a table, all the indexes for that table will have to be updated. So in general, indexes should not be applied on tables that have many write operations compared to reads.

If a SELECT statement has to retrieve more than about a third of the rows in a table, an index will not help. For example, selecting on gender from a table of people might retrieve about half the rows, so indexing the gender column would be pointless. When using an index, MySQL has to perform a disk seek to go from each index entry to the corresponding row in the table, and if it has to do this for a high proportion of rows, it might as well do a table scan.

A further consideration is that indexes take up disk space. If an index does not benefit performance, it might as well be dropped because it will make your database larger than it needs to be.

Finally, there will be no performance advantage from applying indexes to tables with just a few rows of data; a table with just a few rows would not be worth indexing.

Managing Indexes in MySQL

MySQL supports four kinds of indexes:

- PRIMARY KEY
- UNIQUE
- INDEX
- FULLTEXT

The first two allow only unique values to be used in the column to which they apply. Only one unique index can be designated the PRIMARY KEY, but several indexes can be designated UNIQUE. The third kind permits the reuse of the same value in that column and is denoted by the keyword INDEX.

The fourth index type, FULLTEXT, is intended for speeding up full-text searches within VARCHAR or TEXT type columns. It works with the MATCH function of a WHERE clause, as was explained in Day 8, "Querying Data." FULLTEXT was added in MySQL version 3.23.23.

As you will see in a moment, you can apply an index on a single column of a table, or on multiple columns. With a text column, you can create an index based on the first few characters of the values in that column (known as a *partial index*).

You can have several indexes on the same table. The MyISAM table type permits 32 indexes on a table by default, and no MySQL table type restricts you to fewer than 16 indexes.

Syntax for Adding and Dropping Indexes

You can add indexes at table creation time using CREATE TABLE, or later using ALTER TABLE. You can also drop an index from a table. Let's look at the syntax for doing these things.

Adding Indexes During Table Creation

It's common to create an index at table creation time. Let's recall the syntax for creating a table (simplified a little):

```
CREATE TABLE table_name (create_definition,...)
```

As well as declaring the columns, to define an index (or indexes), you would have at least one *create_definition* with syntax like one of these:

```
PRIMARY KEY (column_list)

UNIQUE [index_name] (column_list)

INDEX|KEY [index_name] (column_list)

FULLTEXT [index_name] (column_list)
```

where *column_list* is the name of a single column to be indexed, or for a multiple-column index, several column names separated by commas.

You can optionally specify *index_name*, the name of the index. If you do not, the name of the column being indexed will be used, or the first column if there are multiple columns being indexed. (If you want to drop an index, you will need to refer to it by its index name.)

For a non-unique index, you can use the keywords INDEX and KEY equally.

If you are adding several indexes to the table at once, remember to put a comma after the *create_definition* for each index, unless it's the last thing in the list for CREATE TABLE.

If you're defining a primary key on a column, that column will not be able to contain any null values, and the column must be declared NOT NULL. In MySQL version 3.23.2 and later and with the MyISAM table type, you can have null values in unique and non-unique keys (that is, UNIQUE and INDEX) but not in a PRIMARY KEY. However, in other versions and with other table types, null values are not allowed, and the definitions of the relevant columns must contain NOT NULL.

For example, let's create a table called products, with one key of each type for illustration. You might write the CREATE TABLE like this:

```
CREATE TABLE products (
  product_id INT NOT NULL,
  name VARCHAR(30) NOT NULL,
  color VARCHAR(10) NOT NULL,
  price FLOAT(6,2),
  PRIMARY KEY (product_id),
  UNIQUE (name),
  INDEX (color))
```

In this definition, name and color are declared NOT NULL, and this works with earlier versions of MySQL and all table types. However, in version 3.23.2 or later with a MyISAM table type, these could be allowed to have null values, thus the definitions for these columns could legally be

```
name VARCHAR(30) NULL,
color VARCHAR(10) NULL,
```

Adding Indexes to Existing Tables

To add an index to a table that already exists, the syntax is similar to creating indexes with CREATE TABLE. You just use ALTER TABLE and add the word ADD before the index specification. You should recall how to alter a table:

```
ALTER TABLE table_name action_list
```

The *action_list* would include any or all of the following, each one working like its counterpart when used during table creation:

```
ADD PRIMARY KEY (column_list)
```

```
ADD UNIQUE [index_name] (column_list)
```

```
ADD INDEX|KEY [index_name] (column_list)
```

```
ADD FULLTEXT [index_name] (column_list)
```

MySQL also supports CREATE PRIMARY KEY, CREATE UNIQUE, and CREATE INDEX syntax for compatibility with other implementations of SQL. These are identical in operation to the ALTER TABLE forms. See the MySQL Technical Reference for more about using these.

Note   Adding an index to a table that has a lot of data can take some time! This is not surprising because MySQL has to scan the entire table, creating the index as it goes.

Showing the Indexes on a Table

It's easy to see what indexes exist on a table. You can use either the DESCRIBE or SHOW statements. Using DESCRIBE (or its shortened form, DESC) works like this:

```
mysql> DESC products;
+------------+-------------+------+-----+---------+-------+
| Field      | Type        | Null | Key | Default | Extra |
+------------+-------------+------+-----+---------+-------+
| product_id | int(11)     |      | PRI | 0       |       |
| name       | varchar(30) |      | UNI |         |       |
| color      | varchar(10) | YES  | MUL | NULL    |       |
| price      | float(6,2)  | YES  |     | NULL    |       |
+------------+-------------+------+-----+---------+-------+
```

Using SHOW, you could type this:

```
mysql> SHOW INDEXES FROM products;
```

Here's a sample of the output (shortened for clarity):

```
+----------+------------+----------+--------------+-------------+
| Table    | Non_unique | Key_name | Seq_in_index | Column_name |
+----------+------------+----------+--------------+-------------+
| products |          0 | PRIMARY  |            1 | product_id  |
| products |          0 | name     |            1 | name        |
| products |          1 | color    |            1 | color       |
+----------+------------+----------+--------------+-------------+
```

As you can see, in both cases the `product_id` column is shown as the primary key (marked `PRI` or `PRIMARY`, respectively), `name` is a unique index (`UNI` or `Non_unique` set to 0), and `color` is a non-unique index (`MUL`, for multiple value, or `Non_unique` set to 1).

You can also see whether a query is using an index, by adding `EXPLAIN` before a query:

```
mysql> EXPLAIN SELECT * FROM products WHERE name LIKE "Sweater%";
+----------+--------+---------------+------+---------+------+------+-------+
| table    | type   | possible_keys | key  | key_len | ref  | rows | Extra |
+----------+--------+---------------+------+---------+------+------+-------+
| products | system | name          | NULL |    NULL | NULL |    1 |       |
+----------+--------+---------------+------+---------+------+------+-------+
```

You'll learn how to use the `EXPLAIN` statement and how to ensure that your queries are making best use of indexes in Day 18, "Optimizing Performance."

Dropping Indexes

Dropping an index destroys the index and the values it stores but does not affect the data in any indexed columns. Again you can use `ALTER TABLE`:

```
ALTER TABLE table_name action_list
```

Your `action_list` would now include any of the following:

```
DROP PRIMARY KEY
```

```
DROP INDEX index_name
```

For example:

```
ALTER TABLE products DROP INDEX color
```

would drop the index called `color`.

Disabling and Enabling Indexes

MySQL 4.0 brings two new ways of handling indexes on `MyISAM` tables: within the context of an `ALTER TABLE` command, you can disable and enable non-unique indexes. The syntax for an item in your `action_list` would be like this:

```
DISABLE KEYS
```

or

```
ENABLE KEYS
```

If you are performing a bulk insert, disabling indexes prior to the insert speeds up performance. (Because only non-unique indexes are disabled, unique key integrity is still ensured.) With these indexes disabled, MySQL does not need to create an index entry after inserting each record, thus saving performance overhead.

After the bulk insert is finished, you would enable keys again by using the ALTER TABLE...ENABLE KEYS command, which creates the missing indexes in one go. Overall, this is a far more efficient way to perform a bulk insert of data.

Note

Indexes slow down performance during write operations. If you are performing a batch import of thousands of rows, you could benefit by dropping or disabling the indexes on a table before the import and reapplying them afterward. This saves rebuilding the index after every INSERT and minimizes the downtime while the table is being repopulated.

9

Multiple-Column Indexes

An index can apply to a single column, but you can also create multiple-column indexes: in other words, you can have an index that is a combination of the values of several columns.

As you saw in the syntax for creating indexes during CREATE TABLE and ALTER TABLE, the parameter *column_list* can contain a list of column names.

For example, in the products table you saw earlier, you could create an index on columns name and color:

```
CREATE TABLE products (
  product_id INT NOT NULL,
  name VARCHAR(30) NOT NULL,
  color VARCHAR(10),
  price FLOAT(6,2),
  PRIMARY KEY (product_id),
  UNIQUE desc_idx (name,color))
```

This multiple-column index, desc_idx, would speed up operations that use

name

or

name...AND...color

in the WHERE portion of a SELECT statement, or in a JOIN that uses either combination to relate to another table.

In general, if a multiple-column index has been added on table columns *col1*, *col2*, and *col3* (although there could be more than three), it speeds up operations that refer to

col1

```
col1...AND...col2
```

```
col1...AND...col2...AND...col3
```

However, operations that refer to *col2* but not *col1*, or *col3* but not both *col2* and *col1*, will not use the index. Likewise, operations that have OR instead of AND, such as *col1*...OR...*col2*, will not use the index, and thus not be any faster than a table scan.

If you're using multiple-column indexes, it is good practice to place the most restrictive column first. We did this just now in the products table, in which we placed name before color (because a product name is likely to be more specific than a color, which might apply to many products). This helps database performance in any read operation that uses this index.

Partial Indexes

For CHAR and VARCHAR columns, you can create partial indexes. Rather than indexing the entire width of the column, a partial index holds just the first few characters of the values in a column.

In MySQL 3.23.2 and newer versions using the MyISAM table type, you can have partial indexes on BLOB and TEXT columns (which are designed to hold much longer values), but you cannot have indexes on the whole width of the column.

Although theoretically you can index many characters of a text column (or in some cases the whole width), you probably would never need to do this. If you're storing people's names, the headline of a news article, email addresses, or even city names, it's unlikely that you would benefit from storing more than the first 10 characters, after which point the values are likely to be different anyway. Keeping indexes short saves disk space and minimizes the impact on write operations.

You specify a partial index by putting the number of characters to be indexed in parentheses after the name of the column. For example:

```
ALTER TABLE products
  ADD INDEX (name(8))
```

creates an index called name on the first eight characters of the values in the column name. It speeds up operations such as

```
SELECT * FROM products WHERE name LIKE 'Sweater%'
```

Note   You can have multiple-column indexes that include partial indexes on some or all of the columns.

Summary

Today you saw two important and related concepts in relational database design, and learned how to apply them using MySQL.

You saw how to join tables when retrieving data, the resulting data set cross-referencing rows between tables. You saw several kinds of join operations, with the INNER JOIN and LEFT JOIN being of greatest interest.

You also learned how to apply indexes. It should be clear by now that it's always a good idea to consider using indexes, an aspect of database design that is sometimes overlooked. A database will work without indexes—to a point—but it is unlikely to reach its best possible performance without them. They will usually speed up both straightforward SELECTs and joins.

You can now apply the four kinds of indexes that MySQL supports: PRIMARY KEY, UNIQUE, INDEX, and FULLTEXT. You saw how to add them to a table, how to display what indexes exist on a table, and how to drop them. Furthermore, you saw how to specify partial and multiple-column indexes.

Q&A

Q I have run a join but get many thousands of rows of data in my resultset, when each table only has a few hundred rows. Help!

A You probably didn't use the JOIN keyword, but listed several tables in your FROM clause. You may have done something like this:

```
SELECT * FROM table1, table2
```

Right? This is a common mistake. You performed a cross join when you meant to do a different type of join. You forgot to specify the relationship between the two tables.

The solution is to change your SQL to look like this:

```
SELECT * FROM table1, table2
  WHERE table1.id_col = table2.id_col
```

or to write your SQL using the JOIN keyword, like this:

```
SELECT *
  FROM table1
  INNER JOIN table2
  ON table1.id_col = table2.id_col
```

Q Can I join more than two tables?

A Yes, you can join any number of tables. You would write your query like this:

```
SELECT *
  FROM table1 AS t1
  INNER JOIN table2 AS t2
    ON t1.id_col = t2.id_col
  INNER JOIN table3 AS t3
    ON t2.id_col = t3.id_col
```

Q Can I perform a join only on a column that is indexed? And does it have to be some kind of ID number?

A No and no! You can join on any kind of column, although it's a little unusual to perform joins on values that are not some sort of reference number or name. There's no need for the columns on which you perform a join to be indexed, but you will get speed benefits if they are, and even greater benefit if they are unique, provided that the nature of your data allows this.

Q What's the difference between a primary key and a unique key?

A Very little, except in certain versions and table types where MySQL permits NULL in a UNIQUE key but not in a PRIMARY KEY. A table can have many unique keys, but can have only one primary key.

Note that if you apply a UNIQUE key to a column that is NOT NULL, it will actually be made a PRIMARY KEY. (Try this for yourself and do a DESCRIBE on that table, and you will see that it has assigned the Key to MUL.)

Workshop

The quiz and exercises are provided to help you solidify your understanding of the material covered today. Try to understand the quiz and exercise answers before continuing to tomorrow's lesson.

Quiz

1. What is the default type of join called?

2. In the following statement, which are the best columns to index?

```
SELECT u.name, u.email, o.id, o.total_cost
  FROM users AS u
  LEFT JOIN orders AS o ON u.user_id = o.user_id
  WHERE o.order_id = 1002;
```

3. True or False: it is essential to use a table alias using AS when doing a join.

Quiz Answers

1. The default type of join is an INNER JOIN.

2. The best columns to index are user_id on the users table, and user_id and order_id on the orders table.

3. False. An alias is only used to make SQL more compact.

Exercises

1. Write the SQL to query the table articles and display each headline together with the name of its author, as held in the table users. Use ANSI-92 syntax.

2. Modify the query from Exercise 1 to sort them into alphabetical order by headline.

3. Modify the query from Exercise 1 to list only people of type writer in the users table, listing them in name order together with the number of articles they have written, including people who have written none.

4. Write ALTER TABLE queries to add the most appropriate index or indexes to the columns in the tables used in Exercise 3.

Exercises Answers

1. You should have this:

```
mysql> SELECT a.headline, u.name
       FROM articles AS a
       INNER JOIN users AS u USING (user_id);
```

2. You should have this:

```
mysql> SELECT a.headline, u.name
       FROM articles AS a
       INNER JOIN users AS u USING (user_id)
       ORDER BY a.headline;
```

3. You should have this:

```
mysql> SELECT u.name, COUNT(a.headline)
       FROM users AS u
       LEFT JOIN articles AS a USING (user_id)
       WHERE u.auth_group = 'writer'
       GROUP BY u.name;
```

4. The most appropriate indexes are articles.user_id, users.user_id, and users.name. You would not index on users.auth_group because it would not narrow the search significantly (at least when searching for the group writer, whose rows occupy a large proportion of the total).

The articles table would have a non-unique index on user_id:

```
ALTER TABLE articles ADD INDEX (user_id);
```

The users table would have a primary key on user_id, and a non-unique index on name:

```
ALTER TABLE users ADD PRIMARY KEY (user_id);
ALTER TABLE users ADD INDEX (name);
```

DAY 10

Operators and Functions in MySQL

Today you will go on a tour of MySQL's extensive operator and function library. You will learn how to process data using numerical, string, logical, comparison, time, and other operations.

Today's lesson provides an overview of the principal operators and functions with explanations and examples of how to use them. It is not meant to be an exhaustive list; for a more thorough list, refer to Appendix C, "Function and Operator Reference."

How to Use This Lesson

The examples in today's lesson will usually show constants where you would normally put a column name. For example, you may be shown this:

```
SELECT 2 < 3
```

where in real life you would probably put something like

```
SELECT * FROM mytable WHERE amount < 3
```

In this example, we're studying the < (less than) operator, but using constants in the first instance so that you can see precisely how it behaves. You can follow these examples yourself in the `mysql` console. In the preceding example, you would simply type the query and view the output as follows:

```
mysql> SELECT 2<3;
+-----+
| 2<3 |
+-----+
|   1 |
+-----+
1 row in set (0.00 sec)
```

As you can see, the `mysql` console returns a small table with the expression or query in the first line and the result in the body of the table. The preceding example returns 1, which means a logical `true` (because 2 is less than 3). (A result of `0` would mean `false`.)

The last line of the output shows `1 row in set` or something similar, and the elapsed time to run the query. For our purposes today this line is not important, so you won't see it in the examples given.

When you put today's techniques into practice, remember that when doing a `SELECT` with the operator or function before a `WHERE`, you will probably want to make an alias for the returned value, thus making it easier to process the resultset in your script. For example:

```
SELECT (item_cost * num_items) + postage AS total
```

This line evaluates the expression and makes an alias to it called `total`.

You may also find you need to nest functions and combine several types of functions. The following example totals up sales. It uses the `*` (multiplication) operator inside the aggregating function `SUM()`:

```
SELECT SUM(item_cost * num_items) AS total
```

Although in today's lesson we will write function examples in uppercase, they are not case sensitive. The following queries are equivalent:

```
SELECT "abc" LIKE "a%"

SELECT "abc" Like "a%"

SELECT "abc" like "a%"
```

Finally, you may recall that aggregating functions such as `SUM()` and `COUNT()` were covered in Day 8, "Querying Data."

Operators

There are several types of operators: for comparison, arithmetic, logical operations, pattern matching, type casting, and bitwise operations. Let's go through these types one at a time.

Comparison Operators

The comparison operators have their syntax as follows:

- = (equal to)
- <=> (NULL-safe equal to)
- != or <> (not equal to)
- < (less than)
- <= (less than or equal to)
- >= (greater than or equal to)
- > (greater than)
- *expr* IS [NOT] NULL (is or is not NULL)
- *expr* IN (*expr1, expr2, ...*) (expression in range of possible values)
- *expr* BETWEEN *expr_min* AND *expr_max* (expression between two given values)

Comparison operators return 1 if the result of a comparison is true, or 0 if the result is false. Here are a few examples with = (equals):

```
SELECT 1 = 1 returns 1.
SELECT 1 = "1" returns 1.
SELECT 1 = 1.00000 returns 1.
SELECT 1 = 0 returns 0.
SELECT 1 = 0 returns 1.
```

But beware! Watch out for these conditions:

```
SELECT NULL=0 returns NULL.
SELECT NULL=NULL returns NULL.
```

As you can see, whenever a comparison uses NULL as an operator, you get a NULL result. You might consider the last of the preceding examples to be unsatisfactory. If so, use <=>, the NULL-safe equals operator:

```
SELECT NULL <=> NULL returns 1.
SELECT NULL <=> 0 returns 0.
```

The other comparison operators can be used with predictable results with numerical terms, but again beware comparing a NULL. Here are a few examples:

```
SELECT 1 != 2 returns 1.

SELECT 1 <= 2 returns 1.

SELECT 1 > 2 returns 0.

SELECT 1 > 2 returns 0.

SELECT 1 > NULL returns 0.
```

When used with strings, an alphabetical comparison is made. To be precise, this is in the order of the ISO-8859-1 Latin1 character set by default:

```
SELECT "a" > "b" returns 0.

SELECT "a" < "b" returns 1.

SELECT "A" < "b" returns 1.

SELECT "a" < "B" returns 1.

SELECT "abz" < "abc" returns 0.

SELECT "Bertie" < "Bettie" returns 1.
```

Note

For German language applications, MySQL 4 introduces the latin_de character set, which puts character sorting in the same order as a German language telephone book. To enable this, you should start mysqld with the --default-character-set=latin_de option.

For more information on setting server variables for mysqld, see Day 15, "Administration."

You can use the comparators to compare dates and times, the least one being the earlier in time. Whether in string or numeric format, the result is the same. For example:

```
SELECT '2002-06-31' <= '2002-10-09' returns 1.

SELECT 20020631 <= 20021009 returns 1.
```

But you must make sure that your dates are formatted properly. Beware comparing dates without their leading zeros, or years in two-digit format; the following would both be bad practice:

```
SELECT '2002-6-31' <= '2002-10-9' returns 0.

SELECT '99-06-31' <= '02-10-09' returns 0.
```

You can test whether an expression is NULL, using

```
expr IS [NOT] NULL
```

For example, this query would find all people who have an email address in some table:

```
SELECT * FROM friends WHERE email address IS NOT NULL
```

You can test whether an expression is in one of a list of values, using

```
expr IN (expr1, expr2, ...)
```

You use IN like this—for example, this would normally be true:

```
SELECT * FROM wines WHERE color IN ("red", "white", "rose")
```

or with NOT, such as:

```
SELECT * FROM students WHERE age NOT IN (21, 22, 29, 30)
```

You can find out whether an expression is between two values using BETWEEN, which takes the format

```
expr BETWEEN expr_min AND expr_max
```

For example:

```
SELECT (14.5 * 2) BETWEEN 25 AND 50 returns 1.
```

Arithmetic Operators

MySQL can do basic arithmetic, with the following operators:

- *x* * *y* (multiplication)
- *x* / *y* (division)
- *x* + *y* (addition)
- *x* - *y* (subtraction)
- *x* % *y* (modulo)

The arithmetic operators expect numbers rather than strings to be passed to them. However, a string containing a numerical value at the beginning of the string will still be processed: Each value is evaluated to a number, which will be non-zero if the string starts with numeric information. Thus:

```
SELECT 9+2
```

will return 11 but

```
SELECT "4.5abc" - 0.5 + "two2"
```

would be the same as

```
SELECT 4.5 · 0.5 + 0
```

and will therefore return 4.

The · (minus) operator can also be used as a unary minus, by putting it to the left of the term. Thus

```
SELECT 4.5 * · 2
```

returns -9.0.

The % (modulo) operator works like this:

```
x % y
```

x is divided by y, and the remainder is returned. For example:

```
SELECT 10 % 4
```

returns 2.

Logical Operators

The logical (or boolean) operators NOT, OR, and AND (with equivalents as !, ||, and &&) have their syntax as follows:

- NOT *expr* (not), which is equivalent to
- ! *expr*
- *expr1* OR *expr2* (or), which is equivalent to
- *expr1* || *expr2*
- *expr1* AND *expr2* (and), which is equivalent to
- *expr1* && *expr2*

NOT or ! does logical negation of the operand that it precedes, returning 1 for true or 0 for false. It expects the operand to be numeric and will convert a string to a number before evaluating. Note that any negation of NULL also returns NULL. Some examples:

```
SELECT NOT 1 returns 0.
SELECT NOT 0 returns 1.
SELECT NOT "xyz" returns 1.
SELECT NOT "" returns 1.
SELECT NOT NULL returns NULL.
```

The logical OR takes two operands and returns 1 if either is true, or 0 otherwise. The logical AND returns 1 if both its operands are true, or 0 otherwise. As with NOT, strings are converted to numbers first. Some examples:

```
SELECT 1 OR 0 returns 1.
SELECT 1 AND 0 returns 0.
SELECT "a" AND "b" returns 0.
```

Note the behavior when comparing NULL:

```
SELECT NULL OR NULL returns NULL.
SELECT NULL OR 1 returns 1.
SELECT NULL AND 1 returns NULL.
SELECT NULL AND "a" returns NULL.
SELECT NULL AND NULL returns NULL.
SELECT 1 AND NULL returns NULL.
SELECT "a" AND NULL returns 0.
```

10

Pattern Matching and Cast Operators

MySQL provides a set of pattern matching operators, ranging from the simple LIKE to the powerful regular expression operator REGEXP (or its equivalent RLIKE). Here's the syntax of the operators:

- *string* LIKE *pattern* (simple pattern match)
- *string* REGEXP *pattern* (regular expression comparator), same as
- *string* RLIKE *pattern*
- BINARY *string* (interpret string as binary to force case sensitivity)

You can use LIKE to do simple, pattern matching that is not case sensitive. You would typically use LIKE to find whether one pattern contains another, or whether two patterns are similar (perhaps ignoring case). It returns a 1 for true (a match) or 0 for false.

You will find the % wildcard character useful, either before or after the pattern. For example, to find whether a string is equivalent to another except for case:

```
SELECT "Felix" LIKE "felix" returns 1.
SELECT "Felix Mendelsohn" LIKE "felix" returns 0.
```

Or to determine whether a string contains that name, at the beginning, end, or anywhere, respectively:

```
SELECT "Felix Mendelsohn" LIKE "felix%" returns 1.
```

```
SELECT "Felix Mendelsohn" LIKE "%felix" returns 0.
```

```
SELECT "Felix, John, Bruno" LIKE "%john%" returns 1.
```

To force a case-sensitive comparison, use the BINARY operator on either *string* or *pattern*. This converts either one to binary. For example:

```
SELECT "Felix, John, Bruno" LIKE BINARY "%john%" returns 0.
```

You can also use the _ (underscore) operator, which matches any single character. For example:

```
SELECT "abc" LIKE "ab_" returns 1.
```

```
SELECT "abcd" LIKE "ab_" returns 0.
```

```
SELECT "abc" LIKE "___" returns 1.
```

You can use % and _ in combination:

```
SELECT "abcd" LIKE "a__%" returns 1.
```

but

```
SELECT "ab" LIKE "a__%" returns 0.
```

 Caution

Pattern matching operators can be used as powerful text search tools, such as for building a search engine that finds rows in a table that contain a given piece of text. But beware the performance impact it will have because any string comparison will inevitably take a good deal of processor time owing to the multiple comparisons it must make.

If your pattern matching operator looks for a pattern only at the beginning of a string (for example, SELECT * FROM table WHERE text_column LIKE "pattern%"), you can build an index for that column and make your search faster.

But an index will not help if you will be searching for the pattern anywhere in the text (for example, SELECT * FROM table WHERE text_column LIKE "%pattern%"). If you want to run a search for a complete word (or words) occurring anywhere in a text column, consider using a full-text search, as described in Day 8, "Querying Data."

For more sophisticated pattern matching, you can use the REGEXP operator (or RLIKE, which is the same). REGEXP does extended regular expression matching, returning a 1 for true (if the *string* contains the regular expression *pattern*), 0 otherwise, but NULL if either is NULL.

Regular expressions are powerful pattern matching algorithms and are also found in Perl, PHP, and Unix programs such as grep. They go beyond the simple LIKE operator, allowing you to specify, for example, how many instances of a given pattern element are required to qualify as a match.

Table 10.1 shows the regular expression sequences available to you.

TABLE 10.1   REGEXP Regular Expressions

Sequence	Meaning
.	(A dot) Matches any single character.
[...]	Matches any character or characters that appear between the brackets.
	For example, [Aa] matches the letter a in upper- or lowercase.
[^...]	Matches any character other than those that appear between the brackets.
	For example, [^0-9] matches any string lacking a non-numeric character.
^	Matches at the beginning of the string.
	For example, ^John matches strings beginning with "John".
$	Matches at the end of the string.
	For example, Smith$ matches strings ending with "Smith".
element	Matches *element*.
	For example, John matches strings containing "John" anywhere in its length.
element1|element2	Matches *element1* or *element2*.
	For example, a|b|c matches strings containing "a", "b", or "c" anywhere.
element*	Matches 0 or more instances of *element*.
	For example, [0-9]* matches any number of digits (including none).
element+	Matches 1 or more instances of element.
	For example, [0-9]+ matches at least one digit anywhere in the string.
element?	Matches 0 or 1 instances of *element*.
element{n1}	Matches exactly *n1* instances of *element*.
element{n1,}	Matches at least *n1* instances of *element*.
element{,n2}	Matches from 0 to *n2* instances of *element*.

10

TABLE 10.1 continued

Sequence	Meaning
element{n1,n2}	Matches from *n1* to *n2* instances of *element*.
()	Use parentheses to group patterns, with inner patterns to be evaluated before outer patterns.

Here are a few more examples:

```
SELECT "John Smith" REGEXP "x" returns 0.
SELECT "John Smith" REGEXP "^John" returns 1.
SELECT "John Smith" REGEXP "Smith$" returns 1.
SELECT "John Smith" REGEXP "^Smith" returns 1.
SELECT "John Smith" REGEXP "^john smith$" returns 1.
SELECT "John Smith" REGEXP "[0-9]+" returns 0.
SELECT "John" REGEXP "J...." returns 0.
SELECT "John" REGEXP "J..." returns 1.
SELECT "John" REGEXP "J.." returns 1.
SELECT "John" REGEXP ".o.." returns 1.
```

Look for a four-letter word where the second letter is "o":

```
SELECT "John" REGEXP "^.o..$" returns 1.
SELECT "Johnathan" REGEXP "^.o..$" returns 0.
```

Look for at least one "J", first not case sensitive and then case sensitive:

```
SELECT "John" REGEXP "j{1,}" returns 1.
SELECT "John" REGEXP BINARY "J{1,}" returns 1.
```

Look for the last name after at least one space:

```
SELECT "Robert Grant" REGEXP " +Grant$" returns 1.
SELECT "Grant" REGEXP " +Grant$" returns 0.
```

Bitwise Operators

You can perform operations at a binary level. Here is the syntax of the bitwise operators, where *expr* should be a BIGINT:

- *expr* << *num* (shift bits of *expr* left by *num* bits)

- *expr* >> *num* (shift bits of *expr* right by *num* bits)

- *expr1* | *expr2* (perform bitwise OR of *expr1* and *expr2*)

- *expr1* & *expr2* (perform bitwise AND of *expr1* and *expr2*)

Order of Operator Precedence

Expressions are evaluated strictly in the following order (operators higher up the list are performed first):

```
BINARY
NOT !
- (unary)
* / %
+ -
<< >>
&
|
= <=> != <> < <= >= > LIKE REGEXP IS IN
BETWEEN
AND &&
OR ||
```

Thus, for example, SELECT 9+2*5 returns 19 because * is evaluated before +.

You may use parentheses to affect the order of evaluation. For example, SELECT (9+2)*5 returns 55.

Logical and Conditional Functions

MySQL provides three logical and conditional functions, IF(), IFNULL(), and CASE. Here's an overview of their syntax:

- IF(*expr1, expr2, expr3*)

- IFNULL(*expr1, expr2*)

- CASE value WHEN [compare-*value1*] THEN *result1* [WHEN [compare-*value2*] THEN *result2* ...] [ELSE *result3*] END

IF() takes the format

```
IF(expr1, expr2, expr3)
```

If *expr1* is true (not NULL or 0), the function returns *expr2*. If false, it returns *expr3*. For example, to test whether there are any items in a table products:

```
SELECT IF(COUNT(product_id), "yes", "none") FROM products
```

10

Beware that if *expr1* is a floating-point number that evaluates to less than one but not zero, it will be rounded to zero and thus equate to false.

Note that you may want to nest IF() functions. In a programming language, it's normal to have nested IF()'s, and here you would simply replace any of the expressions with another IF(). For example:

```
SELECT IF(10>5,
  IF(2>3, "yes", "no"),
  "sorry")
```

would return no.

The syntax for IFNULL() is

```
IFNULL(expr1, expr2)
```

It tests *expr1*, and if not NULL, it returns *expr1*; otherwise, *expr2*. If you think an expression *expr1* may evaluate to NULL, such as when you do a division by zero, it can be a handy function to avoid an IF(). For example:

```
IFNULL(1, 2) returns 1.

IFNULL(0, 2) returns 0.

IFNULL(NULL, 2) returns 2.

IFNULL("something", "something else") returns something.

IFNULL(100/0, "infinity") returns infinity.
```

But note that NULL is not the same a zero-length string:

```
SELECT IFNULL("", "something else") returns something else.
```

The CASE function can be used like this:

```
CASE value
  WHEN [compare-value1] THEN result1
  [WHEN [compare-value2] THEN result2 ...]
  [ELSE result3] END
```

It tests *value* against a list of possible *compare-values*. When it finds a match, it returns that *result*. For example:

```
SELECT CASE 1
  WHEN 0 THEN "zero"
  WHEN 1 THEN "one"
  WHEN 2 THEN "two"
  ELSE "none of these"
  END;
```

returns one.

Caution

Be careful with the use of spaces when using MySQL's functions. Never put a space before the function name and the opening parenthesis, or the query will cause a syntax error:

Correct: *FUNCTION()*

Wrong: *FUNCTION ()*

However, spaces within a function's parentheses—for example around a comma—are allowed.

String Functions

MySQL contains a considerable number of string functions. They are listed in Appendix C. We will consider a small subset of them here to give you a flavor of what you can do. Here is the syntax of some of the more popular functions:

- LEFT(*string*, *num*) and RIGHT(*string*, *num*)
- LENGTH(*string*)
- SUBSTRING(*string*, *position* [,*length*])
- CONCAT(*string1*, *string2*, ...)

LEFT() and RIGHT() return the leftmost or rightmost *num* characters. The return will be an empty string if *num* is less than 1. Thus:

    SELECT LEFT("abcde", 4) returns abcd.

    SELECT RIGHT("abcde", 1) returns e.

LENGTH() determines the length of a string, so

    SELECT LENGTH("abcde") returns 5.

SUBSTRING() allows you to extract from character *position* in *string* and optionally specify a *length*. Some examples:

    SELECT SUBSTRING("abcde", 3) returns cde.

    SELECT SUBSTRING("abcde", 3, 1) returns c.

CONCAT() joins any number of strings together. For example:

    SELECT CONCAT("Sarah", "Jane") returns SarahJane.

10

Date and Time Functions

MySQL gives you a range of date and time related functions. In essence, the types of functions boil down to

- Get current date and time
- Format dates or times
- Extract information (for example, name of a month of a given date)
- Add and subtract date and time
- Compare dates and times

It's worth noting that your data doesn't have to be in a MySQL table for you to use date functions! For example, if your programming language doesn't have some of the powerful functions that MySQL has—the capability to add and subtract dates, say—you can perform the query through MySQL just by using a SELECT statement on the data directly.

When passing a date or time to MySQL, it should be formatted slightly differently, depending on whether you are passing it as a string or as a number, as shown in Table 10.2.

TABLE 10.2 Passing Date and Time Formats

Format Passed	Passed as a String	Passed as a Number
DATE	YYYY-MM-DD	YYYYMMDD
TIME	hh:mm:ss	hhmmss
DATETIME	YYYY-MM-DD hh:mm:ss	YYYYMMDDhhmmss

It's not essential to use the - and : separators for dates and times, although you are recommended to stick with these for consistency with MySQL's default output format.

We'll now look at each of the functions in more detail.

Getting the Current Date and Time

Several functions are available for obtaining the current date and time. In all cases, there are various ways to ask for the same thing:

- NOW() or SYSDATE() or CURRENT_TIMESTAMP (current date and time)
- CURDATE() or CURRENT_DATE (current date)
- CURTIME() or CURRENT_TIME (current time)

The answer can be returned as a string, as follows in a request for the current date and time:

    SELECT NOW() could return 2002-09-08 09:50:13.

It can be returned as a number, by adding 0 to the result, as in the following request for the date only:

    SELECT CURDATE()+0 would return something like 20020908.

Formatting Dates and Times

You can use the following two functions for formatting dates and times in almost any way you want:

- DATE_FORMAT(*date*, *format*)
- TIME_FORMAT(*time*, *format*)

DATE_FORMAT() is the most versatile because you can pass either a date, time, or date and time to it. TIME_FORMAT() only accepts a time or a function such as NOW(); otherwise, a NULL results.

Table 10.3 shows the possible formats for the second parameter, *format*.

TABLE 10.3 DATE_FORMAT() and TIME_FORMAT() Options

format Parameter	Output Format	Example
%a	Weekday name, abbreviated	Sun, Mon
%b	Month name, abbreviated	Jan
%c	Month without leading 0	1, 2...12
%D	Day of month, suffixed	1st, 2nd
%d	Day of month with leading 0	01, 02
%e	Day of month without leading 0	1, 2
%h or %I	Hour with leading 0 (12h)	01, 02...12
%H	Hour with leading 0 (24h)	00, 01...23
%i	Minutes	00, 01...59
%j	Day of year with leading 0's	001, 002...366
%k	Hour without leading 0 (24h)	0, 1...23
%l	Hour without leading 0 (12h)	1, 2...12
%M	Month name	January
%m	Month with leading 0	01

10

TABLE 10.3 DATE_FORMAT() and TIME_FORMAT() Options

format Parameter	Output Format	Example
%P	AM or PM	AM, PM
%r	12-hour time	10:30:21 PM
%S or %s	Seconds	00, 01...59
%T	24-hour time	22:30:21
%U	Week number in the year*	01, 02...52
%u	Week number in the year**	01, 02...52
%X and %V	Year and week number*	2001 52
%x and %v	Year and week number**	2001 52
%W	Weekday name	Sunday, Monday
%w	Weekday number*	0, 1...6
%y	Numeric year, 2-digit	02
%Y	Numeric year, 4-digit	2002
%%	Literal % symbol	%

*in which Sunday is the first day of the week, or day 0.

**in which Monday is the first day of the week.

Use the functions like this:

```
SELECT TIME_FORMAT(NOW(), "%H:%i:%s") returns 21:30:15.
SELECT DATE_FORMAT(NOW(), "%a %D %M") returns Wed 9th January.
```

All *format* parameters must be prefixed by a %, but you can insert your own separators between the parameters, such as / or : and words such as "on." Table 10.4 shows a few handy formats.

TABLE 10.4 A Few Useful DATE_FORMAT() Formats

Use	Format	Example Output
American style date	%c/%d/%Y	3/31/2000
British style date	%d/%c/%Y	31/3/2000
24h time	%T	22:30:21
Full date	%W %D %M %Y	Friday 31st March 2000
Full date and time	%r on %W %D %M %Y	11:00:00 AM on Friday 31st March 2000

Extracting Date and Time Information

Here is a quick synopsis of the functions MySQL provides for extracting information from dates and times. First are the date extraction functions, which should be fairly self-explanatory:

- DAYOFYEAR(*date*)
- DAYOFMONTH(*date*)
- DAYOFWEEK(*date*)
- WEEKDAY(*date*)
- DAYNAME(*date*)
- YEAR(*date*)
- MONTH(*date*)
- MONTHNAME(*date*)
- QUARTER(*date*)
- WEEK(*date*[,*firstday*])
- YEARWEEK(*date*[,*firstday*])

There are just a few time extraction functions:

- HOUR(*time*)
- MINUTE(*time*)
- SECOND(*time*)

For slightly more unusual applications, you may need the following:

- TO_DAYS(*date*)
- FROM_DATE(*number_of_days*)
- TIME_TO_SEC(*time*)
- SEC_TO_TIME(*seconds*)
- UNIX_TIMESTAMP([*date*])
- FROM_UNIXTIME(UNIX_*timestamp*[,*format*])

Many of these extraction functions are a somewhat longhand way of doing what you could do more generically with DATE_FORMAT(). But they can be useful nevertheless. Here's an example of DAYNAME():

```
SELECT DAYNAME('2002-03-31')
```

returns Sunday.

Date extraction functions require a date, but the time portion is ignored. Here's an example with MONTH():

```
SELECT MONTH('2002-03-31 23:45:56')
```

returns 3.

The examples here are somewhat predictable (you already knew the last response would be "3," right?). These functions become more useful when applied to a database. Say that you want to find all items in a table of articles from a given month (for example, January):

```
mysql> SELECT DATE_FORMAT(date_post, '%e %b %Y'), headline
    -> FROM articles
    -> WHERE MONTH(date_post)=1;
+------------------------------------+--------------------+
| DATE_FORMAT(date_post, '%e %b %Y') | headline           |
+------------------------------------+--------------------+
| 6 Jan 2002                         | MySQL 4 Released    |
+------------------------------------+--------------------+
```

The time extraction functions are straightforward. You can extract the hour, minute, and second components of a time or date/time combination, for example:

```
SELECT HOUR('2002-03-30 23:45:56')
```

returns 23.

The more unusual functions can do things such as tell you how many days it's been between 1 A.D. and the dawn of this millennium, such as:

```
SELECT TO_DAYS(20000101)
```

returns 730485.

Note that there was no Year Zero. The opposite effect is obtained by using FROM_DAYS(), so

```
FROM_DAYS(1000000)
```

returns 2737-11-28 as the millionth day after 1 A.D.

The TO_DAYS() and FROM_DAYS() are only meant to be used on dates after 1582 when the Gregorian calendar was introduced.

TIME_TO_SEC() returns the number of seconds since the beginning of the day, and SEC_TO_TIME() converts the number of seconds into a time.

Finally, if you want to work in Unix time (the number of seconds since 1 January 1970), UNIX_TIMESTAMP() should be useful. You can optionally specify a date and time; otherwise, the current time is used:

```
SELECT UNIX_TIMESTAMP('2020-10-04 22:23:00')
```

returns 1601850180.

FROM_UNIXTIME() has the opposite effect. When used with the *UNIX_timestamp* parameter alone, it returns the date and time in standard format—for example, the billionth Unix second:

```
SELECT FROM_UNIXTIME(1000000000)
```

returns 2001-09-09 01:46:40.

Using FROM_UNIXTIME() with its optional *format* parameter causes the output to be formatted according to the rules of the FORMAT_DATE() function, like this:

```
SELECT FROM_UNIXTIME(1000000000, '%r on %W %D %M %Y')
```
returns 01:46:40 AM on Sunday 9th September 2001.

Adding and Subtracting Date and Time

MySQL offers a number of ways to take a date (with time optionally specified, but not time alone) and add or subtract an amount of time. The following options are available for adding, all with identical meanings:

- DATE_ADD(*date*, INTERVAL *expression type*), which is equivalent to
- ADDDATE(*date*, INTERVAL *expression type*), which is equivalent to
- *date* + INTERVAL *expression type*

Likewise for subtracting, there are several equivalent forms:

- DATE_SUB(*date*, INTERVAL *expression type*), which is equivalent to
- SUBDATE(*date*, INTERVAL *expression type*), which is equivalent to
- *date* - INTERVAL *expression type*

MySQL also offers some period-based functions (a *period* being a year and month combination) for finding the difference in months between two dates and adding a number of months to a period:

- PERIOD_DIFF(*period1*, *period2*) (find difference in months)
- PERIOD_ADD(*period*, *months*) (add months to a period)

Here are a few examples. First add an interval to a date (both statements are equivalent):

```
SELECT '1980-07-04' + INTERVAL 15 YEAR
```

returns 1995-07-04.

```
SELECT ADDDATE('1980-07-04', INTERVAL 15 YEAR)
```

returns 1995-07-04.

Now subtract, this time with a composite interval consisting of hours and minutes:

```
SELECT '2002-01-10' - INTERVAL '01:30' HOUR_MINUTE
```

returns 2002-01-09 22:30:00.

Similarly, in the more verbose format:

```
SELECT DATE_SUB('2002-01-10 15:00:00', INTERVAL 1 HOUR)
```

returns 2002-01-10 14:00:00.

The *expression* and *type* that you specify must be of a standard format, with *expression* being a number or string (for example, "01:30" for hours and minutes in a string format) and *type* being one of the values given in Table 10.5 (for example, HOUR_MINUTE). The possibilities are as specified in Table 10.5.

TABLE 10.5   Values for *expression* and *type* when Adding and Subtracting Date and Time

Required Format for *expression*	INTERVAL *type*
SECONDS	SECOND
MINUTES	MINUTE
HOURS	HOUR
DAYS	DAY
MONTHS	MONTH
YEARS	YEAR
"MINUTES:SECONDS"	MINUTE_SECOND
"HOURS:MINUTES"	HOUR_MINUTE
"DAYS HOURS"	DAY_HOUR
"YEARS MONTHS"	YEAR_MONTH
"HOURS:MINUTES:SECONDS"	HOUR_SECOND
"DAYS HOURS:MINUTES"	DAY_MINUTE
"DAYS HOURS:MINUTES:SECONDS"	DAY_SECOND

If you want to find the time difference between two dates, you can use `PERIOD_DIFF()`. You cannot pass it a standard date format; only a year and month combination will be read, so use only the format *YYYYMM*. (Don't expect a calculation of precise differences, such as to the day.) For many calculations, it may be sufficient to have the answer in months.

For example, how old are you, in months:

```
SELECT PERIOD_DIFF(200202, 196412)
```

returns 446.

The opposite effect is obtained by using `PERIOD_ADD()`, which takes a period and adds (or subtracts) months. This example adds 12 months:

```
SELECT PERIOD_ADD(200202, 12)
```

returns 200402.

This takes 12 months away:

```
SELECT PERIOD_ADD(200302, -12)
```

returns 200202.

Nesting Date and Time Functions

At times, you might need to nest one date or time function within another. Why would you want to do this? One reason is that it's better than performing several queries, and another is that it may be the only way to do what you want.

Let's look at an example of nesting functions. Imagine that you have a table of customers who have purchased an annual subscription for a magazine. You record the start date of the subscription and want to automatically send an email to the customer 10 days before his subscription is up. You have a program scheduled to run once a night to find all relevant people and send them a reminder.

How do you do the date comparison? You might imagine subtracting each subscription date in the table from today so as to find how long ago each one was, and then select all those whose time interval is greater than a certain amount. But MySQL has no function to do this, and it would be highly inefficient if there were one.

Here's a solution, which we'll build up gradually.

Write a query that finds a critical date: "one year ago less 10 days." Any subscriptions begun prior to that will be up for renewal. This query uses only MySQL's date functions and does not yet query the data:

10

```
SELECT
  DATE_ADD(DATE_SUB(NOW(), INTERVAL 12 MONTH),
  INTERVAL 10 DAY);
```

Note that the output of DATE_SUB() and DATE_ADD() are in MySQL's standard DATETIME format with four-digit years and leading zeros. As pointed out earlier in today's lesson, this is important for correct comparison.

To find the subscriptions, you now need to turn it into a WHERE clause to find those that are ready for renewal:

```
SELECT start_date, sub_id
FROM subscriptions
WHERE start_date <=
DATE_ADD(DATE_SUB(NOW(), INTERVAL 12 MONTH),
  INTERVAL 10 DAY);
```

> **Tip**
>
> Building up nested functions can create sophisticated and powerful queries, but they can be difficult to debug. Build up your queries one level at a time, ideally at the mysql console.
>
> Also remember that thorough testing is required, especially where you use DATE_FORMAT() in conjunction with date calculations or nesting. This can return shorter, more human-friendly formats without the leading 0 for days and months, but this is dangerous where another query may process its output!

Encryption, Encoding, and Checksum Functions

MySQL has a number of commands for creating encrypted and encoded versions of an expression. Here are the commands with their syntax:

- PASSWORD(*string*) (returns encrypted form of a password)
- ENCRYPT(*string* [,*salt*]) (encrypts a string)
- ENCODE(*string*, *password*) (encodes a string)
- DECODE(*string*, *password*) (decodes an encoded string)
- MD5(*string*) (returns MD5 checksum)

The PASSWORD() function encrypts a string and returns the encrypted result using MySQL's own encryption algorithm. The Password column of MySQL's user authentication table mysql.user contains passwords in the MySQL password format. (You were introduced to this in Day 4, "Getting Hands-On with MySQL," but it will be explained more thoroughly in Day 14, "Security." Here's an example of its use:

```
SELECT PASSWORD("mypass")
```

returns `6f8c114b58f2ce9e`.

After the string is converted to a password, there is no way to undo it! It's strictly a one-way process.

It's important to understand that `PASSWORD()` does not perform the same encryption as `ENCRYPT()`, which uses the Unix `crypt()` function. Look at how `ENCRYPT()` works:

```
SELECT ENCRYPT("secret word")
```

returns `AWKLJbk2ZvuYM`.

But let's run `ENCRYPT()` again:

```
SELECT ENCRYPT("secret word")
```

now returns `MWgAzAeDlaKwM`.

Each time you use `ENCRYPT()`, the result is different! You can optionally pass `ENCRYPT()` a "*salt*", which flavors the encryption algorithm. (In Unix, the *salt* is normally two characters, but in MySQL it can be longer than two.) If not specified, a random *salt* will be used, and the encrypted result is not predictable. But if specified, the *salt* will cause the result to be the same each time. Try running the following query twice:

```
SELECT ENCRYPT("secret word", "MW")
```

always returns `MWgAzAeDlaKwM`.

By specifying *salt*, you get a predictable result. There is no way of decrypting, but you can check whether an encrypted string corresponds with an unencrypted string tested against it.

For example, if you have an encrypted version of a secret message or passphrase stored in your database but no plain-text version of it, you can still establish whether a passphrase tested against it corresponds.

Let's write a query to test whether the typed-in string secret word matches the one we know (and store) only in an encrypted form:

```
SELECT ENCRYPT('secret word', LEFT('MWgAzAeDlaKwM', 2))
  = 'MWgAzAeDlaKwM'
```

returns `1`.

10

indicating that `secret word` is the correct passphrase, whereas

```
SELECT ENCRYPT('wrong word', LEFT('MWgAzAeDlaKwM', 2))
  = 'MWgAzAeDlaKwM'
```

returns 0 because the wrong word, encrypted, does not equal the encrypted string.

The `ENCODE()` function encodes a given string with *password* as the access password. It returns a binary string. `DECODE()` does the opposite, enabling you to unlock the binary string provided that you know the password.

For example, to encode, try this:

```
SELECT ENCODE('private number', 'mypass')
```

returns æt bÁI'7 ¸?.

Being binary, the result is not nice to look at, and you should store it as a `BLOB` datatype in your database.

To decode, try with the correct password:

```
SELECT DECODE(ENCODE('private number', 'mypass'), 'mypass')
```

returns `private number`.

Decoding with the wrong *password* gives a spurious binary result.

`MD5()` returns the MD5 checksum for a given string. This is a 32-character hexadecimal number. For example:

```
SELECT MD5('abcde')
```

returns ab56b4d92b40713acc5af89985d4b786.

Why would you ever need this? Well, here's one example. Suppose that you are sending a message across the Internet by email. Although the message is not top secret, when it's received, you want to establish whether the message is genuine.

One solution is this: Both the sending end and the receiving end know the same private key and keep it in a well-protected place. By adding the key to the message and doing an MD5 checksum, you can test the validity of the message. The private key is never sent across the Internet, but the MD5 checksum is appended to the message by the sender.

The receiving end reads the message, separates the message content from the checksum, adds its version of the private key to the message, and performs an MD5 check. If the newly calculated checksum is the same as the one that came with the message, the message can be trusted.

Here's the procedure, using a sample message and key. The sending end takes the original message and joins it with the key, MyKey using the MySQL CONCAT() function. It does this:

```
SELECT MD5(CONCAT('Original message.', 'MyKey'))
```

produces 842620dbe651d749314bb6ddeb18db5b.

The email that is sent looks like this:

```
Original message.
842620dbe651d749314bb6ddeb18db5b
```

Remember that the key is never sent! When it arrives at the receiver, the application separates the checksum from the message, gets the private key from the database, and tests the message to see whether it's genuine:

```
SELECT MD5(CONCAT('Original message.', 'MyKey'))
  ='842620dbe651d749314bb6ddeb18db5b'
```

returns 1.

What would happen if the message is not genuine? The checksums would not match because a fake sender would not have been able to append the private key to its message, and without this the checksums would be different.

Finally, note that MD5 is a *lossy* routine. In other words, the outcome does not in any way include the original data, and theoretically, many possible strings could produce the same checksum. It is thus not reversible, and you can never reliably retrieve the original string from the checksum. This is a valuable characteristic for us using it as a "trusted source" function.

Tip

> Beyond the functions you have seen, there is a wide range of other functions. These include mathematical functions (such as SIN() and SQRT(), for sine and square root, respectively), other numerical functions (such as ROUND() for rounding off floating-point numbers), string functions (such as LCASE() for converting a string to lowercase), and administrative functions (such as DATABASE(), for returning the name of the database selected). See Appendix C for details of all available functions.

Summary

Today you examined some of the operators and functions available in MySQL. You should now be able to do many things with your data using MySQL's operators:

- Make comparisons of numeric and string data
- Test whether an expression is in a range or list of values
- Use MySQL to perform arithmetic, logical, and bitwise operations
- Determine whether a string contains a given pattern, and apply regular expressions to do complex pattern comparisons

You were introduced to MySQL's function library and should be able to do the following:

- Use IF() and similar constructs to perform conditional operations
- Perform string operations
- Format date and time, extract elements of date and time information, and perform addition and subtraction of date and time
- Use MySQL's password, encryption, encoding, and MD5 functions
- Know where to look for other MySQL functions

Some operators, such as = (equals), might appear obvious in function at first, but their behavior may be a little surprising to the unwary programmer—for example, when one of the operands is NULL. As you saw, it is worth studying the behavior of operators carefully to get full benefit from them and to be able to use them to write powerful and reliable SQL.

Q&A

Q I keep getting a SQL error whenever I try to use a function, such as

```
mysql> SELECT CURTIME ();
ERROR 1064: You have an error in your SQL syntax near '()' at line 1
```

A Functions should never have a space between the name of the function and the opening parenthesis.

Q Regular expressions seem complicated, but powerful. Do I really need to learn about them?

A Agreed, regular expressions may not appear to be the most friendly things. For simple string comparisons, you may find the LIKE operator does what you want, or perhaps MySQL's string functions such as LENGTH(). However, remember regular expressions are powerful and can detect patterns that other functions cannot.

Q How can I display dates and times in a user-friendly format?

A Use the DATE_FORMAT() and TIME_FORMAT() functions. They offer considerable flexibility for formatting date and time information according to how you want to present them.

Workshop

The quiz and exercises are provided to help you solidify your understanding of the material covered today. Try to understand the quiz and exercise answers before continuing to tomorrow's lesson.

Quiz

1. Is it possible to decode a string that has been encrypted with PASSWORD()?

2. What's wrong with the query:

```
SELECT ADD_PERIOD (200304, 8)
```

3. What is returned by:

```
SELECT 'Hello' - '22'
```

4. What is the result of:

```
SELECT 'Hello World' RLIKE 'b|c|d'
```

10

Quiz Answers

1. No.

2. The function should be PERIOD_ADD(), and there cannot be a space before the opening parenthesis.

3. The number -22.

4. 1, meaning true.

Exercises

1. Write a query to run on a table invoices that returns all columns where the invoice was produced more than one week ago (according to the column invoice_date).

2. What will be the output of the following query? Why?

```
SELECT 1 - 10 * 2
```

3. Write an expression, without using regular expressions, that returns 1 if a string has only a single character; otherwise, 0.

4. Repeat Exercise 3 using REGEXP, but this time only return a 1 if the string has just one letter, upper- or lowercase.

5. Why is the following statement badly formatted?

```
SELECT * FROM friends WHERE birth_date > '80-01-01'
```

Answers to Exercises

1. `SELECT * FROM invoices WHERE NOW() - INTERVAL 7 DAY > invoice_date`

2. `-19`. The multiplication (`*`) is evaluated first, and the subtraction (`-`) second.

3. `SELECT LENGTH("string")=1`

4. `SELECT "string" REGEXP "^[a-zA-Z]$"`

5. It will yield an incorrect result. The dates will be compared as strings and give an incorrect result because only two-digit years are being used. Always use four-digit years in comparisons, and always use leading zeros in dates and times.

WEEK 2

DAY 11

Using PHP

Today's lesson introduces you to PHP, a server-side scripting language that can be embedded into HTML pages to create dynamic Web sites.

PHP is a powerful language: You can use it together with MySQL as the foundation for a sophisticated database-driven Web site. Today's lesson introduces you to the language and shows you how to use it with MySQL.

Today, you will learn the following:

- PHP's principles of operation
- How to embed PHP within HTML files on a Web server
- An overview of the PHP language
- How to use PHP to interact with a MySQL database, including making a database connection, running queries, processing the results of queries, and handling errors

What Is PHP?

PHP stands for *PHP: Hypertext Preprocessor*. It is a language that came out of the open source stable, with elements taken from C, Perl, and Java. Fast growing in popularity, PHP is an excellent partner to MySQL and competes with Perl, ASP, and other server-side languages.

Interactivity can be achieved using CGIs (Common Gateway Interfaces). These programs can be written in a number of languages, such as Perl and C (both of whose MySQL APIs you will study in later lessons). However, with CGIs, a program is purely a program and cannot be a Web page.

PHP allows you to embed lines of code within an HTML page. When the Web server receives a request for an HTML file containing PHP, it does not simply serve up the page to the user, but first executes the PHP script within the page.

The script usually results in an HTML page being served back to the user, but it can be generated or customized on-the-fly according to the instructions in the script. At a more complex level, the script may include instructions to interrogate a database, update data stored on the server, send email, make background calls to other servers, and even generate graphics.

The result is totally transparent to the user; there is no indication that the page has been generated especially for the user! The user never gets to see the PHP script and may not even realize it's there.

PHP has a well-developed function library and a range of APIs that enable it to interface with many other server systems, such as databases, POP and IMAP systems, graphic manipulation modules, and much more.

Because PHP is an easy language to learn and experiment with, today's lesson provides a quick guided tour that enables you, even if you are new to PHP, to start writing your own scripts. This is merely an introduction to PHP and leaves considerably more to learn, but the sections on the MySQL API should be sufficient for you to start writing powerful database scripts. For more information on PHP, read one of the many books on the subject such as Sams Publishing's *PHP and MySQL Web Development*.

Installing and Running PHP

Versions of PHP will run on the various versions of Microsoft Windows, Unix, and Linux, and for the most popular Web servers, including Apache and IIS. PHP can also be used for free under an open source license, whether it's for personal, educational, or commercial use.

The latest version of PHP (currently version 4.2.2) is available from the official PHP Web site at http://www.php.net/. This site is an excellent source of online documentation. Also visit PHP Builder at `http://www.phpbuilder.com/`, which contains how-tos, discussion archives, and other resources for PHP developers.

This section concentrates on using PHP with Apache. For a guide to installing PHP with Apache, consult the installation notes in the PHP distribution that you download from `http://www.php.net/`. You should also read the installation notes for Apache, which are available at the Apache Web site, `http://httpd.apache.org/`, and will be found in the Apache distribution that you download.

Tip

> The combination of Linux, Apache, MySQL, and PHP is often known as *LAMP*. This is a popular combination of software packages among developers who write software for open source platforms.
>
> You should find many resources on the Web for LAMP servers, such as the Web site `http://www.onlamp.com/`.

A Quick Guide to PHP

11

Here's a guide to the PHP language, designed to get you started quickly. To keep this guide lightweight, this section assumes that you are comfortable with the principles of programming in general and that you can hand-code simple HTML pages.

You will look at a useful but nonexhaustive set of PHP syntax—there's much more than can be included here! Nevertheless, you should be able to build powerful scripts after digesting today's lesson.

To get the most out of this guide, you should have at least PHP version 4.1. The general principles covered apply to PHP from version 3 onward, and we've noted wherever something has only been introduced in version 4. But the later versions of PHP contain much more functionality and have inherently better security than earlier versions. It's recommended that you upgrade to version 4.2.2 or later if you can.

How PHP Works

With Apache, PHP can be used either as a module linked into the Apache binary, or as a standalone interpreter (like a CGI).

When run as a module and an HTTP request comes to a PHP-enabled Web server, the Web server does a number of things:

- It receives the request from the client's browser.
- It locates the requested page on the server, passing any data to it that came as part of the request (for example, in a POST or GET operation).

- If the filename ends in a PHP extension (typically .php), the Web server invokes the PHP interpreter, which executes any PHP code contained between PHP script tags in the page.
- The Web server compiles the output and sends the resultant page back to the client.

PHP Basics

PHP scripts must be given an appropriate filename for a Web server to recognize it as such. Typically, this extension is .php, but .php3 and .phtml have also been used in the past. Apache's httpd.conf configuration file defines which filename extensions cause the PHP interpreter to be invoked. Valid extensions may even include .htm and .html if you want all HTML pages on your server to be treated as PHP scripts. (If they contain no PHP code, they will simply be output as ordinary HTML, but with a slight performance overhead.)

PHP requires special tags to denote a section of PHP code as opposed to plain HTML. There are several ways to denote this, as shown in Table 11.1.

TABLE 11.1 PHP Script Tags

Tag Style	Example
Normal tag style	`<?php echo "PHP mode now\n"; ?>`
Short tag style	`<? echo "PHP mode with short tags\n"; ?>`
Script tag style	`<SCRIPT LANGUAGE="php">`
	`echo "PHP mode with script tags\n";`
	`</SCRIPT>`
ASP style	`<?% echo "PHP mode with ASP tags\n"; %>`

An HTML page containing some PHP might look like this:

```
<HTML>
<?
echo "Some PHP here\n";
?>
<P>Some HTML here</P>
</HTML>
```

You can place the opening and closing PHP tags on the same line as PHP code, or on a separate line. The effect is the same. ASP-style tags and (in some earlier installations) short tags may not be enabled by default; you will need to change your php.ini file to change these options if you want to use them. Consult the PHP documentation for more about customizing your configuration.

Note PHP can optionally have a `php.ini` file, which contains settings that define how PHP should behave. For example, you can define whether short tags and ASP tags can be used, the maximum allowed execution time for a script, whether to allow HTTP file uploads, and so on.

Without a `php.ini` file, PHP behaves in the default way. A `php.ini` file is normally placed in `/usr/local/lib`.

Consult the PHP documentation for more about this file.

The script tag style is more verbose than the others but can make life easier when using HTML editors that interfere with things they don't recognize, such as the PHP tags and code. If you never edit your PHP files with such an editor (for example, if you always use a text editor), you probably won't want to use script-style tags.

The examples in Table 11.1 use the echo language construct, which prints the specified text to output, to appear on a Web page in the user's browser. It is important to notice the semicolon (;) after every PHP statement. However, PHP doesn't mind if you put several statements on one line, spread one statement across several lines, or indent statements to make nested code easier to read.

Types

PHP supports integers, floating-point numbers, strings, arrays, and objects to represent different types of data. When PHP accesses a variable, it decides which type to interpret it as according to the context in which it is used. This is known as *type juggling*.

It's unusual for the programmer to set the variable type: There's often no need to do this—called *type casting*—although it can be done if you need to.

You don't need to formally declare a variable before you can use it: you simply start using the variable (just call it by name!), and it comes into being. The following example creates some variables, assigning them automatically in various types:

```
$num = 20;  # integer
$price = 14.95;  # floating-point
$size = 'large';  # string
$myarray[0] = "red";  # array, first element a string
$myarray["qty"] = 6;  # associative array, element "qty" an integer
```

Notice the # symbol, which denotes that everything after it on that line is a comment.

Note

> There are several ways to indicate comments in PHP code. You can use # and
> // to make the rest of the line on which they are used a comment. You can
> also use /*...*/ for multiline comments.
>
> These examples illustrate how to use them:
>
> ```
> # this line is a comment
> // this line is a comment too
> /* this comment...
> spans...
> several lines */
> ```

When handling string values, either double (") or single (') quotes can be used, but the results are subtly different. With double quotes, any variables contained within the quotes will be evaluated. With single quotes, they will not. So if you have a variable $price set to 14.95 and you want to display it,

```
echo "red $price";
```

produces the following output:

```
red 14.95
```

However,

```
echo 'green $price';
```

produces the following:

```
green $price
```

You can also use objects. Use the new statement to create an object. In the following example, the class myclass is defined and the object $var created, a member of myclass:

```
class myclass {
    function do_myclass ($p) {
        echo "Doing myclass with parameter $p.\n";
    }
}
$var = new myclass();
$var->do_myclass(5);
```

The final line of the preceding code calls the operation do_myclass with the parameter 5. This produces the following output:

```
Doing myclass with parameter 5.
```

PHP variables can also be equated to Boolean types (TRUE and FALSE). If a variable is undefined, null or zero, it equates to FALSE. If it contains some value, it equates to TRUE.

Comparing a variable with TRUE or FALSE is useful in conditional expressions and loops, as you will see later in the section "Control Structures."

Variables

Variables (both scalar or array) are denoted by a dollar sign ($) before the name of the variable. Variable names are case sensitive.

By default, variables are available to the script in which they are used and in any subsidiary scripts incorporated into it. (In a moment, you'll look at how to use the include statement to incorporate one script inside another.) Specifically:

- A global variable declared in a script will be visible throughout the script, but not in functions within that script.
- A variable declared within a function is visible only within that function.
- A variable declared as global within a function will refer to a global variable of that name.

For example, you can set a variable, declare a function with a second variable of the same name, and call it like this:

```
$some_var = 0;

function my_func () {  # define the function
    $some_var = 2;
}

my_func();  # call the function
echo "value is $some_var\n";
```

When you define the function my_func(), the variable $some_var is by default local to that function, and its value is not available outside. It's independent from the other variable of the same name. Therefore the output produced would be

```
value is 0
```

However, if you declare the variable as global within the function, your code might look like this:

```
$some_var = 0;

function my_func () {  # define the function
    global $some_var;  # make variable global
    $some_var = 2;
}

my_func();  # call the function
echo "value is $some_var\n";
```

11

Now the function declares $some_var as global, which makes every instance of $some_var inside the function refer to the global variable called $some_var. Therefore the output would be

```
value is 2
```

As you can see, it takes its eventual value (2) from the assignment within the function. The assignment takes effect on the global variable, not just a local one within the function.

External and Form Variables

You've seen some user-defined variables, but a number of variables come from outside your script. You can view the values of these variables on your system by inserting the following line into a PHP script:

```
phpinfo();
```

This single line of code produces a substantial output. You will find the values of many variables relating to your PHP configuration, settings for the MySQL API, your Apache configuration, and information about the HTTP request that requested the page. You can isolate some of these variables. For example, try the following:

```
echo "$HTTP_USER_AGENT\n";
```

This returns information about the user's browser, such as:

```
Mozilla/4.75 (Macintosh; U; PPC)
```

You can use the variables to find out useful information about the clients visiting your site, where visitors came from ($HTTP_REFERER), the name of the script being run ($SCRIPT_FILENAME), what request method was used ($REQUEST_METHOD), the exact query that was sent ($QUERY_STRING), and so on.

PHP makes it easy to ascertain the values of user input from an HTML form. Forms use the common name=value structure, and any query string values create a variable of a corresponding name in PHP. Consider the HTML form called form_example.php in Listing 11.1. It's a simplified order form that asks the user to enter his name and choose a size.

LISTING 11.1   form_example.php

```
1: <HTML>
2: <FORM ACTION="process_order.php" METHOD="POST">
3: Enter your name: <INPUT TYPE="TEXT" NAME="username">
4: What size would you like to order? <SELECT NAME="size">
5: <OPTION VALUE="S">small
```

LISTING **11.1** continued

```
 6: <OPTION VALUE="M">medium
 7: <OPTION VALUE="L">large
 8: </SELECT>
 9: <INPUT TYPE="SUBMIT" name="submit" value="Place order">
10: </FORM>
11: </HTML>
```

The user views the Web page, types his name into a text box, makes his choice from a select box, and clicks the Submit button. Submitting the form requests process_order.php and sends it the chosen values from the form. When process_order.php is run, the $_POST array will be set (because the form does a POST operation; in a GET operation, the $_GET array would be set).

We'll take a look at process_order.php in a moment, but no matter what the script does, the variables $_POST["username"] and $_POST["size"] will already be set when it is invoked.

Caution

In PHP versions prior to 4.1, submitting the preceding form to a PHP script would cause the variables $username and $size to be set automatically when that script starts. This might seem convenient but is a potential security flaw because there may be other variables within your code, which, unless you set them to an undefined or safe value when your script starts, could be faked by a user who modifies the form he is submitting.

However, from version 4.1 onward you can set the register_globals system variable in your php.ini file. If it is On, the program variables (such as $size) will be set. This is risky, so you are encouraged to set register_globals to Off so that program variables are not set by user input. You must then go to the $_POST or $_GET array to get the value.

register_globals is off by default as of version 4.2.2.

11

The process_order.php script, which is called by form_example.php (refer to Listing 11.1), could look like Listing 11.2.

LISTING **11.2** process_order.php

```
1: <?
2: $username = $_POST["username"];
3: $size = $_POST["size"];
4:
5: echo "$username, you ordered size $size.\n";
6: ?>
```

This produces output like this:

```
Tony Butcher, you ordered size M.
```

You can even transmit an entire array of data from a form. You do this with an HTML SELECT MULTIPLE tag, adding brackets ([]) after the name of the array. You could add the following into the form on your form_example.php page:

```
What do you want on your pizza?
<SELECT MULTIPLE NAME="topping[]">
<OPTION VALUE="A">anchovies
<OPTION VALUE="O">onions
<OPTION VALUE="P">pepperoni
<OPTION VALUE="C">cheese
</SELECT>
```

In PHP 4.1 and later, this would create the array $_POST["topping"] in the process_order.php script. (In earlier versions of PHP, it would be stored as $HTTP_POST_VARS["topping"] and as $topping.)

Altogether, PHP 4.1 and later versions set the following arrays, all of which are automatically available globally:

- $_GET—Form variables sent through a GET operation.
- $_POST—Form variables sent through a POST operation.
- $_COOKIE—HTTP cookie variables.
- $_REQUEST—A combined set of the GET, POST, and COOKIE variables, thus all the information coming from the user.
- $_SERVER—Server variables.
- $_ENV—Environment variables.
- $_SESSION—Contains HTTP variables registered by the session module. (This is used to keep track of a visitor's activity using a cookie or propagated through the URL of each page.)

Assignment Operators

The simplest type of expression in PHP is equality, which you can set by using the equals sign (=), like this:

```
$size = 10;
```

This sets the $size variable to the integer 10. You can do multiple assignments in the same way:

```
$leftcolor = $rightcolor = 'brown';
```

This sets both the $leftcolor and the $rightcolor variables to the string brown.

There are arithmetic and string operators:

- + for addition
- - for subtraction
- * for multiplication
- / for division
- % for modulo arithmetic
- . for string concatenation

For example, if $a and $b are numeric values,

```
$difference = $a - $b;
```

subtracts $b from $a and places the result in $difference.

There are some shortcuts for doing simple variable assignments in a compact way. Here are a few examples of doing arithmetic on the variable $n, all of which set $n to the resultant value:

- $n++ returns the value of $n and then increments it by 1.
- $n-- returns the value of $n and then decrements it by 1.
- ++$n increments $n by 1 and then returns its new value.
- --$n decrements $n by 1 and then returns its new value.
- $n += 6 increments $n by 6.
- $n -= 2.5 decrements $n by 2.5.
- $n /= 10 divides $n by 10.
- $n *= 3 multiplies $n by 3.

Similarly, with a string variable you could do this:

- $text .= "yours sincerely" appends the given text to the end of the string $text.

Comparison Operators

PHP supports a number of comparison operators. They return TRUE or FALSE according to the result of the comparison. Here is their syntax:

- $a == $b for testing whether $a equals $b.
- $a === $b for testing whether $a is identical to $b, equal, and of the same type (introduced in PHP 4).

11

- `$a != $b` for testing whether `$a` is not equal to `$b`.

- `$a !== $b` for testing whether `$a` is not identical to `$b` (PHP 4).

- `$a < $b` for testing whether `$a` is less than `$b`.

- `$a <= $b` for testing whether `$a` is less than or equal to `$b`.

- `$a > $b` for testing whether `$a` is greater than `$b`.

- `$a >= $b` for testing whether `$a` is greater than or equal to `$b`.

You can use these operators for both numeric and string comparisons. Strings are compared in alphabetical order. "Greater than" means "later in the alphabet" (so b is greater than a), and lowercase comes after uppercase (so a is greater than A). Comparisons are case sensitive.

PHP has built-in string comparison functions, such as `strcmp()` and `strcasecmp()`, which do case sensitive and not case sensitive comparison, respectively. These are more versatile ways of testing, returning a positive or negative value or zero, depending on the result of the comparison. Study a more detailed PHP manual (or try `http://www.php.net/strcmp`) for more on how to use these functions.

> **Caution**
>
> Don't confuse = with ==. For example, if your code contains the following:
>
> `if ($name='John') { echo "Hello, John"; }`
>
> your output will always be `Hello, John`, no matter what value `$name` had before.
>
> Why? It's because = does an assignment, whereas what you probably meant to do was a comparison. So you should use ==:
>
> `if ($name=='John') { echo "Hello, John"; }`

Control Structures

Control structures allow you to control the flow of execution through your PHP script. There are conditional control structures (`if`) and looping control structures (`while`, `for`).

The `if` Statement

There are a number of means of controlling the flow of your script. The simplest of these is `if`, which you can use in its simplest form as follows:

```
if (expression) {
    statement;
    ...
}
```

For example:

```php
if ($price > 100) echo "This is expensive\n";
```

The *expression* may contain comparison and assignment operators but is evaluated to be either TRUE or FALSE, and the following statement (in this case echo) is executed if it is TRUE.

You need to use braces if you have a code block of several statements that are executed if the condition succeeds. Your code might now look like this:

```php
if ($price > 100) {
    echo "This is expensive\n";
    echo "Another time, thanks.\n";
}
```

You can optionally control flow using elseif and else. There can be any number of elseif conditions. Your syntax looks like this:

```php
if (expression1) {
    # do this
} elseif (expression2) {
    # do that
} elseif (expression3) {
    # do something else
} else {
    # do default thing
}
```

Execution keeps evaluating the various expressions (*expression1* then *expression2* and so on) until it finds one that is TRUE. If none is TRUE, the code block after else is executed. (You can have an elseif but no else, however.)

if statements can be nested, as in this example:

```php
if ($price > 100) {
    if ($price > 200) {
        echo "This is very expensive.\n";
    } else {
        echo "This is expensive.\n";
    }
}
```

The while Loop

You can create a simple loop structure using the while statement. A while loop has the following syntax:

```php
while (expression) {
    statement;
}
```

When entering the loop, *expression* is evaluated. It is evaluated to be either TRUE or FALSE. If TRUE, the statements in the code block are executed. Braces are required if more than one statement is in the code block.

The while statement is similar to if. It executes the statements in the code block only if *expression* evaluates to TRUE, but having executed the code once goes back and evaluates *expression* again. It keeps doing this until *expression* evaluates to FALSE, whereupon the loop exits.

Consider a simple example that counts down from 3 to 0:

```
$n = 4;
while (--$n) echo "...$n";
```

This produces the following output:

```
...3...2...1
```

Each time execution enters the while loop, the $n variable is decremented by 1 and then evaluated as TRUE or FALSE. The first time into the loop, after being decremented, it evaluates to 3 (which is TRUE), so the echo statement is executed. The loop keeps running until $n is decremented to zero, which evaluates to FALSE. Then, instead of doing the echo, the loop terminates.

A second form of the while loop is to write it in reverse, as do...while. This takes the following form:

```
do {
    statement;
    ...
} while (expression);
```

Using do...while, you can guarantee that your code block gets executed at least once because *expression* is evaluated only after the first iteration. If *expression* evaluates to TRUE, the loop is repeated. Looping continues in this way until *expression* evaluates to FALSE.

The for Loop

Another method of looping is available using the for loop, which has the following syntax:

```
for (expression1; expression2; expression3) {
    statement;
    ...
}
```

As before, you need braces if your code block has several statements. The expressions are used as follows:

- *expression1* is evaluated exactly once, when execution enters the loop for the first time.
- *expression2* is evaluated once for each iteration of the loop, upon entry. If it evaluates to TRUE, execution continues within the code block; if not, the loop terminates.
- *expression3* is evaluated each time execution finishes the statements in the code block. If TRUE, execution starts the loop again; if not, the loop terminates.

Consider how you could rewrite the simple countdown loop that prints values from 3 down to 1:

```
for ($n=4; --$n; 1) echo "...$n";
```

When execution enters the loop for the first time, $n is set to 4. Then the second expression decrements $n to 3. This evaluates to TRUE, so the echo is executed.

The third expression is not used in this example: It is always TRUE, but the loop exits when $n equals 1, and --$n decrements it to zero. This evaluates to FALSE, which causes the loop to terminate without doing an echo again.

You could also have written this loop as

```
for ($n=3; $n; $n--) echo "...$n";
```

This sets $n to 3 the first time into the loop and then checks that it's non-zero, as it does for each subsequent iteration of the loop. Each time after executing the echo, it decrements its value with $n-- and tests the result. When the result of decrementing is zero (FALSE), the loop terminates.

Optional Controls for Loops: `break` and `continue`

You can modify the behavior of while and for loops, causing execution to break out of the loop either immediately or after completion of the current iteration.

When using a while or a for loop, you can insert a break statement to make it terminate immediately, like this:

```
do {
    statement;
    ...
    if (expression2) break;
} while (expression1);

statement;
# execute here after "break"
```

break is a drastic way to exit a loop, letting you exit at any point during the loop's execution. No more statements will be executed in the code block, and the loop will not be iterated again.

The continue statement is similar but more elegant: it forces execution to skip out of the code block (in other words, to curtail this iteration), but then to do the expression evaluation again and keep iterating the loop if conditions are again met.

```
do {
    # code block of repeatable statements
    if (expression2) continue;
} while (expression1);  # evaluate this again after "continue"
# execute here after loop exits
```

If you want to terminate the entire script, you can use the statement

```
exit;
```

Incorporating Other Files: include and require

The include and require statements allow you to incorporate a second file into the first.

For example, you may have a Web page called index.php in which you include a file for displaying a Web site header from an HTML file called header.html, a navigation bar from a PHP file called navbar.php, and so on. Your Web page might look like this:

```
<HTML>
<?
include ("header.html");
include ("navbar.php");
?>
Content here
<?
include ("footer.html");
?>
</HTML>
```

The string passed to include can be the full path to the included file. Without the full path (as in the example), PHP looks for a file of the name given in the current directory (where the main script is). It also looks in include_path, a variable set in the php.ini file.

You can use require in much the same way, like this:

```
require ("header.html");
```

The two statements differ in that with require the contents of the referenced file replaces the require statement once and for all. With include, the file is read and evaluated each time the include statement is encountered.

It may be more efficient to use `require` if the subsidiary file's contents do not change (as with an HTML file). However, if your script executes the same line several times and the contents of the file need to be evaluated each time (as may be the case with a PHP file), you will need to use `include`. Also, if you want to specify the name of the included file as a variable (for example, `include ($file)`), you will need to use `include` so that the filename is evaluated each time the line is executed.

Functions

PHP has a large library of built-in functions. These cover all sorts of uses, including mathematical, string, array processing, image processing, connectivity to databases and other systems, and much more. There are too many to be covered here, but you should consult one of the PHP Web sites or a more detailed book on PHP if you want to explore them. Today, the built-in functions we will cover will mostly be limited to those for interfacing with MySQL.

You can also create user-defined functions. When defined, they work in the same way as built-in functions. These are blocks of code defined once and invoked from many different places in your code, including from another PHP file.

When you define a function, you specify how it should execute and what values it should return, if any. You can optionally define parameters that will be passed to it and specify how they will be processed.

You define a function as follows:

```
function function_name (parameter1, parameter2, ...) {
    statement;
    ...
    return variables;  # optional variables to be returned
}
```

You can invoke the function using the following syntax:

```
$var = function_name (parameter1, parameter2, ...);
```

This is the same way you invoke one of PHP's built-in functions.

Suppose that you want to create a function to subtract a percentage from a number (such as applying a discount). You could pass it two values: the original price and the percentage discount. You might define the function `discount` like this:

```
function discount ($price, $percent) {
    $newprice = $price * (1 - ($percent / 100));
    return $newprice;
}
```

11

Let's see how to invoke it. To apply a 6% discount to a price of $150:

```
echo "The discounted price is $". discount (150, 6) ."<BR>\n";
```

This produces the output

```
The discounted price is $141
```

The code `discount (150, 6)` is all you need to invoke the function and return its result.

Arrays

You will use arrays a good deal when you start using PHP to access a MySQL database, so it's a good idea to look at arrays on their own first to get an understanding of the basics.

PHP has two kinds of arrays: *numerically indexed* and *associative*. Numerically indexed arrays contain elements starting at the "zeroth" element (for example, `$myarray[0]`). You could create a simple array like this:

```
$size = array ("small", "medium", "large");
```

In this example, `$size[1]` represents the second element and equals `medium`. An alternative way of doing the same thing is like this:

```
$size[] = "small";
$size[] = "medium";
$size[] = "large";
```

In the preceding example, you populated the array sequentially. You can also define it by numerically referencing each element (which removes the need to define them in the same order):

```
$size[1] = "medium";
$size[0] = "small";
$size[2] = "large";
```

You could write a simple script to display the contents of an array by stepping through it with a loop. This example uses PHP's built-in `count()` function to find out how many items are in the array, and a `for` loop to iterate through each element:

```
for ($i=0; $i<count($size); $i++) {
    echo "Element $i is $size[$i]<BR>\n";
}
```

This produces the following output:

```
Element 0 is small
Element 1 is medium
Element 2 is large
```

You can also use associative arrays. These allow you to use more meaningful indexes to the arrays, and typically you would use strings for these indexes. You could create an associative array like this:

```php
$color = array ("red"=>"FF0000", "green"=>"00FF00", "blue"=>"0000FF");
```

In this example, $color["green"] has the value 00FF00 (which happens to be the hexadecimal value for displaying green in HTML). You could also write this as:

```php
$color["red"] = "FF0000";
$color["green"] = "00FF00";
$color["blue"] = "0000FF";
```

To pass through an associative array and display each element, you can use list. This is a construct that assigns elements of an array to a list of variables. In this case, the elements are a key=value pair (not to be confused with the entire array $color). The list of variables you assign them to are the variables $name and $hex. Here's the code:

```php
while (list ($name, $hex) = each ($color)) {
    echo "$name has hex value $hex<BR>\n";
}
```

Notice that the function each() is used, which is handy for single-stepping through the array $color. Arrays in PHP have an internal pointer, and each time you call each(), the element referenced by the pointer is returned, and the pointer is moved onto the next element. This is handy because it means that you don't need a separate variable to keep track of the index number of the array, as with the for loop.

Each time the while expression is evaluated, another key=value pair is taken from the array and the pointer moved on. Provided that you haven't reached the end of the array, the code then echoes the pair to the output. When you reach the end of the array, the while loop terminates.

Functions similar to each()—called next(), prev(), and array_walk()—give you other ways of single-stepping through an array, moving the internal pointer accordingly each time the function is called. You can return to the beginning of an array with reset().

The output of the preceding code looks like this:

```
red has hex value FF0000
green has hex value 00FF00
blue has hex value 0000FF
```

This simple introduction covered only one-dimensional arrays, although PHP does have the capability to handle multidimensional arrays. PHP also has a good range of functions for array processing, including sort functions. It's worth exploring other PHP resources to learn more about the possibilities.

11

The PHP API for MySQL

PHP has a suite of built-in functions for interfacing with MySQL database servers. You can get by with a small subset of them, but we'll try to cover the full function list for completeness.

Connecting to a MySQL Database

Table 11.2 shows the functions for connecting to and disconnecting from a MySQL database server and for selecting a database.

TABLE 11.2 Functions for Connecting to a MySQL Database

Function	Action
mysql_connect()	Opens a connection to a MySQL server
mysql_pconnect()	Opens a persistent connection to a MySQL server
mysql_select_db()	Selects a MySQL database
mysql_close()	Closes a connection to a MySQL server

You can use the following syntax to connect to a MySQL server:

```
mysql_connect ([server[,username[,password]]]);
```

Or, to make a persistent connection:

```
mysql_pconnect ([server[,username[,password]]]);
```

where *server* is of the form *hostname*[:*port*][:/*path/to/socket*]. Calling the function returns a link identifier if a successful connection is made or FALSE if there is a failure. You typically precede the function with the @ symbol; this allows you to handle a connection failure elegantly in your own code rather than have the default PHP warning text printed to your output. (You can place the @ symbol before any expression in PHP, the effect being that any error will be suppressed.)

For example, to connect to a database on localhost, with the database username and password in the variables $dbuser and $dbpass, respectively, you might do this:

```
$link_id = @mysql_pconnect ("localhost", $dbuser, $dbpass);
if ($link_id) {
    echo "Link id is $link_id<BR>\n";
} else {
    echo "Failed to connect<BR>\n";
}
```

If you use valid connection parameters, this prints:

```
Link id is Resource id #1
```

You can use either `mysql_connect()` or `mysql_pconnect()`. The former makes a simple database connection that is closed when the PHP script exits or when `mysql_close()` is encountered. `mysql_pconnect()` creates a *persistent* connection.

A persistent connection will not be closed when your script exits or when a `mysql_close()` is encountered. The next time a script tries to do a `mysql_pconnect()` using the same connection parameters, if it can find an existing link with these parameters, that link will be used again.

This is more efficient because it saves having to open a new connection each time your script is run and close it when the script finishes. However, beware that on a system that has busy peak periods, a number of persistent connections will be left open after the peak activity is over. You may thus want to set a low `wait_timeout` period in MySQL's variables rather than have inactive connections stay open for a long time after they are actually required. (See Day 15, "Administration," for more about administering MySQL and setting variables that govern its behavior.)

As well as connecting to the MySQL server, you will need to select a MySQL database for use. You can do this by specifying the name of the database to the function `mysql_select_db()`. For example, to select the content management system database `cms`:

```
if (mysql_select_db ("cms")) {
    echo "Connected to cms!<BR>\n";
}
```

In practice, you will probably find it most useful to keep your database connection script as an included file for a variety of scripts to use rather than embed the connection parameters and error handling in each PHP script that you write. This has a number of advantages:

- You keep the database name, username, and password in one place; if you change the password, you only need to change one file.

- You can keep the connection parameters outside the Web tree where your main scripts reside, making it more difficult for them to be revealed should a server misconfiguration ever arise.

- You keep your main scripts simpler and can have a standardized routine in the included file for handling connection errors.

11

You might want to have an include called `mysqlsubs.inc`, which is placed in a non-Web directory (in other words, it can never be viewed via a Web browser) and contains all database connection and selection routines (and possibly other shared database routines). It might look like Listing 11.3.

LISTING 11.3   mysqlsubs.inc

```
 1: <?
 2: function connect_to_cms () {
 3:     $link_id = @mysql_pconnect ("localhost", "cms_user", "mypass");
 4:     if (!$link_id) {
 5:         echo "Failed to connect to MySQL!<BR>\n";
 6:         exit;
 7:     }
 8:     if (!mysql_select_db ("cms")) {
 9:         echo "Failed to select database cms!<BR>\n";
10:         exit;
11:     }
12: }
13: ?>
```

In your main script, you then have the following lines:

```
include ("/nonweb/mysqlsubs.inc");
connect_to_cms ();
```

As you can see, by using the `include` statement and a user-defined function, you can improve the security of your site and keep the code tidier in your main PHP pages.

Tip

mysqlsubs.inc could be improved by passing a link identifier back to the calling program, using `return` in a line like this, inserted just before the end of the function definition:

`return $link_id;`

It could also do error handling in more elegant ways. For example, instead of simply printing an error message onscreen and exiting rather abruptly, it might perform a browser redirect to take the user to a completely different Web page. You could do this using the `header()` function, like this:

`header ("Location: http://www.mysite.com/errorpage.php");`

`exit;`

Running Database Queries

The most commonly used function for running queries is `mysql_query()`, which runs a query on the current database (the one already selected with `mysql_select_db()`). The basic syntax is as follows:

```
mysql_query (querystring)
```

where `querystring` is the SQL query to be run. Alternatively, if you want to specify the name of the database within the statement, you can use `mysql_db_query()`:

```
mysql_db_query (database_name, querystring)
```

The first form, `mysql_query()`, is probably the most convenient unless your script jumps between several different databases.

If your query is a `SELECT` statement, the function returns a resource identifier if the query is processed successfully, or `FALSE` if it fails. In a moment, you'll learn how to use this resource identifier to access the resultset of data.

For other kinds of queries, the result is either `TRUE` for success or `FALSE` for failure.

11

> **Note**
>
> By "success" we mean that the query was successfully executed. It does not mean that any data was affected (for example, in an UPDATE statement). Equally, you could run a SELECT statement that returns no data, but it would still be successful. A query can succeed without it necessarily having the effect the programmer intended!
>
> There may be a number of reasons leading to the failure of a query:
>
> - The SQL may contain syntax errors.
> - The query may be meaningless, such as trying to select from a table that does not exist.
> - The database user may not have sufficient privileges to perform the query (although that user may have successfully connected, other actions may be prohibited).
>
> In a moment, you'll learn how to determine the effects of a query that modifies data and how to determine the nature of any errors that occur.

Running Queries That Return a Resultset

When you run a `SELECT` query, a resultset is created, provided that the query is run successfully. Table 11.3 lists the most useful functions for handling a resultset.

TABLE 11.3 Functions for Handling Results from Queries

Function	Action
`mysql_fetch_row()`	Fetches one row of data from a resultset as a numerical array
`mysql_fetch_array()`	Fetches one row of data from a result row as an associative or numeric array (or both)
`mysql_fetch_object()`	Fetches one row of data from a resultset as an object
`mysql_num_rows()`	Returns the number of rows in the resultset

Consider a simple example of querying articles for display from the content management system. First we'll use `mysql_query()` to run the query and `mysql_fetch_row()` within a `while` loop to fetch the resulting rows one at a time, as shown in Listing 11.4.

LISTING 11.4 Displaying the Resultset from a SELECT Query

```
 1: <?
 2: include ("/nonweb/mysqlsubs.inc");
 3: connect_to_cms ();

 4: $sql = "select date_post, headline
 5:         from articles";
 6: $result = mysql_query ($sql);
 7:
 8: while ($row = mysql_fetch_row ($result)) {
 9:     echo "Date $row[0]: $row[1]<BR>\n";
10: }
11: ?>
```

This code executes the query using `mysql_query()` and puts the resource identifier into `$result`. (The code should really do some error checking at this point, but for now just assume that the query executes successfully.)

Then we used a `while` loop with `mysql_fetch_row()` in its expression (line 5). This fetches one row of the resultset each time it is called and places the result into the array `$row`. The elements in the row are numerically referenced, so we can access the two fields using $row[0] and $row[1].

After iterating through the resultset, when we try to go beyond the last row, `mysql_fetch_row()` returns FALSE, and the `while` loop terminates.

You could use the following `while` loop in place of the one in Listing 11.4. It does the same thing, but this time using `mysql_fetch_array()` to fetch each row of the resultset into an associative array:

```
while ($row = mysql_fetch_array ($result)) {
    echo "Date ".$row["date_post"].": ".$row["headline"]."<BR>\n";
}
```

Using `mysql_fetch_array()` is more convenient and is really an extension of `mysql_fetch_row()`. It fetches the data into an array that you can access either associatively, using the field names as keys (for example, `$row["headline"]`) or numerically (for example, `$row[1]`).

If your SELECT query references column names that are preceded by the table name and a period (for example, SELECT `articles.headline...`), such as may occur when performing a join across tables with columns with identical names, you will have to use either an alias in your SQL (such as SELECT `articles.headline AS arthead...`) or use a numerical reference to that element in the array (for example, `$row[0]`).

A third way of fetching the resultset is by using `mysql_fetch_object()` to fetch each row as an object. To use the preceding example again, the code for the fetch looks like this:

```
while ($row = mysql_fetch_object ($result)) {
    echo "Date $row->date_post: $row->headline<BR>\n";
}
```

Here you can access the data by the field names (such as `$row->headline`), but you can no longer access them by their numeric indexes. You will therefore find that `mysql_fetch_array()` is the most versatile of these functions because it gives both ways of accessing the resultset.

The final function considered here is `mysql_num_rows()`. Rather than return an array of data, this returns just the number of rows retrieved as a result of the query.

You can use it like this:

```
$num = mysql_num_rows ($result);
echo "Rows in result set = $num<BR>\n";
```

Running Queries That Return No Resultset

If you run a query that returns no resultset, such as one that performs an UPDATE, INSERT, or DELETE, you may want to check what effect the query had on your data.

Although `mysql_query()` returns a TRUE for success, this only indicates whether the query succeeded, not whether it made any change. To see what effect the query had, you need to use the function `mysql_affected_rows()`.

You can use `mysql_affected_rows()` like this:

```
$sql = "DELETE FROM articles
        WHERE article_id=2";
$result = mysql_query ($sql);
if ($aff = mysql_affected_rows ()) echo "$aff row(s) deleted<BR>\n";
else echo "Nothing deleted<BR>\n";
```

In the preceding code (assuming that `mysql_query()` is successful), the scalar variable `$aff` will be populated with the number of rows deleted as a result. You can do the same with any kind of query that performs some kind of modification to a database.

If you run a query that performs an `INSERT` on a table with an auto-increment primary key, you may want to determine which key value was generated as a result of the `INSERT`.

PHP has a function that tells you exactly this: `mysql_insert_id()`. You can use it like this:

```
$sql = "INSERT INTO articles
        SET headline='Some headline'";
$result = mysql_query ($sql);
if ($id = mysql_insert_id ()) echo "Insert ID = $id<BR>\n";
```

The preceding examples left out one vital aspect: how to know whether an error occurred when running the query and how to handle it. Let's look at this now.

Handling Query Errors

Correct handling of errors is imperative when writing almost any database query. You cannot assume that your query will execute successfully, and your code must handle the error condition in a suitable way.

In the preceding examples, we wrote something like this:

```
$result = mysql_query ($sql);  # no error handling!
```

whereas we should have written something like this:

```
if ($result = mysql_query ($sql)) {
    # query worked okay, keep going
} else {
    # handle error
}
```

Because `mysql_query()` returns `FALSE` when a query fails, you can place it within an `if` condition as shown here and handle the error in a predictable way.

If an error occurs, you may want to know what went wrong. This is useful for debugging, and you may even build in functions for sending the user to a different Web page or even sending an alert to a system administrator.

Table 11.4 shows the functions available for reporting on an error that occurred.

TABLE 11.4   Functions for Handling Errors from Queries

Function	Action
mysql_error()	Returns the error message text from the previous MySQL operation
mysql_errno()	Returns the error message number from the previous MySQL operation

Thus, you might have an error routine like this:

```
if ($result = mysql_query ($sql)) {
    # query worked okay, keep going
} else {
    echo "A database error occurred!<BR>\n";
    echo mysql_error() ." (error no. ". mysql_errno() .")<BR>\n";
    exit;
}
```

The preceding code produces an error report like this:

```
A database error occurred!
Table 'cms.notable' doesn't exist (error no. 1146)
```

Tip

> It's good practice to always store your SQL in a variable (say $sql, as in the preceding example) rather than to pass it directly to mysql_query(). You can then display your SQL in your error report just by printing $sql along with mysql_error().

11

Remember, always put error handling into your code, and you will benefit from easier debugging and safer, more resilient scripts.

Summary

Today you had a crash course in PHP, learning the basics of the language, how to incorporate PHP scripting into your Web pages, and how to use it to communicate with a MySQL database.

You should now be able to write PHP scripts that use the `include` statement for incorporating one file into another. You saw how to create user-defined functions and how to use the control structures `if`, `for`, and `while`. You learned how to handle arrays, both in general use and when created as a result of a `SELECT` query from a database.

You saw how to connect to a MySQL database and how to run queries, iterating through a resultset of data and processing it row by row. You also learned how to run database queries that return no resultset while determining what effect they had on the data.

Finally, you learned how to handle errors that result from database queries so that you are now able to write resilient database access scripts.

Q&A

Q Where can I learn more about PHP?

A Visit `http://www.php.net/`, the official PHP Web site, and `http://www.phpbuilder.com/`, which contains some excellent resources. There are also other Sams titles on the subject that are worth studying if you want to put PHP to serious use.

For more hands-on experience with PHP, you will need a Web server that runs Apache onto which you can install PHP. Visit `http://httpd.apache.org/` and search for "LAMP" resources, this being an acronym for the Linux, Apache, MySQL, and PHP combination of software.

Q Why should I use PHP rather than another language?

A A wide range of server-side languages currently are on the market. PHP has the advantage that it's free, easy to learn, and fast to develop in, and can be installed onto the most popular platforms, including Linux, Unix, and Windows. It can be used in almost any Web-based application and is ideally suited to database-access applications.

Q Are there times when I should not use PHP?

A Remember that PHP is designed to run Web applications. It is possible to write standalone scripts in PHP, but it's seldom used this way. If a standalone program is your main objective, consider a different language such as Perl or C.

Because PHP is an interpreted language, it may not be as fast as a compiled language such as C. If you are writing a program that will be used intensively, and speed is important, a compiled language may be a better option.

Workshop

The quiz and exercises are provided to help you solidify your understanding of the material covered today. Try to understand the quiz and exercise answers before continuing to tomorrow's lesson.

Quiz

1. Which of the following are correct tags for marking the beginning of a section of PHP in an HTML page:

   - <<
   - <php
   - <?
   - <!

2. If you have an associative array called $arr with elements defined by

   ```
   $arr = array ("J"=>"John", "S"=>"Susan", "T"=>"Thomas");
   ```

   which of the following is correct syntax for referencing the first element?

   - $arr["John"]
   - $arr["J"]

3. True or False: If you run a DELETE query like this:

   ```
   $x = mysql_query ("DELETE FROM mytable");
   ```

   the result in $x will be the number of rows deleted.

4. What statement could you use within a while loop if you want to terminate it prematurely?

Quiz Answers

1. <php and <? are correct.
2. $arr["J"] is correct.
3. False. $x would be TRUE if the SQL statement was executed successfully or FALSE if it failed. You would need to call mysql_affected_rows() to determine the number of rows deleted.
4. You could use break or continue. exit terminates the entire script.

Exercises

1. Write a PHP function for connecting to a MySQL database on localhost and returning the link identifier to the calling program. It should connect to MySQL and should make a persistent connection. Assume that the database user is called myuser and the password is mypass. Your script should print an appropriate error message (but suppress any server error messages) if the connection fails.

2. Write a section of PHP script that performs an UPDATE on a table articles, tests for the query being run successfully, and prints the number of rows that were affected.

11

3. Write a section of PHP script that performs a SELECT on a table called products. The table includes the columns name and price. Your query should retrieve all products whose price is less than 50. You should allow for an error condition and display the MySQL error if one occurs.

Answers to Exercises

1. Your code should look something like this:

```
function connect_to_database () {
    $link_id = @mysql_pconnect ("localhost", "myuser", "mypass");
    if (!$link_id) echo "Failed to connect to MySQL!<BR>\n";
    return $link_id;
}
```

2. Your code should look something like this:

```
<?php
$sql = "UPDATE articles
        WHERE some condition
        SET some column=some_value";
if ($result = mysql_query ($sql)) {
    if ($aff = mysql_affected_rows ()) echo "$aff rows updated<BR>\n";
    else echo "Nothing updated<BR>\n";
} else echo "Query failed: ". mysql_error() ."<BR>\n";
?>
```

3. Your code should look something like this:

```
<?php
$sql = "SELECT name, price
        FROM products
        WHERE price < 50";
if ($result = mysql_query ($sql)) {
    while ($row = mysql_fetch_array ($result)) {
        echo "Product: ".$row["name"]." price: $".$row["price"]."<BR>\n";
    }
} else echo mysql_error() ."<BR>\n";
?>
```

DAY 12

Using the Perl DBI

Today's lesson serves different purposes, depending on your existing level of skill with Perl:

- If you already know how to write scripts in Perl, even if only at a rudimentary level, you will learn how to use the Perl DBI interface to MySQL.
- If you don't, and you're considering what language to write your applications in, today's lesson introduces Perl and explains the benefits of using it.

Today's lesson contains simple Perl scripts that will run in their own right and communicate with a MySQL database. It is not meant as a tutorial on Perl itself. However, whatever your previous knowledge of Perl, today you will learn

- How and when to use the Perl DBI interface to MySQL
- How to build queries and how to work on the results

At the end of today, you should be able to fully integrate a MySQL database into your scripts.

Even if you don't know Perl already, you will understand its benefits and limitations when used in building a MySQL application. If Perl is for you, it is recommended that you consult a more detailed tutorial to further develop your skills in Perl.

What Is Perl?

Perl is a programming language. It was originally designed to make it easier to extract data and generate reports. Over the years, Perl has been considerably developed and enlarged, but it retains its powerful text manipulation capabilities. Perl has come to be widely used in an Internet environment for the simple reason that many Internet tasks require the processing of text: verifying and analyzing input, communicating with other systems, and generating textual output.

Well suited to use in an Internet environment, Perl is most often used to write CGI (Common Gateway Interface) scripts for Web servers. Nevertheless, you can use Perl to write standalone programs for a wide range of applications.

CGI is a protocol that, combined with a scripting language, can be used to make Web sites dynamic. Such scripts can query a database, perform file operations, and generate Web pages on-the-fly, thus allowing you to build a Web site that interacts with the user. CGI scripts do not have to be written in Perl, and indeed C, Visual Basic, Java, and other languages can be used. But because of Perl's qualities, it is highly suited to most CGI tasks.

 Note

Perl is an acronym for Practical Extraction and Report Language.

Things written in Perl are usually called *Perl scripts* or *CGI scripts*, although the term *Perl program* is also correct. The main reason that the word "script" is more commonly used than "program" is simply because the Perl language is usually interpreted rather than compiled.

The Perl Interface to MySQL

Applications written in Perl use a two-level interface to communicate with MySQL and other databases.

The DBI (database interface) is a generic programming interface. It is not MySQL-specific, and Perl and DBI can be used to interface with a wide range of databases.

There is a second database-specific level called DBD (database driver). For MySQL and mSQL, support is provided by a software package called `Msql-MySQL-modules`.

A simple example illustrates how DBI and DBD work. Suppose that a user is browsing a Web site, perhaps an online store that uses a database to hold its catalog. He clicks on a link to view a page of items in the catalog for which the Web server must go to the database, find out what's there, and present the information to the user.

The user initiates the request, which goes over the Internet to the Web server. The particular page he asked for is a CGI written in Perl, and his request causes the Web server to invoke the Perl interpreter and run the Perl program.

The Perl interpreter reads the program and begins executing its instructions. In the program, there is some SQL for querying a database. The SQL is passed down through the DBI and DBD levels to MySQL. MySQL performs the query on its database, forms the response, and passes it back up the chain via DBD and DBI to the Perl application. The Perl program forms its response by packaging MySQL's response into a Web page that can be sent to the user.

When the program finishes, control passes back to the Web server that invoked it, and it sends the result back to the user. The result is a dynamically created Web page, which can allow a user to interact with a remote database in all sorts of ways.

The program doesn't have to be run via a Web server, and some programs may be run standalone, such as from the command line. However, the principle is the same, just without the involvement of the Web server in the preceding process. Figure 12.1 illustrates the process.

FIGURE 12.1

Querying a database.

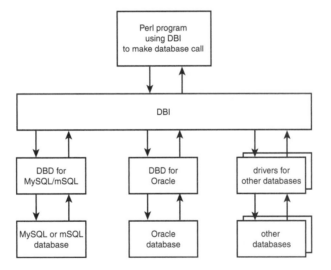

12

Installing DBI and DBD on Linux

To try out the Perl DBI, you need to install it. Although Perl is usually preinstalled on a Unix or Linux system, DBI and DBD usually are not. We'll go through the procedure for installing from source on a Unix or Linux system.

The following software components are essential for interfacing between Perl and MySQL:

- `DBI-version`, the compressed download called something like `DBI-1.18.tar.gz`
- `Msql-Mysql-modules-version`, the compressed download called something like `Msql-Mysql-modules-1.2216.tar.gz`

Also recomm]ended is

- Data-ShowTable-*version*, the compressed download called something like Data-ShowTable-3.3.tar.gz

First get the tar.gz files by downloading them from the Internet (for example, the API section of http://www.mysql.com/downloads/contrib.html). It doesn't matter where you save them in your directory structure because they will be installed into the Perl directory anyway. Unzip and untar, as in the following:

```
# gunzip DBI-1.18.tar.gz
# gunzip Data-ShowTable-3.3.tar.gz
# gunzip Msql-Mysql-modules-1.2216.tar.gz
# tar -xvf DBI-1.18.tar
# tar -xvf Data-ShowTable-3.3.tar
# tar -xvf Msql-Mysql-modules-1.2216.tar
```

Compile and install DBI:

```
# cd DBI-1.18
# perl Makefile.PL
# make
# make test
# make install
```

Now compile and install Data-ShowTable:

```
# cd ../Data-ShowTable-3.3
# perl Makefile.PL
# make
# make install
```

Then compile and install the DBD module, which is named Msql-Mysql-modules-*version*. You will have the option of installing support for MySQL, mSQL, or both. In the example, we'll choose just MySQL. Here's a sample:

```
# cd ../Msql-Mysql-modules-1.2216
# perl Makefile.PL
Which drivers do you want to install?
    1)  MySQL only
    2)  mSQL only (either of mSQL 1 or mSQL 2)
    3)  MySQL and mSQL (either of mSQL 1 or mSQL 2)
    4)  mSQL 1 and mSQL 2
    5)  MySQL, mSQL 1 and mSQL 2
Enter the appropriate number:  [3] 1
Do you want to install the MysqlPerl emulation? You might keep your old
Mysql module (to be distinguished from DBD::mysql!) if you are concerned
about compatibility to existing applications! [n] N
Where is your MySQL installed? Please tell me the directory that
contains the subdir 'include'. [/usr/local/mysql]
Which database should I use for testing the MySQL drivers? [test]
On which host is database test running (hostname, ip address
or host:port) [localhost]
User name for connecting to database test? [undef] tonyb
Password for connecting to database test? [undef]
```

After this, you should see several messages that refer to writing a `Makefile`. At this point, you can compile, test, and install:

```
# make
# make test
# make install
```

You have installed the Perl DBI for MySQL.

DBI Methods

With DBI installed, a number of methods are now available through Perl. Every Perl script that uses DBI must include the following line before it tries to use any DBI methods:

```
use DBI;
```

You can then invoke a DBI method using the general format:

```
$var = DBI->method ($parameters, ...)
```

or with reference to a handle as well as a method:

```
$var = handle->method ($parameters, ...)
```

> **Note**
>
> It's important that you understand what is meant by the terms *handle*, *object*, and *method*.
>
> A *handle* is a pointer variable that points to a data structure (or *object*). The object will typically be a database or a statement object (say a resultset from a query), and you can think of the handle as a convenient way of getting hold of that object when you want to do something with it.
>
> You'll normally only use a handle together with a *method* (the action that you're performing on the object). For example, later today you'll see how to perform a SQL query given by *$statement* like this:
>
> `$dbh->do ($statement);`
>
> This shows the do() method being performed on a database object referred to by the handle $dbh.
>
> A *method* is the object-oriented word for what you might otherwise know as a function.

12

We will go through the various DBI methods, examining them in logical groups so that you learn how to use them a few at a time. We'll start with the method for connecting to a database.

Note You can get help on DBI and the MySQL DBD from the Linux or Unix command line, using

```
$ perldoc DBI
$ perldoc DBI::FAQ
$ perldoc DBD::mysql
```

Connecting to MySQL with the DBI

With the architecture installed, we will start by writing a Perl program that uses DBI to connect to the MySQL database.

Perl communicates with MySQL using a database handle. The connect() method uses a general format:

```
$dbh = DBI->connect($data_source, $username, $auth [, %attr]);
```

So we may use this format:

```
$dbh = DBI->connect("DBI:mysql:$db_name:hostname:port", $db_user, $db_pass);
```

or with additional parameters:

```
$dbh = DBI->connect("DBI:mysql:$db_name:hostname:port", $db_user, $db_pass,
  { RaiseError => 1, PrintError => 0 } );
```

where $dbh is the database handle returned (if connection is successful), and the parameters are used like this:

- $db_name holds the name of the database to connect to.
- *hostname* is the name of the host machine (can be omitted to default to localhost), and *port* is the port number to connect to (can be omitted to default to MySQL's default port).
- $db_user, the database user, and $db_pass, the user's password, would normally be included but can be left undefined, defaulting to the user executing the program.
- RaiseError and PrintError can optionally be added to modify the way DBI handles error conditions. We'll examine these later today in the section "Handling Query Errors."

Let's create a simple Perl program called test_connect.pl, which queries the database in a content management system (CMS).

Later in this lesson, after connecting, we will run some example queries. The SQL that will be performed will include queries to find out which articles in the CMS should be emailed to subscribers and queries that return and update data about subscribers.

The first few lines of the connection script, which connects to a database called cms, are
shown in Listing 12.1.

LISTING 12.1 test_connect.pl, First Part of Script

```
 1: #!/usr/bin/perl -w
 2:
 3: use DBI;
 4:
 5: print "Content/type: text/plain\n\n";
 6:
 7: my $dsn = "DBI:mysql:cms";
 8: my $db_user = "cms";
 9: my $db_pass = "mypass";
10:
11: # Connect to the database
12: my $dbh = DBI->connect ($dsn, $db_user, $db_pass)
13:    or die "Couldn't connect to MySQL.\n";
```

Line 1 of the script tells us it's a Perl script and contains the path to Perl on your system—
in this case, /usr/bin, which is usual on a Linux system (but can be /usr/local/bin).

Line 5 is necessary if you want to call the script via Apache, so as to view the output in
your browser. (You don't need it if you invoke the script standalone.) It specifies the
header and the type of document that Apache is about to handle.

Line 3 tells Perl to use DBI, and lines 7–9 declare the database name, the database user,
and its password. This must be a valid database user already set up. (Valid users will
appear in the User grant table of the database called mysql. See Day 4, "Getting Hands-
On with MySQL," and Day 14, "Security," for more about user privileges). The user
specified here typically would not be the root user for security reasons.

Lines 12–13 execute the database connection: They call DBI's connect method with the
parameters we just set up. Within the $dsn parameter, the first part, DBI:mysql:..., tells
the DBI to use the MySQL driver rather than any other DBDs it may have available.

12

Tip

If you run the script from the command line using

$ ./test_connect.pl

(which requires execute permission to be set on the script), or

$ perl test_connect.pl

all errors and output will be printed on the screen. Alternatively, you can
put the script in your Web server's cgi-bin directory and invoke the script
through your Web browser. You will then see normal response through your

browser, but errors will be written to the Web server's error log. You can view the last few lines of the Apache error log like this (adjust to suit the directory where your error log is located):

```
$ tail /usr/local/apache/logs/error_log
```

If you get an error like this when you run this script:

```
install_driver(mysql) failed: Can't locate DBD/mysql.pm
 in @INC (@INC contains:
/usr/lib/perl5/5.6.0/i586-linux
/usr/lib/perl5/5.6.0
/usr/lib/perl5/site_perl/5.6.0/i586-linux
/usr/lib/perl5/site_perl/5.6.0
/usr/lib/perl5/site_perl .) at (eval 1) line 3.
Perhaps the DBD::mysql perl module hasn't been fully installed, or
perhaps the capitalisation of 'mysql' isn't right.
Available drivers: ADO, ExampleP, Multiplex, Proxy.
 at /home/sites/cms/web/cgi-bin/test_connect.pl line 25
```

you have not correctly installed DBD/DBI. You will need to complete the installation before proceeding.

The result of trying to connect, if successful, is the database handle $dbh. This is represented as a scalar variable in Perl. Several database methods are associated with it, which we will look into in a moment.

You must always handle the failure condition, in which Perl might be unable to connect to MySQL. If this failure occurs, the Couldn't connect error text will be appended to the server's error log, and the script will terminate (die).

If connection fails, you'll want to debug the code. It's a good idea to insert the following line just before line 12 (the connect line):

```
print "Variables: $dsn, $db_user, $db_pass\n";
```

When you run the script again, you should get a dump of the variables on the screen. If they appear correctly, go to your MySQL monitor and try logging in with these values manually. Remember, they must represent a valid MySQL user in the User table.

Finally, our simple script will disconnect. Here are the last few lines we'll need in the script:

```
# Disconnect from database
$dbh->disconnect;
exit;
```

This disconnects from the database and destroys the $dbh handle. The exit statement tells the Perl interpreter to terminate.

Note

> This simple program is nonmodular! In a typical installation, you might have several programs all talking to the same database; therefore, these lines should be placed in a central "environment" file. Such a file would contain details that are specific to a particular server, leaving other scripts generic.
>
> This makes maintenance easier should you want to change the database password, for example, and makes it easier for you to port the program to another system.

Assuming that the script is functioning correctly and connecting to the database, you should get an output like this:

```
Variables: DBI:mysql:cms, cms, mypass
Connection successful: $dbh=DBI::db=HASH(0x81b877c)
```

500 Internal Server Errors

If you invoke your script through Apache and your Web browser, and it generates an Internal Server Error, don't panic!

These errors are generated by Apache when it tries to run a Perl script and fails. Taken at face value, they appear unhelpful because they do not report specifically what the error is. But help is at hand:

- There will usually be some report of the error in your server error log. On Linux, type **tail /usr/local/apache/logs/error_log** (or adjust the path or filename to suit your system). This shows you the last few lines and should contain a more helpful report on the error.

- Check the permissions on your Perl script. On a typical Linux installation, you will need to do a chmod to change the file permissions and have the script executable by anyone (for example, chmod +x test_connect.pl sets permissions to -rwxr-xr-x).

- Remember to include the line print "Content/type: text/html\n\n"; (note the two new lines) before any other output. Any other output before this line will count as a bad header as far as Apache is concerned.

12

Basics of Database Queries

Now that you've mastered creating a Perl script and connecting to and disconnecting from your database, you're ready to do some simple database queries.

Running Queries That Return a Resultset

DBI has a number of methods (shown in Table 12.1) that help you handle a query that returns a resultset.

Table 12.1 shows the methods for running queries, which you will learn how to use.

TABLE 12.1   DBI Methods for Running Queries

DBI Method	Meaning
`$sth = $dbh->prepare ($statement);`	Prepare query
`$rv = $sth->execute ();`	Execute query
`$rv = $dbh->do ($statement);`	Prepare and execute query, and finish
`$rv = $dbh->do ($statement, %attr);`	Prepare and execute query, and finish (with extra attributes)

Running Queries with `prepare()` and `execute()`

We'll start with a simple SELECT query that we might use. Assume that we want a query to find article summaries that have not been emailed from the CMS:

```
my $sql = "select headline, text_summary, date_post
           from articles
           where sent_flag != 1";
```

We'll use DBI's prepare() and execute() methods to handle the query:

```
my $sth = $dbh->prepare ($sql)
  or die "Couldn't prepare statement $sql.\n";
$sth->execute ()
  or die "Couldn't execute statement $sql.\n";
```

This code calls the prepare() method on the database object referenced by $dbh, which passes the SQL to the DBD for preprocessing. If there's an error in the query, prepare() returns undef (meaning undefined), and the script dies, leaving a message in the error log.

Tip

If prepare() fails, try running your SQL directly through the mysql console to check it; it may give some more helpful explanation of what's wrong.

It's also worth remembering that the error report from the script should contain the actual SQL that was passed, with any Perl variables converted to their values at the time.

Errors can also emerge from the incorrect handling of single and double quotes, ' and ". If your SQL contains quotes, consider using the DBI quote() method or Perl's qq{} method. See your system documentation for more on these (perldoc DBI and man perlop, respectively).

Provided that the SQL is prepared successfully, it returns the statement handle $sth, and our script calls the execute() method, which sends the query to be executed. If it executes correctly (irrespective of whether any rows were returned), the resultset becomes available through the $sth statement handle. If execute() fails, it returns undef, and the or die condition tells the script to exit.

After running execute() on our statement handle, we'll tidy up using the method finish(). This frees up system resources and prevents a warning from appearing:

```
$sth->finish;
```

The whole script should now look like Listing 12.2.

LISTING 12.2   test_connect.pl, Entire Script

```
 1: #!/usr/bin/perl -w
 2:
 3: use DBI;
 4:
 5: my $dsn = "DBI:mysql:cms";
 6: my $db_user = "cms";
 7: my $db_pass = "mypass";
 8:
 9: print "Content/type: text/html\n\n";
10:
11: # Connect to the database
12: my $dbh = DBI->connect ($dsn, $db_user, $db_pass)
13:    or die "Couldn't connect to MySQL.\n";
14:
15: print "Connection successful: \$dbh=$dbh\n";
16:
17: my $sql = "select headline, text_summary, date_post
18:             from articles
19:             where email_sent != 1";
20: my $sth = $dbh->prepare ($sql)
21:    or die "Couldn't prepare statement $sql.\n";
22: $sth->execute ()
23:    or die "Couldn't execute statement $sql.\n";
24: $sth->finish;
25:
26: # Disconnect from database
27: $dbh->disconnect;
28:
29: exit;
```

12

You've not yet learned how to handle the result of the query. Before going into this, let's look at an alternative and shorter method of query handling.

Running Queries with do()

The do() method is just a shorter way to run prepare(), execute(), and finish() in a single statement. Here's how we might remove prepare(), execute(), and finish() and replace them with a single line:

```
my $sth = $dbh->do ($sql)
    or die "Couldn't do statement $sql.\n";
```

Simple, isn't it? At least the code looks simpler. But why not use it every time and forget about prepare() and execute()?

The do() method is not useful for queries that return a resultset, because by implicitly calling the finish() method, our statement handle is lost. When we handle the resultset, as you'll see in a moment, it's essential that this statement handle is preserved until we've finished fetching the resulting data. do() is therefore most useful when running queries that don't produce a resultset, such as INSERT, DELETE, and UPDATE.

Another reason we don't always use do() is because DBI gives you a technique for running similar queries multiple times without having the overhead of doing a prepare() each time (and remember that prepare() is implicit within do()), which would be highly inefficient. This technique is called *parameter binding*, and you will learn how to use it later today.

In summary, do() is efficient to use when you're dealing with a single query that doesn't return a resultset. Where there is a resultset or you need to run multiple similar queries, other DBI methods are better.

For now, you're probably eager to see how to get at the result of our query, so let's see how to handle the resultset.

Handling the Resultset

After we have run a query and created a resultset, we need to process it. Table 12.2 shows an overview of the DBI methods that we can use to handle the resultset of the query.

TABLE 12.2 DBI Methods for Handling Resultsets

DBI Method	Meaning
$hash_ref = $sth->fetchrow_hashref;	Reference to hashed array containing one row of resultset keyed by column name
@row_ary = $sth->fetchrow_array;	Array containing one row of resultset
$ary_ref = $sth->fetchrow_arrayref;	Reference to object containing one row of resultset
$ary_ref = $sth->fetchall_arrayref;	Reference to object containing all rows of resultset
$ary_ref = $dbh->selectall_arrayref();	Prepare and execute query, return reference to object containing all rows of resultset, and finish

Handling the Resultset Row-by-Row

In many applications, you'll probably find that it's convenient to write code that deals with one row of the resultset at a time.

Look at how to process the resultset using the convenient `fetchrow_hashref` method, which creates an array hashed by the names of the columns in the query:

```
my $hash_ref;
while ($hash_ref = $sth->fetchrow_hashref ()) {
  print "$hash_ref->{'date_post'}: ";
  print "$hash_ref->{'headline'}\n";
  print "$hash_ref->{'text_summary'}\n\n";
}
```

The `fetchrow_hashref()` method returns a hashed (otherwise known as *associative*) array, referenced by `$hash_ref`. Each time we call the method, it returns one row of the data retrieved. We can easily reference the values in this array by using their column names in the database because they are held in a `name=value` relationship. Thus in general we can use

```
$hash_ref->{'column_name'}
```

The lines within the `while` loop in the previous example print out the values retrieved in each row of the resultset. It loops through the resultset, printing each row, until it has done them all.

A `while` loop is a convenient way of going row-by-row through the resultset. When it reaches the last line, the statement handle `$sth` equates to a boolean `false`, and the loop terminates.

Don't try to access the resultset `$hash_ref` after the loop has terminated; it will be empty, because of being set to null on the last iteration. If you have to use a `while` loop and want to save the last set of data, you will need to save the resultset while still inside the loop. However, note that if you are retrieving a single row (that is, you're sure that you want only one row returned), you don't need the `while` loop at all.

The `fetchrow_hashref()` method is useful because you can call each column by name: You don't need to keep count of how many columns are returned in your query or in what order. But it can get tricky to use if your SELECT query is a join, and fields from different tables have the same names, requiring the `tablename.fieldname` construct. However, you can use aliases to get around this—for example, SELECT a.name AS a....

On the downside, `fetchrow_hashref()` is also not the most processor efficient. A more efficient way to retrieve the resultset would be using `fetchrow_array()` and reference array elements like this:

```
$row_ary[num]
```

12

where *num* is the column number. For example, we could do as follows:

```
while (@row_ary = $sth->fetchrow_array ()) {
    print "$row_ary[2]: $row_ary[0]\n";
    print "$row_ary[1]\n\n";
}
```

This achieves the same thing in terms of program output, but this time we used the index of the array (for example, `$row[0]`) to access each field in the resultset, with the index number corresponding to the order of fields in our SELECT statement, starting at 0. This method is arguably less friendly, but it may make your code a little more compact and has the benefit that the code should still work if you change the name of a column in the database. It also enables you to loop through the columns using a numeric variable.

There's a third method, `fetchrow_arrayref()`. In this method, you get a reference to the resultset array. You can use `fetchrow_arrayref()` and reference the returned elements as follows:

```
$ary_ref->[num]
```

For example:

```
my $ary_ref;
while ($ary_ref = $sth->fetchrow_arrayref ()) {
    print "$ary_ref->[2]: $ary_ref->[0]\n";
    print "$ary_ref->[1]\n\n";
}
```

Running Queries with Parameter Binding

Parameter binding may sound like a mouthful, but don't be put off. It's just an easy way of executing the same query repeatedly, without having to reprepare the statement each time. Think of it as preparing a template and then running it multiple times with the data filled in at the last minute.

Table 12.3 shows the DBI methods for parameter binding that we'll look at.

TABLE 12.3 DBI Methods for Parameter Binding

DBI Method	Meaning
`$rc = $sth->bind_columns` `(@list_of_refs_to_vars_to_bind);`	Bind the list of named variables to the columns of the resultset
`$rc = $sth->bind_col` `($col_num, $col_variable);`	Bind the named variable `$col_variable` to resultset column number `$col_num`

Why would we use parameter binding? Suppose that we want to write a routine that finds and prints out the dates, titles, and summaries of all the articles written by a particular writer in the CMS. Listing 12.3 shows the complete script, now with parameter binding.

LISTING 12.3   Program for Running a Query with Parameter Binding

```
 1: #!/usr/bin/perl -w
 2:
 3: # Simple program to run a query using parameter binding
 4:
 5: use DBI;
 6:
 7: my $dsn = "DBI:mysql:cms";
 8: my $db_user = "cms";
 9: my $db_pass = "mypass";
10:
11: print "Content/type: text/plain\n\n";
12:
13: # Connect to the database
14: my $dbh = DBI->connect ($dsn, $db_user, $db_pass)
15:     or die "Couldn't connect to MySQL.\n";
16:
17: print "Connection successful: \$dbh=$dbh\n";
18:
19: my $sql = "select headline, text_summary, date_post
20:             from articles
21:             where email_sent != 1";
22: my $sth = $dbh->prepare ($sql)
23:     or die "Couldn't prepare statement $sql.\n";
24: $sth->execute ()
25:     or die "Couldn't execute statement $sql.\n";
26:
27: my ($headline, $text_summary, $date_post);
28: $sth->bind_columns (\$headline, \$text_summary, \$date_post);
29: print "$date_post: $headline\n$text_summary\n"
30:    while $sth->fetchrow_array ();
31:
32: $sth->finish;
33:
34: # Disconnect from database
35: $dbh->disconnect;
36:
37: exit;
```

This routine prepares and executes the query (lines 19–25). It then calls the bind_columns() method (line 28) and binds the elements of the resultset from the SELECT statement to the variables in bind_columns(), $headline, $text_summary, and $date_post, respectively. Each time we call fetchrow_array() (line 30), those variables get repopulated.

With `bind_columns()`, the order of the variables in the list defines which variable gets populated with which column from the resultset. Make sure that you have the same number of variables as columns, or an error will result.

There's a similar method for binding selected column variables, `bind_col()`. The difference is subtle, and with this method you use a number specifying which column relates to which variable (starting at 1), as follows:

```
my $sth = $dbh->prepare ($sql)
    or die "Couldn't prepare statement $sql.\n";
$sth->execute ()
    or die "Couldn't execute statement $sql.\n";
my ($headline, $text_summary, $date_post);
$sth->bind_col (1, \$headline);
$sth->bind_col (2, \$text_summary);
$sth->bind_col (3, \$date_post);
print "$date_post: $headline\n$text_summary\n"
  while $sth->fetchrow_array ();
```

This method allows you to pick out columns one at a time for binding, using a numeric value.

Handling a Resultset as a Complete Set of Data

Processing the resultset a row at a time may not be the most convenient for your application. For example, you may need to process the resultset once in its entirety, or perhaps just find out how many rows have been returned and then go back to a specific row or rows to process them only. A helpful method is available:

```
$ary_ref = $sth->fetchall_arrayref ();
```

With `fetchall_arrayref()`, the reference returned points to a two-dimensional array of the rows and columns of the entire resultset.

To illustrate this by example, assume that we want to extract a list of subscribers to the content management system and assemble them into a single 2D array. Our code might look like Listing 12.4.

LISTING 12.4   Program for Running a Query Using `fetchall_arrayref()`

```
1: #!/usr/bin/perl -w
2:
3: # Simple program to run a query using fetchall_arrayref()
4:
5: use DBI;
6:
7: my $dsn = "DBI:mysql:cms";
8: my $db_user = "cms";
```

LISTING 12.4 continued

```
 9: my $db_pass = "mypass";
10:
11: print "Content/type: text/plain\n\n";
12:
13: # Connect to the database
14: my $dbh = DBI->connect ($dsn, $db_user, $db_pass)
15:    or die "Couldn't connect to MySQL.\n";
16:
17: my $sql = "select *
18:            from subscribers";
19: my $sth = $dbh->prepare ($sql)
20:    or die "Couldn't prepare statement $sql.\n";
21: $sth->execute ()
22:    or die "Couldn't execute statement $sql.\n";
23:
24: my $ary_ref = $sth->fetchall_arrayref ();
25: my ($rows, $cols, $r, $c);
26:
27: # find number of rows
28: if (defined ($ary_ref)) {
29:    $rows = scalar (@{$ary_ref});
30: } else { $rows = 0; }
31:
32: # find number of columns
33: if ($rows != 0) {
34:    $cols = scalar (@{$ary_ref->[0]});
35: } else { $cols = 0; }
36:
37: # print all rows, and all columns within each
38: for ($r = 0; $r < $rows; $r++) {
39:    for ($c = 0; $c < $cols; $c++) {
40:       print $ary_ref->[$r][$c];
41:       print " ";
42:    }
43:    print "\n";
44: }
45:
46: $sth->finish;
47:
48: # Disconnect from database
49: $dbh->disconnect;
50:
51: exit;
```

In Listing 12.4, lines 28–30 find how many rows are in the resultset. If non-zero, lines
33–35 find out how many columns there are. The for loop in lines 38–44 then iterates
through the rows and within that lines 39–42 iterate through the columns, printing them
as rows and columns on the screen.

There is an even more compact method for achieving much of the output, but besides fetching the resultset, this method even does the prepare(), execute(), and finish() for you. The method is called selectall_arrayref().

In our example, lines 17–46 of Listing 12.4 would look like this:

```
my $sql = "select *
           from subscribers";
my $ary_ref = $dbh->selectall_arrayref ($sql)
  or die "Couldn't selectall_arrayref $sql.\n";

# find number of rows
if (defined ($ary_ref)) {
  $rows = scalar (@{$ary_ref});
} else { $rows = 0; }

# find number of columns
if ($rows != 0) {
  $cols = scalar (@{$ary_ref->[0]});
} else { $cols = 0; }

# print all rows, and all columns within each
for ($r = 0; $r < $rows; $r++) {
  for ($c = 0; $c < $cols; $c++) {
    print $ary_ref->[$r][$c];
    print " ";
  }
  print "\n";
}
```

Note that these methods revealed how to find out the number of rows and columns in the resultset. With $ary_ref as our 2D array reference, we can display the number of rows and columns in the resultset like this:

```
print "Rows = ". scalar (@{$ary_ref}) ."\n";
print "Cols = ". scalar (@{$ary_ref->[0]}) ."\n";
```

Queries That Return No Resultset

Now that you've mastered SELECT queries, you should find that queries to update, delete, and insert data and even queries to create tables are straightforward. However, they have the characteristic that they return no resultset. As you'll see, you need to look carefully at the result returned so that you know whether your query failed with an error, or whether it succeeded, and if so what difference it made to the database.

In the next simple example, we'll write a query that creates a temporary table. Let's assume that we may want to do an UPDATE and get some feedback that the query has worked. This feedback comes via the statement handle:

```
my $sql = "UPDATE subscribers
          SET name='New name',
              email='New\@email'
          WHERE subscriber_id=4";  ## id 4 doesn't exist
my $sth = $dbh->prepare ($sql)
  or die "Couldn't prepare statement $sql.\n";
my $aff = $sth->execute ()
  or die "Couldn't execute statement $sql.\n";
print "$aff rows were affected.\n";
```

Look at the subscriber_id we've put in the WHERE clause (4). The query tries to update
a record that (deliberately) doesn't exist, and the result we get from running the script is

```
0E0 rows were affected.
```

0E0 is the equivalent of zero in a numeric context, but otherwise means true in the conditional sense; it means that the query succeeded without error, but no rows were affected.

In contrast, if the query fails, $sth returns undef. Here's an example using do() in
which we try to insert data that would infringe a primary key, thus generating an error:

```
my $sql = "INSERT INTO subscribers
          SET name='New name',
              email='New\@email',
              subscriber_id=3";   ## duplicate primary key
if (my $aff = $dbh->do ($sql)) {
  print "$aff rows were affected.\n";
} else {
  print "The insert failed.\n";
}
```

12

Note

> If you write a query and want to see in a more user-friendly way how many
> rows were affected (avoiding 0E0), the statement
>
> $aff += 0;
>
> would convert this variable to a numeric, thus displaying either a number or
> 0 to the user.

Handling Query Errors

It can be useful to control DBI's error-handling behavior for a particular database connection. The connection method looks like this:

```
$dbh = DBI->connect ($data_source, $username, $auth, %attr);
```

The last attribute, a hash, can be left unspecified (as we've done until now), or can be specified, like this, for example:

```
$dbh = DBI->connect ($data_source, $username, $auth,
  { RaiseError => 0, PrintError => 1} );
```

RaiseError and PrintError are error-handling attributes that determine how DBI should handle errors in queries within that connection:

- RaiseError being set to 1 causes the Perl script to exit with an error message if a DBI error occurs. Default = 0 (off).

- PrintError being set to 1 generates an error message if a DBI error occurs, but the Perl script continues executing. Default = 1 (on).

Thus in the default states (as shown in the connect() line in the preceding example), a Perl script will log an error but continue executing if a DBI error occurs. In our scripts earlier today, you may recall that we added the die statement after every DBI method, something like this:

```
$var = $sth->some_method ()
  or die "Error message";
```

In general it's wise to stop further database processing after an error because if it keeps going, a script could have unpredictable effects on your database or produce spurious output. By using RaiseError and PrintError, you could have connected to the database a little differently, standardized error handling, and saved program lines. Consider Listing 12.5.

LISTING 12.5 testerror1.pl, Program to Demonstrate the Effect of Inserting a Duplicate Primary Key

```
 1: #!/usr/bin/perl -w
 2:
 3: # Simple program to try to insert a duplicate primary key
 4:
 5: use DBI;
 6:
 7: my $dsn = "DBI:mysql:cms";
 8: my $db_user = "cms";
 9: my $db_pass = "mypass";
10:
11: print "Content/type: text/plain\n\n";
12:
13: # Connect to the database
14: my $dbh = DBI->connect ($dsn, $db_user, $db_pass,
15:   { RaiseError => 1, PrintError => 1 });
16:
17: my $sql = "INSERT INTO subscribers
```

LISTING 12.5   continued

```
18:              SET name='New name',
19:                  email='New\@email',
20:                  subscriber_id=3";   ## duplicate primary key
21: $aff = $dbh->do ($sql);
22: print "$aff rows were affected.\n";
23:
24: exit;
```

In Listing 12.5, the connection attributes in lines 14–15 mean that error conditions are no longer handled longhand, as we did in previous programs with some lines of Perl after, for example, a do(). In Listing 12.5, if the do() in line 21 fails, we would instead get rather unfriendly messages like this:

```
DBD::mysql::db do failed: Duplicate entry '3' for key 1 at
/home/sites/cms/web/cgi-bin/testerror1.pl line 29.
DBD::mysql::db do failed: Duplicate entry '3' for key 1 at
/home/sites/cms/web/cgi-bin/testerror1.pl line 29.
```

If the script is run standalone, both messages would be printed to the console; but if called as a CGI script through the Web server, the messages would be printed to the Web server's error log. The script would terminate with no output to the user's browser telling him of the error.

Although the error occurs only once because both RaiseError and PrintError are set, an error is logged once, and the script exits with that error logged again. We could turn PrintError off, in which case, only a single message from RaiseError would be logged when the script dies.

To handle the error in a more user-friendly way, we can insert the following lines before any DBI calls. They define a subroutine that handles the error in a more elegant way by telling Perl to process any DIE signals through the handle_error subroutine. First, we'll define the subroutine; then we'll tell Perl to invoke it for all DIE signals:

```
sub handle_error {
  print "Database error... we\'ll tell sysadmin...\n";
  ## and mail the system administrator for example
  die "Database error... $DBI::err: $DBI::errstr.\n";
}
$SIG{__DIE__} = \&handle_error;
```

With RaiseError and PrintError both on, if the script is called through a Web browser and if DBI causes Perl to terminate, a friendly message will be printed to the screen (you may also want to email the system administrator or do other things), and some useful information will be put in the error log, such as this:

12

```
DBD::mysql::db do failed: Duplicate entry '3' for key 1 at /home/sites/cms/
web/cgi-bin/testerror1.pl line 29.
Database error... 1062: Duplicate entry '3' for key 1.
```

Deciding precisely how to handle errors is in the end a matter of what the application requires and even down to the programmer's own taste. However, by learning the various options offered by Perl and DBI, you should be able to find the most elegant solution for your application.

When to Use Perl

When designing an interactive Web site, you have a wide choice of languages to develop in. Not even CGIs have to be written in Perl. Some languages, such as PHP and ASP, are embedded into HTML pages, and other languages, such as C, are compiled and can offer high performance. So when should you use Perl?

There are some circumstances in which it is convenient to be able to write standalone scripts with no need for a Web server; for instance:

- You may want to invoke programs directly from the command line; you can do this easily with Perl.
- You may want to invoke programs from the cron scheduler. If, for example, you have a database that needs a regular update, perhaps a once-nightly process to be run, you can write the application in Perl and invoke it from cron.
- Your program may take a long time to run. Perl processes, when invoked directly, do not have the timeout limitations of programs invoked via Apache.

There are also performance benefits in some circumstances:

- Perl has powerful text processing routines (regular expressions); this makes it particularly useful for handling user input from a form on a Web site, verifying and analyzing it.
- Because Perl is an interpreted language, it is generally quicker to develop Perl programs than programs in a compiled language such as C because you do not have the overhead of recompiling the program every time you want to retest it.

However, there are a few downsides. Perl is not the easiest language to learn quickly, and for the inexperienced coder, it can be daunting to view the code left by another developer. There are those enlightened ones who are addicted to Perl, but more simple folk will probably find languages such as PHP easier to learn, without losing much functionality (indeed PHP has much in common with Perl).

Perl is not embedded into HTML pages (although versions of Perl do operate like this). This means that to compile an HTML output, complete with all the HTML tags required for page layout, navigation, and images (usually static content) can be a tedious exercise. HTML can either be directly output from Perl, or held in a template file that Perl can parse, inserting dynamic content as it goes. Although there are tools to help with Web interfacing matters (such as `CGI.pm`), the implications of this are that it's less elegant to generate a Web page from Perl than PHP, and you may prefer to do things an easier way. The upshot is, development times for Web applications are often shorter in PHP than for Perl.

Furthermore, if an application must run fast and demands that every last ounce of performance is squeezed out of the system, a compiled language might be a better option. When a Perl script is invoked, the Perl interpreter must first be loaded into memory, which is an additional performance overhead. These things may be issues with programs that are run frequently on a busy Web site. If this is the case, a compiled language such as C may be the fastest option.

Summary

In today's lesson, you had a short tour of Perl and the DBI interface to MySQL.

Perl is a vast subject, and for the beginner this lesson has only been a taste of the language itself. However, you should now be able to create and run a simple Perl program that connects and communicates with a MySQL database.

You learned some methods for doing queries through DBI, for processing and displaying the resultset where there is one, for ascertaining the success or failure of your query, and for handling errors where they occur.

Finally, you looked at the pros and cons of using Perl versus other languages.

12

Q&A

Q Some new languages appear better than Perl. Is it about to become obsolete?

A Unlikely. Although some languages do certain things better, Perl is flexible enough to be used in a wide range of situations. Compiled languages are faster, and some people find HTML-embedded languages such as PHP and ASP more convenient for Web use. But Perl has such a large library of functions and third-party modules that it can be easily deployed across a range of applications.

Q **I'm having problems installing DBI and DBD. What should I do?**

A Some systems can be more difficult than others to install software on, although it has to be said that the DBI is usually straightforward. The World Wide Web has many discussion archives on Perl, DBI, and MySQL, their installation and use. Go to a search engine such as Google and search on the error text you receive. You should easily find a reference to the problem, and hopefully a solution.

Workshop

The quiz and exercises are provided to help you solidify your understanding of the material covered today. Try to understand the quiz and exercise answers before continuing to tomorrow's lesson.

Quiz

1. What's wrong with the following code?

```
my $dsn = "DBI:mysql:mydb";
my $db_user = "some_user";
my $db_pass = "some_pass";
my $dbh = $dbh->connect ($dsn, $db_user, $db_pass)
or die "Couldn't connect to MySQL.\n";
```

2. If you have the following lines to perform a prepare():

```
$sth = $dbh->prepare ($sql)
  or die "Couldn't prepare statement $sql.\n";
```

which of the following lines performs an execute()?

```
$sth->execute ()
  or die "Couldn't execute statement $sql.\n";

$sth = $dbh->execute ()
  or die "Couldn't execute statement $sql.\n";

$sth- = execute ()
  or die "Couldn't execute statement $sql.\n";
```

3. Which of the following allow(s) you to reference columns in a resultset by name?

```
@row_ary  = $sth->fetchrow_array;
$hash_ref = $sth->fetchrow_hashref;
$ary_ref  = $sth->fetchall_arrayref;
$ary_ref  = $sth->fetchrow_arrayref;
```

Quiz Answers

1. The `connect()` method should reference DBI, not the database handle `$dbh`. The `connect()` line should read:

```
my $dbh = DBI->connect ($dsn, $db_user, $db_pass)
or die "Couldn't connect to MySQL.\n";
```

2. The first one is correct:

```
$sth->execute ()
   or die "Couldn't execute statement $sql.\n";
```

The second one is wrong because it tries to call the `execute()` method on the database handle `$dbh` (which is wrong), and the third one tries to call a Perl function called `execute()`, (which will not have the desired effect!).

3. The second one, `fetchrow_hashref()` is the only one that allows you to reference columns of the resultset by name.

Exercises

1. Write out the lines of Perl that will connect to your database with the following parameters:

```
$dsn = "DBI:mysql:cms"
$db_user = "your_user"
$db_pass = "your_password"
$hostname = "localhost"
```

2. Write a query that performs an update on a table in your database. Then put it into a Perl program that connects to the database, using `RaiseError` and `PrintError` set to keep running if an error occurs. Use the `do()` method to do the update, and then print out how many rows were affected.

Specify your connection line and the `do()` line.

3. In Exercise 2, what would `0E0` mean as the value returned from `do()`?

Answers to Exercises

1. Your code should look something like this:

```
my $dbh = DBI->connect ("$dsn:$hostname", $db_user, $db_pass)
   or die "Couldn't connect to MySQL.\n";
```

2. Your code should look something like this:

```
## connect
my $dbh = DBI->connect ($dsn, $db_user, $db_pass,
   { RaiseError => 0, PrintError => 0 });
## perform query and print result
$aff = $dbh->do ($sql);
print "$aff rows were affected.\n";
```

3. `0E0` means "query successful, nothing affected."

12

DAY 13

Using the C API

C is a powerful language and the choice of many people who write applications that interact with a database such as MySQL. Much of MySQL and its client programs has been written in C, and the API is included with the MySQL distribution. A knowledge of the C API is essential for those writing applications in C, and C itself is a language you should consider if you are creating high-performance or standalone database applications.

Today you will learn:

- When to use C to write MySQL applications, and the key principles of the C API
- The datatypes provided by the `mysqlclient` library
- How to connect to a MySQL database, run queries, and process the results
- How to determine whether errors occurred during database interaction, and how to handle them

This lesson assumes that you already have a knowledge of C programming and is not a tutorial on the language itself. It is intended to teach you how to use the API so that you can easily start building powerful MySQL applications.

C and MySQL

If you're using C to write MySQL database applications, you will need the C API to communicate with the MySQL server. Like all APIs, it is the lowest common denominator for passing instructions and information between your application and a MySQL database.

The C API is distributed with MySQL. Unlike other languages, such as Perl with its DBI, there is no need to download or install it separately.

The administrative clients that come with MySQL, such as the mysql client program, are written in C and based on this API. If you installed MySQL from source, you may be interested to look at the C code of these programs, which you'll find in your MySQL source directory, in mysql-*VERSION*/client.

With the advent of MySQL version 4, it is now possible to embed MySQL into a C application. Although today's lesson shows you how to build a C application that uses the API to talk to MySQL, in Day 20, "Embedding the MySQL Server," you will learn how to create an application that embeds an entire MySQL server into your C program.

Note

In today's lesson, I will refer frequently to NULL. Note that this means a C NULL pointer rather than a NULL value in a MySQL table.

In addition, note that the terms *column* and *field* are synonymous. Many of the API's functions include the word field, which makes it easier to refer to a *field* than a *column*, even though the meaning is the same.

When to Use C, and When Not To

C is a widely used, general-purpose language that has found use in many kinds of applications. Compiled languages inherently produce faster code than interpreted languages such as Perl or PHP. Another advantage of C is that because it is a relatively low-level language, a skilled programmer can write code that makes most efficient use of system resources. Provided that an application merits a slightly longer development time—such as applications that will be frequently or intensively used—C is an excellent candidate.

Because C is a compiled language, development time in C tends to be longer than with an interpreted language. The simple reason is that a C program must be compiled and linked each time a change is made, before it can be run and tested. With an interpreted program, you simply make your changes to the program and run it.

C lacks the memory management capabilities built into Perl and PHP. In C, you often need to write your own code for handling data structures that can grow dynamically. C also lacks most of the powerful text processing capability of Perl and PHP, whose routines are indispensable when building dynamic Web sites that process user input and other textual input.

All this means that C may not be the language of choice for building a dynamic Web site with multiple scripts making up the various pages of the site. However, it lends itself well to standalone and high-performance applications.

Datatypes

When you create a C program that uses the API for MySQL, you will need to include the `mysql.h` header file. By doing so, a number of MySQL datatypes become available that are representative of the data you will handle during the interaction with a MySQL server.

The datatypes include representations for

- A database connection
- An entire resultset of data
- A single row of data from a resultset
- Information about field descriptions
- A number of rows (for example, how many rows were affected or returned by a query)

Table 13.1 shows the API's datatypes.

TABLE 13.1 The C API Datatypes for MySQL

Datatype	Description
MYSQL	Used for almost all MySQL interaction, this datatype represents a database connection handle.
MYSQL_RES	Represents the resultset of any query that returns a resultset. It contains both data (the resultset itself) and metadata (information about the resultset, such as column types).
MYSQL_ROW	Represents a pointer to one row of data. The structure contains an array of counted-byte strings. Note that if resultset data contains binary data (which can contain nulls), you cannot assume that the row comprises null-terminated strings.
MYSQL_FIELD	Represents a set of data about a field (column), including its name, type, and size. We'll look at this further under mysql_fetch_field().

13

TABLE 13.1   continued

Datatype	Description
MYSQL_FIELD_OFFSET	When using MYSQL_FIELD, this represents an offset (beginning at zero) into a MySQL field list.
my_ulonglong	A long integer that represents a number of rows. This number is returned from functions such as mysql_affected_rows(), mysql_num_rows(), and mysql_insert_id().

This is not an exhaustive explanation of the datatypes. For example, the MYSQL_FIELD structure has many component datatypes that can be distilled out, and careful processing may be required for a MYSQL_ROW that may contain binary data. Consult the MySQL Technical Reference Manual for more details on the data structures themselves and for functions that can access them in particular ways.

Compiling and Linking

Before we delve into the various functions that you can use for interacting with MySQL, let's spend a few moments studying the structure of the sample code that we will create to demonstrate them. We will pay attention to compiler options and the means of linking to the library and include what our programs require.

Our code will consist of the following source files:

- main.c, the main program that we will use to demonstrate the API
- common.c, in which we will define common functions, such as for connecting to a MySQL server
- common.h, a header file that contains prototypes for those common functions
- The MySQL header files and client library
- stdio.h, the library of standard input/output routines

You will need to ensure that the MySQL header file, mysql.h, and the MySQL client library are available on your system. On a Unix system, the header file will normally be found (depending on where you installed MySQL) in /usr/local/mysql/include/mysql/ or /usr/local/include/mysql/. Similarly, the client library will be in /usr/local/mysql/lib/mysql/ or /usr/local/lib/mysql/. When building your application, you will need to include the correct paths to these directories.

In the examples, we will assume that you're using gcc as your compiler (this assumes that you have a Unix-type system), although if you are familiar with C on a Windows system you should still be able to compile, with minor adjustments.

We'll also assume that you are using make, which means that you can place complex compile options and paths to linked files in a file called Makefile, which resides in the same directory as your C source code. Create a Makefile like this (although you may have to modify the paths to the MySQL files to suit your system):

```
CC = gcc
INCLUDES = -I/usr/local/mysql/include/mysql
LIBS = -L/usr/local/mysql/lib/mysql -lmysqlclient -lm
all: myapp
main.o: main.c common.h
    $(CC) -c $(INCLUDES) main.c
common.o: common.c common.h
    $(CC) -c $(INCLUDES) common.c
myapp: main.o common.o
    $(CC) -o myapp main.o common.o $(LIBS)
clean:
    rm -f myapp main.o common.o
```

To run the compiler, you just need to type a single word at the command prompt:

```
$ make
```

Here's a sample output from make:

```
gcc -c -I/usr/local/mysql/include/mysql main.c
gcc -c -I/usr/local/mysql/include/mysql common.c
gcc -o myapp main.o common.o -L/usr/local/mysql/lib/mysql -lmysqlclient -lm
```

These lines are what you would have typed if you hadn't used make! gcc compiles the files, creating main.o and common.o, and the linking process creates the executable binary myapp.

Note

You may get a compile error on certain systems if the mysql library isn't found in your library path.

To fix this, you can edit the /etc/ld.so.conf file (if you are root), add the path to the library (such as /usr/local/mysql/lib/mysql), and run ldconfig to reload it. Alternatively, set the $LD_LIBRARY_PATH to the mysql library path. Then run make to compile again.

13

If you run make and get output free of errors such as the preceding output, you will be able to run the executable like this:

```
$ ./myapp
```

or if it's in your $PATH variable for your system, just this:

```
$ myapp
```

We'll develop myapp throughout this lesson, so what it does and what it produces as output will evolve according to the functions in main.c at the time. The functionality will include connecting to a database and running various types of queries, getting more complex as the lesson progresses.

To clean up your directory of old compiled files (in fact to delete them) but leave your source files alone, you may want to run the following:

```
$ make clean
```

Connecting to Your Database

Connecting to a MySQL database has two stages. First you initialize a connection handler; then you connect to the MySQL server. In the second step, you can optionally specify which database to use. Let's look at this procedure in detail.

You first need to call mysql_init() to initialize a connection handler. Its syntax is

```
*mysql_init (*mysql)
```

where *mysql is a database connection handle, although typically we pass it NULL to initiate a new connection. The result is an initialized MYSQL* handle.

We'll embed this function into common.c, which holds our common functions. The relevant lines within the function look like this:

```
MYSQL   *mysql;
    if ((mysql = mysql_init (NULL)) == NULL) {
        fprintf (stderr, "mysql_init() failed.\n");
        return (NULL);
    }
```

Here the first line declares mysql as a pointer to our database handler of type MYSQL. Then we call mysql_init() and test the result. By passing it a NULL pointer, mysql_init() initializes a new object suitable for mysql_real_connect(), which we'll use in a moment to make a connection. It returns NULL if it fails, which indicates that there was too little memory to allocate a new object. But if successful, it returns a MYSQL* type, which we store in mysql, our initialized connection handle.

Now let's see how to connect to the database. The function mysql_real_connect() attempts to make a connection to a MySQL server. It returns a MYSQL* connection handle if it succeeds or NULL if it fails.

`mysql_real_connect()` takes several parameters. For clarity, I will show it spread across several lines. Again to be added to `common.c`, the function looks like this:

```
mysql_real_connect (
    mysql,
    db_host,
    db_user,
    db_pass,
    db_name,
    db_port,
    unix_socket,
    db_flags)
```

> **Note**
>
> In the preceding code example, the C declarations of the parameters were omitted for simplicity. You'll see these when we put the connection program together.

The parameters passed are as follows:

- `mysql` is the `MYSQL` structure we created from `mysql_init()`; it'll be our database connection handle provided that connection is successful.

- `db_host` is the server hostname or IP address, defaulting to `localhost` if `NULL`. If the operating system supports sockets (Unix) or named pipes (Windows), this method is used rather than TCP/IP.

- `db_user` is the MySQL user's username, defaulting to the current user if `NULL`.

- `db_pass` is the MySQL user's password (unencrypted).

- `db_name` is the name of the database to use by default within this connection; it can also be `NULL`, and you can specify the database name later.

- `db_port` is the port number for TCP/IP connection (if not `0`).

- `unix_socket` if not `NULL` specifies the socket or named pipe to be used.

- `db_flags` is usually `0` but can be used to modify the behavior of MySQL for this connection, such as modifying the timeout period (closing the connection if inactive) or specifying the use of SSL encrypted protocol. See the MySQL Technical Reference for details of these options.

Because db_name is optional, you can simply connect to the MySQL server and select which database to use later. Should you need to select or change the name of the default database after calling `mysql_real_connect()`, you can use the function `mysql_select_db()`. You would use it with the following syntax:

```
mysql_select_db (*mysql, *db_name)
```

13

where *mysql* is again our database connection handle, and *db_name* is the new database to connect to. The function returns an integer: zero for success or non-zero if an error occurred. So we might use it as follows, with a connection mysql and database db_name:

```
mysql_select_db (mysql, db_name)
```

Disconnecting from a Database

To disconnect from the MySQL server, we use the mysql_close() function. Here's the line of code we'll use:

```
mysql_close (mysql);
```

It's not complicated: This line closes the MySQL connection referenced by the argument passed here as mysql.

Handling Errors

We're nearly ready to put our program together! There's just one more important thing to include: error handling.

Nearly all the API's functions return a value indicating success or failure. If a function fails, you can use mysql_error() and mysql_errno() to report on what went wrong.

For example, we will test the result of mysql_real_connect(). As you saw just now, it returns a MYSQL* connection handle if the connection attempt succeeds, or NULL if it fails. Let's add some error handling to our connection routine, which should now look like this:

```
if (mysql_real_connect (
    mysql,
    db_host,
    db_user,
    db_pass,
    db_name,
    db_port,
    unix_socket,
    db_flags) == NULL ) {
    fprintf (stderr,
        "mysql_real_connect() failed!\nError %u: %s\n",
        mysql_errno (mysql),
        mysql_error (mysql));
    return (NULL);
}
```

The functions mysql_error() and mysql_errno() return the error message and error code, respectively, for the most recent API call that could succeed or fail. They take the MYSQL* database connection handle as their argument.

The preceding code example tests the result of `mysql_real_connect()` and prints an error message if the connection fails together with some error information. For example, a failed connection attempt might generate the following output:

```
Error 1045: Access denied for user: 'tonyb@localhost' (Using password: YES)
```

A Simple Connection Script

Now it's time to put the code together into a suite of small programs that we can use. As a reminder, the three programs we will create are as follows:

- `main.c`—The main program
- `common.c`—In which we will define common functions
- `common.h`—A header file that contains prototypes for the common functions

The code examples you saw just now came from `common.c`. Listing 13.1 shows the full program.

LISTING 13.1 `common.c`

```
 1: /* common.c */
 2:
 3: #include <stdio.h>
 4: #include <mysql.h>
 5: #include "common.h"
 6:
 7: MYSQL * db_connect (
 8:     char *db_host,
 9:     char *db_user,
10:     char *db_pass,
11:     char *db_name,
12:     unsigned int db_port,
13:     char *unix_socket,
14:     unsigned int db_flags )
15: {
16: MYSQL    *mysql;
17:
18:     if ((mysql = mysql_init (NULL)) == NULL) {
19:         fprintf (stderr, "mysql_init() failed.\n");
20:         return (NULL);
21:     }
22:     if (mysql_real_connect (
23:         mysql,
24:         db_host,
25:         db_user,
26:         db_pass,
```

13

LISTING 13.1   continued

```
27:          db_name,
28:          db_port,
29:          unix_socket,
30:          db_flags) == NULL ) {
31:      fprintf (stderr,
32:      "mysql_real_connect() failed!\nError %u: %s\n",
33:      mysql_errno (mysql),
34:      mysql_error (mysql));
35:      return (NULL);
36:    }
37:    return (mysql);
38: }
39:
40: void db_disconnect (MYSQL *mysql)
41: {
42:      mysql_close (mysql);
43: }
```

This program defines the subroutines for connecting to (db_connect(), lines 7-38) and disconnecting from (db_disconnect(), lines 40-43) the database. These wrapper functions are held in common.c so that they may be shared by any number of application programs.

Because db_disconnect() holds a one-line routine only, it is arguable that you don't need it; you could just call mysql_close() directly each time you want to disconnect. However, this is just good program structure because at some time in the future, if you want to add other features to the disconnection routine, you would only have to change code in this one program.

Now let's look at the main application, main.c, which is shown in Listing 13.2.

LISTING 13.2   main.c

```
1: /* main.c */
2:
3: #include <stdio.h>
4: #include <mysql.h>
5: #include "common.h"
6:
7: #define def_db_host      NULL
8: #define def_db_user      NULL
9: #define def_db_name      NULL
10: #define def_db_port      0
11: #define def_unix_socket NULL
12:
13: MYSQL    *mysql;
14:
```

LISTING 13.2 continued

```
15: int main (int argc, char *argv[])
16: {
17: MYSQL_RES    *res_set;
18: char         *db_pass;
19:
20:     db_pass = get_tty_password (NULL);
21:
22:     mysql = db_connect (
23:         def_db_host,
24:         def_db_user,
25:         db_pass,
26:         def_db_name,
27:         def_db_port,
28:         def_unix_socket,
29:         0);
30:     if (mysql == NULL) {
31:         exit (1);
32:     } else {
33:         fprintf (stdout, "Connected.\n");
34:
35:         /* Do the work here */
36:
37:     }
38:
39:     db_disconnect (mysql);
40:     exit (0);
41: }
```

Lines 3 through 5 include standard I/O and MySQL routines, and the common.h header file, which we'll look at in a moment.

Lines 7 through 11 define values for the MySQL server, the database user, the database name, the port to use, and the Unix socket. You will immediately notice that all these values are NULL or 0. This means that the server localhost will be used, and the MySQL username specified will be the same as the Unix login name of the user running the script.

Why do we do this? On a Web application, such as you saw with PHP and Perl, this would not make sense. In a Web application, you would typically put your database connection parameters into a common file that is locked away from view as much as possible. But here we're putting those parameters into the main application program.

We're doing this because a C program is more likely to be used as a standalone application than a Web application, and the user who runs the program may well be logged in at the console of the client machine where the program is running. Our script is simple! It assumes that he has a username that will be a MySQL username and, for even greater simplicity, that the MySQL server is running on that same machine.

13

Naturally the script would have some shortcomings in the real world: We'd want to be able to specify a different username, connect to databases on other machines, and specify which database to use. (The `mysql` monitor is a good example of a similar program that can do these things.) But the objective here isn't to get so clever, so let's concentrate on how to use the API.

The connection routine needs a password, so we declare the string variable `db_pass` on line 18 of `main.c` and in line 20 use the `get_tty_password()` function to ask the user to enter a password. This routine gets user input without echoing what he types to the screen. `get_tty_password()` and many other useful routines are defined in the MySQL client library, which you may want to study if you are building C applications in earnest.

Starting at line 22, the `db_connect()` function defined in `common.c` is invoked, with the values we established for the connection being passed to it. The function should return `mysql`, the database connection handle. The program tests for `NULL` in line 30, indicating failure to connect, but if successful, it executes the code in the body of the program at line 35. This is where we will soon insert some more interesting code.

To complete the three files, Listing 13.3 contains the code for `common.h`.

LISTING 13.3   common.h

```
 1: MYSQL * db_connect (
 2:     char *db_host,
 3:     char *db_user,
 4:     char *db_pass,
 5:     char *db_name,
 6:     unsigned int db_port,
 7:     char *db_socket,
 8:     unsigned int flags );
 9:
10: void db_disconnect (
11:     MYSQL *mysql);
```

This header file contains prototypes for the `db_connect()` and `db_disconnect()` functions, which we defined in `common.c`.

To compile and link your programs, type the following:

```
$ make
```

If this proceeds without errors, it creates object files `main.o` and `common.o`, and the executable `myapp`. If it fails, go back and look for where the error occurred, following guidance from the compiler's error report.

When compiled and linked, run your application like this:

```
$ ./myapp
```

If you enter a valid password and the connection succeeds, you see this:

```
Enter password:
Connected.
```

Output looks like this if the connection fails:

```
Enter password:
mysql_real_connect() failed!
Error 1045: Access denied for user: 'tonyb@localhost' (Using password: YES)
```

Provided that your program compiled and ran correctly, you have now successfully built a simple database connection program. We will now enhance this program to make it run queries on a database.

Running Queries That Return a Resultset

When a program has a live connection to a MySQL database, two functions are available for running a query: mysql_query() and mysql_real_query().

You can use these functions to run any kind of query: those that return a resultset (such as the SQL statements SELECT, DESCRIBE, and SHOW) and those that don't (such as INSERT, UPDATE, and DELETE). Initially we'll concentrate on queries that return a resultset, so you'll see how to run the query and process the data that is returned.

mysql_query() expects a string terminated by a null, whereas mysql_real_query() takes a counted string. For our simple examples, you can use mysql_query(); however, if you need to create a query that contains binary data (which may contain null bytes), you must use mysql_real_query().

The syntax for these commands is

```
mysql_query (*mysql, *query)
```

```
mysql_real_query (*mysql, *query, length)
```

where *mysql is a database handle, *query is the SQL, and unsigned integer length is the length in bytes of the query. Both return an integer result: zero for success, or non-zero if there was an error. (The result is not an indication of whether a resultset was returned.)

For example, you might run a query like this:

```
mysql_query (mysql, "SHOW DATABASES")
```

In a moment, we'll incorporate this line into our program. But first, let's look at the functions for processing a resultset.

13

Therec are two functions: `mysql_store_result()` and `mysql_use_result()`. Their syntax follows:

`mysql_store_result (*mysql)`

`mysql_use_result (*mysql)`

where `*mysql` is a database handle. We'll look at the behavior of these two functions in a moment, but for the time being, we'll assume that we're using `mysql_store_result()`.

If a resultset is fetched (even with no rows of data!), a structure of the datatype `MYSQL_RES` will be returned. In other words, even if you run a query like `SELECT * FROM mytable WHERE 0`, a `MYSQL_RES` structure will be returned.

If a `NULL` is returned, this can be because the query wasn't meant to return data: It could have been an `INSERT` or `DELETE`, for example. Alternatively, it could be `NULL` because `mysql_store_result()` failed. So how do you tell?

To find out whether the query should have returned some data, use `mysql_field_count()`. Its syntax is

`mysql_field_count (*mysql)`

It returns an integer indicating the number of columns retrieved as a result of the query. If it's non-zero, it indicates that a resultset was expected (so if `mysql_store_result()` returned `NULL` and a resultset was expected, something went wrong!). But if it returns zero, it's because no resultset was expected.

Let's put this knowledge together into some code that should help clarify things:

```
if (mysql_query (mysql, "SHOW DATABASES") == 0) {
    printf ("Query succeeded. About to fetch result.\n");
    res_set = mysql_store_result (mysql);
    if (res_set != NULL) {
        /* Result set obtained, so process */
        /* Do something with the result set */

    } else {
        /* No result set, see what happened */
        if (mysql_field_count (mysql) > 0) {
            /* Should have had some fields
             * so an error must have occurred */
            fprintf (stderr,
                "No result set, mysql_store_result() failed: %s\n",
                mysql_error (mysql));
        } else {
            /* Field count is 0,
             * so no result was expected from the query */
            printf ("Query was not meant to return data.\n");
        }
    }
```

```
   } else {
      fprintf (stderr,
      "Query failed: %s\n", mysql_error(mysql));
   }
```

As you can see, we run the query with `mysql_query()` and test the result for success or failure of the query itself. If successful, we do `mysql_store_result()`. If it returns a resultset (not NULL), we process it (you'll see how to do this in a moment). But if there's no resultset, we have to find out why.

So we test `mysql_field_count()` to see what value it has. A zero value means that the query wasn't meant to return a resultset (this would be the case with a DELETE, INSERT, and so on). But a non-zero result means that some fields were expected and something went wrong with `mysql_store_result()`.

You don't have to write your code in a way that appears ignorant of the SQL it's running! However, it can be useful to use this technique, especially if you're writing a client program that allows the user to write his own SQL. Such a program (such as the `mysql` monitor) needs to be resilient and handle any result that may be produced.

More About `mysql_store_result()` and `mysql_use_result()`

These two result-processing functions work in slightly different ways. `mysql_store_result()` retrieves the entire resultset at once; in other words, it fetches all the rows of data that result from the query. `mysql_use_result()`, on the other hand, only initializes the retrieval, which must then be done row-by-row, using the function `mysql_fetch_row()`.

Of the two functions, `mysql_store_result()` is the most memory-hungry in its demands on the client, because it fetches a potentially large two-dimensional array into memory on the client system. `mysql_use_result()` is less burdensome on the client; however, it causes the entire resultset to be loaded into the server's memory, and the data will stay there until the last row has been fetched by the client.

`mysql_use_result()` is therefore a less than ideal choice on a database server that may serve multiple clients. Although `mysql_store_result()` shifts the memory demands to the client, it is in general a better choice and is the most commonly used as a result.

A Simple Query Program

Now that you understand how to retrieve a resultset and check whether it was fetched without error, let's update the programs so that you can compile and run them with their new functionality.

13

The common.c and common.h programs are the same as before, although main.c now has more code, as shown in Listing 13.4.

LISTING 13.4   main.c

```
 1: /* main.c */
 2: /* Connect, run a query and check the result set */
 3:
 4: #include <stdio.h>
 5: #include <mysql.h>
 6: #include "common.h"
 7:
 8: #define def_db_host      NULL
 9: #define def_db_user      NULL
10: #define def_db_name      NULL
11: #define def_db_port      0
12: #define def_unix_socket NULL
13:
14: MYSQL    *mysql;
15:
16: int main (int argc, char *argv[])
17: {
18: MYSQL_RES    *res_set;
19: char         *db_pass;
20:
21:     db_pass = get_tty_password (NULL);
22:
23:     mysql = db_connect (
24:         def_db_host,
25:         def_db_user,
26:         db_pass,
27:         def_db_name,
28:         def_db_port,
29:         def_unix_socket,
30:         0);
31:     if (mysql == NULL) {
32:         exit (1);
33:     } else {
34:         fprintf (stdout, "Connected.\n");
35:
36:         if (mysql_query (mysql, "SHOW DATABASES") == 0) {
37:             printf ("Query succeeded. About to fetch result.\n");
38:             res_set = mysql_store_result (mysql);
39:
40:             if (res_set != NULL) {
41:                 /* Result set obtained, so process */
42:
43:                 /* Do something with the result set */
44:
45:                 mysql_free_result (res_set);
46:             } else {
```

LISTING 13.4   continued

```
47:                    /* No result set, see what happened */
48:                    if (mysql_field_count (mysql) > 0) {
49:                        /* Should have had some fields
50:                         * so an error must have occurred */
51:                        fprintf (stderr,
52:                            "No result set, mysql_store_result() failed: %s\n",
53:                            mysql_error (mysql));
54:                    } else {
55:                        /* Field count is 0,
56:                        so no result was expected from the query */
57:                        printf ("Query was not meant to return data.\n");
58:                    }
59:                }
60:            } else {
61:                fprintf (stderr,
62:                    "Query failed: %s\n", mysql_error(mysql));
63:            }
64:
65:        }
66:
67:        db_disconnect (mysql);
68:        exit (0);
69: }
```

Lines 36 through 63 should look familiar; they are almost identical to the code example you looked at previously. Notice the function mysql_free_result() in line 45. When you finish processing your resultset, you must use this to free up the memory allocated as a result of functions such as mysql_store_result() or mysql_use_result().

> **Note**
>
> There are also other functions that produce resultsets that we've not covered here.
>
> For example, the API has functions to retrieve information about fields (columns) in a resultset and information about the client, server, and connection protocol. There are also functions to list databases on the server, to show information about processes running on the server, and so on.
>
> Consult the MySQL Web site or the MySQL Technical Reference for more information about other available functions.

13

mysql_free_result() has the syntax

mysql_free_result (*result)

where *result is a resultset of the datatype MYSQL_RES. It doesn't return a value, and there's no need to check for errors.

You should be able to compile and run this program, although its output still shows only the connection routine and does not display any data from our query. Let's see how to do that.

Handling Resultsets

Although the program in Listing 13.4 retrieves and tests a resultset from a query, it doesn't do anything with it. We need some functions for processing the data in a resultset.

You saw that you can use `mysql_store_result()` or `mysql_use_result()` to fetch the result of your query. Whichever you use, you can access one row of that data at a time using the function `mysql_fetch_row()`.

The syntax for `mysql_fetch_row()` is as follows:

```
mysql_fetch_row (*result)
```

It returns the next row of data in the datatype `MYSQL_ROW`. Each time the function is called, it returns the next row, until there are no more rows, whereupon it returns `NULL`.

If you use `mysql_store_result()`, you have the advantage of some extra functions that let you move backward and forward within the resultset. These commands and their syntax are

```
mysql_data_seek (*result, offset)
```

```
mysql_row_seek (*result, offset)
```

in which `*result` is a resultset of the datatype `MYSQL_RES`, and `offset` is an unsigned long integer indicating the number of the row in the resultset to be retrieved, between `0` and `mysql_num_rows(result)`-1.

`mysql_num_rows()` is used with this syntax:

```
mysql_num_rows (*result)
```

and it returns the number of rows in a resultset (in datatype `my_ulonglong`). If you use `mysql_store_result()`, this number is available immediately; but if you use `mysql_use_result()`, it returns the correct value only when all rows have been retrieved with `mysql_fetch_row()`.

Modifying the Script to Process a Resultset

In Listing 13.4, we fetched a resultset but didn't do anything with it. Now we'll do some processing to go through the resultset and print it to the screen.

The program will now define a new function, print_result_set(). This requires a prototype in the shared header file, so the following lines need to be appended to common.h:

```
void print_result_set (
    MYSQL *mysql,
    MYSQL_RES *res_set);
```

In Listing 13.5, look out for the addition of the print_result_set() function.

LISTING 13.5   main.c

```
 1: /* main.c */
 2: /* Program to connect to database, run a query,  */
 3: /* fetch and display the result set */
 4:
 5: #include <stdio.h>
 6: #include <mysql.h>
 7: #include "common.h"
 8:
 9: #define def_db_host     NULL
10: #define def_db_user     NULL
11: #define def_db_name     NULL
12: #define def_db_port     0
13: #define def_unix_socket NULL
14:
15: MYSQL    *mysql;
16:
17: int main (int argc, char *argv[])
18: {
19: MYSQL_RES    *res_set;
20: char         *db_pass;
21:
22:     db_pass = get_tty_password (NULL);
23:
24:     mysql = db_connect (
25:         def_db_host,
26:         def_db_user,
27:         db_pass,
28:         def_db_name,
29:         def_db_port,
30:         def_unix_socket,
31:         0);
32:     if (mysql == NULL) {
33:         exit (1);
34:     } else {
35:         fprintf (stdout, "Connected.\n");
36:
37:         if (mysql_query (mysql, "SHOW DATABASES") == 0) {
38:             printf ("Query succeeded. About to fetch result.\n");
39:             res_set = mysql_store_result (mysql);
```

13

LISTING 13.5   continued

```
40:
41:                if (res_set != NULL) {
42:                    /* Result set obtained, so process */
43:
44:                    print_result_set (mysql, res_set);
45:                    mysql_free_result (res_set);
46:
47:                } else {
48:                    /* No result set, see what happened */
49:                    if (mysql_field_count (mysql) > 0) {
50:                        /* Should have had some fields
51:                         * so an error must have occurred */
52:                        fprintf (stderr,
53:                            "No result set, mysql_store_result() failed: %s\n",
54:                            mysql_error (mysql));
55:                    } else {
56:                        /* Field count is 0,
57:                         * so no result was expected from the query */
58:                        printf ("Query was not meant to return data.\n");
59:                    }
60:                }
61:            } else {
62:                fprintf (stderr,
63:                    "Query failed: %s\n", mysql_error (mysql));
64:            }
65:
66:        }
67:
68:    db_disconnect (mysql);
69:    exit (0);
70: }
71:
72: void print_result_set (MYSQL *mysql, MYSQL_RES *res_set)
73: {
74: unsigned int    f;
75: MYSQL_ROW       row;
76:
77:    while ((row = mysql_fetch_row (res_set)) != NULL) {
78:        f = 0;
79:        while (f<mysql_num_fields (res_set)) {
80:            if (f>0) fputc ('\t', stdout);
81:            fprintf (stdout, "%s", row[f]);
82:            f++;
83:        }
84:        fputc ('\n', stdout);
85:    }
86:
87:    if (mysql_errno (mysql) == 0)
88:        fprintf (stdout, "Number of rows returned: %lu.\n",
89:            (unsigned long) mysql_num_rows (res_set));
```

LISTING 13.5 continued

```
90:    else
91:        fprintf (stderr, "mysql_fetch_row() failed.\n");
92: }
```

In line 44 of `main.c` we call `print_result_set()`, which is defined in lines 72 through 92 of the code. Let's analyze what this code does.

When we call the function in line 44, we pass it the connection handle pointer and the resultset pointer. The function calls `mysql_fetch_row()` repeatedly (line 77) to get each row of data, each time placing it in the array `row`. The inner `while` loop (line 79) goes through each of the elements of `row` until it reaches the last one (corresponding to the last column), the last element number being referenced by `mysql_num_fields()` less one.

When the outer `while` loop finishes (line 85), the result of `mysql_fetch_row()` will be `NULL`. However, after exiting the loop, we don't know whether the `NULL` resulted from an error occurring or simply from reaching the last row. If an error occurred, we should handle it, so line 87 tests the value of `mysql_errno()`. If it's zero, there was no error, and lines 88–89 report the number of rows returned, from `mysql_num_rows()`. Otherwise, line 91 reports the error.

> **Caution**
>
> Because of problems on certain operating systems, you should convert values of datatype `my_ulonglong` to type `unsigned long` if you want to print them to the screen.
>
> Hence in line 89, we convert the integer returned from `mysql_num_rows()` to `unsigned long` before printing it.

After compiling your program with `make`, run your program. You may get a dialog like this:

```
$ ./myapp
Enter password:
Connected.
Query succeeded. About to fetch result.
store
contacts
mysql
test
Number of rows returned: 4.
```

13

As you can see, the program asked for my password and then ran the query to display the names of all the MySQL databases on my system. You can start experimenting with this script—for example, by changing the database name in line 11 (for example, put the database name `"store"` rather than `NULL`) and changing the SQL in line 37 to run some `SELECT` statements that return multiple columns.

Queries That Return No Resultset

So far you've learned how to run a query and check whether it ran successfully. You've also seen how to fetch the resultset, and, in the case of a `NULL` result, how to check whether this was because of an error or because the query wasn't meant to produce a result, such as with an `INSERT` or `DELETE`.

As a result, you've built some resilient code that can run a query of either type. You can modify the SQL query in any of the preceding listings to make it an `INSERT`, `DELETE`, and so on, and the code still runs. If there's no resultset from the query, the code produces a message telling you whether this is okay, or whether an error occurred.

However, if you do run a query that is meant to modify your data, how can you tell what effect it had?

You can use two important functions: `mysql_affected_rows()` and `mysql_insert_id()`. Their syntax is as follows:

```
mysql_affected_rows (*mysql)
```

and

```
mysql_insert_id (*mysql)
```

`mysql_affected_rows()` returns an integer of datatype `my_ulonglong`, which contains the number of rows affected from the query.

If you are performing an `INSERT` into a table with an `AUTO_INCREMENT` column, `mysql_insert_id()` returns an integer of datatype `my_ulonglong`, which is the ID generated in that column as a result.

Here's a code example that you could modify and use to handle an `INSERT` query (or an `UPDATE`, `DELETE`, and so on, although in these cases the `mysql_insert_id()` function would not be used).

It's much the same as the previous code you have seen, but a little trimmed down for simplicity (it assumes that you're doing a query that returns no resultset). If the query works without error, it prints out how many rows were affected by the `INSERT`, and the ID created in an `AUTO_INCREMENT` column as a result:

```
if (mysql_query (mysql,
    "INSERT INTO some_table VALUES (...)"   /* put an INSERT query here */
    ) == 0) {
    printf ("Query succeeded.\n");
    if ((res_set = mysql_store_result (mysql)) == NULL) {
        /* No result set (should be the case with INSERT) */
        if (mysql_field_count (mysql) == 0) {
            /* Field count is 0 (should be the case with INSEERT) */
            fprintf (stdout, "Rows affected: %lu\n",
                (unsigned long) mysql_affected_rows (mysql));
            fprintf (stdout, "Insert ID: %lu\n",
                (unsigned long) mysql_insert_id (mysql));
        }
    }
} else {
    fprintf (stderr,
        "Query failed: %s\n", mysql_error (mysql));
}
```

You can try this yourself, performing an INSERT into a table of your choice. It should give an output something like this:

```
$ ./myapp
Enter password:
Connected.
Query succeeded.
Rows affected: 1
Insert ID: 24
```

Summary

Today you learned how to use the C API for MySQL. You saw which code libraries to include and tried one method of structuring your code, using make to compile and link your application.

You had an introduction to the datatypes used by the API and learned how to make a connection to a MySQL server. You should now understand how to run queries and check for and report on error conditions. You learned how to process resultsets where they are returned, or, for queries that return no resultset, to determine what effect a query had on your data.

Although this study of the API covered its main functions and usage rather than its every detail, you should have enough knowledge to write powerful database applications using the C API.

13

Q&A

Q **Is a program in C that interacts with MySQL always going to run faster than a program in another language?**

A Not necessarily. It is true that in general a compiled language produces a program that executes faster than a script written in an interpreted language such as Perl or PHP. In this respect, a C program generally runs faster.

However, C lacks certain functionality that is present in Perl or PHP, such as text processing. If your C program has to implement in code that has core functionality in another language, any advantage will usually be lost, and the resulting program may be slower. Also, bear in mind that a significant amount of processing time may be spent running SQL queries. If these queries are complex, MySQL itself takes time to run them, no matter what language is chosen.

Q **Do I really need to check whether a query runs successfully (it seems awfully complicated)?**

A Checking for the successful completion of a database action is essential. If the program simply marches on after an error occurs, the results could be unpredictable, returning ugly results to the user and even corrupting data.

To put it simply, when you run `mysql_query()` or `mysql_real_query()`, they return a zero if the query executes successfully.

If you know your query was one that returns no result (such as an INSERT or UPDATE), you don't need to do further checking. However, you may want to call `mysql_affected_rows()` to find out how many rows were inserted, modified, or deleted.

If you know your query should return some data, you'll be doing a `mysql_store_result()`. This returns NULL if an error occurred; otherwise, a data structure of the type MYSQL_RES.

In today's lesson, we tested `mysql_field_count()` to determine whether an error occurred; however, this process is only necessary if you don't know what kind of query was being run (which is the case in a generic SQL handler like the mysql monitor).

Workshop

The quiz and exercises are provided to help you solidify your understanding of the material covered today. Try to understand the quiz and exercise answers before continuing to tomorrow's lesson.

Quiz

1. Which function makes the server do more work: `mysql_store_result()` or `mysql_use_result()`?

2. True or False: When connected to a MySQL database using `mysql_real_connect()`, you can still change the default database.

3. True or False: You have to use `make` to create C programs for MySQL.

Quiz Answers

1. `mysql_use_result()` is harder on the server because the server has to store the entire resultset while the client retrieves them a row at a time. In contrast, `mysql_store_result()` returns the whole resultset to the client in one go.

2. True. Use `mysql_select_db()`.

3. False! `make` just makes life easier by putting many compiler options into one place, the `Makefile`. You could run the compiling and linking manually by invoking your C compiler directly if you prefer.

Exercise

1. Modify Listing 13.5 to return the number of rows affected if the SQL is a query that affects data but returns no result.

Exercise Answer

1. Insert the line
   ```
   fprintf (stdout, "Rows affected: %lu\n",
       (unsigned long) mysql_affected_rows (mysql));
   ```
   into the `if()` statement in the condition where `mysql_field_count()` is zero.

13

WEEK 2

DAY 14

Security

Today you will learn about security on a MySQL server. MySQL has a powerful security system that can create globally powerful users or precisely control their privileges.

In particular, you will learn:

- How the MySQL privilege system works
- How to set up and manage database users using GRANT, REVOKE, and SHOW GRANTS
- How to set up some typical users and their privileges
- How to exercise good practices to keep your MySQL installation secure
- How to configure your MySQL server to use secure connections

The MySQL User Privilege System

MySQL has a sophisticated user privilege system that allows precise control of user privileges, whether users have powers across the server or are restricted to one or a number of its databases. Although MySQL complies with ANSI-92, its user privilege system goes beyond the ANSI standard.

Under the MySQL privilege system, you can grant a user access across the server, or you can limit users at a database, table, or even column level, with close control over what each user is allowed to do and where, such as whether the user can view or modify data. You can require users to connect to MySQL from a specific host machine or domain, and you can vary their level of privilege according to where they connect from.

For example, you may give a user root privileges to do absolutely anything when he connects from localhost. (Connecting from localhost means that he is physically at the server console, or is logged in to that machine via Telnet or SSH.) Yet when the same root user connects from another machine, say in the company.com domain, you might let him do nothing more than perform SELECT queries.

As another example, if a user tom connects from his private machine tomsmachine.shop.com, you can allow him access to his toms_db database, to create, alter, and drop tables as well as to run normal database queries. However, when connecting from anywhere else, you might limit his access to the database toms_db to perform only SELECT, INSERT, UPDATE, and DELETE queries. This improves security by conferring less power when the user is connecting from a less trusted location.

Many scenarios like this are possible under the MySQL privilege system. It will help your security setup if you have a clear understanding of how it works, so we'll try to explain it step-by-step.

Five special tables in the mysql database control user privileges. They're called *grant tables* and are named as follows:

- user
- db
- host
- tables_priv
- columns_priv

We'll go through what each table does in a moment, but for now you just need to know that in rough terms, each one has a finer level of control than the one preceding it.

Each grant table has *scope fields* and *privilege fields*. The entries in the scope fields determine the scope of each entry (when to apply them), whereas the privilege fields determine what operations may be performed by the user.

Note   If you're using MySQL 4 or later, you will find an additional table in the mysql database called func. This is not really a grant table but is used for enabling user-definable functions (UDFs). For more about UDFs, see Day 21, "Extending MySQL's Function Library."

The user Table

The user grant table contains all users who may connect to a MySQL server. It stores their usernames, their passwords, and the host machines from which they can connect. You may have several entries for the same user, specifying different hosts and potentially different privileges as consequence.

Table 14.1 lists the scope fields and the most important privilege fields in the user table.

TABLE 14.1 The user Table

Scope Fields	Privilege Fields
Host	Select_priv
User	Insert_priv
password	Update_priv
	Delete_priv
	Create_priv
	Drop_priv
	Reload_priv
	Shutdown_priv
	Process_priv
	File_priv
	Grant_priv
	References_priv
	Index_priv
	Alter_priv
	Show_db_priv
	Super_priv
	Create_tmp_table_priv
	Lock_tables_priv
	Execute_priv
	Repl_slave_priv
	Repl_client_priv

The scope fields in the user table work like this:

- Host contains the hostname from which a user can connect, such as localhost for the server itself, or % for "any host." See later in this section for more examples.

14

- User contains the MySQL username.
- Password contains the encrypted version of that user's password.

Host can take a number of different forms, especially when the % wildcard character is used. Here are some examples of things that Host can contain:

- A fully qualified domain name such as office.tribalinternet.com, or 192.168.1.20 for the IP address of a specific machine
- A host name with a wildcard, such as '%.tribalinternet.com' for any host in the given domain (always use single or double quotation marks when including the % wildcard or other special characters such as -)
- An IP address with a wildcard, such as '123.231.1.%' for any host within the given IP address range
- '%' to mean any host at all

It is important to remember that there may be several entries for any given user (that is, several rows in the user table), with different values for Host (and perhaps with different passwords). The username, host, and password that are offered at connection time are compared with entries in the table, and if a match is found, the connection is allowed. That entry's privilege fields are then used to determine what the user is allowed to do. If no match is found for the three values, the connection is refused.

The privilege fields with names such as Select_priv correspond with SQL statements (such as SELECT) and administrative actions (such as shutting down the server) that the user may or may not do. Each one contains a Y if the operation is permitted, or N if not.

See Table 14.2 for an explanation of the main privileges.

TABLE 14.2   The Main Privileges Allowed from the user Table

Privilege	What the User Is Allowed to Do
Select_priv	Perform SELECT queries
Insert_priv	Perform INSERT queries
Update_priv	Perform UPDATE queries
Delete_priv	Perform DELETE queries
Create_priv	Create databases or tables
Drop_priv	Drop databases or tables
Reload_priv	Reload the grant tables, flush logs, and caches
Shutdown_priv	Shut down the MySQL server
Process_priv	View the MySQL processes running and also kill these processes
File_priv	Read and write files that reside on the server (not just MySQL's data files)

TABLE 14.2 continued

Privilege	What the User Is Allowed to Do
Grant_priv	Grant privileges to other users
References_priv	Not currently used
Index_priv	Create and drop indexes on tables
Alter_priv	Change a table definition using ALTER TABLE (excluding the creation and dropping of indexes)
Show_db_priv	Perform SHOW DATABASES queries (MySQL 4.0.2 onward)
Super_priv	Kill MySQL processes (MySQL 4.0.2 onward)
Create_tmp_table_priv	Create temporary tables (MySQL 4.0.2 onward)
Lock_tables_priv	Lock tables (MySQL 4.0.2 onward)
Execute_priv	Run stored procedures (for MySQL 5)
Repl_slave_priv	Be a replication slave (ability to read from replication master) (MySQL 4.0.2 onward)
Repl_client_priv	View where slaves and masters are (MySQL 4.0.2 onward)

Note

In MySQL version 4.0.2 and later, you will also find the following fields:

- max_questions
- max_updates
- max_connections
- ssl_type
- ssl_cipher
- x509_issuer
- x509_subject

The fields beginning with max are additional privilege fields. They can be used for setting a maximum number of queries, updates, and connections per hour. These fields take integer values instead of being either Y or N, and default to 0. If set to any value other than 0, they place a restriction—a quota per hour—on the rate at which a user can utilize the MySQL server. In this lesson, you'll concentrate on understanding the main privilege fields, so we won't cover the max fields in detail.

The ssl and x509 fields are additional scope fields. If completed, they require a user to authenticate to MySQL using a secure connection. You will learn about this later today.

If you are migrating from an earlier version of MySQL, you will need to run the script mysql_fix_privilege_tables. You'll see how to do this too, later in this lesson.

14

The privileges in Table 14.2 range from the fairly innocuous to the very dangerous! Allowing a user to perform SELECT queries is relatively harmless, whereas being able to add or modify data, add indexes, and alter or drop tables are progressively more serious affairs. The ability to create and drop entire databases is still more heavyweight.

The entries in Table 14.2 from Select_priv down to Drop_priv, as well as Index_priv and Alter_priv, represent the database-related operations, listed in approximate order of seriousness. Privileges such as Reload_priv, Shutdown_priv, Process_priv, and Grant_priv are administrative and are global powers across the database server.

Grant_priv must be used sparingly: it gives one user the ability to increase the permissions of another user. File_priv also must be issued with great care because it means that a MySQL user can read or write to any Linux or Windows file to which the mysql user (the user under which the MySQL daemon runs) has access. The administrative privileges from Grant_priv downward are seldom issued to any user other than the MySQL superuser—that is, root.

The user table is powerful: Any privileges granted to a user in this table allow him to exercise that privilege on all databases and all tables on the server.

So how can you control access at a finer level?

Most ordinary users in the user grant table are listed there for only one purpose: to connect. The privileges of most users are actually turned off (to N) in the user table, but turned on elsewhere at more specific levels. That's where the db and host tables come in.

Tip

If you're upgrading your database from version 3.x to version 4.x, you may find that non-root users cannot do a CREATE TEMPORARY TABLE or cannot perform a LOCK TABLE.

Because Create_tmp_table_priv, Lock_tables_priv, and other privileges have been added to the user grant table in MySQL 4.0.2, you will need to set these entries to Y to allow users to exercise this privilege.

Caution

Think of the user table as the master privilege table. If you grant a privilege to a user in this table, say, Delete_priv, he will be able to delete rows from any table in any database on the server.

You should therefore keep all privilege fields set to N unless you're creating a superuser who will have powers extending across all databases.

The db and host Tables

The db and host tables are used together to work out what privileges a user has at a database-specific level. Just like the user table, db and host have scope fields and privilege fields.

Table 14.3 shows the db table's fields. Its scope fields contain entries for host, database, and username, determining who can access what from where.

TABLE 14.3   The db Table

Scope Fields	Privilege Fields
Host	Select_priv
Db	Insert_priv
User	Update_priv
	Delete_priv
	Create_priv
	Drop_priv
	Grant_priv
	References_priv
	Index_priv
	Alter_priv

Let's look at how db works by example. You might have an entry in db with the values localhost, tonys_db, and tony in the respective scope fields. This entry defines the privileges for user tony on the database tonys_db when he's connecting from localhost.

You may prefer to place a % in the Host entry, which means that tony can connect to the tonys_db database from any host. In other words he can connect from anywhere, but his privileges on that database are the same.

If you don't have an entry at all for a given user in db, that user will have access to all databases on the server. This may sound worrying, but remember that as long as a user's privileges are turned off in the user table, the user will be denied global privileges wherever there's an N in the user table privilege.

Now let's look at the host table. The host table is a way of fine-tuning the entries in the db table. Although a wildcard entry of % in the Host field of db means "any host," you can have a blank entry, which means "consult the host table."

14

Entries in the host table will then determine the privileges on that database granted to that user when connecting from each given host.

Table 14.4 lists the fields of the host table.

TABLE 14.4   The host Table

Scope Fields	Privilege Fields
Host	Select_priv
Db	Insert_priv
	Update_priv
	Delete_priv
	Create_priv
	Drop_priv
	Grant_priv
	References_priv
	Index_priv
	Alter_priv

As you can see, the scope fields specify the host and database. When a match is found for the database requested and the host from which the request is made, the privileges emerge from the privilege fields.

So if you want a user to be able to access a given database from several hosts, you would put a single entry in the db table, specifying Db and User but leaving Host blank. The blank entry would tell MySQL to consult the host table and look for an entry that matches the user's host against the value for Host, and the requested database against the value for Db.

In summary, you can use the db table to grant a user privileges on a given database. You can use the host table in conjunction with it to make the privileges different according to specific hosts that he may connect from.

The tables_priv and columns_priv Tables

The final two tables of the privilege system, tables_priv and columns_priv, work in much the same way as the db table. They allow you to control access at finer levels of granularity, down to individual tables and, optionally, to columns within those tables.

Table 14.5 shows the fields in the table tables_priv. It has scope fields that are the same as those in the db table, but with the addition of a Table_name field.

TABLE 14.5 The `tables_priv` Table

Scope Fields	Privilege Fields	Informational Fields
Host	Table_priv	Timestamp
Db	Column_priv	Grantor
User		
Table_name		

The `columns_priv` table, shown in Table 14.6, has scope fields that are again the same as the db table, but with the addition of both `Table_name` and `Column_name` fields.

TABLE 14.6 The `columns_priv` Table

Scope Fields	Privilege Fields	Informational Fields
Host	Column_priv	Timestamp
Db		
User		
Table_name		
Column_name		

When matching the user parameters against the scope fields in the tables, a comparison is now done not just for host, database, and username but also for the table requested and possibly for the column referenced in the user's query.

In both tables, the privilege fields works a little differently from the previous grant tables we have seen. Instead of containing `Y` or `N`, each entry contains a number of possible values. (In fact, they are a `SET` column type, as described in Day 5, "MySQL Data Types.")

In the `tables_priv` table, the `Table_priv` field can be any number of the following: `Select`, `Insert`, `Update`, `Delete`, `Create`, `Drop`, `Grant`, `References`, `Alter`, and `Index`.

The `Column_priv` field of both tables can be any number of the following: `Select`, `Insert`, `Update`, and `References`.

In summary, these two tables work just like the db table, but they set privileges according to the table and column referenced in a query.

How the Grant Tables Work Together

You won't be alone if you're wondering what takes precedence over what. How does everything fit together?

To understand how the various grant tables work together, you need to understand the process MySQL goes through when considering a request.

14

MySQL first checks whether the user is allowed to connect to the server at all. If so, it goes on to look at the nature of the request he's making (such as a SELECT query, a DELETE, or a database shutdown) and uses the grant tables to work out whether he's allowed to perform that request.

It works like this:

1. A user tries to connect to the MySQL server. The user table is consulted, and on the basis of his username, password, and the host from which he's connecting, the connection may be either refused or accepted. (MySQL actually sorts the table and looks for the first match; we'll look at what implications this has in a moment.)

2. If the connection is accepted, any privilege fields in the user table that are set to Y will allow the user to perform that action on any database in the server. For administrative actions (for example, shutdown, reload), the entry in the user table is deemed absolute, and no further grant tables need be consulted.

3. Where the user makes a database-related request and the user table does not allow him to perform it (the privilege is set to N), MySQL consults the db table.

4. The db table is consulted to see whether there's an entry for the user, database, and host. If there's a match, the db privilege fields determine whether the user can perform his request.

5. If there's a match on the db table's Db and User fields but Host is blank, the host table is consulted to see whether there's a match on all three fields. If there is, the privilege fields in the host table will determine whether the user can perform his request. Corresponding entries in the db and host tables must both be Y for the request to be granted (thus an N in either table will block the request).

6. If the user's request is not granted, MySQL checks the tables_priv and columns_priv tables. It looks for a match of the user, host, database, and table to which the request is made (and the column, if there's an entry in columns_priv). It adds any privileges it finds in these tables to the privileges already granted. With the sum of these privileges, it decides whether the request can be granted.

Phew! That may sound like a long list of decisions, but in many cases the decision is made by just the user and db tables. Most sysadmins seldom use the tables_priv and columns_priv tables.

Note   MySQL reads the contents of the user, db, and host grant tables into memory when it starts up. If you make modifications to the entries in these tables directly, you will need to ensure that the grant tables are reloaded.

The following command run from Linux or Windows accomplishes this:

```
# mysqladmin reload
```

Sorting of Entries in the Grant Tables

As just mentioned, some sorting occurs in the grant tables. This takes place with the user, db, and host tables when they are read, at startup or at reload time.

When MySQL reads any of these (sorted) tables, it finds the first matching entry and acts on that. It's worth spending a moment to understand the implications of this.

The user table is sorted on Host and then on User. So you may have a user table that looks like this:

```
mysql> SELECT Host,User FROM user;
+---------------------+-------+
| Host                | User  |
+---------------------+-------+
| %.anotherdomain.com | tonyb |
| %.somedomain.com    | tonyb |
| host.somedomain.com |       |
| linux               |       |
| localhost           |       |
| localhost           | root  |
+---------------------+-------+
6 rows in set (0.00 sec)
```

As you can see, names preceded with a wildcard % appear first, with more specific Host names later. When a user attempts a connection, MySQL looks through the entries in order until a match is found.

As soon as a match is found, that entry will be read, and its privileges will define what requests may be performed. MySQL looks no further. The first match is used, even though more than one valid match may be in the table.

In the preceding example, if user tonyb is connecting from somedomain.com, he will get the privileges prescribed by the user table entry

```
| %.somedomain.com    | tonyb |
```

rather than the line

```
| host.somedomain.com |       |
```

This is often the source of some confusion among sysadmins. To make life simpler, you may want to delete all entries from the user table that have no User value:

```
DELETE FROM user WHERE User=''
```

14

Managing User Privileges with GRANT and REVOKE

You've seen how the grant tables work together, in some detail. Although it's possible to create, delete, and modify users by making changes to these tables directly (and prior to version 3.22.11 of MySQL, this was the only way), MySQL now has the GRANT and REVOKE commands, which make user management much easier.

Granting Privileges with GRANT

The GRANT statement has the following syntax:

```
GRANT privileges [(column_list)]
  ON database_name.table_name
  TO username@hostname [IDENTIFIED BY 'password']
  [REQUIRE [SSL | X509]
    [CIPHER cipher [AND]]
    [ISSUER issuer [AND]]
    [SUBJECT subject]]
  [WITH GRANT OPTION |
    MAX_QUERIES_PER_HOUR num |
    MAX_UPDATES_PER_HOUR num |
    MAX_CONNECTIONS_PER_HOUR num ]
```

GRANT has enough options to make it look more intimidating than it really is. For a start, look at it again without the REQUIRE part, which is used only for encrypted connections to MySQL and for limiting the hourly usage:

```
GRANT privileges [(column_list)]
  ON database_name.table_name
  TO username@hostname [IDENTIFIED BY 'password']
  [WITH GRANT OPTION]
```

Let's look at what each part means.

privileges means which privileges you want to assign to the user. They can be taken from the list shown in Table 14.7. Notice that some are new to MySQL 4 (actually 4.0.2) and some are reserved for MySQL and other future use.

TABLE 14.7 Privileges

Value for privilege	Operation Permitted
ALL or ALL PRIVILEGES	All privileges (but not Grant_priv).
ALTER	Change a table definition using ALTER TABLE (excluding the creation and dropping of indexes).
CREATE	Create databases or tables.
CREATE TEMPORARY TABLES	Create temporary tables (MySQL 4).

TABLE 14.7   continued

Value for privilege	Operation Permitted
DELETE	Perform DELETE queries.
DROP	Drop databases or tables.
EXECUTE	Run stored procedures (MySQL 5)
FILE	Read and write files that reside on the MySQL server.
INDEX	Create and drop indexes on tables.
INSERT	Perform INSERT queries.
LOCK TABLES	Lock tables (MySQL 4).
PROCESS	View the MySQL processes running.
REFERENCES	Not currently used.
RELOAD	Reload the grant tables, flush logs and caches.
REPLICATION CLIENT	View where slaves and masters are (MySQL 4).
REPLICATION SLAVE	Be a replication slave (ability to read from replication master) (MySQL 4).
SELECT	Perform SELECT queries.
SHOW DATABASES	Show all databases (MySQL 4).
SHUTDOWN	Shut down the MySQL server.
SUPER	Kill MySQL processes (MySQL 4).
UPDATE	Perform UPDATE queries.
USAGE	No privileges; user can only connect to the server.

You can use the ON *database_name.table_name* part to specify what the user has privileges on. You can write:

- ON *.* to specify all databases on the server
- ON *database_name.** to specify all tables in one database
- ON *database_name.table_name* to specify all columns of one table

username@hostname is the name and host of the user whose privileges you are setting. As you saw in the way MySQL reads the user table when calculating privileges, the hostname is always considered along with the username. However, you can be more or less specific, for example:

- tonyb@host.somedomain.co.uk means the user tonyb at a specific host.
- tonyb@"%host.somedomain.co.uk" means the user tonyb at any host within that domain (remember to specify quotes if you use the % wildcard or other special characters).

14

- `tonyb@"%"` means `tonyb` connecting from anywhere.
- `tonyb@localhost` means `tonyb` connecting from the server.

You can optionally specify `IDENTIFIED BY "password"`. This sets the password for that user/host combination. If that user and host already exist, it changes the password to that given.

Note GRANT encodes the password for you (don't try to use PASSWORD()). Also, if you don't use IDENTIFIED BY when creating a new user, an empty password will be entered into the user table, which means that user has no password. This is a security risk.

The clause `WITH GRANT OPTION` gives the user the ability to grant to other users any privileges he has himself. He can't grant a privilege that he doesn't already have, but two or more users with this ability could collaborate to enhance each other's privileges. This is a security risk; use this clause with caution.

Let's look at a few examples of using `GRANT`. The following allows the user `tonyb` to connect from any host in the domain `somedomain.co.uk` and perform `SELECT`, `INSERT`, `UPDATE`, and `DELETE` operations on the database `cms`:

```
GRANT SELECT,INSERT,UPDATE,DELETE ON cms.* TO tonyb@'%.somedomain.co.uk'
```

Remember, this leaves the entry without a password and is not secure!

You might grant the ability to modify the database `store` to an administrator, providing that he is logged in to `localhost`, this time more wisely specified with a password:

```
GRANT SELECT,INSERT,UPDATE,DELETE,INDEX,ALTER,CREATE,DROP,
  CREATE TEMPORARY TABLES,LOCK TABLES
  ON store.*
  TO admin@localhost IDENTIFIED BY "mysecret"
```

On a Web server with several Web sites, you might well allow Apache to access the database using a different username for each site that it serves. For example, for a Web site called `mysite`, we'll allow Apache access to this database, but not allow it to alter any tables:

```
GRANT SELECT,INSERT,UPDATE,DELETE,INDEX
  ON mysite.*
  TO mysite@localhost IDENTIFIED BY "web"
```

Notice how we restricted this user to connect from `localhost`, because that's where Apache connects from. If you did this in practice, you would put the `mysite` user's login details in your application (that is, into Perl or PHP) and keep them stored outside the Web directory.

Note

Unless a hostname is explicitly supplied, your Web server always connects to a MySQL server on the same machine as *username*@localhost. There's no need to make any Host entries except for the one with the Web server's username and localhost.

Keep privileges down to those that you want Web applications to be able to do. So you might not want CREATE and DROP, for example.

If you need to do database changes, do them in a more secure way, such as via the server console or through an SSH connection to the server.

It's also worth noting that if you use a Telnet or SSH connection to a server and connect to MySQL from there (through the mysql monitor), it will count as a connection from localhost. The Host field in the grant tables only refers to connections made from a host directly to the MySQL server.

You'll probably want to use this statement only for a single user on your machine:

```
GRANT ALL ON *.*
  TO root@localhost IDENTIFIED BY "rootpass"
  WITH GRANT OPTION
```

This is a typical grant setup but should be reserved for the MySQL superuser.

As you've seen, you can limit access to tables and columns. Here's an example of using GRANT to create a user called payroll who can view an employee's name and salary on an employee table, but not modify it:

```
GRANT SELECT(emp_id,name,salary)
  ON company.employee
  TO payroll@"%.company.com"
  IDENTIFIED BY "PayMaster321";
```

You may like to study the effect the preceding examples have on the user, db, host, tables_priv, and columns_priv tables.

Displaying Privileges with SHOW

You can use the SHOW SQL command to display privileges for a given user. You use it like this:

```
SHOW GRANTS FOR username@hostname
```

For example, to see what privileges the payroll user has:

```
mysql> SHOW GRANTS FOR payroll@"%.abc.com";
+-------------------------------------------------------------------------+
| Grants for payroll@%.abc.com                                            |
+-------------------------------------------------------------------------+
| GRANT USAGE ON *.* TO 'payroll'@'%.abc.com' IDENTIFIED BY PASSWORD '28dd6f3'|
| GRANT SELECT (emp_id, name, salary) ON abc.employee TO 'payroll'@'%.abc.com'|
+-------------------------------------------------------------------------+
```

14

Removing Privileges with REVOKE

To remove privileges from a user who already exists in the user table, you can use the REVOKE command:

```
GRANT privileges [(column_list)]
  ON database_name.table_name
  FROM username@hostname
```

For example, to revoke the privilege of payroll to see the employee's name, you could do this:

```
REVOKE SELECT (name)
  ON company.employee
  FROM payroll@"%.company.com"
```

To revoke all privileges from the user, you could do this:

```
REVOKE ALL
  ON company.employee
  FROM payroll@"%.company.com"
```

Caution

Using wildcards, such as in REVOKE ALL ON *.* FROM user, will not necessarily revoke all privileges where access has been granted to specific databases or tables. The simple solution is, after running REVOKE, you should always check the remaining grants using SHOW GRANTS as described previously.

Also note that revoking all privileges will not remove the user from the user grant table. The user will still be able to connect to the MySQL server, even if he has no privileges.

To completely remove a user, you will need to run a DELETE FROM user WHERE... to delete the user directly from the table and reload the grant tables for the change to take effect.

Keeping a MySQL Installation Secure

Running a MySQL database server can be a major responsibility. The greater the value of the information stored in its databases, and the greater the number of users of the system, the more emphasis you'll need to place on keeping the system secure. It can be serious, even disastrous, that the server can be shut down or its data modified by a malicious hacker. In some cases, it may be just as bad that a user can simply view data that's outside his privileges. Here are a few guidelines for good practice when securing a MySQL server.

- Always run the MySQL daemon under the user `mysql`, never as `root` or as `nobody` (as Apache does). If you run the daemon as `root`, any MySQL user who has `File_priv` privileges will be able to read and write to *any* file on the server. By running the daemon as `mysql`, even if an intruder gains access to the MySQL `root` account he won't automatically be able to break the operating system.

- Keep your operating system secure. Just because someone is a MySQL user doesn't mean that he should be allowed to log in to Linux or Windows. Making him an OS user means that he can read the machine's file system, so restrict him to MySQL access only.

- Check the permissions of the MySQL data directory, which (on Linux) should always be `drwx------`, with the owner being `mysql`. This prevents anyone other than the system user `mysql` (and `root`) from reading the directory's contents.

- Where possible, avoid using `%` in hostnames. Try to make hosts as specific as possible, and use an IP address rather than a domain name if you can.

- Avoid granting the administrative privileges, especially `File_priv` and `Grant_priv`, to anyone but `root`. Whenever logging in to the `mysql` monitor as the superuser, always use

```
# mysql -u root p
```

and never this (even though it's more convenient):

```
# mysql -u root ptopsecret
```

The latter can make the `root` password visible to Linux programs such as `ps`, and it stores the entire line, with password, in your command log file (`.bash_history` if you're using `bash`).

- You may have Linux users on the server who access databases. For convenience, they may safely place their password in a `.my.cnf` file in their home directory. This file contains their password plus other options. The password should be in the `[client]` section of the file, like this:

```
[client]
password      = mysecret
```

The permissions of the `.my.cnf` file should prevent it from being group- or world-readable, thus `-r--------` or `-rw-------` on Linux, and it should be owned by that user. (You'll learn more about the `.my.cnf` file in Day 15, "Administration.")

- When creating users, restrict them to a single database if you can, and even to individual tables or columns if practical. However, there will be a limit to this level of granularity: Many table and column privileges will eventually slow down access because they need to be interpreted for every request. Too many privileges can also become difficult to manage.

14

- Finally, never allow anyone other than the MySQL root user access (even read access) to the user grant table itself. If an entry can be read, and if a hacker can gain access to the host that is listed, he will be able to gain access as that user.

Making Secure Connections to MySQL

MySQL supports the use of SSL and the X509 standard, allowing you to make an encrypted connection to a MySQL server.

> **Note**
>
> SSL stands for Secure Sockets Layer and is a way of transmitting data across the Internet using an encryption protocol. Any system receiving data via an SSL connection immediately knows whether the data has been tampered with in transit, or whether the data is bona fide.
>
> X509 is a standard that enables a system to ascertain the identity of another system over the Internet with a good level of certainty.
>
> Combining SSL and X509 enables the setting up of ecommerce applications that have a high level of trust, so a system knows who it's talking to and can be sure that the data it's receiving is trustworthy.

By default, a connection to a MySQL server is unencrypted, meaning that data is transferred in plain text or binary, and theoretically someone can "sniff" packets of information passing between client and server across the public Internet. If a hacker can do this, he can also modify the data before sending it on, or send it on multiple times.

Using SSL, you can send data in a way that makes it practically unreadable to anyone other than the intended recipient. Any change in the data post-encryption, and the recipient will be aware that the data has been compromised since leaving the sender and cannot be trusted.

The recipient's public key is used by the sender to encrypt the data when it's sent, and the recipient has a private key that he uses to decrypt the message.

SSL encryption can optionally use an X509 Certificate, issued by a certificate authority. This is a trusted public body that ascertains a system owner's real identity before granting a certificate.

Any receiving machine will send an SSL public key to any host trying to send it encrypted data. The public key means "encrypt your data like this."

A host sending data must encrypt the data using the public key, but the data is safe from prying eyes on the Internet because it can be decrypted only by using the SSL private key, which is kept secret and in a secure place on the receiving system.

In MySQL, you declare that a user must connect using SSL and/or X509 by using a REQUIRE clause in the GRANT statement. This defines whether that user and host combination must connect using just SSL, and whether that user must hold an X509 Certificate. It may specify the Certificate Issuer, the Certificate "Subject," or that a specific cipher method has to be used when connecting.

To use SSL and X509 on MySQL, you must first prepare your server for it.

Preparing Your Server for Secure Connections

To use secure connections, you will need to do the following:

1. Install the openssl library.
2. Reconfigure and recompile MySQL with openssl.
3. Ensure that the user grant table is updated to the new format with extra fields for encryption requirements.

If you're ready to do these things, let's go through it step-by-step.

Installing MySQL with openssl

You can download openssl, the SSL library that MySQL requires, from http://www.openssl.org/. At the time of writing, the latest version is 0.9.6g.

Locate and download the file openssl-0.9.6g.tar.gz, become root using su, and move the file to wherever you like to keep your source files, such as /usr/src or /usr/local/src. Unzip and extract the archive using tar.

You should read the instructions in INSTALL, but in essence, configure using the directory locations shown (MySQL likes these) and run make:

```
# ./config --prefix=/usr/local --openssldir=/usr/local/openssl
```

```
# make
```

```
# make test
```

```
# make install
```

If everything goes well, openssl should be installed on your machine. Now change to the MySQL source directory and configure with the options --with-vio and --with-openssl. For example:

```
# ./configure \
# --prefix=/usr/local/mysql \
# --enable-assembler \
# --with-mysqld \
# --with-ldflags=-all-static \
# --with-vio \
# --with-openssl
```

14

This compilation should work on most Unix systems, but if not, you will need to read the MySQL and OpenSSL documentation and possibly related Web sites. Compilation problems usually arise when libraries are located in different places from where the compiler expects.

You can refresh your memory on the `configure` command by referring to Day 2, "Installing MySQL." Now run `make`:

```
# make
```

If compilation goes without error, shut down your MySQL server. Then install the new binary as follows:

```
# make install
```

Updating the Grant Tables to the New Format

Now you'll need to update the `user` grant table to the new format that allows for encryption fields. If your MySQL version is currently 3.x, your user table may look similar to this (in the `mysql` monitor):

```
mysql> DESC user;
+-----------------+-----------------+------+-----+---------+-------+
| Field           | Type            | Null | Key | Default | Extra |
+-----------------+-----------------+------+-----+---------+-------+
| Host            | char(60) binary |      | PRI |         |       |
| User            | char(16) binary |      | PRI |         |       |
| Password        | char(16) binary |      |     |         |       |
| Select_priv     | enum('N','Y')   |      |     | N       |       |
| Insert_priv     | enum('N','Y')   |      |     | N       |       |
| Update_priv     | enum('N','Y')   |      |     | N       |       |
| Delete_priv     | enum('N','Y')   |      |     | N       |       |
| Create_priv     | enum('N','Y')   |      |     | N       |       |
| Drop_priv       | enum('N','Y')   |      |     | N       |       |
| Reload_priv     | enum('N','Y')   |      |     | N       |       |
| Shutdown_priv   | enum('N','Y')   |      |     | N       |       |
| Process_priv    | enum('N','Y')   |      |     | N       |       |
| File_priv       | enum('N','Y')   |      |     | N       |       |
| Grant_priv      | enum('N','Y')   |      |     | N       |       |
| References_priv | enum('N','Y')   |      |     | N       |       |
| Index_priv      | enum('N','Y')   |      |     | N       |       |
| Alter_priv      | enum('N','Y')   |      |     | N       |       |
+-----------------+-----------------+------+-----+---------+-------+
17 rows in set (0.00 sec)
```

If so, you'll need to run a script called `mysql_fix_privilege_tables` to change the tables to the required format. (If you installed from source, it will be in your `scripts` directory, or the `bin` directory if you installed the binary.)

Run it like this (with the response shown):

```
# ./scripts/mysql_fix_privilege_tables rootpass
```

```
This scripts updates the mysql.user, mysql.db, mysql.host and the
mysql.func table to MySQL 3.22.14 and above.

This is needed if you want to use the new GRANT functions,
CREATE AGGREAGATE FUNCTION or want to use the more secure passwords in 3.23

If you get Access denied errors, you should run this script again
and give the MySQL root user password as a argument!
Converting all privilege tables to MyISAM format

If your tables are already up to date or partially up to date you will
get some warnings about 'Duplicated column name'. You can safely ignore these!

...
```

There will probably be a lot more output, but you can ignore any Duplicate column name errors.

Now go back into the mysql console and look at the effect on your mysql.user table:

```
mysql> DESC user;
```

Field	Type	Null	Key	Default	Extr
Host	varchar(60) binary		PRI		
User	varchar(16) binary		PRI		
password	varchar(16)				
Select_priv	enum('N','Y')			N	
Insert_priv	enum('N','Y')			N	
Update_priv	enum('N','Y')			N	
Delete_priv	enum('N','Y')			N	
Create_priv	enum('N','Y')			N	
Drop_priv	enum('N','Y')			N	
Reload_priv	enum('N','Y')			N	
Shutdown_priv	enum('N','Y')			N	
Process_priv	enum('N','Y')			N	
File_priv	enum('N','Y')			N	
Grant_priv	enum('N','Y')			N	
References_priv	enum('N','Y')			N	
Index_priv	enum('N','Y')			N	
Alter_priv	enum('N','Y')			N	
Show_db_priv	enum('N','Y')			N	
Super_priv	enum('N','Y')			N	
Create_tmp_table_priv	enum('N','Y')			N	
Lock_tables_priv	enum('N','Y')			N	
Execute_priv	enum('N','Y')			N	
Repl_slave_priv	enum('N','Y')			N	
Repl_client_priv	enum('N','Y')			N	

14

```
|ssl_type         |enum('','ANY','X509','SPECIFIED')|   |   |       |   |
|ssl_cipher       |blob                             |   |   |       |   |
|x509_issuer      |blob                             |   |   |       |   |
|x509_subject     |blob                             |   |   |       |   |
|max_questions    |int(11) unsigned                 |   |   |0      |   |
|max_updates      |int(11) unsigned                 |   |   |0      |   |
|max_connections  |int(11) unsigned                 |   |   |0      |   |
+-----------------+---------------------------------+---+---+-------+---+
31 rows in set (0.00 sec)
```

Your server should now be ready to accept secure connections. To test this, do the following:

```
mysql> SHOW VARIABLES LIKE '%openssl%';
+---------------+-------+
| Variable_name | Value |
+---------------+-------+
| have_openssl  | YES   |
+---------------+-------+
```

If the Value shows YES, MySQL is prepared. If it's NO, go back and check that you followed every step of the procedure. Failure to convert the grant tables, or even to link the openssl library properly can prevent it from succeeding.

Setting Up SSL/X509 Users

Turn your attention now to the REQUIRE clause of the GRANT statement, including the three lines that follow REQUIRE:

```
GRANT privileges [(column_list)]
  ON database_name.table_name
  TO username@hostname [IDENTIFIED BY 'password']
  [REQUIRE [SSL | X509]
    [CIPHER cipher [AND]]
    [ISSUER issuer [AND]]
    [SUBJECT subject]]
```

For SSL connections without an X509 Certificate, you just need to specify the user with

```
REQUIRE SSL
```

So for example:

```
GRANT ALL ON *.*
  TO root@localhost IDENTIFIED BY "rootpass"
  REQUIRE SSL
```

You can specify X509 instead, requiring a valid certificate, but with no particular requirements placed on the certificate, like this:

```
GRANT ALL ON *.*
  TO root@localhost IDENTIFIED BY "rootpass"
  REQUIRE X509
```

If you want to require the certificate to be from a particular authority, for it to have a specific subject, or for a particular cipher method to be used (avoiding older ciphers whose codes are considered crackable these days), you can do this using the keywords given in the preceding syntax. Use the keyword AND to enforce multiple conditions.

The SSL Client

After you set a user grant table entry to require an encrypted connection from a given user and host, the client making that connection must connect in the way specified, or the connection will fail.

Depending on what kind of client you are using, this will be implemented in various ways. But let's look at building an example program using the C API.

You may recall our small C client program from Day 13, "Using the C API." We used it to connect to the MySQL server, taking the username from the identity of the logged-in Linux user and requesting his password from the console when the program was run.

main.c was the connection script, which used mysql_real_connect() to make the database connection using a number of parameters including username, password, hostname, and so on. At the time, for simplicity, we left the last argument in the list, *db_flags*, at 0.

We can use *db_flags* to indicate that an SSL connection is to be made. You simply have to set its value to CLIENT_SSL.

To implement this, add this line to your main.c listing, in the section that defines constants:

```
#define def_db_flags    CLIENT_SSL
```

Also modify the connection routine in main.c to look like this:

```
mysql = db_connect (
          def_db_host,
          def_db_user,
          db_pass,
          def_db_name,
          def_db_port,
          def_unix_socket,
          def_db_flags);
```

The last line contains def_db_flags where it used to be 0. It is now effectively CLIENT SSL.

Make these changes to your main.c and recompile using make. Your client will now use SSL for all its connections to MySQL.

14

Although the example here is simple, it shows you the basics of running MySQL with applications using secure connections. For a database containing information that must be well protected, this may be the only viable way to allow access to it from across the public Internet.

Summary

Today you learned about security on a MySQL server. You learned the principles of the user privilege system and saw that you can use it to not only authenticate users with their passwords but also to base the level of privilege on the host from which the user is connecting. On the basis of these three parameters, privileges can be granted globally, or for a specific database, table, or columns. This allows you to set up some users with wide-ranging privileges, and others with their privileges limited to a database or part of it.

You learned how to use the GRANT, REVOKE, and SHOW GRANTS commands to manage user privileges. Finally, you saw how to use MySQL to make secure connections.

Q&A

Q Are GRANT and REVOKE the only ways of managing user privileges?

A No, there are other ways, and prior to MySQL 3.22.11, these commands weren't even implemented.

You can modify user privileges by editing the grant tables directly. For example, you would create a new user in the user table like this:

```
INSERT INTO user SET Host="localhost",
  User="someuser",
  Password=PASSWORD("somepass"),
  Select_priv="Y"
  Insert_priv="Y"
```

For database-specific privileges (which you ought normally to be doing), you would also insert an entry into db, and there may well be entries into host, tables_priv, and even columns_priv.

Although there's no technical difference in the outcome, these commands can be lengthy and prone to minor errors. GRANT and REVOKE make life a little easier.

Q The privilege system seems complex. I just want to set up a user for simple learning purposes.

A It's a good idea to learn the privilege system at some point. But for simple purposes (such as a system that's not going to be used in production), you can make the following simplifications:

- At its simplest, just create a `root` user who can do everything (for example, `GRANT ALL ON *.* TO root@localhost`), but remember this is not secure for anything but an offline system.

- Set up users on a by-database basis, and don't worry about tables and columns privileges.

- If you're happy for users to authenticate by password only and you don't care about their host, just put `%` as the host (for example, `GRANT USAGE ON database.* TO user@"%"`).

Q **I'm typing this but get an error:**

```
mysql> SHOW GRANTS FOR user@%;
ERROR 1064: You have an error in your SQL syntax near '%' at line 1
```

What am I doing wrong?

A The `%` wildcard counts as a special character, so you must enclose any strings containing it in single or double quotes. Thus you should do the following:

```
mysql> SHOW GRANTS FOR user@"%";
```

Q **If I type this:**

```
mysql> SHOW GRANTS FOR payroll@"%";
```

will it show me all grants for the `payroll` user, with all of that user's possible host locations?

A No. It shows only entries for the user `payroll@"%"`, not for the user `payroll@"%.company.com"`, which is a different entry in the user grant table. Because they have different *username@hostname* combinations, MySQL treats them as different accounts.

To find all grants for that user (no matter what host), you would have to query the tables directly, for example:

```
mysql> SELECT * FROM mysql.user WHERE User='payroll';
```

Q **There's a lot about setting up secure connections on MySQL, but not much about how to make the client secure. Where can I learn more?**

A In today's lesson, we concentrated on how to set up SSL and, briefly, X509 on a MySQL server. You saw how our simple client written in C (from Day 13) can be modified to make a secure connection. Study Day 13, "Using the C API," for more information on this program. If you have a prior knowledge of C, that lesson and today's lesson should now enable you to build database clients with secure connections.

14

Many good books about encryption and SSL in general are available, and a quick search on the Internet will uncover many more resources.

It's beyond the scope of this book to create more sophisticated clients (using X509, certificates, and so on). Study your development environment (for example, Perl, Visual Basic, or whatever) to learn how to implement secure connections in them.

Workshop

The quiz and exercises are provided to help you solidify your understanding of the material covered today. Try to understand the quiz and exercise answers before continuing to tomorrow's lesson.

Quiz

Consider the following GRANT statement, and use it to answer Quiz questions 1–4:

```
GRANT ALL
  ON mydb.*
  TO admin@localhost
```

1. What is not secure about the privileges set by this statement? Specify one way in which it's not secure.

2. Would the user admin be able to grant privileges to other users?

3. Would the user admin be able to drop the mydb database?

4. Would admin be able to connect from a host in the company.com domain?

Consider the following GRANT statement, and use it to answer Quiz questions 5–6:

```
GRANT ALL
  ON *.*
  TO admin@localhost
  IDENTIFIED BY "sk2934jkh"
```

5. What is the biggest security risk to your system now?

6. What can admin@localhost do to the mydb database?

Quiz Answers

1. The user has no password set, so anyone at localhost will be able to log in as admin without a password.

2. No. Although ALL is specified, this does not include Grant_priv, which would have to be specified by appending WITH GRANT OPTION to the statement.

3. Yes.

4. No.

5. When logged in at `localhost`, `admin` will have `File_priv`, so it can access any file on the operating system to which the `mysql` system user has access.

6. This user can do everything to the `mydb` database, including dropping it.

Exercises

1. Write a `GRANT` statement to create a user `yvonne` who can only log on from a host in the `company.com` domain. You want the user to have access to the `shop` database, and to be able to do all kinds of database viewing and modification, including creating and dropping tables, but not creating and dropping the database. Remember to set a password, `ypass`.

2. Write a `GRANT` statement to create a user `john` who can log on from only one specific host in the `company.com` domain, called `jmachine`. You want the user to have access to the `shop` database, and to be able view all database tables, but not to make any modifications. Remember to set `john` a password, `johnspass`.

Answers to Exercises

1. Your code should look something like this:

```
GRANT ALL ON shop.* TO yvonne@"%.company.com" IDENTIFIED BY 'ypass'
```

2. Your code should look something like this:

```
GRANT SELECT ON shop.* TO john@jmachine.company.com

  IDENTIFIED BY 'johnspass'
```

or you may use the optional quotes:

```
GRANT SELECT ON shop.* TO "john"@"jmachine.company.com"
  IDENTIFIED BY 'johnspass'
```

14

WEEK 3

At a Glance

DAY **15**

Administration

Today's lesson will look at how to administer a MySQL database. It will touch on a number of things, some of which you will study in more detail in later chapters.

Today you will look closely at `mysqladmin`, the principal tool for administering MySQL. You will be introduced to `mysqldump` and `mysqlhotcopy`, and briefly meet programs such as `myisamchk`. However, some of these deal with repair and maintenance and other topics, and so will be dealt with more thoroughly in other lessons.

Particular topics you will study today are

- The tools for administering MySQL
- Looking at the status of a MySQL server
- Setting MySQL server variables using `my.cnf`
- The structure of MySQL's data directory
- Backing up and relocating a database

Managing a Database with `mysqladmin`

The `mysqladmin` utility can be used to perform a wide range of administrative operations on a MySQL database. It is usually run from a command-line prompt.

When invoked, you should pass `mysqladmin` a number of options and commands to tell it how to run, and what to do.

How to Use `mysqladmin`

The following is the basic syntax for `mysqladmin`:

```
mysqladmin [options] cmd1 [cmd1_opts] cmd2 [cmd2_opts] ...
```

Remember that you may need to prefix `mysqladmin` with the path to your `mysql/bin/` directory where it resides. This will be true for the other utilities as well.

Here are a couple of sample invocations:

```
$ mysqladmin -u root -p create newdb
```

```
$ /usr/local/mysql/bin/mysqladmin -u root -p variables
```

The first of the preceding examples creates a new database (`newdb`), whereas the second displays `mysqld`'s variables.

> **Note**
>
> Using `mysqladmin` to administer your MySQL server is really just a convenient way of running the equivalent command in SQL. For example, the preceding commands are identical to the following commands in SQL:
>
> `mysql> CREATE DATABASE newdb;`
>
> `mysql> SHOW VARIABLES;`
>
> Furthermore, the username you supply to `mysqladmin` must have sufficient privilege to perform whichever command you are asking for.

As you can see from its syntax, you may pass `mysqladmin` a number of *options*: Often these include `-u` *username* (if your MySQL username is not the same as your Unix username), `-p` to indicate that you will supply a password, and sometimes `-h` *hostname* to indicate a different host. (But note that there are potentially more options than I'm showing you here.)

You should recall from Day 6, "Manipulating a Database," the various ways you can pass usernames and passwords to the `mysql` program (using `-u`, `-p`, and so on). The same principles apply when invoking `mysqladmin` and the other programs introduced today.

After the *options*, you can issue one or more commands (shown previously as *cmd1*, *cmd2*, and so on), each possibly with its own options.

Table 15.1 lists the various commands you can pass to `mysqladmin`.

TABLE 15.1 Commands That Can Be Passed to `mysqladmin`

Command	Meaning
create database_name	Create a database with the name specified
drop database_name	Drop (delete) a database with the name specified
extended-status	Give a detailed message about the status of the MySQL server
flush-hosts	Flush all cached hosts
flush-logs	Flush all logs
flush-tables	Flush all tables to disk
flush-privileges	Reload the grant tables
kill thread1, thread2, ...	Kill the given MySQL threads (threads numbered as displayed with processlist, not Unix threads)
password new_password	Change the user's password to new_password
ping	Check whether mysqld is running
processlist	Display a list of active threads on the server
reload	Make MySQL reload its grant tables
refresh	Make MySQL flush all grant tables and log files
shutdown	Shuts down mysqld
slave-start	Begin replication as a slave
slave-stop	Stop replication as a slave
status	Give a brief message about the status of the MySQL server
variables	Display a list of MySQL's current server variables
version	Display server version information

The meanings of most of `mysqladmin`'s commands should be clear from Table 15.1, but some require a little more explanation. We'll go through the more advanced ones in the following sections.

Thread Information

The `mysqladmin processlist` command displays information about threads currently executing on the MySQL server.

Here's an example interaction, running as `root`:

```
# mysqladmin -p processlist
Enter password:
+----+------+-----------+---------+---------+------+-------+------------------+
| Id | User | Host      | db      | Command | Time | State | Info             |
+----+------+-----------+---------+---------+------+-------+------------------+
| 12 | tony | localhost | product | Sleep   | 5    |       |                  |
| 20 | root | localhost |         | Query   | 0    |       | show processlist |
+----+------+-----------+---------+---------+------+-------+------------------+
```

The first line of the preceding output indicates that a thread with `Id` `12` is being run by user `tony` connected to the server from `localhost`. He has selected the database `product`.

The `Command` column tells you what's going on: `Sleep` in this column indicates that this thread is currently idle. He has connected but is not currently running a query. The `Time` column shows the time the thread has been connected, in the case of `tony`, `5` seconds.

The second line shows `root`'s own thread. Its `Command` is given as `Query` because it is doing a `SHOW PROCESSLIST` query. It's the `mysqladmin processlist` command itself.

It's unusual to see much more than your own `processlist` thread and perhaps some other threads in the state of `Sleep`. In theory, you can see queries running, and if so the SQL appears in the `Info` column. But unless queries take a significant time to run, they're unlikely to be running at the precise time `mysqladmin` generates the list.

You may see threads running more complex (and hence slower) queries, or a thread that is waiting for another thread that has locked a table it needs. For example

```
# mysqladmin -p processlist
+----+------+-----------+---------+---------+------+--------+------------------+
| Id | User | Host      | db      | Command | Time | State  | Info             |
+----+------+-----------+---------+---------+------+--------+------------------+
| 12 | tony | localhost | product | Sleep   | 5    |        |                  |
| 19 | bob  | localhost | product | Query   | 2    | Locked | SELECT * FROM tbl |
| 20 | root | localhost |         | Query   | 0    |        | show processlist |
+----+------+-----------+---------+---------+------+--------+------------------+
```

In this example, thread 12 (`tony`) has locked some tables, and thread 19 (`bob`) is trying to run a `SELECT` query on table `tbl`:

```
SELECT * FROM tbl
```

But `bob` has to wait until `tony` has finished and unlocked the table `tbl`.

But suppose that thread 12 is taking too long (perhaps the application has a bug and has gone into an infinite loop). How can you get rid of thread 12?

Should you want to terminate a thread, you can issue a `kill` command like this for `root` to kill the thread owned by `tony`:

```
# mysqladmin -p kill 12
```

Server Status Information

The `mysqladmin status` command displays summary information about the state of the MySQL server.

Its output looks like this:

```
Uptime: 69192  Threads: 1  Questions: 34381  Slow queries: 0  Opens: 230
Flush tables: 1  Open tables: 46  Queries per second avg: 0.497
```

These numbers are mostly statistics of things that have happened since `mysqld` was last started, or about the current status. In the order as shown previously, they show

- `Uptime`—`mysqld`'s uptime in seconds
- `Threads`—The number of connections currently open (including the `mysqladmin` command itself)
- `Questions`—The number of queries that have been run since `mysqld` was started
- `Slow queries`—The number of "slow" queries (taking longer than a specified time, the default being 10 seconds)
- `Opens`—The number of tables that have been opened
- `Flush tables`—The number of times that the `flush`, `refresh`, and `reload` commands have been run
- `Open tables`—The number of tables currently open
- `Queries per second avg`—The average number of queries per second since `mysqld` was started

Extended Server Status Information

To get more detailed information about the current state of `mysqld` and what it has been doing since it was last started, use

```
mysqladmin -p extended-status
```

This is the same as the following SQL:

```
mysql> SHOW STATUS;
```

The output contains around 100 pieces of information about precisely what's going on inside the server.

Table 15.2 lists the variables returned and explains their meanings. Nearly all variables are numbers. For the most part, these reflect the total number of times an event has occurred since `mysqld` came up, whereas a few of them express the current state.

TABLE 15.2   Interpreting Data from `mysqladmin extended-status`

Name	Meaning
Aborted_clients	Number of aborted connections.
Aborted_connects	Number of failed attempts to connect to `mysqld`.
Bytes_received	Number of bytes received by `mysqld` from all clients.
Bytes_sent	Number of bytes sent to all clients from mysqld.
Com_command	Number of times each command has been executed.
Connections	Number of connections made (successful or otherwise) to `mysqld`.
Created_tmp_disk_tables	Number of temporary tables created implicitly on disk to execute queries.
Created_tmp_tables	Number of temporary tables created implicitly in memory to execute queries.
Created_tmp_files	Number of temporary files created by `mysqld`.
Delayed_insert_threads	Current number of delayed insert handler threads.
Delayed_writes	Number of rows written using INSERT DELAYED.
Delayed_errors	Number of rows written using INSERT DELAYED in which an error occurred.
Flush_commands	Number of FLUSH commands that have been executed.
Handler_commit	Number of internal COMMIT commands that have been executed.
Handler_delete	Number of rows deleted from any table.
Handler_read_first	Number of requests to read the first entry of an index.
Handler_read_key	Number of requests to read a row based on an index.
Handler_read_next	Number of requests to read the next row based on an index.
Handler_read_prev	Number of requests to read the previous row based on an index.
Handler_read_rnd	Number of requests to read a row based on the row's position.
Handler_read_rnd_next	Number of requests to read the next row in the datafile.
Handler_rollback	Number of internal ROLLBACK commands.
Handler_update	Number of requests to update a row in a table.
Handler_write	Number of requests to insert a row into a table.
Key_blocks_used	Number of blocks used in the index (key) cache.
Key_read_requests	Number of requests to read a block from the index cache.
Key_reads	Number of physical reads of an index block from disk.

TABLE 15.2 continued

Name	Meaning
Key_write_requests	Number of requests to write a block to the index cache.
Key_writes	Number of physical writes of an index block to disk.
Max_used_connections	Maximum number of connections that have been open simultaneously.
Not_flushed_key_blocks	Current number of blocks in the index cache that have been modified but not yet saved (flushed) to disk.
Not_flushed_delayed_rows	Current number of rows in INSERT DELAYED queues that are waiting to be written.
Open_tables	Current number of open tables.
Open_files	Current number of open files.
Open_streams	Current number of open streams (applies to log files only).
Opened_tables	Number of tables that have been opened.
Select_full_join	Number of joins made without keys. (If this is 0, you should carefully check the index of your tables.)
Select_full_range_join	Number of joins where a range search was used on a reference table.
Select_range	Number of joins where a range was used on the first table.
Select_scan	Number of joins where a full scan was performed on the first table.
Select_range_check	Number of joins without keys where key usage is checked after each row.
Questions	Number of queries sent to the server.
Slave_open_temp_tables	Number of temporary tables currently open by the slave thread.
Slave_running	ON or OFF according to whether this server is a slave.
Slow_launch_threads	Number of threads that have taken more than server variable slow_launch_time to create.
Slow_queries	Number of queries that have taken more than server variable long_query_time.
Sort_merge_passes	Number of merge passes required for sorts.
Sort_range	Number of sorts performed with range arguments.
Sort_rows	Number of rows that have been sorted.
Sort_scan	Number of sorts performed by scanning the table.
Table_locks_immediate	Number of occurrences of a table lock being acquired immediately.
Table_locks_waited	Number of occurrences of a table lock not being acquired immediately.

TABLE 15.2   continued

Name	Meaning
Threads_cached	Number of threads stored in the thread cache.
Threads_connected	Current number of connections open.
Threads_created	Number of threads created to handle connections.
Threads_running	Current number of active threads (that is, not in a state of Sleep).
Uptime	How long mysqld has been up, in seconds.

Status information like that returned from mysqladmin extended-status can have a number of uses. You may want to see certain "health check" information (such as the maximum number of concurrent connections that have been occurring), or you might want to improve the speed with which MySQL runs.

Here are some telltale signs that MySQL is running inefficiently. Use them as pointers for improving your SQL, improving your table designs, or tuning MySQL's server variables:

- Aborted_clients and Aborted_connects—These can be an indication of someone trying to hack your server.

- Handler_read_rnd and Handler_read_rnd_next—If these are high, your queries are doing many table scans, suggesting that your queries are not making use of table indexes, or that more table indexes are required. See the EXPLAIN command in Day 18, "Optimizing Performance."

- Handler_read_key—If this is high, it shows that indexes are being well used.

- Key_reads—If this is big, it's because indexes are being repeatedly read from disk, where they should be held in memory. Consider increasing the server variable key_buffer_size to store more indexes in RAM.

- Slow_queries—If there are several of these, several queries are taking a long time to run. Study the slow log, as explained previously in this lesson.

- Table_locks_waited—If this is high compared to Table_locks_immediate, performance will suffer because threads are having to wait before attaining a lock. You may need to design your table structure or optimize queries.

- Opened_tables—If this is big, tables are having to be opened more than they should. Look at the server variable table_cache and consider increasing it so that more tables can be held open at once.

> **Tip**
>
> If you want `mysqladmin` to execute repeatedly, give it an option of `-i` or `--sleep`, plus your desired interval in seconds between executions, like this:
>
> ```
> $ mysqladmin -u root -p --sleep=1 processlist status
> ```
>
> or the equivalent in shortened form:
>
> ```
> $ mysqladmin -u root -p -i 1 processlist status
> ```
>
> These commands make `mysqladmin` display both its thread list and summary status information, repeating once per second until cancelled with a Ctrl-C.
>
> To make `mysqladmin` display extended status data with *relative* values (that is, the change since last time), type
>
> ```
> $ mysqladmin -u root -p -i 60 -r extended-status
> ```
>
> This runs `mysqladmin` once every 60 seconds and displays the change in values so that you can see on a live basis how the server is behaving.
>
> For a full list of `mysqladmin`'s options, just type
>
> ```
> $ mysqladmin
> ```

MySQL's Server Variables

As well as status information (what's happening and what has happened), you can use `mysqladmin` to display the MySQL server variables—the settings with which `mysqld` is running.

You can use `mysqladmin` to display a list of these variables like this:

```
# mysqladmin -p variables
```

Performance can be influenced by adjusting MySQL's server variables. For example, you can "tune" MySQL to make better use of the system's resources by adjusting its use of memory and disk.

Try running `mysqladmin variables` and have a look at the output. It's beyond the scope of this book to explain the meaning of all of these variables. However, some critical ones can be used for optimizing MySQL. These key variables, their meanings, and implications are explained in Day 18.

Setting Variables for MySQL

Without being set explicitly, the variables for the MySQL server and other MySQL programs will be at their default values. However, for various reasons, you may want to adjust these from the default: to improve performance, to turn on or off things, or simply to make programs run more conveniently.

The easiest way to set variables is by using a my.cnf file (or for Windows, it may be my.cnf or my.ini).

The my.cnf or my.ini file may contain several sections' worth of variables: usually a section for mysqld itself; and optionally sections for other programs, such as mysql, mysqldump, and myisamchk. Here's a short extract of one, including sections for client and mysqld:

```
# Settings for all MySQL clients:
[client]
port            = 3306
socket          = /tmp/mysql.sock

# Settings for MySQL server:
[mysqld]
port            = 3306
socket          = /tmp/mysql.sock
```

As well as a my.cnf file, which is global, on Unix you can also create a .my.cnf file to set variables specific to an individual user.

On Unix, my.cnf resides in /etc. If you want to set user-specific options, the .my.cnf file should be placed in that user's home directory.

On Windows, all options are set in a single file. If the machine boots from drive C:, you should call the file my.cnf and place it in C:\. However, if the system does not boot from C:, your file must be called my.ini, and it must be placed in the Windows WINDIR directory. You may need to run a DOS SET command to display the value of WINDIR, which is probably something like C:\WINDOWS. Do *not* create both my.cnf and my.ini.

If you don't already have my.cnf set up, look in your MySQL distribution for a support-files subdirectory. There you will find some sample my.cnf files, with names like my-small.cnf and my-huge.cnf. These are get-you-started configurations for various sizes of machines, according to the amount of RAM you have.

Have a look at these configuration files and find the one best suited to your server. Then copy the file to the location where MySQL can read it as described previously.

To do this, first change to the MySQL source directory (if you installed from source) or the binary installation directory (if you installed the binary), for example:

```
# cd mysql-4.0.2-alpha
```

Then choose which my.cnf file to use; for example, on a system with 1GB of RAM, copy my-huge.cnf:

```
# cp support-files/my-huge.cnf /etc/my.cnf
```

Then restart MySQL. Perform a shutdown with the following:

```
# mysqladmin -u root -p shutdown
```

Then start MySQL again, for example:

```
# /usr/local/mysql/bin/mysqld_safe &
```

(Remember that you will need to use safe_mysqld if you're using MySQL version 3.)

How does a my.cnf file work? It contains a list of settings, one per line. Here's an extract from the my.cnf file on my system:

```
# Settings for all MySQL clients:
[client]
#password        = your_password
port             = 3306
socket           = /tmp/mysql.sock

# Settings for MySQL server:
[mysqld]
port             = 3306
socket           = /tmp/mysql.sock
skip-locking
set-variable     = key_buffer=384M
set-variable     = max_allowed_packet=2M
set-variable     = table_cache=512
set-variable     = sort_buffer=2M
set-variable     = record_buffer=2M
...
log-bin
server-id        = 1
...
```

As you can see, there are lines containing names in square brackets, such as [mysqld]. This means that whatever follows refers to settings for mysqld.

The first section of the preceding file, [client], contains settings that declare things for all clients (such as for them to all use port 3306 and the socket file at /tmp/mysql.sock). The mysqld section declares the same port and socket. It sets several server variables (see the set-variable lines), turns on binary logging (log-bin), and declares the server-id to be 1.

You may also have a .my.cnf file in your home directory. This is something often done for convenience: You can use it to store your password in a private place and avoid having to type it each time you use one of MySQL's utilities. For example, here's the .my.cnf from my /home/tonyb directory:

```
[mysql]
password         = secret
```

The section under [mysql] declares my password for use with mysql, and this enables me to run mysql without a password. So I can just type

```
$ mysql
```

to access the mysql monitor program.

Tip

If you want, you can change the way the mysql prompt appears. For example, to remind you which database you're connected to, add the following line to your .my.cnf file in the section beneath [mysql]:

```
prompt          = [\d]>\_
```

You will then see the name of the database you're connected to whenever you interact with the mysql console:

```
$ mysql
Welcome to the MySQL monitor.  Commands end with ; or \g.
Your MySQL connection id is 6132 to server version: 4.0.2-
alpha-log

Type 'help;' or '\h' for help. Type '\c' to clear the buffer.

[(none)]> use store
Database changed
[store]>
```

Setting Variables at `mysqld` Startup Time

You can also change MySQL's system variables by declaring a variable when you invoke mysqld_safe. Just add -O (or --set-variable) and the variable setting.

For example, to start the server and set the server variable key_buffer to 16MB, you could invoke MySQL like this:

```
# /usr/local/mysql/bin/mysqld_safe -O key_buffer=16M
```

Remember that a variable set in this way will lose its value after the current mysqld_safe process terminates.

Other Administration Tools

`mysqladmin` is just one of a suite of administration tools distributed with MySQL. Here are some others that are included:

- `myisamchk`—A tool for checking and repairing a database. (See Day 16, "Repair and Maintenance," for more about this.)

- `myisampack`—A utility for compressing a database into a high-speed, read-only format. (See "Creating Fast, Compressed Tables Using `myisampack`" later in this lesson.)

- `mysqlbinlog`—A utility for displaying a MySQL binary update log. (See "Binary Update Logs" later in this lesson.)

- `mysqlbug`—Used for reporting bugs in MySQL. (It gathers information about your system and creates a template for submitting the bug report in a standard way.)

- `mysqlcheck`—A tool for checking and repairing `MyISAM` tables. (See Day 16 for more about this.)

- `mysqldump`—For dumping the structure of tables and their data. (See "Backing Up" later in this lesson.)

- `mysqldumpslow`—For dumping the contents of the slow log in a summarized format. (See "The Slow Log" later in this lesson.)

- `mysqlhotcopy`—A utility for quickly making a backup of a database while `mysqld` is running. (See "Backing Up with `mysqlhotcopy`" later in this lesson.)

- `mysqlimport`—A utility for importing data in CSV or other character-delimited format. (See Day 7, "Inserting and Updating Data," for more about this.)

- `mysqlshow`—For displaying information about a database or its tables. (For an example, see "Symbolic Linking," later in this lesson.)

As you can see from this list, there are many programs for a variety of purposes. It's not the intention to explain every one of them, although those for backing up a database will be explained later today. Many of the other tools are described elsewhere in this book, as noted in the preceding list.

Apart from the programs included with MySQL that are console-based, there is a whole range of other tools from third-party software authors. You will find programs designed for Windows or other desktop systems, such as `MysqlFront`, and others that are browser-based.

To recommend one single tool for all purposes, I would have to name `phpMyAdmin`. It is a browser-based tool written in PHP. It is highly versatile, allowing you to perform just about any administrative operation or query with just a couple of mouse clicks. The beauty of it is, you don't need to remember perfect SQL syntax! Although it doesn't let you perform table joins without typing some SQL, you can perform joins just like in any other SQL interpreter. No developer who writes database software for the Web should be without this versatile program.

You can get `phpMyAdmin` and other tools by visiting the Contributed Software section at `http://www.mysql.com/downloads/`.

The MySQL Data Directory

After you start administering MySQL in anything but the most simple way, it becomes important to understand the structure of the MySQL data directory.

If you installed from a source distribution, this will be called `var/` (such as `/usr/local/mysql/var/`), but if you installed a binary distribution, it will be called `data/` (such as `/usr/local/mysql/data/`). There's no difference between the two, just the name, which has stayed different for historical reasons.

What's in the data directory? Not surprisingly, there's data, but there's a lot more besides.

Here's a sample directory listing:

```
# ls -l
total 20888
-rw-rw----  1 mysql   mysql       25088 Aug 12 09:33 ib_arch_log_0000000000
-rw-rw----  1 mysql   mysql     5242880 Aug 24 14:00 ib_logfile0
-rw-rw----  1 mysql   mysql     5242880 Aug 12 09:33 ib_logfile1
-rw-rw----  1 mysql   mysql    10485760 Aug 24 14:00 ibdata1
-rw-rw----  1 mysql   mysql        5743 Aug 12 09:32 linux-bin.001
-rw-rw----  1 mysql   mysql         702 Aug 12 12:54 linux-bin.002
-rw-rw----  1 mysql   mysql          98 Aug 12 12:58 linux-bin.003
-rw-rw----  1 mysql   mysql         544 Aug 24 14:00 linux-bin.index
-rw-rw----  1 mysql   mysql         162 Aug 24 14:00 linux-slow.log
-rw-rw----  1 mysql   mysql          79 Aug 24 14:00 linux.001
-rw-r--r--  1 mysql   root        48234 Aug 24 14:00 linux.err
-rw-rw----  1 mysql   mysql         162 Aug 24 14:00 linux.log
-rw-rw----  1 mysql   mysql           5 Aug 24 14:00 linux.pid
drwx------  2 mysql   mysql        4096 Aug 20 21:24 mysql/
drwx------  2 mysql   mysql        4096 Aug 16 17:28 products/
drwx------  2 mysql   mysql        4096 Aug 12 09:32 test/
```

Let's go through these files and explain what each of them is.

InnoDB Files

The files with names beginning `ib` are used by the transaction-based `InnoDB` table handler for logging and keeping track of transactions. `InnoDB` tables are explained in more detail in Day 17.

Binary Update Logs

There are many files called

hostname-xxx

or

hostname.xxx

In this example, all such files have names beginning with `linux`, because `linux` is the hostname of the sample machine. On your system, this will be replaced with your machine's hostname.

The `linux-bin.00n` files are binary update logs. These files are produced because the line

```
log-bin
```

exists in the `my.cnf` file. The files themselves contain a binary representation of all data updates (any command that has modified data). The file `linux-bin.index` contains other information about this logging process.

You can display a binary update log in human-readable format using the `mysqlbinlog` utility, like this:

```
# mysqlbinlog linux-bin.001
```

The binary update log can be used as part of a backup strategy. It is also used for master-slave replication, which you will learn more about in Day 19, "Replication."

The Update Log

The file `linux.001` is an "old-fashioned" kind of update log. It contains all updates to the data in a textual format. Although it can be useful to turn on this log now and again so that you can get an idea what the server is doing, its use is otherwise limited.

The update log is less useful than the binary update log because it cannot be run against another database with a guarantee of the same result each time. For example, if an update contains `NOW()` or `RAND()`, the values will be computed differently each time the log is run. For this reason, this update log is more or less superceded by the binary update log.

The Slow Log

The file `linux-slow.log` contains a record of all slow queries that have been processed. By default a "slow" query is one that takes longer than 10 seconds to run. However, you can change this value from the default. Here are the lines from `my.cnf` that enable the slow log and declare that all queries taking more than 2 seconds should be logged:

```
log-slow
set-variable    = long_query_time=2
```

The slow log is useful when optimizing performance because it can help you spot queries that take a long time to run. You can get a summarized version of the slow log using `mysqldumpslow`, like this:

```
# mysqldumpslow linux-slow.log
```

However, the slow log's use is limited because it may ignore queries that are inefficient but executed frequently.

The Error Log

The file `linux.err` is the so-called error log. It contains a log of when `mysqld` was started and stopped, as well as details of any errors it encountered. If your server crashes, study the log for information about what happened.

The General Log

`linux.log` is the general log of just about everything that happens on your server. It logs when `mysqld` is started and stopped, and logs every query—both read queries and updates. To enable the general log, you just need the following line in `my.cnf`:

```
log
```

Because it logs so many things, the general log tends to get large quickly. It can be useful if you need to get a feel for what queries are being processed on the server, for optimizing slow queries, or for tracing problems. But leaving it enabled on a busy server could easily fill up your hard disk!

The Database Directories and Other Files

The file `linux.pid` contains the Unix process ID of the `mysqld` process.

After the numerous logs and other files described previously, you're probably pleased to finally see where the data is actually stored! `mysql/`, `test/`, and `products/` are the directories containing the actual databases with these respective names. Let's descend into the `mysql/` directory to look at how the `mysql` database is represented:

```
# cd mysql
linux:/usr/local/mysql/var/mysql # ls -l
total 116
-rw-rw----    1 mysql    mysql           0 Aug 12 09:50 columns_priv.MYD
-rw-rw----    1 mysql    mysql        1024 Aug 23 23:59 columns_priv.MYI
-rw-rw----    1 mysql    mysql        8778 Aug 12 09:50 columns_priv.frm
-rw-rw----    1 mysql    mysql         302 Aug 12 09:50 db.MYD
-rw-rw----    1 mysql    mysql        3072 Aug 23 23:59 db.MYI
-rw-rw----    1 mysql    mysql        8982 Aug 12 09:50 db.frm
-rw-rw----    1 mysql    mysql         975 Aug 16 17:25 func.MYD
-rw-rw----    1 mysql    mysql        2048 Aug 23 23:59 func.MYI
-rw-rw----    1 mysql    mysql        8641 Aug 12 09:50 func.frm
```

```
-rw-rw----   1 mysql    mysql            0 Aug 12 09:50 host.MYD
-rw-rw----   1 mysql    mysql         1024 Aug 23 23:59 host.MYI
-rw-rw----   1 mysql    mysql         8958 Aug 12 09:50 host.frm
-rw-rw----   1 mysql    mysql            0 Aug 12 09:50 tables_priv.MYD
-rw-rw----   1 mysql    mysql         1024 Aug 23 23:59 tables_priv.MYI
-rw-rw----   1 mysql    mysql         8877 Aug 12 09:50 tables_priv.frm
-rw-rw----   1 mysql    mysql           60 Aug 20 21:24 user.MYD
-rw-rw----   1 mysql    mysql         2048 Aug 23 23:59 user.MYI
-rw-rw----   1 mysql    mysql         9806 Aug 12 09:50 user.frm
```

Because the mysql database is common to all installations, your mysql/ directory should look similar to the preceding one. However, if you study a directory holding a different database (such as products/ in the previous listing), you should see the same pattern, of .MYD, .MYI, and .frm files.

.MYD files are MyISAM data files. These contain the actual data of the table whose name is given by the part of the name before the period (.)—for example, user.MYD holds data from the grant table mysql.user.

Files ending .MYI are MyISAM index files, and files ending with .frm are "format" files; they hold the table definition.

If your database uses different table types, such as merge, InnoDB, and ISAM tables, you will see different files here. These different table types are covered in Day 17.

Symbolic Linking

MySQL allows you to place a symbolic link to a database directory, meaning that you don't have to actually store those databases in MySQL's var/ (or data/) directory.

Why would you want to do this? If your database is growing to a size you had not anticipated, you may find it easier to add a second hard disk than move the database to a new machine.

To make a symbolic link to a database, shut down mysqld, move the database to a new location, add a symlink to the new location, and restart mysqld.

Here's an example of moving the products database to a new location (/var/newdisk):

```
# mysqladmin -p shutdown
Enter password:
020824 15:23:05  mysqld ended

[1]+  Done                    /usr/local/mysql/bin/mysqld_safe
# cd /usr/local/mysql/var
# mv products /var/newdisk
# ln -s /var/newdisk/products/ .
# /usr/local/mysql/bin/mysqld_safe &
[1] 28359
```

```
linux:/usr/local/mysql/var # Starting mysqld daemon with databases
 from /usr/local/mysql/var
# mysqlshow -p
Enter password:
+-----------+
| Databases |
+-----------+
| mysql     |
| products  |
| test      |
+-----------+
```

Don't forget to check that the symlink is working, either by using mysqlshow as used here, or by connecting to the symlinked database and verifying that things are still working properly.

Although it's possible to symbolically link whole databases in this way, it is not recommended that you do this for individual tables.

Backing Up

Backing up is a vital part of the administration of any database system. Reasons for creating a backup can range from fire and theft to accidental user corruption of data. But whatever the reason and the perceived risk, making a backup addresses a real business issue, and backups must be regarded as a core part of any IT strategy.

Just as important as the backing-up process is the intended method of restoring data. Any survival plan must have at its core the intended means of getting data back onto the system—or onto a new system—in an appropriate time scale. In these days of online databases, a downtime of just minutes can be a serious issue, so your plans must have system recovery as their key deliverable, not merely a library of historic backups that are locked so safely away that they're impossible to access!

MySQL includes several utilities for backing up and restoring data. The ones we will look at today are mysqldump and mysqlhotcopy. These produce a snapshot of whatever is in a database or table at the time they are run. However, you should not neglect other important methods.

Backing Up with mysqldump

mysqldump is a useful utility for dumping (that is, saving to a file) a MySQL database. It can be used both for backup or for saving a database so as to relocate it to another SQL database (not necessarily MySQL).

You can run mysqldump from a command line, or it can be invoked by a scheduler such as Unix's cron or the At program in Windows.

The syntax for `mysqldump` can be any one of the following forms, depending on whether you want to back up a single database (or some of its table), several named databases, or all databases:

```
mysqldump [options] database_name [tables]

mysqldump [options] --databases [options] database_name1 [database_name2 ...]

mysqldump [options] --all-databases [options]
```

The first case is probably the one most commonly used, and you must specify a database name. If you run the program without any options or tables specified, it dumps the entire database given by *database_name*.

What does `mysqldump`'s output look like? `mysqldump` creates a file full of CREATE and INSERT SQL statements. These can be used as instructions to re-create the table definitions and their component data.

Usually, you will want to store the output to a file. You should therefore invoke `mysqldump` like this:

```
mysqldump [options] database_name [tables] > filename.sql
```

This creates a file called *filename.sql* (in the current directory if its path is not specified), which contains the dump. (It's not essential to have .sql as its suffix, but you might find it convenient to do this, to remind you that it contains SQL.)

After you have the dump file, you can preserve it for backup purposes, or move it to its new destination if you are moving a database.

Table 15.3 shows the most useful options with which you can run `mysqldump`.

TABLE 15.3   Principal Options for `mysqldump`

mysqldump *option*	*Meaning*
-?, --help	Display the full list of options for `mysqldump`
--add-locks	Add the LOCK TABLE command before INSERT, and UNLOCK TABLES afterward. Speeds up import at the destination.
--add-drop-table	Precede each CREATE TABLE statement with a DROP TABLE statement. Ensures that no duplication occurs at the destination if tables already exist, and ensures that the table definition is updated.
-C, --compress	Compress data. Requires both databases to support compression.

TABLE 15.3 continued

mysqldump *option*	*Meaning*
-d, --no-data	Omit dumping data and dump only the CREATE TABLE definitions.
-e, -extended-insert	Use multiline INSERT syntax for more compact dumps and faster inserts.
-F, --flush-logs	Flush the MySQL server logs before starting the dump. This option can be useful for synchronizing full and incremental backups.
-f, --force	Ignore any SQL errors during the dump and continue.
--fields-terminated- by='*delimiter*'	Specify the delimiter to use as a separator after each field. Default is \t (tab). Used with --tab.
--fields-enclosed- by='*delimiter*'	Specify the delimiter to enclose each field. Used with --tab.
--fields-optionally- enclosed-by='*delimiter*'	Specify the delimiter to enclose each CHAR and VARCHAR field. Used with --tab.
--fields-escaped- by='*esc_char*'	Specify the escape character to place before any special character. Default is '\\' (amounting to one backslash). Used with --tab.
-h=*hostname*, --host=*hostname*	Specify a database on a host other than localhost to perform the dump.
-K, --disable-keys	Put DISABLE KEYS and ENABLE KEYS statements around the data for each table. This disables indexes while the data is being imported, making for a faster import. Will be ignored where the target database is not MySQL 4.x or later.
-l, --lock-tables	Lock all tables before beginning the dump. If you have complex updates occurring on your system, this ensures that you get a consistent dump.
--lines-terminated- by='*delimiter*'	Specify the delimiter to use as a separator after each line. Default is '\n' (newline). Used with --tab.
--opt	Same as --add-locks --add-drop-table --extended-insert --quick --disable-keys. The most convenient way to get a fast dump.
-p[*password*], password[=*password*]	Specify a password when connecting to MySQL. Note the absence of a space after -p. Better to avoid typing the password here; you will be prompted for it separately.
-q, --quick	Dump the result directly to stdout instead of buffering in memory. This prevents memory getting filled up if your database is large or memory is short.

TABLE 15.3   continued

mysqldump *option*	*Meaning*
-t, --no-create-info	Omit CREATE TABLE statements, thus dumping only the data.
--tab=/*path*/*to*/*dir*, -T=/*path*/*to*/*dir*	Save the dump in files in the directory /*path*/*to*/*dir*. Each table is dumped in a file called *table_name*.sql and contains the CREATE TABLE statements, and a file called *table_name*.txt containing the data.
	The data format will be tab-separated by default; otherwise, as given by the --fields-terminated-by, --fields--enclosed-by, and similar options.
	Can only be run on the same machine as the target mysqld, and the mysql user must have write permissions in /*path*/*to*/*dir*.
	See also the LOAD DATA INFILE command in Day 7, "Inserting and Updating Data," for a more detailed explanation of the delimiters that can be used.
-u *username*, --user=*username*	Specify a username when connecting to MySQL. Default is Unix username.
-w='*condition*', --where='*condition*' --xml	Dump only rows meeting the WHERE condition. Create XML format in the dump.

You can get an exhaustive list of mysqldump's options by running

```
# mysqldump --help
```

Here's an example of running a dump from a database named photo:

```
$ mysqldump -p --opt photo > /home/tonyb/photo.sql
Enter password:
```

It runs with a connection to MySQL that is the same as my Unix username because -u is not given. The -p option indicates that I want to be prompted for my password. It creates a file of SQL in /home/tonyb.

--opt as used here is probably the option you will use most often. It is the same as adding the options:

```
--add-drop-table --extended-insert --quick --add-locks --disable-keys
```

It causes mysqldump to use minimal memory while dumping. mysqldump produces compact output, and because the dump contains commands for locking tables and temporarily disabling indexes (keys), the import process should be as fast as possible.

Here's a sample file produced in this way, for a database called store:

```
$ mysqldump -p --opt store
Enter password:

-- MySQL dump 9.06
--
-- Host: localhost    Database: store
--------------------------------------------------------
-- Server version       4.0.2-alpha-log


--
-- Table structure for table 'products'
--

DROP TABLE IF EXISTS products;
CREATE TABLE products (
  name varchar(20) default NULL,
  value int(11) default NULL
) TYPE=MyISAM;


--
-- Dumping data for table 'products'
--

/*!40000 ALTER TABLE products DISABLE KEYS */;
LOCK TABLES products WRITE;
INSERT INTO products VALUES ('sweater',13) ,('jeans',120) ,('socks',10);
UNLOCK TABLES;
/*!40000 ALTER TABLE products ENABLE KEYS */;
```

The pattern /*!40000...*/ tells the destination server to process this enclosed statement only if it's MySQL version 4.0.0 or later.

You can use such a file for populating another database (in this case again store) by typing this on the destination server:

```
$ mysql store < store.sql
```

As an alternative to a single file of SQL, you may want to save your database as separate files, with files of SQL table definitions and character-delimited files of data. You might type the following:

```
# mysqldump --tab=/home/tonyb store
```

For each table in the store database, two files are now produced. For example, the products table will have a products.sql file for the table definition, and a products.txt file for its contents. The same will be true for each other table.

The .txt data files in this example will be tab-delimited because no additional delimiter options were given. However, you could use commas or other characters to delimit the fields, and \n (newline) or other characters to mark the end of each record.

15

You can import this character-delimited file into just about any SQL or table-based system (even spreadsheets or word processors), or of course you can get it back into a MySQL database using `mysqlimport`, as described in Day 7.

Backing Up with `mysqlhotcopy`

`mysqldump` is a Perl utility that allows you to rapidly make a backup of a database while `mysqld` is running. It may be useful to use this on a busy server where you cannot stop the database but need a full, consistent backup.

Because it flushes tables to disk and locks them, it ensures that the data is consistent across tables; and because it copies the files from the data directory, it's very fast.

You would use it with the following syntax:

```
mysqlhotcopy [options] database_name /path/to/destination/directory
```

As with `mysqldump`, options can include `-p` and `-u` for username and password, respectively.

Because `mysqlhotcopy` is written in Perl, you will need to have DBD/DBI installed. See Day 12, "Using the Perl DBI," if you don't already have this installed.

Other Backup and Relocation Methods

Using `mysqldump` is an easy way of getting a complete snapshot of your database. However, transferring the entire thing off to a backup system on a regular basis—daily, or even more often—means a lot of repetitive data transfer.

Using the binary update log can help you keep a record of all changes that have been applied to a database. If you save this log on a regular basis (and preferably copy it to a remote machine), then if disaster strikes you should be able to apply the changes in the log to the last full copy of the database. It goes without saying that you must take a complete snapshot of your database from time to time and that you must keep all the update files; any gaps in the update record will lead to data corruption. But by backing up the update log, you reduce the amount of data that regularly transfers from your server.

Apart from using a utility such as `mysqldump`, it's also possible for you to simply copy the files from the MySQL data directory. There's no reason not to do this, but you must make sure that you lock tables, flush tables to disk, perform the copy, and then unlock table again afterward. (Failing to do this can result in your dump not having a consistent set of data.) This is effectively what `mysqlhotcopy` does.

Another alternative is to use the MySQL SQL commands BACKUP TABLE and RESTORE TABLE. The syntax of these commands is given in Appendix C, "Function and Operator Reference."

Finally, an important technique to consider, which is a little different from a static backup, is replication. This is a system whereby your system continually replicates its database updates to other machines, thus maintaining any number of identical copies. This technique is described in Day 19, "Replication."

Tip

> If you simply want to relocate a database—that is, take a copy of a database from the source host and load it into a MySQL database at another location—you can do it with just a single-line command.
>
> First, create the database at the destination with the name you'll want to use. Then create a user there that can connect to MySQL and perform inserts from the source host.
>
> Then on the source machine, issue your command like this:
>
> `mysqldump --opt database_name | mysql --host=destination-host database_name`
>
> This performs a `mysqldump` on the source machine, and invokes `mysql` in batch mode to connect to the destination machine, piping the SQL from the dump into it. With a single command, you have copied your database to another server.

Creating Fast, Compressed Tables with `myisampack`

By now you'll be familiar with the MyISAM table type. MySQL has the facility for creating compressed, faster versions of MyISAM tables using a utility called `myisampack`.

`myisampack` creates tables that are around 50% smaller in disk size than normal MyISAM tables. They are therefore faster to access because disk seek time is reduced. You can use `myisampack` as part of an optimization strategy for your database.

The main limitation of packed MyISAM tables is that they are read-only. They really are only useful in situations where you have a large table containing information that doesn't change.

For example, you may have a table called `cities` that holds data about cities around the world. The following sample listing from a MySQL data directory is taken from a real-world system:

```
# ls -l cities*
-rw-rw----   1 mysql    mysql      896068 Sep  8 14:12 cities.MYD
-rw-rw----   1 mysql    mysql      702464 Oct  7 14:06 cities.MYI
-rw-rw----   1 mysql    mysql        8820 Sep  8 14:11 cities.frm
```

The syntax for running `myisampack` is as follows, if run within the data directory of the relevant database:

```
myisampack [options] table_name
```

The *options* are not essential and won't be covered here. However, you must specify a *table_name* of which there exists a `.MYI` file for that table.

Here is `myisampack` being run on the table `cities`:

```
# myisampack cities
Compressing cities.MYD: (24610 records)
- Calculating statistics
- Compressing file
55.62%
Remember to run myisamchk -rq on compressed tables
```

After it has been run, you must re-create the table's indexes. You should use the `myisamchk` utility (which you will see in more detail in Day 16, "Repair and Maintenance"):

```
# myisamchk -rq cities
- check key delete-chain
- check record delete-chain
- recovering (with sort) MyISAM-table 'cities'
Data records: 24610
- Fixing index 1
- Fixing index 2
```

Now the table has been compressed, and its indexes have been rebuilt:

```
# ls -l cities*
-rw-rw----  1 mysql    mysql       397689 Sep  8 14:12 cities.MYD
-rw-rw----  1 mysql    mysql       622592 Oct 14 20:39 cities.MYI
-rw-rw----  1 mysql    mysql         8820 Sep  8 14:11 cities.frm
```

As you can see, the `citied.MYD` file, which contains the data, has been reduced considerably (from 896068 to 397689 bytes).

Tip

> When compressed, tables packed with `myisampack` cannot be updated.
> Should you ever need to change them back to a `MyISAM` format, simply cre-
> ate a new table using syntax like this:
>
> `INSERT INTO new_table SELECT * FROM compressed_table`

For more detailed information about `myisampack` and the options that can be passed to it, see the MySQL Technical Reference. For more about optimizing performance, see Day 18 in this book.

Summary

Today's lesson covered a lot of ground in the diverse topic of administration. Some parts were elementary and showed you commands that you'll use often, whereas other parts were more advanced.

You studied the all-important `mysqladmin` command in detail. It enables you to do just about anything, from creating a database to studying the performance of your MySQL server.

You looked at the use of `my.cnf` and `my.ini`, the primary way of setting MySQL's server variables.

You also were introduced to a range of the other utilities included with MySQL. These perform a variety of tasks, including displaying logs, importing, and dumping data. Many of these are covered in more detail in other lessons.

Also covered today were the `mysqldump` and `mysqlhotcopy` utilities for making backups of databases, either for safe-keeping or relocation.

Finally, you looked at the structure of the MySQL data directory. You should now be able to look at your own server's directory and pick out the various kinds of logs, as well as the files containing table definitions, data, and indexes.

Q&A

Q I just want to do a simple backup of all my databases for safe-keeping. How should I do it?

A Use the following command:

```
mysqldump -u myusername -p --opt --all-databases > /path/to/myfile.sql
```

This creates a compact and fast backup of all the databases on your MySQL server. The file at `/path/to/myfile.sql` contains SQL for table creation and inserting data. You should save `myfile.sql` to a secure location.

Q How do I restore from this file?

A At a Unix command prompt, change (`cd`) to the directory where you stored `myfile.sql`, and type the following:

```
/path/to/mysql -u myusername -p < myfile.sql
```

When you run this on the destination machine, it creates each database (if it doesn't already exist) and then creates each table with the backed-up data.

Q How much do I need to know about `mysqladmin`?

A `mysqladmin` has many options that can be passed to it. This makes it versatile but sometimes daunting. Probably the first one you will use is `mysqladmin shutdown`, for shutting down your server.

It's worth studying the various options to see what is possible; then try each one to see how it works.

`mysqladmin` is particularly valuable when your server starts to get busy and you need to see clearly what's happening on it. You'll want to look at the threads running (`mysqladmin processlist`), the status of `mysqld` (`mysqlamin status`), and possibly the extended status and variables (`mysqlamin extended-status` and `mysqlamin variables`).

Nearly all of `mysqladmin`'s commands have a SQL equivalent.

Workshop

The quiz and exercises are provided to help you solidify your understanding of the material covered today. Try to understand the quiz and exercise answers before continuing to tomorrow's lesson.

Quiz

1. True or False: `mysqldump` can only create output as SQL.

2. True or False: You cannot insert data into a table that has been compressed with `myisampack`.

3. True or False: Once you set a password for a MySQL user account, it's impossible for that user to connect to MySQL without typing a password (using one of the client utilities).

Quiz Answer

1. False. `mysqldump --tab` creates a file of SQL for table creation and a text file of character-delimited data.

2. True. Tables compressed with `myisampack` are read-only.

3. False. You can place the user's password in a `my.cnf` or `my.ini` file under the section relevant for the client program.

Exercises

1. Write a `mysqldump` command that dumps a database called `photo` but saves only the structure of the database, not its data. It should save the dump to a file called `photo-structure.sql`.

2. Write a `mysqladmin` command that displays basic status information about your server.

3. Write a `mysqladmin` command that displays extended status information about your server and the list of threads, repeating once every 10 seconds.

Answers to Exercises

1. You should have this:

   ```
   mysqldump --no-data photo > photo-structure.sql
   ```

   or

   ```
   mysqldump -d > photo-structure.sql
   ```

2. You should have this:

   ```
   mysqladmin status
   ```

3. You should have this:

   ```
   mysqladmin -i 10 extended-status processlist
   ```

   Stop the process with Ctrl-C.

DAY **16**

Repair and Maintenance

In yesterday's lesson on database administration, you saw how to back up and restore a database. Conducting a regular backup is a good strategy for avoiding disaster, and running MySQL with a binary update log is another because it captures changes to your data that occur between the backups. If the worst happens to your data, you can resort to your backups to re-create your data.

But in the case of table corruption, you shouldn't have to resort to a backup. In most cases, it's possible to repair a database with the tools that MySQL provides, particularly myisamchk.

Today you will learn:

- How to check a database for problems
- How to repair tables that have become corrupted
- How to optimize tables for performance
- How to use the myisamchk utility for the preceding tasks, and the SQL commands CHECK TABLE, REPAIR TABLE, and OPTIMIZE TABLE

Checking and Fixing a Corrupted Database

Tables can become corrupted for a number of reasons. For example, your server might experience a power outage while a write operation is being performed, or `mysqld` might be killed at a critical time like this, leaving data incomplete on the disk. More rarely but still possible, you might hit a software bug in MySQL, your operating system, or encounter a hardware problem.

The first sign of a problem will probably be an error message when you try to run a query (such as `Got error num from table handler`). Alternatively, you might be running a `SELECT` query on a table and retrieve fewer rows than you think it should have.

Before doing anything, remember the immortal words: *don't panic*. Many MySQL users have been there before and have had their data recovered successfully! You'll see how to do this in a moment, but take care to study this lesson in its entirety before diving in to fix problems on a production system.

File Structure: A Quick Recap

You should recall from yesterday's lesson that a `MyISAM` table called *table_name* is comprised of the following files:

- *table_name*`.frm` for the table definition (the `CREATE TABLE` statement)
- *table_name*`.MYD` for the data
- *table_name*`.MYI` for the indexes

The files sit in the MySQL data directory (in this book we've assumed `/usr/local/mysql`) under

`var/`*database_name*`/`

or

`data/`*database_name*`/`

(where the choice of `var/` or `data/` depends on whether you installed MySQL from source or binary).

In practice, the vast majority of database corruptions occur in the index file—the `.MYI` file—of a table. This is because indexes are most often changed in general use.

The `.frm` table definition file is the most seldom corrupted because it usually gets written to only at table creation time.

An Overview of Checking, Repair, and Optimization Methods

The principal tool for MyISAM tables is myisamchk. This is a command-line utility that you run from the console using a number of options that tell it how to run.

To perform any of these tasks, you will need to have read and write access to the files in the data directory. The best way to do this is as the operating system root user.

16

Note

> If you are using ISAM-type tables in a database (the predecessor to MyISAM tables), you need to use isamchk instead. It has identical usage and options. If you're using this lesson as a guide to isamchk, you should be able to take the myisamchk instructions and apply them to isamchk.

Beside the command-line utilities, there is a SQL-based method for doing the identical things (in fact a little more), using the CHECK TABLE and REPAIR TABLE commands. They contain a few minor options that are new to MySQL version 4 and are available only through the SQL commands.

How to Use myisamchk

myisamchk has many modes in which it can be used. The following is its basic syntax:

```
myisamchk [options] table_name [table_name2 ...]
```

Or you can use wildcard characters on the names of the directories and files:

```
myisamchk [options] /path/to/mysql/data/*/*.MYI
```

Using the first syntax, you can run myisamchk on a single table, whereas the second syntax pattern enables you to run it on several tables at once, including across several databases.

You can run it with or without a number of *options*, whose meanings you will see in a moment.

To use the first syntax given previously—where you refer to a table by *table_name*—you must be in the data directory of the MySQL database you're working on. If you're not, myisamchk won't know where your database resides or even which table or database you're referring to. For example:

```
# cd /usr/local/mysql/var/store
# myisamchk products
```

runs myisamchk on the table products in the database store.

But using the second syntax, with wildcard characters, you can invoke `myisamchk` like this:

`myisamchk [options] /path/to/data/directory/*.ISM`

Here is a sample usage:

 # myisamchk -r -q /usr/local/mysql/var/*/*.MYI

This runs `myisamchk` with options `-r` and `-q` on all `.MYI` (index) files in all databases on the server.

For now, you should hold back from trying out `myisamchk`: it's better for you to first understand the scope and meaning of the various options.

Table 16.1 lists the various options you may pass to `myisamchk`. You will see from the table that the options fall into several categories: checking, repair, optimization, and general modifiers.

TABLE 16.1 Options That Can Be Passed to `myisamchk`

Option	Type	Meaning
-?, --help	general	Show a full list of `myisamchk` options.
-a, --analyze	optimization	Analyze the distribution of values in indexes. Can be useful to speed up some join queries.
-c, --check	check	Default if no other options given. Check table for errors.
-C, --check-only- changed	check	Check tables for errors if they have changed since the last check. See also -U.
-d, --description	general	Display descriptive information about the state of the table.
-e, --extend-check	check, repair	Perform an extended check. During data file recovery, try to repair every row. It can take time to run and return a lot of deleted rows, so try other options first.
-f, --force	check, repair	If checking, start a repair with -r if errors found. If repairing, overwrite temporary files.

TABLE 16.1 continued

Option	Type	Meaning
-F, --fast	check	Only check tables that have not been properly closed.
-i, --information	check	Display statistical information about the table.
-k=*num*, --keys-used=*num*	optimization	Disable all indexes except *num*, where each bit of the binary representation of *num* refers to an index, starting from the least significant bit (that is, bit 0 is the first index). Set *num* to 0 to do the same as ALTER TABLE ... DISABLE KEYS. Can speed up inserts.
-m, --medium-check	check	Perform a medium check. Finds virtually all errors, thus recommended for most checks.
-o, --safe-recover	repair	Recover a table using an older though more thorough method than -r. Try -r first.
-O *var=option*, --set-variable *var=option*	general	Set the value of a variable, such as key_buffer_size, when running myisamchk.
-q, -qq, --quick	repair	Used with -r for faster repairs. -q tells myisamchk to repair only index files. -qq tells myisamchk to also fix duplicate keys in the data file too.
-r, --recover	repair	Recover a table. The main option for performing a repair, which should be tried before other options. An alternative is -o.
-R*index_num*, --sort- records= *index_num*	optimization	Sort data file, so that the data records are in the order of the given index, where *index_num* is the number of the index to use.
-s, -ss, --silent	general	Use silent mode: display errors only. Use -ss for very silent.

16

TABLE 16.1 continued

Option	Type	Meaning
-S, --sort-index	optimization	Sort the index files into order. Speeds up operations that use the index to locate data records or use ORDER BY queries.
-U, --update-state	checking	Record date and time of when table was checked. See also -c.
-u, --unpack	repair	Unpack a file packed with myisampack.
-v, -vv, -vvv, --verbose	general	Used with -d and -e to be verbose. Use -vv and -vvv for more and more verbose.
-V, --version	general	Display the version number of myisamchk.
-W, --wait	general	Wait for table to be unlocked (if it is, such as by another myisamchk command) rather than returning an error.

Tip

Some options to myisamchk require you to refer to indexes by number. To find out what indexes a table has, run SHOW INDEX or SHOW KEYS. This produces a list of indexes on a table, and the order of the indexes determines this index_num, as required by some myisamchk options.

The first index listed will have an index_num of 1.

Note

The -c, -F, -m, and -U options to myisamchk are not available in the older isamchk utility for ISAM tables. The -C option has a different meaning in isamchk (it sets the default character set).

Now that you have an overview of what options are available, it's time to look at some scenarios to illustrate which options you would use.

Checking a Table

| Caution | myisamchk is a powerful tool and will recover your data from the vast majority of corruptions. However, before running it to repair or optimize a table, and preferably before checking a table, you should do the following: |

1. Shut down mysqld if you can. If mysqld is accessing the table (and worst of all, writing) while myisamchk is trying to do a recovery or optimization, it may cause data corruption. If myisamchk is checking, it may think there's a problem when there isn't.

2. If you can't shut down mysqld, you should perform a mysqladmin flush-tables to save tables to disk and ensure that no other client is accessing the table when you run myisamchk.

3. If you can't be sure nobody else is accessing the table, make copies of the .frm, .MYD, and .MYI files for that table. Use myisamchk to work on the copies; then stop mysqld briefly and replace the original (suspect) ones with the repaired ones. However, if users write to the live copies of the tables while you're doing the repair, you'll have data concurrency issues, and their updates will be lost.

4. If you are working on the original files rather than copies, back up the files to a safe place before doing the recovery.

16

Before you repair a table, it's a good idea to know whether it needs repairing! There are several ways of checking a table, each with its own merits:

1. Use myisamchk with no options. For example, to check the table people:

```
# myisamchk people
Checking MyISAM file: people
Data records:      10   Deleted blocks:       0
- check file-size
- check key delete-chain
- check record delete-chain
- check index reference
- check data record references index: 1
- check record links
```

myisamchk used with no options checks only the index file. It won't pick up problems in the data file or table definition file.

The preceding output indicates that there are no errors with the table people, but if there are problems, you may get output like this:

```
# myisamchk people
Checking MyISAM file: people
Data records:       0   Deleted blocks:       0
myisamchk: warning: Table is marked as crashed
```

```
- check file-size
- check key delete-chain
- check record delete-chain
- check index reference
- check data record references index: 1
myisamchk: error: Found 10 keys of 0
- check record links
myisamchk: error: Record-count is not ok; is 10    Should be: 0
myisamchk: warning: Found          10 parts    Should be: 20 parts
MyISAM-table 'people' is corrupted
Fix it using switch "-r" or "-o"
```

2. Use myisamchk with -i for information. Here's an example with a corrupted table:

```
# myisamchk -i people
Checking MyISAM file: people
Data records:       0    Deleted blocks:       0
myisamchk: warning: Table is marked as crashed
- check file-size
- check key delete-chain
- check record delete-chain
- check index reference
- check data record references index: 1
myisamchk: error: Found 10 keys of 0
- check record links
myisamchk: error: Record-count is not ok; is 10    Should be: 0
myisamchk: warning: Found          10 parts    Should be: 20 parts

Record blocks:      10    Delete blocks:       0
Record data:       245    Deleted data:        0
Lost space:         14    Linkdata:           37
MyISAM-table 'people' is corrupted
Fix it using switch "-r" or "-o"

User time 0.00, System time 0.00
Maximum resident set size 0, Integral resident set size 0
Non-physical pagefaults 24, Physical pagefaults 206, Swaps 0
Blocks in 0 out 0, Messages in 0 out 0, Signals 0
Voluntary context switches 0, Involuntary context switches 0
```

The preceding output shows that the table has been marked as crashed; in fact, SELECT * FROM people returns the following error:

```
ERROR 1016: Can't open file: 'people.MYD'. (errno: 145)
```

MySQL knows that the table is "crashed" and cannot run queries on it. The output suggests that you repair the table, which you'll do in a moment.

3. Use myisamchk with -m for medium checking. -m checks each data record against its index entry, finding just about all errors.

Here's an example:

```
# myisamchk -m people
Checking MyISAM file: people
Data records:        0    Deleted blocks:       0
myisamchk: warning: Table is marked as crashed
- check file-size
- check key delete-chain
- check record delete-chain
- check index reference
- check data record references index: 1
myisamchk: error: Found 10 keys of 0
- check record links
myisamchk: error: Record-count is not ok; is 10     Should be: 0
myisamchk: warning: Found          10 parts      Should be: 20 parts

MyISAM-table 'people' is corrupted
Fix it using switch "-r" or "-o"
```

As before, the output tells you that the table is marked as crashed. You could also run it with both -m and -i for more information:

```
# myisamchk -m -i people
Checking MyISAM file: people
Data records:        0    Deleted blocks:       0
myisamchk: warning: Table is marked as crashed
- check file-size
- check key delete-chain
- check record delete-chain
- check index reference
- check data record references index: 1
myisamchk: error: Found 10 keys of 0
- check record links
myisamchk: error: Record-count is not ok; is 10     Should be: 0
myisamchk: warning: Found          10 parts      Should be: 20 parts

Record blocks:          10    Delete blocks:        0
Record data:           245    Deleted data:         0
Lost space:             14    Linkdata:            37
MyISAM-table 'people' is corrupted
Fix it using switch "-r" or "-o"

User time 0.00, System time 0.00
Maximum resident set size 0, Integral resident set size 0
Non-physical pagefaults 59, Physical pagefaults 206, Swaps 0
Blocks in 0 out 0, Messages in 0 out 0, Signals 0
Voluntary context switches 0, Involuntary context switches 0
```

4. In rare cases, if the error is such that -m has not found it, but you still suspect a corruption and want to test further, you can perform an extended check with -e. This takes considerably longer if the table is large.

Here's an example again:

```
# myisamchk -e people
Checking MyISAM file: people
Data records:        0   Deleted blocks:       0
myisamchk: warning: Table is marked as crashed
- check file-size
- check key delete-chain
- check record delete-chain
- check index reference
- check data record references index: 1
myisamchk: error: Found 10 keys of 0
- check records and index references
myisamchk: error: Record at:        0  Can't find key for index:  1
MyISAM-table 'people' is corrupted
Fix it using switch "-r" or "-o"
```

You can get more information with myisamchk -e -i:

```
# myisamchk -e -i people
Checking MyISAM file: people
Data records:        0   Deleted blocks:       0
myisamchk: warning: Table is marked as crashed
- check file-size
- check key delete-chain
- check record delete-chain
- check index reference
- check data record references index: 1
myisamchk: error: Found 10 keys of 0
- check records and index references
myisamchk: error: Record at:        0  Can't find key for index:  1
MyISAM-table 'people' is corrupted
Fix it using switch "-r" or "-o"

User time 0.00, System time 0.00
Maximum resident set size 0, Integral resident set size 0
Non-physical pagefaults 59, Physical pagefaults 207, Swaps 0
Blocks in 0 out 0, Messages in 0 out 0, Signals 0
Voluntary context switches 0, Involuntary context switches 0
```

You can get even more detailed information by adding the verbose option, -v.
Here's a sample output:

```
# myisamchk -e -v people
Checking MyISAM file: people
Data records:        0   Deleted blocks:       0
myisamchk: warning: Table is marked as crashed
- check file-size
- check key delete-chain
block_size 1024:
- check record delete-chain
No recordlinks
- check index reference
- check data record references index: 1
```

```
myisamchk: error: Found 10 keys of 0
- check records and index references
myisamchk: error: Record at:            0  Can't find key for index: 1
myisamchk: error: Record at:           20  Can't find key for index: 1
myisamchk: error: Record at:           40  Can't find key for index: 1
myisamchk: error: Record at:           60  Can't find key for index: 1
myisamchk: error: Record at:           80  Can't find key for index: 1
myisamchk: error: Record at:          104  Can't find key for index: 1
myisamchk: error: Record at:          128  Can't find key for index: 1
myisamchk: error: Record at:          152  Can't find key for index: 1
myisamchk: error: Record at:          256  Can't find key for index: 1
myisamchk: error: Record at:          276  Can't find key for index: 1
myisamchk: error: Record-count is not ok; is 10     Should be: 0
myisamchk: warning: Found        10 parts        Should be: 20 parts
MyISAM-table 'people' is corrupted
Fix it using switch "-r" or "-o"
```

The preceding output is reassuring: MySQL knows that there's a corruption but clearly knows a good deal about the problem.

Having conducted a check and found a problem, you'll need to repair the table.

Repairing a Table

To perform any kind of repair, you can use myisamchk with either -r or -o. -r is the fast, modern recovery method to be used in most cases. (There are a few cases where the older -o will work but -r won't.)

You should attempt repairs according to the following strategy.

Quick Repair

In most cases, corruption exists purely within the index file. You should first attempt to do a "quick repair" using myisamchk -r -q.

A quick repair fixes only the index file without touching the data file. Here's an example, using the preferred method of shutting down mysqld before starting the repair:

```
# mysqladmin -p shutdown
Enter password:
# myisamchk -r -q people
- check key delete-chain
- check record delete-chain
- recovering (with sort) MyISAM-table 'people'
Data records: 10
- Fixing index 1
```

After doing this, you can try one of the previous checks to see whether it fixed the problem.

Caution   If it didn't fix it, now is the time to back up your data! You should not proceed with further repairs without doing this.

Normal Repairs

The next type of repair to attempt is `myisamchk -r`. As well as rebuilding indexes, it deletes any corrupted records from the data file and recovers wasted space (more on this later), thus closing up space occupied by deleted records.

Here's an example where the table `people` has a corruption:

```
# myisamchk -r people
- recovering (with keycache) MyISAM-table 'people'
Data records: 0
Data records: 10
```

There's a confusion about how many data records it has. Alternatively, you may see something like this:

```
# myisamchk -r people
- recovering (with sort) MyISAM-table 'people'
Data records: 10
- Fixing index 1
```

In the second example, the table is fixed.

However, if this doesn't work, it may be worth trying the older repair method `myisamchk -o`, like this:

```
# myisamchk -o people
- recovering (with keycache) MyISAM-table 'people'
Data records: 10
```

Difficult Index Repairs

There may be cases where the index file is so badly damaged that it cannot be repaired. If the preceding attempts fail, follow this procedure:

1. Copy your data file to a safe place outside the data directory.

2. Perform a SQL DELETE FROM *table_name* to empty the table.

3. Do a `mysqladmin flush-tables` or a SQL FLUSH TABLES to ensure that the changes are written to disk.

4. Copy the data file back into the data directory. (If you do this as root, the file will have root ownership, so you will need to change ownership back to the mysql user using chown.) Retain your backup until you know the procedure has worked.

5. Go back and perform quick and then standard repairs on the table; then check whether the repair was successful.

Table Definition Corruption

It's rare for the table definition file (.frm) to get corrupted because table definitions are not often changed. However, it can happen.

If the table definition has become corrupted, follow this procedure:

1. Copy your data file to a safe place outside the data directory.

2. Restore the table definition file from a backup (if you have one), or failing that, issue a CREATE TABLE command if you know the definition of the table.

3. Do a mysqladmin flush-tables or an SQL FLUSH TABLES to ensure that the changes are written to disk.

4. Copy the data file back into the data directory. (You may need to change ownership of the file back to mysql using chown.)

5. Go back and perform quick and then standard repairs on the table; then check whether the repair was successful.

Optimizing a Table

When a table has numerous insert and delete operations performed on it, gaps can appear between the data records. This can arise where a shorter record is occupying the space previously used by a longer record.

You can recover wasted space within a data file by using myisamchk -r.

Here's an example of working on a table people, which has the columns first_name, last_name, and title, with a non-unique index on last_name (which makes it index number 1). First you'll want to flush tables to disk:

```
# mysqladmin -p flush-tables
Enter password:
```

At this point, you should ideally shut down mysqld, or at least lock tables from other users—though for clarity this is not shown here.

Then run myisamchk to get the descriptive information on the table people:

```
# myisamchk -d people
```

```
MyISAM file:        people
Record format:      Packed
Character set:      latin1 (8)
Data records:            10  Deleted blocks:        1
Recordlength:           114
```

```
table description:
Key Start Len Index    Type
1   5    100 multip. char packed stripped NULL
```

As you can see from the preceding output, `Deleted blocks` is 1, so this space (admittedly small) is wasted. To reclaim it, run `myisamchk -r` (remembering to shut down `mysqld` first if at all possible):

```
# mysqladmin -p shutdown
Enter password:
# myisamchk -r people
- recovering (with sort) MyISAM-table 'people'
Data records: 10
- Fixing index 1
```

Now you can get the descriptive information again:

```
# myisamchk -d people

MyISAM file:        people
Record format:      Packed
Character set:      latin1 (8)
Data records:                 10  Deleted blocks:              0
Recordlength:                114

table description:
Key Start Len Index    Type
1   5    100 multip. char packed stripped NULL
```

This time there are no deleted blocks, so the table is better packed than before.

It's a good idea to run `myisamchk -r` regularly on a growing database to minimize any space that is being left among the tables.

Optimizing Performance with Better Indexing

You may want to ensure that the indexes are kept in sort order on the disk. This is a good idea for tables on which you're running queries that use indexes and require a fast seek time.

You can do this by running `myisamchk -S`.

Here's an example:

```
# myisamchk -S people
- Sorting index for MyISAM-table 'people'
```

This action sorts the `.MYI` index file but doesn't affect the data file. You can also sort the data records themselves so that they're arranged in order on the disk. This helps speed up `SELECT` queries (or others) that look for data in a certain range but don't use an index.

You can sort the data file using `myisamchk -R=index_num`, where *index_num* is the number of the index that will govern data order.

Here's an example of using the first index (number 1):

```
# myisamchk -R1 people
```

Checking, Repairing, and Optimizing Using SQL Commands

So far you've looked at how to use `myisamchk` as a convenient command-line utility. However, its commands have SQL equivalents as you will now see, in the form of CHECK TABLE, REPAIR TABLE, and OPTIMIZE TABLE.

Although some of the utilities you've seen earlier today work best with `mysqld` stopped, these commands are SQL queries and therefore need the MySQL server to be running to execute them!

Using CHECK TABLE

The syntax for CHECK TABLE is

```
CHECK TABLE table_name[,table_name,...] [options]
```

You can use it to check a single table or a list of tables separated by commas.

CHECK TABLE checks a table for errors and updates the table's key statistics. Running it returns a resultset showing the status of the table after running the command.

options can be any number of the following, separated by spaces if more than one is specified:

- QUICK is the equivalent of -q with `myisamchk`.
- FAST only checks tables that have not been closed properly, the equivalent of `myisamchk -F`.
- MEDIUM is the equivalent of -m with `myisamchk`.
- EXTENDED is the equivalent of -e with `myisamchk`.
- CHANGED checks only tables that have not been closed properly, or that have been changed since the last check, the equivalent of `myisamchk -C`.

Here's an example of finding a problem with the indexes on table `people`:

```
mysql> CHECK TABLE people QUICK;
+-------------+-------+----------+---------------------------------------------+
| Table       | Op    | Msg_type | Msg_text                                    |
+-------------+-------+----------+---------------------------------------------+
```

```
| cms.people | check | warning | Table is marked as crashed                  |
| cms.people | check | error   | Size of indexfile is: 2046  Should be: 2048 |
| cms.people | check | error   | Corrupt                                     |
+------------+-------+---------+---------------------------------------------+
3 rows in set (0.00 sec)
```

> **Note**
>
> CHECK TABLE, just like any of the table-checking options for myisamchk, updates the status of the table, according to what state it finds it in. It may mark it as corrupt, not closed properly, or okay.

Using REPAIR TABLE

The syntax for REPAIR TABLE is like this:

```
REPAIR TABLE table_name[,table_name,...] [options]
```

options can be any number of the following, separated by spaces if more than one is specified:

- QUICK is the equivalent of -r -q with myisamchk, and thus repairs only the index file.

- EXTENDED is more methodical, creating the index row by row.

- USE_FRM is new to MySQL 4.0.2 and is for dealing with more serious corruption of the index file (or if it's missing); it effectively saves the data file, empties the table, moves the data file back, and performs a quick repair on the index.

```
mysql> REPAIR TABLE people QUICK;
+------------+--------+----------+----------+
| Table      | Op     | Msg_type | Msg_text |
+------------+--------+----------+----------+
| cms.people | repair | status   | OK       |
+------------+--------+----------+----------+
1 row in set (0.00 sec)

mysql> CHECK TABLE people EXTENDED;
+------------+-------+----------+----------+
| Table      | Op    | Msg_type | Msg_text |
+------------+-------+----------+----------+
| cms.people | check | status   | OK       |
+------------+-------+----------+----------+
1 row in set (0.00 sec)
```

Here's an example of using the USE_FRM option to repair a damaged people table:

```
mysql> REPAIR TABLE people USE_FRM;
+------------+--------+----------+------------------------------------+
| Table      | Op     | Msg_type | Msg_text                           |
+------------+--------+----------+------------------------------------+
| cms.people | repair | warning  | Number of rows changed from 0 to 10 |
| cms.people | repair | status   | OK                                 |
+------------+--------+----------+------------------------------------+
2 rows in set (0.00 sec)
```

Using OPTIMIZE TABLE

The syntax for OPTIMIZE TABLE is like this:

```
OPTIMIZE TABLE table_name[,table_name...]
```

It performs a LOCK TABLE before doing its optimization. The optimization work is the same as running

```
myisamchk -q -C -S -a
```

Thus it carries out the following tasks:

- Fixes minor index problems and recovers wasted space (because of -q or --quick)
- Checks only tables that have changed since the last check (-C or --check-only-changed)
- Sorts the indexes (-S or --sort-index) for improved lookup speed
- Analyzes the distribution of values within the indexes (-a or --analyze) for improved range SELECT queries that use an index.

As of MySQL 4.0.2, this command currently works only on MyISAM and BDB tables.

Here's an example:

```
mysql> OPTIMIZE TABLE people;
+------------+----------+----------+----------+
| Table      | Op       | Msg_type | Msg_text |
+------------+----------+----------+----------+
| cms.people | optimize | status   | OK       |
+------------+----------+----------+----------+
1 row in set (0.00 sec)
```

Summary

Today you learned how to check a database for minor problems such as wasted space on this disk ranging up to more serious problems such as corruption.

You learned how to use `myisamchk` to check your tables and perform repairs. You studied not only the options for running `myisamchk` but also a strategy for attempting first simple repairs and then escalating your actions to handle more severe cases of corruption.

You saw how to reclaim wasted space among data records, and how to gain performance improvements by sorting table indexes and data records.

Finally, you studied the CHECK TABLE, REPAIR TABLE, and OPTIMIZE TABLE commands, which are SQL commands, to do the same things as `myisamchk` does as a command-line utility.

Q&A

Q When I run a query, I'm getting a message from MySQL like "Got Error 127 from table handler." Is my database corrupted?

A Probably yes. But don't panic: Use `myisamchk` to check the table you suspect is corrupted without options and then using the `-q`, `-m`, and perhaps `-e` options. You can also add a `-i` for more information.

Ideally you should shut down `mysqld`, or at least flush tables and try to ensure that `myisamchk` is the only thing accessing a table; otherwise, it might tell you that a table is corrupt when it isn't.

If a problem is confirmed by any of these checks, commence the procedure outlined earlier for repairs.

Q How can I find out more about these errors from the table handler?

A If you're getting an error number, you can look it up using `perror`. For example:

```
# perror 126
Error code 126:  Unknown error 126
126 = Index file is crashed / Wrong file format
```

Q Can doing a table repair make the situation worse?

A It is possible for corruption to be made worse if other clients are using the table while you're running `myisamchk`. You should shut down the MySQL server while you're doing the repair, or failing this, flush tables so that they're saved to disk; then make absolutely sure that no other clients are accessing the table while you perform the repair.

Workshop

The quiz and exercises are provided to help you solidify your understanding of the material covered today. Try to understand the quiz and exercise answers before continuing to tomorrow's lesson.

Quiz

1. True or False: `myisamchk` can only check and repair tables.
2. What is the SQL command for repairing a table?

Quiz Answers

1. False. `myisamchk` can also be used to optimize tables. It can reclaim wasted space and re-sort indexes and data records.
2. `REPAIR TABLE`

Exercises

1. Write a `myisamchk` command that performs a table repair that attempts to fix indexes only.
2. Write a `myisamchk` command that performs a table repair that attempts to fix indexes and data files.
3. Write a `myisamchk` command that reveals how much wasted space you have in a table.
4. Write a `myisamchk` command that optimizes all tables in all databases on your server. It should recover wasted space and sort indexes. (Assume that your data is in `/usr/local/mysql/var/`.)

Answers to Exercises

1. You should have this:

   ```
   myisamchk -r -q table_name
   ```

   or this:

   ```
   myisamchk --recover --quick table_name
   ```

2. You should have this:

   ```
   myisamchk -r table_name
   ```

   or this:

   ```
   myisamchk --recover table_name
   ```

16

3. You should have this:

   ```
   myisamchk table_name
   ```

4. You should have this:

   ```
   myisamchk -r -S /usr/local/mysql/var/*/*
   ```

   or this:

   ```
   myisamchk --recover --sort-index /usr/local/mysql/var/*/*
   ```

DAY **17**

Transactions and Table Locking

In today's lesson you will learn about how to process transactions in MySQL using table locking and transaction-safe tables.

Particular topics you will study today are

- What table locking is, why you would want to do it, and how to do it
- The MySQL queries for locking tables, LOCK TABLES and UNLOCK TABLES
- How to do cooperative locking
- How to do transaction processing using transaction-safe InnoDB tables

What Is Table Locking?

Imagine that you have a busy database. Perhaps it's an online store, and clients are performing read and write accesses almost constantly. While some clients are trying to read data from a table (for example, to see what products are available), others are trying to insert data or perform an update (to place an order).

Assume that you have a table containing the stock levels in the online store. There's a table called `stock_level`, and in it there are columns called `product_id`, to identify the product by ID, and `qty`, which holds the current quantity in stock for each item.

If a customer tries to order an item, the server application checks the quantity in stock by running a `SELECT` query on this table. If the number in stock is not less than the number the customer requires, the order can be processed; otherwise, the order is rejected. When processing a successful order, the application decreases the value in `qty` to the new stock level.

Here's what the application code might look like, in which the customer orders three items of a product whose ID is 1234:

```
SELECT qty FROM stock_level WHERE product_id = 1234;
...
# Some code here to check if qty is not less than 3.
# If enough in stock, process order and set qty to qty-3.
# Then...
UPDATE stock_level SET qty = new_qty WHERE product_id = 1234;
```

What's wrong with the preceding code? It has a few weaknesses. Here's why.

Client threads are processed concurrently on MySQL. This means that while this application is being run for client A, there's a chance that client B might be ordering the same product at the same time.

Assume that there's an initial stock level for this product of 10. If Client A orders 3 items, and client B orders 8 items and his thread reads the stock level immediately after client A (but before the update for client A occurs), both threads will think there are 10 items in stock and allow the order to be placed.

In this situation, client A sets the stock level to 7 (because client A orders 3 items from the 10), and immediately afterward client B sets the same stock level to 2 (because client B orders 8 items from 10).

Clearly this is wrong. When the warehouseman goes to the shelf to collect the items for both orders (11 items in all), he'll find only 10 and blame the computer system for the error!

What went wrong here? The main problem is that the application should gain sole use of the stock level information while it's executing. While one client thread is being run, it should not allow other client threads to read the data because the stock level is just about to be changed.

A *table lock* is required on the table while the thread executes. A lock would allow each client to gain sole use of the stock information while the order is being processed; client

B would thus have to wait until client A is completely finished. You'll see how to create a table lock in a moment.

A further problem with the preceding code is the way the update query is performed. Notice how the code says:

```
UPDATE stock_level SET qty = new_qty WHERE product_id = 1234;
```

Because A sets the new quantity to 7, the actual query run by client A is

```
UPDATE stock_level SET qty = 7 WHERE product_id = 1234;
```

The application code passes an *absolute* value to UPDATE.

It would be better to write this:

```
UPDATE stock_level SET qty = qty-3 WHERE product_id = 1234;
```

This time the query sets qty to 3 less than its existing value. It performs an update that is *relative* to the current value. This is much better.

But as stated previously, the main issue is that both threads can read from and write to the store data simultaneously; let's have a look at how table locking can help.

Advantages of Table Locking

How could you use table locking to make the preceding application transaction-safe? Here's the application pseudo-code again for client A that orders three items:

```
SELECT qty FROM stock_level WHERE product_id = 1234;
...
# Some code here to check if qty is not less than 3.
# If okay, process order and set qty to qty-3.
# Then...
UPDATE stock_level SET qty = qty-3 WHERE product_id = 1234;
```

The code needs something to ensure that only one thread at a time can access the stock_level table. It needs a *write lock* so as to block other threads from either reading from or writing to the table.

To perform a write lock, the code would need to be enclosed by table locking statements, like this:

```
LOCK TABLES stock_level WRITE;
SELECT qty FROM stock_level WHERE product_id = 1234;
...
# Some code here to check if qty is not less than 3.
# If okay, process order and set qty to 10-3 = 7.
# Then...
UPDATE stock_level SET qty = qty-3 WHERE product_id = 1234;
UNLOCK TABLES;
```

17

Notice the first line, with the statement LOCK TABLES. This tells the application to take sole possession of the stock_level table before doing the main processing. After it's finished processing, it issues the UNLOCK TABLES command, which releases the tables for other clients to use again.

Locking tables like this prevents client B (or other clients) from reading from or writing to the stock_level table until client A has finished. It enables client A to get a consistent view of the data, and because client A is the sole client that can update the data, it guarantees leaving a consistent view when client A is finished.

Now that you've seen how table locking can help, it's time to see how it is implemented in MySQL, and how to do table locking in practice.

How MySQL Uses Table Locks

The previous code was a simple example of applying a *write lock* to a single table. There are also *read locks*. It is possible to lock any number of tables at once.

An Introduction to LOCK TABLES and UNLOCK TABLES

Here's the syntax (in simplified form) for LOCK TABLES:

```
LOCK TABLES table_name1 {READ | WRITE} [, table_name2 {READ | WRITE} ...]
```

As you can see from the syntax, you can give LOCK TABLES the names of one or more tables. Each named table requires the word READ or WRITE to specify what kind of lock the client thread should obtain on that table.

What's the difference between a read lock and a write lock?

- If a client thread obtains a read lock, that thread and all other threads will only be able to read from that table; no thread can write to the table.

- If a client thread obtains a write lock, it becomes the only thread with either read or write access. No other threads will have read or write access until the lock is released.

Here's an example of locking two tables for read, and one for write:

```
mysql> LOCK TABLES products READ, customers READ, stock_level WRITE;
Query OK, 0 rows affected (0.00 sec)
```

In the preceding query, products and customers were locked with a read lock, and stock_level was locked with a write lock.

When tables are locked, they remain locked until another LOCK TABLES command is issued, the thread exits, or (most commonly) an UNLOCK TABLES command is issued. UNLOCK TABLES is used like this:

```
UNLOCK TABLES
```

So if you try this in the mysql console, you would do this:

```
mysql> UNLOCK TABLES;
Query OK, 0 rows affected (0.00 sec)
```

The Full Syntax for LOCK TABLES

Here's the full syntax of LOCK TABLES, showing all possible options:

```
LOCK TABLES table_name1 [AS alias1] {READ | READ LOCAL | [LOW_PRIORITY] WRITE}
   [, table_name2 [AS alias2] {READ | READ LOCAL | [LOW_PRIORITY] WRITE}]
   ...
```

You'll notice a few extra things in the full syntax (though they're less often used):

- You can give each table an alias; if you do so you will need to use this *alias* to refer to such tables in your queries.

- You can issue a READ LOCAL. This is like a read lock, but allows inserts to be performed by other threads while the lock is in operation.

- You can issue a write lock with LOW_PRIORITY. Write locks are normally obtained before read locks, but LOW_PRIORITY gives a write lock a lower priority. (You'll read more about the process of obtaining locks in a moment.)

Here's an example of a more complex lock statement:

```
mysql> LOCK TABLES products AS p READ,
    -> customers AS c READ LOCAL,
    -> stock_level AS s WRITE;
Query OK, 0 rows affected (0.00 sec)
```

In this example, products has a read lock and alias p, customers has a read local lock and alias c, and stock_level has a write lock and alias s.

Queuing Lock Requests

Issuing a LOCK TABLES command does not mean that the client that issues it gains a lock immediately. The tables requested may be in use or locked by another client, so the client that wants to obtain a lock on those tables will have to wait for the lock to be granted.

In addition, when a client requests a lock, it may have to wait until any other waiting clients have been served their locks. There's a queuing mechanism, so that clients can be served in order.

17

There are actually two queues—you'll see why in a moment. According to a strict set of rules, a client in one queue may have to wait for clients in the other queue to be granted their lock first.

The two queues are a *write lock queue* and a *read lock queue*, and they work in slightly different ways.

When a write lock is issued by a client

- If no locks are currently on the requested tables, the write lock is granted without queuing.
- Otherwise, the write lock request is put into the write lock queue.

When a read lock is issued by a client:

- Where tables have no write locks on them, the read lock is granted without queuing.
- Otherwise, the read lock request is put into the read lock queue.

Whenever a lock is released, clients in the write lock queue are given priority over those in the read lock queue. This is done to help get updates processed as soon as possible.

When no clients are waiting in the write lock queue, clients in the read lock queue are in turn granted their read lock.

Overriding the Lock Request Queue

There are ways to override the lock queuing protocol. For example, you may have an application in which it's important for read locks to be granted with higher priority than write locks.

As you saw in the LOCK TABLES syntax, there is the option of issuing a LOW_PRIORITY WRITE. Issuing a LOW_PRIORITY WRITE lock makes the queuing system behave the other way around for this request: A low priority write lock will have to wait for all read locks to clear the queue before it is granted.

Take care when using this, however. If you have a busy system with a near-continuous stream of read operations, you should ensure that there is time for write operations to occur at some point! Otherwise, you run the risk of write operations being delayed unacceptably if the wait is too long.

Another query that can influence the queuing policy is the SELECT query. When you issue a SELECT (with or without a lock), it normally has to wait behind any write requests that are waiting in the queue.

However, if you issue a SELECT HIGH PRIORITY, it allows the SELECT to read from the table even if a write lock is waiting in the queue.

Locking Multiple Tables

It is important to note that when your application is going to run queries on several tables, you must lock all those tables.

Locking all tables is essential to prevent a *deadlock* situation from arising. How might a deadlock occur?

Imagine that one client is allowed to lock just *table1* of the set of tables, *table1* and *table2*, on which it intends to run a number of queries.

Then another client locks *table2* (before the first client has finished its business) but also wants to run queries on *table1* and *table2*. When it finds *table1* locked, the thread has to wait for the first client to release it.

If the first client then tries to run a query on *table2*, it finds that table locked and has to wait. There's now a situation of two clients, each waiting for the other to release its locks. Neither can make progress, and both *table1* and *table2* are locked by threads that are halted.

This would be a gridlock situation for your database. MySQL prevents it from arising by insisting that when you have a lock on one or several tables, you cannot run queries on any other tables.

Permissions for Locking Tables

Prior to MySQL version 4.0.2, no special client privilege was required to lock tables, although the client should have Select_priv, Insert_priv, Delete_priv, and Update_priv, according to what action your query intends to perform after the lock is granted.

However, in version 4.0.2 and later, with the new-style privilege tables, the client user must also have the Lock_tables_priv privilege.

See Day 14, "Security," for more about MySQL's grant tables and user privileges.

Using Table Locking: A Quick Recap

As you've seen, a client should issue a lock when

- It wants to ensure that it can perform a sequence of queries (often a SELECT and then an UPDATE) without interference from other clients in those tables.

- It wants to ensure that other threads don't see data that is partially updated (it might have to perform UPDATEs on several tables before the overall picture is consistent).

Remember that you must lock all tables that are going to be used by your queries until those tables are unlocked.

Cooperative Locks

MySQL has other kinds of locking arrangements. You can use *cooperative* or *advisory locks* so that client threads can cooperate with one another.

Cooperative locks have nothing to do with table locks; they have no power to block access to tables, and have an effect only if all relevant applications look for the presence of an advisory lock before proceeding. That's why they're called *cooperative*.

You can even think of them as ways of passing information between different instances of an application, but using MySQL to convey the message.

Cooperative locks are implemented by the functions GET_LOCK() and RELEASE_LOCK(). Here's the syntax:

GET_LOCK(*string,timeout*)

RELEASE_LOCK(*string*)

GET_LOCK() attempts to gain a lock with the name given by *string*. This is the agreed-upon lock name, and all clients must use the same lock name for the cooperation to be successful. RELEASE_LOCK() releases the cooperative lock.

In GET_LOCK(), you must specify a timeout given in seconds by *timeout*. The function returns 1 if the attempt is successful, 0 if a timeout occurs, or NULL if an error occurs.

A lock is released when the client thread finishes, when it issues another GET_LOCK(), or when it issues a RELEASE_LOCK().

Here's an example. You may want to follow this yourself using two mysql console windows. Imagine that client A issues the following:

```
mysql> SELECT GET_LOCK("my_lock",5);
+-----------------------+
| GET_LOCK("my_lock",5) |
+-----------------------+
|                     1 |
+-----------------------+
1 row in set (0.00 sec)
```

The result is 1 because the lock is granted successfully on the string my_lock.

At this point, your client may perform some application code, which it wants to do without interference from other clients. This might be any code; for example, writing to a file.

Now client B issues a request for the same lock:

```
mysql> SELECT GET_LOCK("my_lock",5);
+-----------------------+
| GET_LOCK("my_lock",5) |
+-----------------------+
|                     0 |
+-----------------------+
1 row in set (5.10 sec)
```

The result is 0, and the query takes five seconds to run. This is because we passed it a *timeout* of five seconds; it waits this time for client A to unlock (which it doesn't in this case) before giving up. Client A still has the lock.

Now let's make client A release its lock:

```
mysql> SELECT RELEASE_LOCK("my_lock");
+-------------------------+
| RELEASE_LOCK("my_lock") |
+-------------------------+
|                       1 |
+-------------------------+
1 row in set (0.00 sec)
```

The query returns a 1 to indicate that the lock is released successfully.

Now client B tries again:

```
mysql> SELECT GET_LOCK("my_lock",5);
+-----------------------+
| GET_LOCK("my_lock",5) |
+-----------------------+
|                     1 |
+-----------------------+
1 row in set (0.00 sec)
```

This time the result is 1 because the lock on my_lock is granted to client B (and it happens immediately).

To test whether a lock is in place without waiting, you can use GET_LOCK(*string*,0). Giving a timeout of zero means that the lock will be obtained if it is not currently in force, but the client will have to release the lock using RELEASE_LOCK(*string*) if it was successful.

17

Transaction-Safe Table Types

In much of this book, you have studied the MyISAM table type. This is the default table type for MySQL. This table type is well tried and tested; MyISAM tables are fast and compact, but they have one important limitation.

MyISAM tables have no inherent concept of transactions. They ensure safe *atomic* processing: They make sure that a single SQL statement can be executed without interference in the data by other threads.

But other than by locking tables, they cannot help us where we need to perform a sequence of SQL queries, all of which need to be processed to keep the data consistent. We might think of this entire sequence as a single business *transaction*, no part of which should be performed without performing the whole.

Performing Transactions Using Transaction-Safe Tables

Table locking is a somewhat crude mechanism: The client that has obtained the locks it needs can do its work, but other clients have to be held up until the first client is finished. This hampers overall system performance if many clients get held up. A better way of achieving the same goal is to use transaction-safe tables.

A single business transaction may be a sequence of SQL queries, all of which must be performed without interference to keep data consistent. The queries may include any kinds of SQL, such as SELECT, UPDATE, INSERT, and other commands. With transaction-safe tables, the effect of that sequence of queries—the entire transaction—is written to the database in one go.

 Note

> In all MySQL table types, operations are *atomic*.
>
> Atomic operations are indivisible. You can't have a partly completed operation; MySQL won't allow it. For example, if you have an update that affects thousands of rows in a table and may even take a long time to run, no other query can make changes on that data until the first query is running.
>
> In transactional operations (and transaction-safe table types), the difference is that *several* SQL statements in effect have an atomic operation.

There are several advantages of using transaction-safe tables:

- You can group several SQL statements into a single operation, and any write operations can either be implemented in the database (*committed*) or discarded (*rolled-back*).

- If an update fails, the database will be restored to its previous state.
- If MySQL crashes, the database will be restored to its state before the crash.

Newer versions of MySQL (starting with 3.23, and enhanced in version 4) have two transaction-safe table types: `InnoDB` and `BDB`.

MySQL's Transaction-Safe Table Types

`InnoDB` is a transaction-safe table handler distributed with MySQL. It facilitates the commit, rollback, and crash recovery operations, which are central to transaction-safe processing. `InnoDB` has been designed with high volumes of transactions and high performance in mind, and is claimed to have the fasted executing code of any relational database. In this lesson, there is only time to give you an introduction to `InnoDB` (albeit a hands-on one). For more information about it, visit the `InnoDB` Web site at `http://www.innodb.com/`.

The other transaction-safe table type available with MySQL is `BDB`, which stands for BerkeleyDB. `BDB` is developed by Sleepycat and can be used in many other database engines besides MySQL. You can learn more about BDB at `http://www.sleepycat.com/`.

The MySQL interface to `BDB` is not currently considered as advanced as that for `InnoDB`. Therefore in the rest of this lesson, we'll put more emphasis on `InnoDB` than `BDB`; however, the principles of transactions are the same in both cases, so you should be able to apply the skills you learn to either table type.

In summary, transaction-safe tables such as `InnoDB` and `BDB` enable you to group a sequence of queries into an indivisible transaction. In the following examples, you will use the `InnoDB` table type to understand how to do this.

Installing `InnoDB`

If you installed MySQL version 4 or later from source, your `mysqld` binary will already contain support for `InnoDB` tables. With version 3.23, you will need to include the `--with-innodb` option when you run `./configure`; for example:

```
# ./configure \
  --with-innodb
  ...
```

MySQL binaries have `InnoDB` included in the MySQL-Pro and MySQL-Max distributions. If you installed a standard MySQL binary, you should download a `-Pro` or `-Max` distribution, unpack it, and replace your old `mysqld` with the new one. These binary distributions are identical to the normal distributions in all except the `mysqld` executable.

After you have either compiled MySQL or installed the right `mysqld`, you will need to edit the option file `my.cnf` (or `my.ini`). Day 15, "Administration," explains where to find this file.

You will need to add (or in newer versions, just uncomment) the following line in `my.cnf`, in the section under [`mysqld`]:

```
[mysqld]
...
innodb_data_file_path = ibdata1:10M:autoextend
```

This line defines the file that `InnoDB` uses for its data storage area. The preceding example sets this area to 10MB (though you may want to make yours higher), with the capability to auto-extend this space (in other words, grow) if required.

(With versions of MySQL prior to 4.0.2, you will not be able to use the `:autoextend` option shown here.)

Many other options are available for configuring `InnoDB`: You should find these commented-out in your `my.cnf` file, with instructions on how to use these options in the MySQL Technical Reference. However, in this lesson, our aim is to keep things simple. You can get `InnoDB` working with just the one line shown previously; all other options are unnecessary, and they will just set themselves to their default values if left undeclared.

After you have completed these changes, restart `mysqld_safe`. If all is well, MySQL should start up again without any problem. However, if an error is reported or `mysqld` refuses to start, look in the `hostname.err` file of MySQL's data directory for clues as to what went wrong. Also check the `InnoDB` options in `my.cnf` again very carefully.

Creating an InnoDB Table

With `mysqld` started, you're ready to try out `InnoDB` tables and perform some transactions. Start by creating a table of product stock levels; we'll use `InnoDB` tables to repeat the example we looked at earlier in this lesson:

```
mysql> CREATE TABLE stock_level
    -> (product_id INT NOT NULL PRIMARY KEY, qty int NOT NULL) TYPE=InnoDB;
Query OK, 0 rows affected (0.34 sec)
```

The `CREATE TABLE` statement is almost the same as you've seen before, except for the `TYPE=InnoDB` clause, which should be added at the end. This sets the table type to be `InnoDB` rather than the default `MyISAM`.

Alternatively, if the table already exists, you can simply change the table type to `InnoDB` using `ALTER TABLE`, like this:

```
mysql> ALTER TABLE stock_level TYPE=InnoDB;
Query OK, 1 row affected (0.01 sec)
Records: 1  Duplicates: 0  Warnings: 0
```

<table>
<tr><td>Note</td><td>Altering a table type like this has no effect on the data; it just changes the operating system file structure underlying the table.

As you know by now, MyISAM tables have .frm, .MYD, and .MYI files to describe the table structure, data, and indexes, respectively.

InnoDB tables have only a .frm file to describe the table structure, plus a tablespace for the data and indexes of the entire database. This may be one or several files. The tablespace in our example is denoted by the variable innodb_data_file_path. (In this example, the file ibdata1 in MySQL's data directory is used for this tablespace.)</td></tr>
</table>

Running Transaction-Based Queries

You should now have an InnoDB-type table ready to run some transaction-based queries on.

Let's recall the problem of stock levels we had from earlier today. We have two clients querying the table stock_level for the same product. There are 10 items of a particular product line in stock. Client A wants to order 3, and client B wants to order 8.

We're looking to transaction-safe tables to give us a way of processing the requests by the two clients, without allowing a situation of both orders being processed (effectively allowing more products to be ordered than there really are).

First, put some data into your table:

```
mysql> INSERT INTO stock_level SET product_id=1234, qty=10;
Query OK, 1 row affected (0.00 sec)
```

Now open two windows and start a mysql console session in each. The first window represents client A, and the second, client B.

A transaction consists of several queries. To begin a transaction, you have to tell MySQL that the transaction is beginning.

To do this, use the command BEGIN on client A, like this:

```
mysql> BEGIN;
Query OK, 0 rows affected (0.00 sec)
```

It's as simple as that. If you use BEGIN on MyISAM and other non-transaction safe tables, it will have no effect.

The point of BEGIN on a transaction-safe table is that the write queries that follow will not automatically *commit*—update the data files on disk—until you issue a further command to do this.

Now do the same on client B:

```
mysql> BEGIN;
Query OK, 0 rows affected (0.00 sec)
```

Issue a SELECT query on client A to see how many items are in stock:

```
mysql> SELECT qty FROM stock_level WHERE product_id=1234;
+-----+
| qty |
+-----+
|  10 |
+-----+
1 row in set (0.00 sec)
```

As expected, 10 items are in stock. If 3 items are ordered by client A, the stock level of 10 is enough to allow 3 items to be ordered, so the order can be processed. (Imagine that there are some other queries that we don't see here, such as applying a debit to the customer's account because a purchase is taking place.)

The stock level needs to be updated to reduce it by 3. We'll use a relative update:

```
mysql> UPDATE stock_level SET qty=qty-3 WHERE product_id=1234;
Query OK, 1 row affected (0.00 sec)
Rows matched: 1  Changed: 1  Warnings: 0
```

To see what's happening—still in client A's window—check how many items are now left in stock:

```
mysql> SELECT qty FROM stock_level WHERE product_id=1234;
+-----+
| qty |
+-----+
|   7 |
+-----+
1 row in set (0.00 sec)
```

No surprises here. But now switch to client B, and have a look what it sees:

```
mysql> SELECT qty FROM stock_level WHERE product_id=1234;
+-----+
| qty |
+-----+
|  10 |
+-----+
1 row in set (0.00 sec)
```

Client B thinks the stock level is still 10! Why?

Client A is still processing the transaction; it has updated its own picture of the data but hasn't allowed the changes to be committed to disk yet.

The point is, a client may want to process a number of other queries, perhaps on several tables, during which time it must maintain a consistent picture. What client A sees is what existed when it issued the BEGIN, plus the effect of any changes it has made to the data itself, but not changes made by other clients.

Client B now wants to process its own order for 8 items. It thinks there are 10 items in stock and goes ahead (just like client A) with updating the customer's account and other data, but—importantly—without committing to disk yet. Client B updates the stock level:

```
mysql> UPDATE stock_level SET qty=qty-8 WHERE product_id=1234;
```

When you run this, you see that client B's update query hangs without executing. Why? InnoDB allows *row-level locking*. Just as you saw entire tables being locked at the beginning of this lesson, client A is holding a write lock on this one row of the table. So client B has to wait until A releases the lock on the row for product 1234. (If you had updated any other row in the table, thread B would not have been held up, and would have processed the update—through as yet uncommitted—immediately.)

Finally, client A issues a COMMIT. This saves all its changes to disk:

```
mysql> COMMIT;
Query OK, 0 rows affected (0.00 sec)
```

The changes are written to the data file.

Now client B's UPDATE query immediately finishes because A's lock is released, and B is granted access to update the table:

```
mysql> UPDATE stock_level SET qty=qty-8 WHERE product_id=1234;
Query OK, 1 row affected (41.70 sec)
Rows matched: 1  Changed: 1  Warnings: 0
```

The application won't know that it had to wait (or why), although the delay of more than 40 seconds tells a human user that another client has been locking the row while it was waiting!

Client B now checks the stock level again:

```
mysql> SELECT qty FROM stock_level WHERE product_id=1234;
+-----+
| qty |
+-----+
|  -1 |
+-----+
1 row in set (0.00 sec)
```

Ouch. There's clearly something wrong here, as -1 is returned. If these queries were being run by application code, you should at this point (before you commit) run SELECTs to check that the situation is permissible. Just as your code should have checked that the quantity ordered was not more than the stock level before, it also should check that the stock level is not less than zero now.

The current status is not legal within the application. The order should not have been placed. The stock level should not have been updated, neither should the customer's account have been charged nor other update queries been processed. So what can be done to turn back the clock?

The answer is a *rollback*. A rollback restores the state of the database to that which existed when the issuing client issued its BEGIN. So client B, instead of committing the data to disk, issues a ROLLBACK:

```
mysql> ROLLBACK;
Query OK, 0 rows affected (0.00 sec)
```

At this point, the application code might loop back to the beginning and try to process the order again. Issuing another SELECT, client B sees this:

```
mysql> SELECT qty FROM stock_level WHERE product_id=1234;
+-----+
| qty |
+-----+
|   7 |
+-----+
1 row in set (0.00 sec)
```

The rollback has undone all of client B's changes, without saving them to the live database. A quick inspection reveals that with a qty of just 7, an order for 8 items cannot be accepted.

Note

> It should be clear to you that transaction-safe table types such as InnoDB are extremely powerful. They allow you to process a whole sequence of queries in a multithreaded environment, potentially undoing the effect of all the queries before committing them to disk!
>
> However, applications written with transaction-based queries must be written to take these things into account. For example, the simple order-processing application that you might write to run the queries shown just now would have to include a loop mechanism that checks things for legality before committing the updated data to disk, and be prepared to rollback and try again if the situation is deemed unacceptable (such as a stock level of -1).

Why is the solution using transaction-safe tables better than the table locking solution that we saw earlier today?

For a start, InnoDB's row-level locking rather than table-level locking means that only essential rows are locked. So the rest of the table is accessible while one client locks just the rows it needs.

In a real-world situation, two clients of the same application would more typically be updating different rows of the relevant tables. That two clients should be trying to order the same product simultaneously would be a low probability (though it must be guarded against), but by not needing the rest of the table to be locked, performance would be better.

Another reason that this method is better is that execution of all client threads can proceed without having to obtain locks first. A client has to wait only at points when updates interfere directly with another client (as illustrated here), which in most cases might never occur.

In short, transaction-safe tables allow much faster and more efficient processing than other table types.

Summary

17

Today's lesson showed you a number of things:

- You learned how to perform table locking using LOCK TABLES, using both read and write table locks.

- You learned how to use the GET_LOCK() function to perform cooperative locking between applications, or between different instances of the same application.

- You had an introduction to MySQL's transaction-safe table types; you learned how to install InnoDB; how to create an InnoDB table; and how to use the BEGIN, COMMIT, and ROLLBACK commands to manage a multiquery transaction.

Running transaction-based queries is a large subject area. Today you had just a brief introduction to the subject, but by following the practical example given, you should have a good grasp of what transaction processing enables you to do. With this grounding, you should be able to study the subject further using the references suggested.

Q&A

Q Why do I need to be concerned about table locks and transaction-safe tables?

A Locks and transaction-safe tables are important in a multithreaded environment, in which client threads have the job of updating, inserting into, or deleting from the database. If it's important for a thread to perform a sequence of queries and always have a consistent view of the data, consider using locks or transaction-safe tables.

Q Is it better to use table locks or transaction-safe tables?

A If you have a low-traffic system in which there's little contention for getting locks (in other words, clients seldom have to wait), locks may be easier to implement. You can also use the default table type, MyISAM.

In systems with high traffic, in which waiting time for locks impedes performance, it is advantageous to use transaction-safe table types. These are designed for high performance with large volumes of read and write queries.

Q When should I use cooperative locks?

A Think of cooperative (or advisory) locks as more a way of communicating a lock situation between applications, or instances of the same application. MySQL acts as a sort of messenger between applications.

They do not make MySQL lock tables and only take effect when applications honor the state of the lock in a co-operative way: waiting for it to be freed and making sure that they obtain a lock before proceeding.

Workshop

The quiz and exercises are provided to help you solidify your understanding of the material covered today. Try to understand the quiz and exercise answers before continuing to tomorrow's lesson.

Quiz

1. True or False: A table lock, when obtained by one client, prevents other clients from reading from or writing to a table.

2. True or False: When preparing to run a query on several tables, any lock must be obtained on all those tables.

3. True or False: With transaction-safe processing, you must issue a BEGIN to declare the start of a transaction.

4. In transaction-safe processing, what SQL command saves data to disk?

5. In transaction-safe processing, what SQL command undoes all changes without writing to disk?

Quiz Answers

1. True for a write lock. With a read lock, the statement is not true because it allows other threads to read from the table.

2. True. You must obtain suitable locks on all tables that will be used by your queries, until you unlock the tables.

3. True. However, you must use transaction-safe table types (InnoDB or BDB) or BEGIN will have no effect.

4. COMMIT.

5. ROLLBACK.

Exercises

1. Imagine that you have a table called orders. You want to update it while no other threads can read from it. You also have a table called products, which you want to read from but not update. Write the syntax for the appropriate locking and unlocking of the tables.

2. What line must you have in your server's my.cnf file to make it use InnoDB? Assume that you want it to have a 50MB tablespace, auto-extending.

Answers to Exercises

1. You should have this:

```
LOCK TABLES orders WRITE, products READ
...
UNLOCK TABLES
```

2. In the [mysqld] section, you should have this:

```
[mysqld]
...
innodb_data_file_path = ibdata1:50M:autoextend
```

17

WEEK 2

DAY 18

Optimizing Performance

By now you should have learned how to design and build MySQL database applications that serve a variety of different requirements. However, so far you have spent only a little time here and there considering database performance.

In today's lesson, you will focus on attaining the goal of high performance. You will look at the various things that influence it, so that at the end of the lesson you have some techniques for running MySQL with far greater efficiency, even in high-load, performance-critical situations.

In particular, you will learn:

- The principal factors that influence performance
- How to improve your table designs to speed up database access
- How to write applications that run faster
- How to use MySQL's performance commands, EXPLAIN, BENCHMARK, and PROCEDURE ANALYSE
- How to configure your MySQL server, your operating system, and your hardware for optimal performance.

This lesson is not intended to be a study of MySQL's query optimizer. The optimizer is an essential part of the server; it studies each query it is sent and tries to find the best way to execute it. We will look at the effect the optimizer has in a number of places throughout the lesson, but to keep things concise and practical, we will not endeavor to explain the thinking behind the optimizer. You should study the MySQL Reference Manual for more detail on this.

Why Optimize Performance?

It may be too obvious a question to ask, but why should you bother to optimize performance at all?

Let's be honest, in many situations, performance—fast or slow—simply does not matter. You may be building a database that has a small amount of usage, and a fast development time for your application may be the most critical thing. In a "quick fix" situation, you may give database performance a low priority.

However, even systems that are initially quiet can become busy. It may be a database-driven Web site that gradually attracts more traffic, and slow performance will be very off-putting for users, especially if it degrades as traffic grows.

A similar scenario might be a system that you think gets little usage (perhaps its average load is very low), but there may be peaks when it gets many users accessing it simultaneously.

Another reason is that it's just good practice to keep performance in mind when developing any kind of application. You will better develop your skills if you consider performance as you develop your system.

What Do We Mean by Performance Anyway?

It's easy to assume that by "performance" we simply mean speed.

Although this is true in many cases, it's easy to overlook the fact that disk or memory usage may be important in certain situations. (Imagine that you are building an application to run on a PDA, where storage is limited.)

However, the speed issue is the one most frequently confronting developers, especially in this age of Web sites that must stand up to occasionally huge amounts of traffic. Speed is the issue that most of this lesson is devoted to.

Factors Affecting Performance

The performance of your system will be affected by a number of factors. Here are the main factors, roughly in order of impact:

- How your columns and tables are defined, and what table types they have
- How your application uses MySQL
- How your application runs its queries and how the MySQL optimizer processes them
- The MySQL system variables
- Your operating system and hardware
- How `mysqld` is compiled

We will go through these factors in turn. This should enable you to get a good grasp of them, and you will learn what you can do in each respect to improve performance.

Whatever tactics you may come to use, always run benchmark tests to measure the impact of any change. Carry out timings before and after any adjustment. You will usually need to measure query time in milliseconds, and bear in mind that you should try to do so both with and without the impact of other system loads.

Table Design

Table design is probably the biggest influencer of database efficiency. Because databases access disk drives where tables reside, getting data to and from tables is critical. It's also at the top of our list because it's the one factor you, as an application developer, may be most able to influence.

Using Indexes

In Day 9, "Joins and Indexes," you studied how to perform joins and use indexes. Joins are often among the most time-consuming database operations because they involve examining rows from several different tables.

As you saw in Day 9, indexes (in general) improve performance because they preserve a sorted copy of the data in one or more columns. The general rules are that you should apply an index to a column

- When that column appears in a `WHERE` clause
- When that column is used in a `GROUP BY` or `ORDER BY` clause
- When that column is used in a join operation

18

However, indexes should perhaps not be used in some cases:

- Don't apply indexes on very small tables; they won't help.
- Don't apply indexes on columns where a WHERE operation will return more than one-third of the rows.
- Don't apply indexes on tables to which data is added or modified more than it is read; updating indexes wastes time.

Always try to use a primary or unique key if possible, or failing that a non-unique key. Finally, where there are large columns (such as TEXT), use only short indexes.

Column Specifications

When specifying the columns of a table, try to keep data stored in the smallest possible space and use fixed-length columns where possible.

Here are some guidelines:

- Keep columns as small as possible. The less disk access that has to be performed, the better.
- Use fixed-length columns if you can, such as CHAR rather than VARCHAR. If MySQL knows that records are evenly spaced on the disk, it can move from one to the next more efficiently.
- Use NOT NULL columns; it saves on storage and allows faster processing.
- Use an ENUM column type where possible. Because ENUM columns are stored as numeric values, they are faster to access. Use an ENUM where a column can contain a limited number of values from a set that can be specified.

When you create a table, you will often do so with VARCHAR or TEXT columns. Even if you specify a CHAR rather than VARCHAR, under certain circumstances MySQL will perform a silent column change to a VARCHAR type. Tables with VARCHAR columns are known as dynamic tables because they can dynamically adjust column size to suit the data within them.

But dynamic tables are not the fastest. Each row of data has to store not just the raw data but information about the size of the data as well; and the data records themselves are not stored with predictable spacing on the disk.

To optimize speed, you may prefer to create fixed (also known as static) table types. With this kind of table, all columns are of fixed size. A table can be fixed if it has only columns such as CHAR, ENUM, and numeric types, and avoids VARCHAR, TEXT, and BLOB columns.

If you need to store TEXT or BLOB data, but require fast access to it, consider splitting your data into two tables: one that is static and holds summary information, and a second that is dynamic and holds the TEXT or BLOB data. For example, if you had an online library, you might store data about your documents—titles, keywords, creation dates, permissions— in a fast static table, and the contents of the documents in a slower dynamic table.

You can see what types of tables you have by running SHOW TABLE STATUS and looking at the Row_format information for each table, which will be stated as Dynamic or Fixed.

Table Types

The default table type for MySQL is MyISAM. This is a tried-and true table type, and has the least number of restrictions in terms of MySQL functions and commands that cannot be used with all types of tables.

But a faster type is the HEAP table. Although MyISAM tables are stored on disk, HEAP tables exist only in memory. This makes them inherently faster.

For applications that don't require the safety of a table stored on disk (which would preserve data permanently), consider a HEAP table for data that must be accessed with maximum speed.

If your system has tables that are read-only, you should also consider using compressed tables. The myisampack utility can be used to compress tables by a considerable amount. Being smaller on the disk, they are faster to access. See Day 15, "Administration," for more about creating myisampack compressed tables.

How Your Application Uses MySQL

How you write your application, and how you write your queries, will have an immense impact on your system's performance.

For example, don't run queries repetitively if you don't need to; take the processing from your application code into your MySQL queries if you can so that you select only what you need to, rather than sift through it in your application.

Use multitable joins with care (you'll look at how to assess the performance of joins in a moment); as well as being difficult to debug, they may create huge resultsets that consume memory, causing MySQL to automatically create temporary tables on disk. For example, it may be better to remove the join against the smallest table and run a first query to create a short list of comma-separated values, *value1*, *value2*, and so on; then run a second query using WHERE...*column* IN (*value1*,*value2*,...).

In busy systems, you should not only consider which queries take the longest but also those that are run most frequently. A seldom-used query that takes 5 seconds to run may have less adverse impact than one that takes 0.1 seconds but runs 50 times a second!

Perhaps it's obvious, but by no means less important: remember that the language you choose to write your application in will influence its execution speed. See Days 11, 12, and 13 for discussion of the various merits of three possible APIs: PHP, Perl, and C.

Tuning MySQL with Its System Variables

MySQL has tools for helping you improve performance. You can use `mysqladmin` to display the variables with which the server is running:

```
# mysqladmin -p --show-variables
```

The same is accomplished with the query:

```
mysql> SHOW VARIABLES;
```

This returns a long list of items, all of which play some part in performance. However, the essential performance-related variables, and their effects, are described in Table 18.1. The most important of them are `key_buffer_size` and `table_cache`.

TABLE 18.1 Key MySQL Server Variables

Variable	Typical Value	Usage
back_log	5	The number of connection requests that can be made to queue, awaiting connection.
		Increase this for a busy site to allow more to be queued rather than refuse connections.
delayed_queue_size	1000	You can use INSERT DELAYED to place a row to be inserted in a queue rather than hold up the thread while the data is inserted. The client thread is then free to continue processing immediately.
		This variable controls the number of rows that can be queued.
		Increase this value if you use INSERT DELAYED and you find that client threads are having to wait because there's no room left in the queue.
key_buffer_size	16773120	MySQL can hold indexes in memory, using up to this number of bytes for storage. It runs faster when it can find an index in memory rather than going to disk.
		Increase this to improve performance, but not to more than about 25% of system RAM.
max_allowed_packet	1047552	The maximum size, in bytes, of data that can be handled in a single packet.
		Increase this if clients regularly transfer TEXT or BLOB data of several megabytes.
max_connections	100	The maximum number of concurrent connections to mysqld.

TABLE 18.1   continued

Variable	Typical Value	Usage
		Increase this to allow more simultaneous clients, but look carefully at performance that will degrade as more client threads are run.
sort_buffer	524280	Controls the amount of RAM in bytes in which operations to sort indexes are performed.
		Increasing this can improve GROUP BY and ORDER BY operations.
table_cache	384	The number of tables that may be open at once across all threads.
		If the Opened_tables status variable is large, you should increase table_cache (unless your application does a lot of FLUSH TABLES). Ideally should be at least max_connections times the maximum number of tables used in any join.
query_cache_size	20M	MySQL 4 can cache the results of frequently run queries, only rerunning a query on the table when relevant data changes.
		If you have enough memory, set this variable to speed up frequently run queries.

18

You can set these, and other variables, in my.cnf. If you don't already have my.cnf set up, your distribution will contain a support-files subdirectory in which you will find some sample my.cnf files, called things like my-small.cnf and my-huge.cnf. They contain starter setups for various sizes of machines.

Change to your source or binary installation directory and view these configuration files to find the one best suited to your server. Which one you choose will depend principally on how much RAM you have. Copy the file to where MySQL can read it; for example, on a 1GB system:

```
# cp support-files/my-huge.cnf /etc/my.cnf
```

Then restart MySQL. Experiment with setting other variables if you want, restarting to see what effect the change has.

You can also change MySQL's system variables by declaring a variable when you invoke mysqld_safe (or safe_mysqld in MySQL version 3). For example, to start the server and set query_cache_size to 16MB, you could invoke MySQL like this:

```
# /usr/local/mysql/bin/mysqld_safe -O key_buffer=16M
```

Note that a variable set in this way will lose its value after the current invocation of MySQL terminates.

Operating System and Hardware

Look at the operating system and hardware you're running on when addressing performance issues.

Memory is at the top of the list here. MySQL runs faster when it has a lot of memory to work with. As you saw previously when looking at the MySQL server variables, many things can be cached in memory to speed up performance. Give your system as much memory as you can afford. 1GB of RAM will help a busy system work well.

Provided that you have a good deal of RAM, you may also be able to reconfigure your operating system to stop all disk-swap operations. It's pointless to swap temporary files to disk when you have plenty of space in RAM.

Another important consideration is the disk speed. To be precise, it's seek time—the time to move the magnetic head across the surface to the right location—that matters. Disk reading and writing, when in the right place, will be quick by comparison.

If you really need the ultimate in performance, you actually need not one disk but several. Consider a second or third drive, or RAID-0 configuration (in which data is striped across several disks). This allows a read or write to occur on one disk while the other disk performs a seek, so that it's in the right place when the first operation is finished.

Consider the operating system itself. Much of this book is devoted to running MySQL on Linux, but of course it can be run on flavors of Unix and on varieties of Windows. Because MySQL was originally written for Intel machines with Linux, it will run faster on Linux than on Windows.

Finally, on a really heavy-load system, consider using replication. A MySQL database can be replicated across several machines, which with the right load-balancing configuration can make a high-traffic Web site still appear very fast. See Day 19, "Replication," for more about replication.

Compilation Options

How MySQL is compiled affects performance. The binary and RPM distributions of MySQL are compiled for speed and usually hard to beat, but if you have a compiler tuned specifically for your hardware or operating system, you may be able to compile MySQL yourself and squeeze out an improvement of a few percentage points.

If you're compiling from source yourself, two compile-time options can help execution speed. You should run `configure` like this:

```
# ./configure \
> --enable-assembler \
> --with-mysqld-ldflags=-all-static
```

The first option tells the compiler to produce assembler code, and the second tells it to produce statically linked libraries.

Remember, at this level, we're dealing principally with the speed of execution of the compiled binary. Therefore RAM and disk speed typically have a far greater effect.

Commands for Optimization

Now that you've had a tour of the principal things influencing database performance, it's time to spend a little time looking at the commands MySQL offers for improving the speed of your queries and the design of your tables.

Improving Tables for Joins and Other SELECT Queries: EXPLAIN

18

You heard previously that it's usually wise to add indexes to a table. In fact, if you are working with relatively large tables, the use of indexes is one of the biggest influencers of overall database performance.

You've read some rules-of-thumb about where to apply indexes—such as wherever a column is named in a WHERE clause, or where that column may be used as part of a join. But how can you be sure that you've applied them correctly? If you are performing joins and other SELECT queries, how can you be sure that the index is being used? And is it being used the way you expect?

This is where the EXPLAIN command can help you. Placing it in front of a join query gives you information about how the MySQL optimizer will perform the query and in which order they will be joined.

It's worth noting that the tables will not necessarily be joined in the order you write them in your query. The MySQL optimizer decides this for itself (although you can block this behavior by using a STRAIGHT_JOIN).

The syntax for EXPLAIN is simply

```
EXPLAIN SELECT query
```

Let's look at how you would use it by studying an example from the real world. This example is from a busy Web site that uses MySQL to serve up information about tourist attractions in its database.

Suppose that you have a table of attractions that exist in cities whose names are stored in a table of cities. There's also a related table of countries, being a lookup table for the name of the country in which the attraction is located.

Imagine you want to list all tourist attractions in a city whose name begins with "New." The query will be a three-table inner join.

You will probably be familiar with joins by now, so we won't go into how to build the query. More important for this discussion is how MySQL intends to process the join. Here's how you would write the join, preceding the SELECT query itself with EXPLAIN:

```
mysql> EXPLAIN SELECT atts.att_name, cities.city_name, countries.co_name
    -> FROM attractions AS atts INNER JOIN cities ON atts.city_id=cities.city_id
    -> INNER JOIN countries ON cities.co_id=countries.co_id
    -> WHERE cities.city_name LIKE 'New%';
+-----------+--------+--------------+---------+---------+--------------+-------+-----------+
|table      |type    |possible_keys |key      |key_len  |ref           |rows   |Extra      |
+-----------+--------+--------------+---------+---------+--------------+-------+-----------+
|countries  |ALL     |NULL          |NULL     |   NULL  |NULL          |   36| |           |
|atts       |ALL     |NULL          |NULL     |   NULL  |NULL          |14654| |           |
|cities     |eq_ref  |PRIMARY,co_id |PRIMARY  |      4  |atts.city_id  |    1|where used |
+-----------+--------+--------------+---------+---------+--------------+-------+-----------+
```

In the preceding example, it takes a long time to run the query and return 441 rows. There are currently no indexes on the countries and attractions tables.

Has the table design made the best possible use of indexes? (You're right—probably not!) Let's go through what the EXPLAIN information means:

- table is the table name.
- type is the type of join performed (you'll see what these may be in a moment).
- possible_keys indicates which keys MySQL could potentially use for the join.
- key indicates the key MySQL decided to use for the join.
- key_len indicates the length of the key MySQL decided to use.
- ref indicates which column from previous tables, or constants, are to be used to compare against rows in this table.
- rows indicates how many rows MySQL thinks it must examine to run this part of the query.
- Extra contains any additional information about how the query will be executed (you'll see some possible values in Extra in a moment).

At the moment, there are no indexes on the countries and attractions tables.

In the first two rows, the `type` column stating `ALL` indicates that all rows must be analyzed for both the `countries` and `attractions` tables—in other words, a full table scan in each case. This is very time-consuming, especially for the `attractions` table, which has more than 14,000 rows.

However, the `cities` table has a primary key on its `city_id` column and a non-unique index on its `co_id` (country ID) column. In this case, the `key` and `ref` columns state that the `PRIMARY KEY` (`city_id`) will be compared against the `city_id` in the `attractions` table.

This means that things could be worse; there will be no table scan through `cities` because the primary key enables it to go straight to the correct row.

But overall performance is poor. The values under rows indicate that many comparisons have to be made (in fact $36 \times 14,654 \times 1 = 527,544!$). On my machine, this takes 1.16 seconds to run.

So what should be done? With table scans occurring on all 14,000 rows of `attractions`, this table is a clear candidate for an index. Let's try placing an index on `city_id` and see whether it improves things:

```
ALTER TABLE attractions ADD INDEX(city_id)
```

After running the query again, here's the output from `EXPLAIN`:

```
+-----------+------+-------------+-------+-------+-------------+-----+----------+
|table      |type  |possible_keys|key    |key_len|ref          |rows |Extra     |
+-----------+------+-------------+-------+-------+-------------+-----+----------+
|countries  |ALL   |NULL         |NULL   |  NULL |NULL         |   36|          |
|atts       |ALL   |city_id      |NULL   |  NULL |NULL         |14654|          |
|cities_tmp |eq_ref|PRIMARY,co_id|PRIMARY|      4|atts.city_id |    1|where used|
+-----------+------+-------------+-------+-------+-------------+-----+----------+
```

Looking at the `atts` row in the preceding example, you can see that the new `city_id` key is showing up in `possible_keys`, but it's not being used. It doesn't appear in the `key` column.

MySQL is still performing two table scans, and the query takes a barely improved 1.07 seconds to run. What's lacking is a way of efficiently joining `countries` with `attractions`.

So now let's place an index on the `city_id` column of `cities`:

```
ALTER TABLE cities ADD INDEX(city_id)
```

18

After doing this, EXPLAIN gives the following:

```
+---------+------+-------------+-------+-------+------------+-----+---------+
|table    |type  |possible_keys|key    |key_len|ref         |rows |Extra    |
+---------+------+-------------+-------+-------+------------+-----+---------+
|atts     |ALL   |city_id      |NULL   |  NULL |NULL        |14654|         |
|cities   |eq_ref|PRIMARY,co_id|PRIMARY|      4|atts.city_id|    1|where used|
|countries|eq_ref|PRIMARY      |PRIMARY|      3|cities.co_id|    1|         |
+---------+------+-------------+-------+-------+------------+-----+---------+
```

Now you can see that the join is being done in a different order. First MySQL looks at
attractions, then cities, then countries. But a table scan is still being done for all
attractions, which is still bad.

Nevertheless, a join type of eq_ref for both cities and countries is a much better type
of join than before. It's using primary keys to join two of the three tables. In fact, this is
now better by a factor of 36 over the previous run.

Not surprisingly, execution of the query with the next index takes a more healthy 0.41
seconds.

But it can be made better still. Because a WHERE clause is being used against cities (you
can see that MySQL is recognizing this under Extra), let's follow one of the golden
rules: add an index to a column whenever it is to be named in a WHERE clause.

ALTER TABLE cities ADD INDEX(city_name)

After adding the index and running the query again, here's the output from EXPLAIN:

```
+---------+------+----------+---------+-------+---------------+----+---------+
|table    |type  |poss_keys |key      |key_len|ref            |rows|Extra    |
+---------+------+----------+---------+-------+---------------+----+---------+
|cities   |range |PRIMARY,  |city_name|   101 |NULL           | 133|where used|
|         |      |co_id,    |         |       |               |    |         |
|         |      |city_name |         |       |               |    |         |
|atts     |ref   |city_id   |city_id  |      4|cities.city_id |   3|         |
|countries|eq_ref|PRIMARY   |PRIMARY  |      3|cities.co_id   |   1|         |
+---------+------+----------+---------+-------+---------------+----+---------+
```

Study the cities line. Now cities is being examined first. The optimizer has realized that with an index on city_name, if the query is searching for a city name beginning
with New, it can be done very efficiently—quite the opposite from doing a table scan of a
VARCHAR column with no index.

(But remember that the index is beneficial only because our pattern match is left-justified;
a search for cities with "New" anywhere in their name would not have this advantage.)

This action retrieves just 133 rows—the cities with appropriate names.

Now look at the atts line. attractions is now joined, with a type of ref, and the ref column indicating that MySQL joins its city_id column against cities.city_id.

A type of ref is good, but not quite as good as eq_ref: it occurs here because the key used for attractions (city_id) is not unique. Therefore the optimizer knows it can't just retrieve a single row.

Finally, look at the countries line. countries is joined using a join type of eq_ref. This is the best type of join other than a const type because it uses the primary key of countries to join against the co_id of attractions and thus identify a single row to be retrieved.

On my machine, I now have execution in a fairly respectable 0.01 seconds.

> **Caution**
>
> With performance improvements such as those shown here, it's easy to get carried away with EXPLAIN and spend a lot of time experimenting with indexes. Taking a sample query in isolation, as we have done here, can be misleading.
>
> A real system typically runs many different queries, with the same tables being joined in various ways. The difficulty comes because the best index setup for one query may not be the best for another.
>
> For example, an inappropriate index on a column can occasionally degrade performance. Indexes always consume disk space, which may be precious, and when tables are being updated, indexes generate a definite overhead.
>
> You thus need to consider not just the execution times of your various queries but also their frequency of use and the overall performance impact on your system.
>
> There is often not a single "best way" of applying indexes; use EXPLAIN for guidance and do not expect a definitive answer.

18

Timing Query Execution: BENCHMARK()

The BENCHMARK() function permits you to use the mysql console to measure how long a query takes to execute. Its syntax is

```
BENCHMARK(count,expression)
```

where expression is a SQL query, and count is the number of times it should be executed. For example, to see how long it takes to run a SELECT:

```
mysql> SELECT BENCHMARK(1000000000,"SELECT * FROM products ORDER BY price");
+---------------------------------------------------------------+
| BENCHMARK(1000000000,"SELECT * FROM products ORDER BY price") |
+---------------------------------------------------------------+
|                                                             0 |
+---------------------------------------------------------------+
1 row in set (28.42 sec)
```

The value returned is always 0, but the meaningful part is the time elapsed, given in the last row of output to the mysql console. After MySQL returns the time elapsed, you can divide it by count to get the average time required for a single execution of the query.

However, note that BENCHMARK() measures the elapsed time, not the processor time, so if your server is busy it gives you a result that is longer than it should be. You should therefore try to run this command on your system when there are few other processes running.

Defining Your Tables Optimally for Their Data: PROCEDURE ANALYSE()

How do you know whether a table has the best possible column definitions for the data you're storing in it?

You've heard already that column definitions should be no bigger than needed, that they should be NOT NULL if possible, and other rules-of-thumb. PROCEDURE ANALYSE() is a command that you can run to get some free advice from the MySQL query optimizer on a table of your choice, so long as it already has representative data in it.

To run PROCEDURE ANALYSE(), simply place the two keywords at the end of your query. Here's an example.

Suppose that you have a table of countries, holding a country name and an identifier that is the primary key.

```
mysql> DESC countries;
+---------+-------------+------+-----+---------+---------------+
| Field   | Type        | Null | Key | Default | Extra         |
+---------+-------------+------+-----+---------+---------------+
| co_id   | char(3)     |      | PRI |         |               |
| co_name | varchar(30) |      |     |         |               |
+---------+-------------+------+-----+---------+---------------+
2 rows in set (0.00 sec)
```

Here's how you might run PROCEDURE ANALYSE() in the mysql console (adding \G to the end of your query to tell mysql to display the result vertically):

```
mysql> SELECT co_id, co_name FROM countries PROCEDURE ANALYSE()\G
*************************** 1. row ***************************
            Field_name: countries.co_id
             Min_value: AND
             Max_value: YUG
            Min_length: 3
            Max_length: 3
      Empties_or_zeros: 0
                 Nulls: 0
Avg_value_or_avg_length: 3.0000
                   Std: NULL
```

```
            Optimal_fieldtype: ENUM('AND','AUL','AUS','BEL','BUL','CAN','CRO','CYP',
'CZE','DEN','ENG','FIN','FRA','GER','GRE','HUN','IRE','ITY','LIC','LUX','MAC',
'MON','NET','NOR','POL','POR','ROM','SCO','SLO','SLV','SPA','SWE','SWI','USA',
'WAL','YUG') NOT NULL
*************************** 2. row ***************************
                Field_name: countries.co_name
                 Min_value: Andorra
                 Max_value: Yugoslavia
                Min_length: 3
                Max_length: 14
         Empties_or_zeros: 0
                     Nulls: 0
Avg_value_or_avg_length: 7.5000
                       Std: NULL
         Optimal_fieldtype: ENUM('Andorra','Australia','Austria','Belgium',
'Bulgaria','Canada','Croatia','Cyprus','Czech Republic','Denmark','England',
'Finland','France','Germany','Greece','Hungary','Ireland','Italy',
'Liechtenstein','Luxembourg','Macedonia','Monaco','Netherlands','Norway',
'Poland','Portugal','Romania','Scotland','Slovakia','Slovenia','Spain',
'Sweden','Switzerland','USA','Wales','Yugoslavia') NOT NULL
2 rows in set (0.00 sec)
```

Note the `Optimal_fieldtype` suggestions. The MySQL optimizer suggests that you alter the table to have ENUM columns for co_id and co_name. MySQL tells us this because an ENUM column is the most efficient for it to process.

This may be impractical (perhaps you want to add countries at a later date and would rather not alter the table for each country). You may also find it difficult to manage an ENUM column with so many possible values. So you can try limiting the freedom that PROCEDURE ANALYSE() has:

```
mysql> SELECT co_id, co_name FROM countries PROCEDURE ANALYSE(8,64)\G
*************************** 1. row ***************************
                Field_name: countries.co_id
                 Min_value: AND
                 Max_value: YUG
                Min_length: 3
                Max_length: 3
         Empties_or_zeros: 0
                     Nulls: 0
Avg_value_or_avg_length: 3.0000
                       Std: NULL
         Optimal_fieldtype: CHAR(3) NOT NULL
*************************** 2. row ***************************
                Field_name: countries.co_name
                 Min_value: Andorra
                 Max_value: Yugoslavia
                Min_length: 3
                Max_length: 14
         Empties_or_zeros: 0
                     Nulls: 0
```

18

```
Avg_value_or_avg_length: 7.5000
                    Std: NULL
      Optimal_fieldtype: VARCHAR(14) NOT NULL
2 rows in set (0.00 sec)
```

The arguments (8,64) passed to PROCEDURE ANALYSE() tell the optimizer to suggest only ENUM columns with 8 or fewer enumerated values and requiring 64 or fewer bytes to define the column.

Because the list of countries in the data is long, it exceeds the limits specified. So the optimizer suggests the next best thing for each column. For the co_id column it suggests that we use a CHAR(3) NOT NULL column, and for the co_name column a VARCHAR(14) NOT NULL column.

You can now compare these recommendations with the actual definition of the table. In this case, the co_id column is already optimal, but co_name could be shortened from 30 to 16 characters. If you're happy with what the optimizer recommends—or at least you want to get closer to the optimal column definition—you should then alter your table with ALTER TABLE.

Defragmenting: OPTIMIZE TABLE

Not all optimization issues relate purely to speed. You may also want to ensure that MySQL makes best use of your disk's storage capacity.

The OPTIMIZE TABLE command is used to defragment tables that have accumulated a lot of wasted space.

Tables that have many DELETE and UPDATE operations performed on them are particularly susceptible to fragmentation. This is because an update that results in a record getting smaller leaves a gap between the end of that record and the start of the next.

Such "holes" in the data file accumulate, and because the data records become unnecessarily spread out across the disk, performance gradually degrades.

The OPTIMIZE TABLE can be used to rewrite the data in the table and close up the gaps.

Use OPTIMIZE TABLE like in this example, on a table called cities in a database called travel:

```
mysql> OPTIMIZE TABLE cities;
+---------------+----------+----------+----------+
| Table         | Op       | Msg_type | Msg_text |
+---------------+----------+----------+----------+
| travel.cities | optimize | status   | OK       |
+---------------+----------+----------+----------+
1 row in set (0.34 sec)
```

The output from the command tells you whether everything went okay.

On a site with many updates to tables, especially tables with large VARCHAR, TEXT, or BLOB columns, OPTIMIZE TABLE should be run regularly, perhaps once per month.

Summary

In today's lesson, you learned that many things influence performance, from query and table design, to hardware and operating system choices. You looked at these things somewhat in isolation because any analysis has to concentrate on one thing at a time.

However, when trying to improve performance, it's much more difficult to take a single course of action and expect performance to get better. Taking the use of indexes as a case in point, the optimal configuration for one query may not be the best for all.

Most frustrating is that there's no one "right answer." Your strategy needs to consider real-world scenarios and take into account a number of factors. Remember to measure the speed of your system before and after because this is likely to be the best guide of how much improvement an intervention has brought about.

But although performance initiatives may look like a black art, you should by now have a reasonable understanding of the performance influencers and be able to form a plan for addressing the things that matter most on your system.

18

Q&A

Q This all sounds complicated, and I just have a simple system. Do I really need to learn this?

A In systems that you're developing for interest only, or in light-traffic systems, probably No.

However, most serious systems experience more significant traffic and usage at some point in their life span, so performance should be something that's built in to the design in all but the most trivial databases.

Q If I were to do one thing to improve performance, what should it be?

A In almost all cases, add indexes to tables where appropriate.

Workshop

The quiz and exercises are provided to help you solidify your understanding of the material covered today. Try to understand the quiz and exercise answers before continuing to tomorrow's lesson.

Quiz

1. True or False: Adding indexes always improves performance.

2. Why can't you use the BENCHMARK() function in SQL embedded in an application?

3. Put the following factors in order of effect on performance, in terms of which give the best possible scope for improving performance:

   - Disk speed
   - Processor speed
   - Use of indexes

Quiz Answers

1. False. In general adding indexes improves performance, but in some circumstances performance can get worse.

2. BENCHMARK() is intended for use in the mysql console. The output is always 0, although the console will tell you the elapsed time.

3. The factors (most important first) should be ranked in the following order:

   1. Use of indexes
   2. Disk speed
   3. Processor speed

Exercises

1. State the command that you would use for analyzing whether a table has the optimal column definitions for the actual data it holds.

2. Write a query that analyzes the city_id and city_name columns of the table cities, and displays information about the optimal column types for the data held in these columns.

3. State the command that you would use for analyzing whether a join query makes best use of any indexes on tables being joined.

Answers to Exercises

1. PROCEDURE ANALYSE().

2. You should run this:

   ```
   mysql> SELECT city_id, city_name FROM cities PROCEDURE ANALYSE()\G
   ```

3. EXPLAIN.

DAY **19**

Replication

Today's lesson will look at how to replicate a MySQL database.

Particular topics you will study today will be:

- What replication is
- Basic principles of replication in MySQL
- How to set up a simple master-slave replication system
- More complex replication topologies

What Is Replication?

In Day 15, "Administration," you saw how a MySQL database can be backed up and moved to another server. This is a manual process that copies your data to a safe place. But how can you have a seamless, automatic backup that preserves, elsewhere, every last modification to your data? And how can you run a *hot spare* so that your database can never go down? Or spread the load on your systems across several machines?

Replication answers those questions. The principle of replication is this: You can have any number of servers working together. Changes in the database on one server instantly get copied—*replicated*—to the other servers.

Such a system gives you high availability. If one server goes down or its connection is lost, the others keep going and keep responding to client queries. If a server goes down permanently, the other servers have the latest copy of the data.

So there are several reasons to replicate a database:

- Back up, or "hot" back up—So that if your main system should fail you have a backup that is 100% up-to-date
- Load sharing—Rather than refer all your database queries to a single machine, it may be preferable to spread the load across several machines.
- High availability—If you're running a database system that absolutely must not go down, your only option is to have a configuration involving databases at several physically distant sites that run on different Internet connections. In this way, you can guard against most eventualities, from hardware failure to Internet outage to physical disaster.

Limitations of Replication

Having a replicated system necessitates that you have two or more servers (that is, physical machines), and for some situations you should have each server in a different location with its own Internet connectivity. There's a significant hardware cost involved.

What's more, where replication is a one-way process—master to slave—so updates must be applied to a master server first. With many updates, the master itself might be a bottleneck.

Connected with this is the problem of latency of propagation: Although an update to the master will typically be replicated to its slave(s) very quickly (in less than one second), this latency time is not guaranteed and can be influenced by network traffic, system activity, and other factors.

Replication doesn't guarantee better performance. You can't ignore the need to optimize queries and the design and configuration of your database. Failing to do this can also mean that you need more slaves than you otherwise should.

Replication in MySQL

MySQL has implemented replication since version 3.23.15, although version 4 greatly improved the functionality. Replication continues to be developed with new features appearing in just about every release.

MySQL replication works on the principle of a one-way, master-slave relationship. Any database changes made on the master are replicated to the slave. It works like this:

- The master is configured to create a binary log of all updates that occur.

- The slave (or several slaves) is configured to connect to the master and read the binary logs (having started with an initial snapshot of the master's database).

- The slave keeps a record of what *position* it has reached in reading the master's binary update log; should either the slave or the master go down, or the connection between them fail, the slave remembers this position and keeps trying to read from this point onward.

- The slave can itself write to a binary update log, and therefore any number of slaves can look to it as their master.

Setting Up a Master-Slave Replication System

Now that you understand what needs to be achieved, it's time to get hands-on and talk you through the process of setting up a replicated system of one master and one slave.

You will need two servers on which you have installed MySQL. Ideally this should be version 4.0.2 or later, and if possible the same version on each machine.

In essence the following instructions will show you how to

- Set up the master.
- Set up the slave.
- Start replicating.

Master Setup Principles

Setting up the master involves five steps, each of which is straightforward. Here's an overview:

1. Create a user account on the master; this is the user account with which the slave will connect.

2. Shut down `mysqld` on the master.

3. Make a backup or copy of the databases you want to replicate.

19

4. Enable binary logging on the master (in `my.cnf`) and ensure that a `server-id` is set.

5. Restart `mysqld` on the master.

Here's the same process again, with a little more hands-on detail. You should do all of the following on the master server:

1. Create a user account; call it, say, `slave1`. On MySQL version 4.0.2 onward, or on any version using the newer style grant tables, you'll need to grant the slave account `Repl_slave_priv`, like this:

```
mysql> GRANT REPLICATION SLAVE ON *.* TO slave1@'slave.domain.com'
    -> IDENTIFIED BY 'slavepass';
```

If `Repl_slave_priv` is not present in the `mysql.user` grant table (as in older versions), you'll need to assign the slave `File_priv`, like this:

```
mysql> GRANT FILE ON *.* TO slave1@'slave.domain.com'
    -> IDENTIFIED BY 'slavepass';
```

This grants the slave permission to connect to and replicate any database on the master, but in this example (for added security), the slave is restricted to connecting from the `slave.domain.com` host and must provide the given password `slavepass`.

2. Shut down `mysqld` on the master:

```
# mysqladmin -u root -p shutdown
```

If binary logging has previously been enabled on your server (whose name in the following commands is given by *host*), you should remove all previous binary logs to prevent synchronization problems. Go to your data directory and remove any *host*-bin.00*n* files and the *host*-bin.index file:

```
# cd /usr/local/mysql/var
# rm my_host-bin.*
```

3. Take a snapshot (a full backup) of the databases you want to replicate. Probably the best method (on a Linux or Unix system) is to `tar` the directories containing the databases you want to replicate (and if need be, `gzip` to compress). For example, if MySQL's data is in `/usr/local/mysql/var/` and the database you want to replicate is `store`:

```
# cd /usr/local/mysql/var/
# tar -cvf store.tar store
# gzip store.tar
```

(Note that you can replicate any number of databases on the MySQL server, including the `mysql` database with its grant tables. By default, the changes of every database are written to the binary log. You'll see later today in the section "Customizing Replication" how to specify databases to ignore, so that updates to them are omitted from the log.)

Then copy the `.tar.gz` files via FTP or similar means to the slave server.

On Windows, you may want to WinZip the files and then FTP them.

4. Enable binary logging on the master. Edit the `my.cnf` file and ensure that it has the following settings in the `[mysqld]` section:

```
[mysqld]
...
log-bin
server-id  = 1
```

The `server-id` should ideally be 1 (to keep life simple) but actually just needs to be a unique number that is not duplicated by any other server in your replication group.

5. Restart `mysqld` on the master:

 # /usr/local/mysql/bin/mysqld_safe &

You should now have a running master that is writing to a binary log. If you want to confirm this, change to your data directory and look for a file called *host-bin.001*, where *host* is the name of your server.

You can also go in to the `mysql` console and run SHOW MASTER STATUS; you should get something like this:

```
mysql> SHOW MASTER STATUS;
+----------------+----------+--------------+------------------+
| File           | Position | Binlog_do_db | Binlog_ignore_db |
+----------------+----------+--------------+------------------+
| master-bin.001 | 230778   |              |                  |
+----------------+----------+--------------+------------------+
```

The file `master-bin.001` (where the hostname `master` in the preceding output will be the name of your host) is the current binary update log file, and the number under `Position` indicates the master's position as it writes to that file.

Should you want to see what the `master-bin.001` file looks like, you'll find it difficult to read using the normal methods. It's a binary file, so it may look ugly using tools such as Unix's `vi` or `cat`. Instead, you should use the `mysqlbinlog` program, which you'll find in your MySQL `bin/` directory. Use it like this:

 # mysqlbinlog master-bin.001

Slave Setup Principles

On the slave machine, here's an overview of the steps you will need to follow:

1. Define this server as the slave by editing the `my.cnf` configuration file.

2. Shut down `mysqld` on the slave.

19

3. Copy the snapshot of data that you took from the master into the slave's data directory.

4. Restart mysqld on the slave.

Here's the slave setup process in more hands-on detail:

1. Edit the my.cnf configuration file on the slave machine, so that it contains the following lines in the [mysqld] section:

```
[mysqld]
...
master-host       = master.domain.com
master-user       = slave1
master-password   = slavepass
server-id         = 2
```

The preceding shows sample values, which will be different in your system. master-host must be set to the IP or hostname of the master server; master-user must declare the slave's username that you set up previously, with master-password defining his password. The server-id must be another unique number in the replication group, and 2 is suggested here.

2. Shut down mysqld on the slave:

```
# mysqladmin -u root -p shutdown
```

3. Move the snapshot (the full backup) of the store database that you took from the master into the slave's data directory. If you used tar and gzip, you can do this:

```
# mv store.tar.gz /usr/local/mysql/var/
# cd /usr/local/mysql/var
# gunzip store.tar.gz
# tar -xf store.tar
```

4. Restart mysqld on the slave.

```
# /usr/local/mysql/bin/mysqld_safe &
```

You should now have a running slave. You'll want to check that things are working, so go into the mysql console and run a SHOW SLAVE STATUS query, terminating the command with \G (instead of ;) to make the result more readable, like this:

```
mysql> SHOW SLAVE STATUS\G
*************************** 1. row ***************************
          Master_Host: master.domain.com
          Master_User: slave1
          Master_Port: 3306
        Connect_retry: 60
      Master_Log_File: master-bin.001
  Read_Master_Log_Pos: 230778
       Relay_Log_File: slave-relay-bin.003
        Relay_Log_Pos: 4
```

```
Relay_Master_Log_File: master-bin.001
    Slave_IO_Running: Yes
   Slave_SQL_Running: Yes
      Replicate_do_db:
  Replicate_ignore_db:
          Last_errno: 0
          Last_error:
        Skip_counter: 0
 Exec_master_log_pos: 230778
      Relay_log_space: 4
1 row in set (0.00 sec)
```

The two lines in the middle of the output, Slave_IO_Running and Slave_SQL_running, should both be Yes. If not, something is wrong.

Another check you can perform is to run a SQL update query on the master server, such as creating a table or adding some data to a table. Change to the slave and see whether the update has been replicated. If the update you made is not there (and it should normally be there almost immediately), replication is failing.

> **Tip**
>
> Most problems with setting up replication arise at this point. If replication is not happening, check these things:
>
> - Check that the master is creating a binary log, by looking for a host-bin.001 file in its data directory.
> - Check that the slave account can connect to the master; on the slave machine, try to connect to MySQL on the master, for example:
>
> ```
> $ mysql -h master.domain.com -u slave1 -p
> ```
>
> - Ensure that the slave account has the correct user privileges on the master (File_priv or Repl_slave_priv according to MySQL version).
> - Check that both server-id numbers are unique.
> - If no obvious configuration problems are found, look in the MySQL error log on the slave; if errors indicate that the slave is unable to connect or has crashed, you should find helpful messages in the log that suggest what is wrong.
>
> Replication is a complex thing, and early versions of MySQL that implement replication may have minor bugs. However, the vast majority of problems setting up replication in simple configurations are due to improper configurations!

19

If all has gone well, you should now have a working two-machine replication pair. Any change applied to the master should appear in a very short time (less than one second) on the slave.

It is possible for replication to break down after it has started. This may occur if the slave encounters an error in the data it is trying to process. For example, if it encounters a unique key violation when trying to process an update, replication will halt. Such problems most commonly arise if updates are applied to the slave rather than to the master, if the slave is set up incorrectly, or if the slave is out of sync with the binary logs of the master. If problems like this arise, you should study what happened to cause the problem and ensure that your setup is correctly configured.

Using Replication

Now that you have a two-server replication pair working, it's worth noting a few more basic principles.

Most importantly, if you perform any updates on your database, you should make them on the master. If you allow changes to be made on the slave, you run the risk of creating data with duplicate unique keys or other such violation problems. Updating the slave also defeats the object of replication! See the section "Replication Topologies" later in this lesson for alternative architectures.

Your two-server replication pair should be robust. Either machine can go down for several hours, and when it comes back up, replication will resume.

For example, if the master goes down, the slave keeps trying to connect to the master (every 60 seconds by default), but apart from missing its usual feed of new data, it can still respond to client queries that read from its database.

On the other hand, if the slave goes down, the master just won't replicate its changes. It keeps building up its binary log, but the slave has a record of where it left off reading, and when the slave comes back up again, it just continues reading the updates from that point onward.

The same principle applies if an Internet connection goes down. If the two machines can't communicate with each other, they'll just keep trying until they can. This principle applies even if the slave is on a dial-up Internet connection. When the dial-up occurs and the connection is made again, the two systems will resume replicating from the point they last ceased.

Caution

Because replication uses the binary log, it can faithfully duplicate the changes applied on a master database to a slave—but with one minor exception.

If your SQL contains an update based on the random number function RAND(), the update may not be applied in the same way on the slave because the output of RAND() will be different each time. To get around this limitation, you should "seed" RAND() with a value so that the result is the same each time. You can seed it with a Unix timestamp or other integer, for example, RAND(*some_integer*).

However, other functions such as NOW() and LAST_INSERT_ID() are replicated correctly in MySQL.

Customizing Replication

You may want to have a setup that is different from the simple two-server setup described previously. There are a number of options that you can apply to either the master or the slave. This lesson does not cover every possibility, but it covers the most commonly used ones.

You may not want to replicate all the databases on the master. For example, some of your databases may not be worthy of replicating, or you may just want to reduce network traffic and only replicate what is critical.

MySQL lets you tell a master server to ignore logging updates on certain named databases. You do this by placing a line in the [mysqld] section of my.cnf, like this:

```
[mysqld]
...
binlog-ignore-db  = database_name
```

You will need to restart mysqld for the change to take effect. MySQL will now not record updates to the database given by *database_name* in the binary log. Place several such lines in the configuration file if you want the master to skip logging on several databases.

You can do a similar thing from the slave end. You would place the following line in the my.cnf file on the slave:

```
[mysqld]
...
replicate-ignore-db  = database_name
```

This tells the slave to skip updates on the given *database_name*. Place several such lines in the configuration file if you want the slave to ignore several databases.

19

A further possibility is to configure a slave to also be a master. In such a configuration—a *daisy chain*—each slave will be the master of the next. Therefore each slave must be configured to produce a binary log of changes it has replicated, so that those updates can be passed down the line to the next slave. You should include the following line in the `[mysqld]` section of the slave's `my.cnf` file:

```
[mysqld]
...
log-slave-updates
```

SQL Commands for Replication

It is possible to control replication, and to monitor what is going on, using SQL queries. Here are a few SQL commands for doing these things.

You can control and monitor the master using the following SQL commands:

- `SHOW MASTER STATUS` displays information on the state of the master binary logs.
- `RESET MASTER` clears (deletes) all binary logs from the master; this is useful if you want to start with a "clean sheet" and copy a fresh version of the database to the slave.

You can control and monitor the slave using the following commands:

- `SHOW SLAVE STATUS` displays information on the current state of the slave, including whether it is running, the master it is connected to, and what position it is at in reading the master's binary log (this number should increase as updates are processed).
- `SLAVE STOP` tells the slave to cease reading from the master; replication stops immediately.
- `SLAVE START` tells the slave to start replicating again.
- `LOAD DATA FROM MASTER` connects to the master and gets a complete, new copy of its databases; useful if you want to clear the slave's databases and start replicating again from the current position on the master. (Note that in the current version of MySQL, this command obtains a read lock on the master database before transferring the data; this prevents updates from occurring on the master. On a large database or with a slow Internet connection, this may take a considerable time while the transfer is taking place and cause unacceptable downtime on the master.)
- `RESET SLAVE` tells the slave to forget its position in reading the master's logs; this is useful if you want to get a fresh copy of the database from the master.

Try out these commands so that you feel comfortable using a small set of SQL commands for monitoring the state of replication and making some changes to how it's operating.

It's now time to look at some architectures that go beyond the basic two-server model and explore the potentials of replication.

Replication Topologies

So far you have looked at a simple two-server replication topology, like this:

A → B

where machine A is the master, and it replicates to machine B.

This is the simplest, easiest to set up, replicating pair.

Multislave

It's possible to set up a single master with any number of slaves. The architecture would look like this:

A → B

   → C

   → D

   →...

You would configure the master in the same way as explained previously. For the slaves, the only critical thing to ensure is that they each have a unique `server-id`.

In this model, any update that occurs in the master A is replicated to slaves B, C, and D.

Such a system is a good model for a load-balanced system if there are many more client read requests than writes. Client requests would pass through a load-balancing server (not shown), which refers each read request to B, C, or D in turn, whereas write requests would be referred to master server A. (Server A might also process reads.)

The setup is a high availability one, because if any slave system goes down (say, C), the load-balancer would just send requests to the remaining live systems (B and D).

The weakness in the system is that if master server A goes down, updates cannot be processed. To make the system a little more fault tolerant, the configuration needs more than one master.

19

Multislave, Multimaster

As well as having several slaves to share the load of read requests and provide resilience, you can have a second master (or several masters) to ensure high availability of the system to updates, as well as to reads.

You could have a setup like this:

M2 ← M1 → B

→ C

→ D

In this topology, master M1 not only feeds updates to B, C, and D, but also to a backup master, M2. Slave servers B, C, and D know that they must look to master M1 for their updates. But they know that if M1 fails, they should elect server M2 as their new master and replicate changes from it instead.

MySQL has a command, CHANGE MASTER TO, that enables a slave to switch its attention to a new master. However, when several slaves need to be switched to a new master, things can be a little more complicated.

It is important that all slaves "agree" at the same time that they're going to elect a new master. If there's a problem with a network connection, some slaves might think master M1 is down, whereas others know it's still up. If this situation arises, not all slaves will have identical copies of the data.

Currently such master election procedures have to be implemented in application code. However, it is intended that MySQL will soon have a master election process built into its replication system so that issues of this sort are handled in MySQL rather than in your application.

See the MySQL Reference Manual for detailed information about CHANGE MASTER TO and other replication commands.

Circular Replication

It is possible to connect servers in a ring, like this:

A → B → C

↑   ↓

F ← E ← D

To do this, you would need to configure each server, A through F, to do both binary logging and slave update logging. Each machine would have to be configured with both master and slave parameters, effectively a daisy-chain setup that loops back onto itself.

However, such a setup can be prone to problems if you allow clients to perform updates on all machines. If an update is made on A that creates a unique key (perhaps a value got generated in an auto-increment column), and then an update occurs on F a short time after, before replication has occurred, the same unique key value will be generated. When replication of the data from A reaches F, a unique key violation will arise, and replication will stop.

To use circular replication, you need to ensure that updates can occur only on one server. Alternatively, your applications must be written to take this situation into account and ensure that it does not arise.

Summary

Today's lesson looked at replication: what it is and how you can implement it.

You learned some of the strengths of a database that runs in a replicated configuration but also looked at the limitations and costs of replicating databases.

You went through the process of setting up a replicating master-slave pair using two MySQL servers, configuring the master to write to its binary update log and the slave to read updates from this log.

There are several SQL commands for monitoring the status of replication on a server and for modifying the setup. You also encountered the `mysqlbinlog` utility for displaying binary logs.

19

Finally you saw a brief overview of some of the replication topologies that are possible. Although the architectures described do not represent every possible configuration, you saw some of the most useful ones and developed an idea of the possibilities.

Q&A

Q Does a slave always need to be connected to a master?

A No. The connection between the two can go down, or either system can go down, but when they connect again, replication will pick up where it left off.

Of course, the slave will not have an up-to-date copy of the master while it's not connected!

There's no need to tell the slave when the connection resumes; the slave just keeps retrying to connect to the master (once a minute by default).

Q Can I make updates to the slave server?

A In most cases, no. If your slave is replicating all databases from the master, and if a unique key violation may occur, no updates should be made to the slave or replication will eventually break down.

But if your slave is replicating only certain databases from the master, and ignoring others, you can happily update the ignored databases because they won't be overwritten by changes in the master.

Q Can I use replication in a high-load, mission-critical system?

A Yes, that's what many people are doing with replication.

It's wrong to assume that you can ignore other principles: such as good database and application design, and the need for good backups. But replication allows you to have 100% up-to-date backups and systems on which a heavy load can be shared across several machines. If your system is reaching its performance limit as a single-server database, replication should help you fulfill your performance needs.

Q Where can I get more information about replication?

A Replication in MySQL is in its relatively early days. People are finding it easy to set up and very powerful, but there's still a long way to go, and MySQL will be developed a good deal yet.

You can learn more about replication in the MySQL Technical Reference and by searching the Web for other resources, architectures, discussions, and advice.

Workshop

The quiz and exercises are provided to help you solidify your understanding of the material covered today. Try to understand the quiz and exercise answers before continuing to tomorrow's lesson.

Quiz

1. True or False: A master can have any number of slaves.

2. True or False: A slave can have any number of masters.

Quiz Answers

1. True.

2. False. A slave can have only one master at a time. In fault-tolerant setups you may want to reconfigure a slave to get data from a new master.

Exercises

1. Write a GRANT query to be run on a master that allows a slave to connect from IP address 100.11.22.33 with username harry and password hpass23.

2. What lines must you have in the slave's my.cnf file to make it function as a slave? The master's IP will be 200.33.33.33, and the slave's server-id will be 100.

3. What single piece of information must be different in the configuration between the master and all its slaves?

Answers to Exercises

1. You should have this:

```
mysql> GRANT REPLICATION SLAVE ON *.* TO harry@100.11.22.33
    -> IDENTIFIED BY 'hpass23';
```

2. In the [mysqld] section you should have this:

```
[mysqld]
...
master-host     = 200.33.33.33
master-user     = harry
master-password = hpass23
server-id       = 100
```

3. The server-id number must be different on every machine.

19

WEEK 3

DAY 20

Embedding the MySQL Server

In today's lesson you will learn how to embed a MySQL database server into another software package.

This chapter explains the idea of embedding MySQL and shows you how to build a simple MySQL-embedded system.

In particular you will learn:

- What embedding is, and why it's useful
- How to compile MySQL so that it can be used as an embedded server
- How to write and compile an application that includes a MySQL embedded server
- The licensing principles that apply when MySQL is embedded in an application

What Is an Embedded System?

Until now in this book, we have always treated MySQL as a separate entity from other applications, as a server program that runs independently, and to which other users and applications can connect. You have seen how to connect to a MySQL server through the `mysql` client and through the PHP, Perl, and C APIs.

MySQL version 4 introduced the capability to link the program code of MySQL into another program. *Embedding* means that you can put a full-featured MySQL server inside a client application.

If you are a software author writing an application, you can create your application with a MySQL database embedded within it. The client-server paradigm is broken, with application and database becoming a single program.

This can be useful. Here are some scenarios in which you may want to do this:

- Where a software author wants to offer a piece of software for sale, and the customer will install the software on a computer that doesn't have MySQL installed
- Where a software author has no knowledge or control over the version of MySQL present on the user's computer, but the application requires a MySQL database with specific functionality or compiled options
- Where a software author wants the entire application to be as simple to install as possible, with high-speed operation, the minimum size, easy management, and the lowest number of components

When MySQL is embedded, a discrete binary application is created with an entire database inside it. It's ready to be installed on the target computer and run.

Think of embedding as creating a one-box, shrink-wrapped solution, as easy as possible for the customer to install and run.

Licensing

Commercial licensing is principally for developers writing software for sale and distribution. But who can use MySQL for free under the GNU Public License (GPL), and who needs to purchase a commercial license?

There are specific rules that define when MySQL falls under the GPL and can be distributed and used for free, and when a commercial license must be purchased.

Let's look at the principles of GPL and commercial licensing.

Free To Use If Your Application Is 100% GPL

If you write an application that is licensed under the GPL (or a compatible OSI license approved by MySQL AB), you are free to ship MySQL (or any other GPL software of MySQL AB) with your application.

(Where the GPL applies, you must make all source code available with the distribution, as well as comply to other rules of GPL.)

Application means any type of software application, system, tool, or utility. You do not need a specific agreement with MySQL AB because the GPL applies.

Free To Use If You Never Distribute, Modify, or Copy

As long as you *never distribute* the MySQL software in any way (inside your organization or outside), you are free to use it for powering your application. You can do this irrespective of whether your application comes under the GPL (or other OSI approved license).

You are allowed to *modify* MySQL source code. However, if you *distribute* the modified MySQL code, all changes, all interface code, and code relating to it will fall under the GPL. You'll have to comply with the GPL in the way you distribute the package.

You are allowed to *copy* MySQL binaries and source code, but when you do so, the copies will again fall under the GPL.

Commercial Use For All Other Purposes

If your application is *not licensed* under GPL (or other OSI approved license) and you intend to *distribute* MySQL software (inside your organization or outside), you must first obtain a commercial license for the MySQL software in question.

For example:

- If you include the MySQL server in an application that is not open source, you need to purchase a commercial license for the MySQL server.
- If you include any of the MySQL drivers in an application (so that your application can run with MySQL), and the application is not open source, you need a commercial license for those drivers. Examples of MySQL drivers include the ODBC driver, the JDBC driver, and the C language library.

Another reason for purchasing a commercial license is that under such a license MySQL AB takes responsibility for its product. In contrast, under the GPL, there are no warranties or representations from MySQL AB.

20

Note

> You can read more about the specific terms of GNU Public License in the MySQL Technical Reference. For information about the pricing and purchasing of commercial licenses, visit the MySQL Web site at
> `https://order.mysql.com/`.

The embedded server concept means that we may encounter MySQL in anything from PC-based applications to programs running on personal digital assistants (PDAs). Where applications need to have a small footprint, MySQL may just be compiled to have the bare minimum of installed libraries, so it's not difficult to conceive a MySQL-powered application within a wristwatch or a digital camera.

How to Create an Embedded System

The MySQL embedded server library is called `libmysqld`. This library contains everything you need to run MySQL within another application. To embed MySQL, in principle you just compile `libmysqld` and then link it into your application.

In this lesson you will go through the steps for compiling an example application. So that you can concentrate on the principles of embedding rather than be distracted by superfluous code, we'll write a simple application that runs a couple of queries and exits.

Recall from Day 13, "Using the C API," that you created client applications that communicate with a MySQL server. You will do much the same today, although like Day 13, this lesson is aimed at the developer who already has a knowledge of C.

The worked example you're about to see should run on Linux and BSD systems, but if you are using Unix, Windows, or another operating system, it should work with minor changes. Provided that you're familiar with compiling C programs on your platform, you should know the changes that need to be made.

Compiling MySQL for Embedding

To compile MySQL for embedding, you have to download a source distribution of MySQL. See the description as explained in Day 2, "Installing MySQL," if you have not already done so.

You need to compile MySQL with the `--with-embedded-server` option. This tells MySQL to create the `libmysqld` library (as opposed to just `mysqld`). You might change to the source directory and compile like this:

```
# cd /usr/local/mysql-4.0.2-alpha
# ./configure --prefix=/usr/local/mysql --with-embedded-server
```

Then compile by running `make` like this:

```
# make
```

and then install the new binary like this:

```
# make install
```

If you already have `mysqld` running, shut down and start it up again to use the new binary:

```
# mysqladmin shutdown
# /usr/local/mysql/bin/mysqld_safe &
```

In `/usr/local/mysql/lib/mysql`, you will now have a file called `libmysqld.a`. This is the library that we will compile into an application as an embedded server.

> **Tip**
>
> The precise functionality available within your `libmysqld` depends on other options with which you compiled MySQL. For example, to compile a fairly fast-executing server, you could run `configure` like this:
>
> ```
> # ./configure --prefix=/usr/local/mysql \
> > --with-embedded-server \
> > --enable-assembler --with-mysqld-ldflags=-all-static
> ```
>
> A typical `libmysqld` is about 5MB in size, but it can be much smaller if you turn off all unnecessary options. You should do:
>
> ```
> # ./configure -help
> ```
>
> in the MySQL source directory to see a full list of options.

Writing an Application for Use with `libmysqld`

Create a directory called `test_libmysqld` at the same level as the MySQL source directory. Assuming that you placed the source directory under `/usr/local`, you can do this:

```
# cd /usr/local/
# mkdir test_libmysqld
```

You'll then need an application program. Of course, you can write any program you want, but to keep things simple we'll use a slightly modified version of the program we wrote in Day 13. It also has several elements in common with the example that comes with the MySQL distribution (you will find this in the files beginning with the name `manual`, in the `Docs` directory of the source distribution).

Listing 20.1 shows the application program, and for this exercise, you should call it `test_libmysqld.c`.

20

LISTING 20.1   test_libmysqld.c

```
1: /* Simple client, built using the embedded MySQL server library */
2:
3: #include <mysql.h>
4: #include <stdarg.h>
5: #include <stdio.h>
6: #include <stdlib.h>
7:
8: MYSQL *db_connect(const char *dbname);
9: void db_disconnect(MYSQL *mysql);
10: void db_do_query(MYSQL *mysql, const char *query);
11: void print_result_set (MYSQL *mysql, MYSQL_RES *res_set);
12:
13: const char *server_groups[] = {
14:     "test_libmysqld_SERVER", "embedded", "server", NULL
15: };
16:
17: int
18: main(int argc, char **argv)
19: {
20:     MYSQL *one, *two;
21:
22:     mysql_server_init(argc, argv, (char **)server_groups);
23:
24:     one = db_connect(NULL);
25:     two = db_connect("store");
26:
27:     db_do_query(one, "SHOW DATABASES");
28:     db_do_query(two, "SHOW TABLE STATUS");
29:
30:     mysql_close(two);
31:     mysql_close(one);
32:
33:     mysql_server_end();
34:
35:     exit(EXIT_SUCCESS);
36: }
37:
38: static void
39: die(MYSQL *mysql, char *fmt, ...)
40: {
41:     va_list ap;
42:     va_start(ap, fmt);
43:     vfprintf(stderr, fmt, ap);
44:     va_end(ap);
45:     (void)putc('\n', stderr);
46:     if (mysql)
47:         db_disconnect(mysql);
48:     exit(EXIT_FAILURE);
49: }
```

LISTING 20.1   continued

```
50:
51: MYSQL *
52: db_connect(const char *dbname)
53: {
54:     MYSQL *mysql = mysql_init(NULL);
55:     if (!mysql)
56:         die(mysql, "mysql_init failed: no memory");
57:
58:     mysql_options(mysql, MYSQL_READ_DEFAULT_GROUP,"test_libmysqld_CLIENT");
59:     if (!mysql_real_connect(mysql, NULL, NULL, NULL, dbname, 0, NULL, 0))
60:         die(mysql, "mysql_real_connect failed: %s", mysql_error(mysql));
61:
62:     return mysql;
63: }
64:
65: void
66: db_disconnect(MYSQL *mysql)
67: {
68:     mysql_close(mysql);
69: }
70:
71: void
72: db_do_query(MYSQL *mysql, const char *query)
73: {
74: MYSQL_RES *res_set;
75:
76:     if (mysql_query (mysql, query) == 0) {
77:         printf ("Query succeeded. About to fetch result.\n");
78:         res_set = mysql_store_result (mysql);
79:
80:         if (res_set != NULL) {
81:
82:             /* Result set obtained, so process */
83:             print_result_set (mysql, res_set);
84:             mysql_free_result (res_set);
85:
86:         } else {
87:
88:             /* No result set, see what happened */
89:             if (mysql_field_count (mysql) > 0) {
90:
91:                 /* Should have had some fields
92:                  * so an error must have occurred */
93:                 fprintf (stderr,
94:                     "No result set, mysql_store_result() failed: %s\n",
95:                     mysql_error (mysql));
96:
97:             } else {
98:
99:                 /* Field count is 0,
100:                  * so no result was expected from the query */
```

20

LISTING 20.1   continued

```
101:                    printf ("Query was not meant to return data.\n");
102:
103:                }
104:            }
105:        } else {
106:
107:            fprintf (stderr,
108:            "Query failed: %s\n", mysql_error(mysql));
109:
110:        }
111: }
112:
113: void print_result_set (MYSQL *mysql, MYSQL_RES *res_set)
114: {
115: unsigned int    f;
116: MYSQL_ROW       row;
117:
118:     while ((row = mysql_fetch_row (res_set)) != NULL) {
119:         f = 0;
120:         while (f<mysql_num_fields (res_set)) {
121:             if (f>0) fputc ('\t', stdout);
122:             fprintf (stdout, "%s", row[f]);
123:             f++;
124:         }
125:         fputc ('\n', stdout);
126:     }
127:
128:     if (mysql_errno (mysql) == 0)
129:         fprintf (stdout, "Number of rows returned: %lu.\n",
130:             (unsigned long) mysql_num_rows (res_set));
131:     else
132:         fprintf (stderr, "mysql_fetch_row() failed.\n");
133: }
134:
```

What's going on here? Lines 3 through 15 declare C header files, refer to functions defined within the program, and declare a constant.

Lines 17 through 36 comprise the main section, in which mysql_server_init() is called to start the MySQL server and initialize any subsystems that the server may use. You must call mysql_server_init() before anything else, or your program won't run.

In this case, we're passing mysql_server_init() argc and argv (neither of which is used in this case) and the NULL-terminated list server_groups. This has been set in lines 13–15.

The items in the `server_groups` list relate to a section of the user option file (`.my.cnf` for Unix or `my.ini` for Windows, as described in Day 15, "Administration") that contains options for the program. The relevant section of the option file must be headed up by the line:

```
[group]
```

where *group* corresponds with a value in the `server_groups` list.

In the case of our sample program, the first item in the `mysql_server_init()` list is `test_libmysqld_SERVER`. So you should place the following lines in your `.my.cnf` file in your home directory:

```
[test_libmysqld_SERVER]
language = /usr/local/mysql-VERSION/sql/share/english
```

This sets the language for the server's messages. You can also add other options in this section to modify the behavior of the embedded server.

Lines 24 and 25 each make a connection to the embedded server and return connection handles `one` and `two`. The first doesn't select a specific database, but the second selects the database called `store`.

Lines 27 and 28 include the queries that will be run, one query being passed to each connection handle. In lines 30 and 31, the database connections are closed.

Line 33 runs `mysql_server_end()`. This shuts down the embedded server and must be called before the program exits.

Lines 51 through 63 define the connection process to the embedded server. Line 58 uses the `mysql_options()` function to read the option file (`.my.cnf` or `my.ini` as mentioned previously). It looks for another *group* section, this time with the name `[test_libmysqld_CLIENT]`.

So in your user options file, you should include any client options needed within a section of this name. For example, you probably need a password to connect to MySQL, so here's a sample extract from a `.my.cnf` option file that defines the user's password:

```
[test_libmysqld_CLIENT]
password = mypass
```

The client option section is different from the server option section, even if they both sit in the `.my.cnf` file of the user who's invoking the application. They must be kept separate: Think of the application reading its options as a client, and the embedded server reading its section as a server.

Lines 65 through 69 define the code for the program disconnecting from the embedded server.

20

Lines 71 through 111 define how a SQL query will be handled, and lines 113 through 133 define how a resultset from a query should be printed. Both these sections should look familiar to you because they are the same as the relevant sections in `main.c` from Day 13 (in the program's final form). Go back and study that lesson if you need any explanation as to how queries are handled or the resultsets output.

Compiling an Application with `libmysqld`

To compile your application, you will need to instruct the compiler how to operate. On Unix, you should use a makefile, like the `GNUmakefile` shown in Listing 20.2.

LISTING 20.2 GNUmakefile

```
 1: # This assumes the MySQL software is installed in /usr/local/mysql
 2: inc      := /usr/local/mysql/include/mysql
 3: lib      := /usr/local/mysql/lib/mysql
 4:
 5: CC       := gcc
 6: CPPFLAGS := -I$(inc) -D_THREAD_SAFE -D_REENTRANT
 7: CFLAGS   := -g -W -Wall
 8: LDFLAGS  := -static
 9: LDLIBS    = -L$(lib) -lmysqld -lz -lm -lcrypt
10:
11: ifneq (,$(shell grep FreeBSD /COPYRIGHT 2>/dev/null))
12: # FreeBSD
13: LDFLAGS += -pthread
14: else
15: # Assume Linux
16: LDLIBS += -lpthread
17: endif
18:
19: # This works for simple one-file test programs
20: sources := $(wildcard *.c)
21: objects := $(patsubst %c,%o,$(sources))
22: targets := $(basename $(sources))
23:
24: all: $(targets)
25:
26: clean:
27:         rm -f $(targets) $(objects) *.core
```

This makefile is a slightly modified version of the one included in the MySQL source distribution. It should work for Linux and BSD but may require minor platform-specific changes for other operating systems.

Lines 2 and 3 define where the includes and libraries are installed; you may need to modify these to suit your installation if you did not install MySQL under `/usr/local/mysql`.

Lines 5 through 22 set the compiler (in this case, gcc) and various options for it. Lines 11 through 17 set the correct type of threads to use according to whether Linux or BSD is used.

Lines 20 through 27 define how make should run: Running make or make all tells the compiler to start work on all files ending with .c in the current directory, whereas make clean is the cleanup instruction and causes all compiled objects to be removed from the directory.

In line 27, the space before the rm is a tab, not spaces, or the makefile will not work.

You should be able to compile your program like this:

```
# make
```

It may take a few seconds to run. If errors are reported, you will need to debug what went wrong.

If everything goes okay, you find an executable program in the directory called test_libmysqld. Run it like this:

```
# ./test_libmysqld
```

You should get some output, and (depending on what tables you have on your server) it should look something like this:

```
Query succeeded. About to fetch result.
mysql
store
test
Number of rows returned: 3.
invoices      MyISAM Fixed  0      0       0       68719476735    1024
    02002-02-04 16:26:57    2002-02-04 16:26:57    (null)
products      MyISAM Dynamic 5    37      188     4294967295     2048
    0(null)   2002-02-26 13:55:45    2002-09-07 22:07:32    (null)
Number of rows returned: 2.
```

Don't be concerned if the program takes a while to execute: When it starts, the embedded MySQL server has to be started up, and before it exits, the server has to be shut down. (Lines 22 and 33 of test_libmysqld.c do these things.) Just like when a nonembedded MySQL server starts up or shuts down, the program has to be read into memory and other actions are performed, and this takes a few seconds to complete.

20

In most applications, this is not an issue: A typical application starts up and keeps running while interacting with the user, responding to a series of user actions until being shut down.

What an Embedded MySQL Server Cannot Do

There are currently a few restrictions on what can be done with an embedded MySQL server. However, most of these probably won't matter to you:

- The embedded MySQL server will not accept connections from an external client; you can only connect from the application itself.
- You can't use user-definable functions (UDFs; you'll see how to create UDFs in Day 21, "Extending MySQL's Function Library.")
- Replication is not supported.
- You cannot use the older ISAM table format.

Despite these minor omissions, later releases may change some of these limitations, and you should review the MySQL Technical Reference if any of them are important to you.

Building Embedded Server Programs

If you followed the example given today and successfully built and ran the program, you have created a standalone application with an entire MySQL database server inside it.

Combining this with a knowledge of C, you should now be able to build your own embedded applications. Although the example given was carried out on a Linux platform, the principle is the same for compiling on Windows or any other OS.

There is room in this book for only a practical introduction to this subject. If you want to build serious applications, study the MySQL Technical Reference for more details on the behavior of the C API and its function calls.

Summary

In today's lesson you learned how to build an application with an embedded MySQL database.

This is a powerful thing to be able to do: You can create easy to distribute applications that can be deployed to a user's desktop and run, without any of the installation routines normally required for a full MySQL server.

Not only is deployment easier, but it enables you to build fast, compact applications for a range of platforms.

Distributing MySQL in an embedded form is not free: You learned about the licensing requirements for MySQL when embedded and distributed in this way.

Q&A

Q **I'm not a C programmer. Do I need to know about embedding?**

A If it's sufficient for you to be able to run MySQL in client-server mode, as we have done in earlier lessons in this book, then probably not.

Embedding MySQL is essential for developers who want to create a single package, including the desired application and powered by a MySQL database server. However, a knowledge of C is required to do this.

Q **It says somewhere that I have to pay for MySQL. Is this true?**

A You have to pay for a license for each copy of MySQL that you distribute as part of an embedded system. You don't have to pay for MySQL when used as a server, as we've done in the lessons prior to this.

The key things that trigger the need to pay are *embedding* and *distributing*. If you're compiling an embedded server into your application, and you're distributing copies of the program you create, you will have to pay a license fee to MySQL AB. See the Web site at `http://www.mysql.com/` for pricing and more information about licensing.

Workshop

The quiz is provided to help you solidify your understanding of the material covered today. Try to understand the quiz before continuing to tomorrow's lesson.

Quiz

1. True or False: You have to recompile MySQL from source to use the embedded server.

2. What is the name of the embedded server library?

3. What is the essential option that you must pass to `configure` when compiling MySQL to include the embedded server library?

Quiz Answers

1. True (unless you compiled MySQL with it included the first time). You must run `./configure` with the `--with-embedded-server` option.

2. The library is called `libmysqld.a`.

3. You must use

   `./configure --with-embedded-server`

   although you may add other options.

20

WEEK 3

DAY 21

Extending MySQL's Function Library

MySQL has an extensive and varied function library. However, if the function you want is not already included in that library, it is possible to create it yourself, using MySQL's system of user-definable functions (UDFs).

Today you will learn how to create new functions in MySQL using UDFs.

In particular you will learn

- How to prepare MySQL for adding UDFs written in C or C++
- How to add the sample UDFs included with the MySQL distribution as UDFs, including compiling the C programs that define the UDFs and adding them to MySQL using CREATE FUNCTION
- The details of C calling sequences and datatypes for UDFs so that existing C programmers can start writing their own UDFs

Why Create a New Function?

As you will see from Appendix C, "Function and Operator Reference," MySQL has an extensive library of functions. However, there may be times when the precise function that your application requires is not present.

What are your options for implementing this function? You have several options:

- Implement the function in your application code (such as PHP or Perl)
- Ask the company behind MySQL, MySQL AB, to implement the function as a new native function for MySQL itself
- Create a new native function for MySQL yourself
- Write a UDF (user-definable function) for MySQL

The first option—implementing the required function in your application code—is almost certainly the option you will choose most of the time. MySQL applications are frequently written in languages such as PHP, Perl, or ASP, all of which are languages in which you could implement the algorithm you require. If you do this, there's no need to demand anything more from MySQL's functionality.

Moreover, if you are writing your application in one of the Web scripting languages, such as PHP or ASP, you are probably aiming for shortest development time for your product rather than trying to create an application with the absolute fastest execution speed.

However, what if you need a function that can be rapidly executed within SQL statements—perhaps within a WHERE clause? In such cases, it will be beneficial to do the function processing within your SQL rather than retrieve a resultset that gets processed in your application, where it will usually be processed more slowly.

In such cases—usually where performance is critical—it will be better to implement the function within MySQL itself.

The other obvious advantage of adding a function to MySQL itself is that once installed, you can call it just like any other MySQL function. Just as you might call TRUNCATE() or DATE_FORMAT(), or aggregating functions such as AVG() or SUM(), you can create your own function and call it, for example, MY_FUNCTION().

The second option suggested previously—to ask the creators of MySQL to add a new function to the MySQL server software—may not be as extravagant as it sounds. MySQL AB is open to suggestions and requests for additions, and some of the existing functions in MySQL have materialized in this way. However, this option is usually only viable for those developing commercial, heavy-load systems because a financial consideration will usually be involved.

When MySQL AB adds a function to MySQL, they are creating a new native function. But the third option listed previously is a way of doing this yourself. If you are comfortable writing code in C or C++, you can compile a new function into your MySQL server yourself.

However, adding a native function requires you to modify a MySQL source distribution, and whenever you upgrade your MySQL server to a newer release, you will need to reimplement your function in the latest source code.

The fourth option in the preceding list—to write a UDF, or user-definable function—is probably the easiest way to give your new function the speed advantages of C or C++. It's a little more straightforward than writing a native function: You can install it into MySQL distribution, and you won't have to reimplement it each time you upgrade to a newer version of MySQL.

The writing and installation of UDFs are the techniques you will learn today.

An Overview of Installing UDFs

Because the MySQL source distribution contains a C file with a number of sample UDFs, you can easily start experimenting with UDFs right away. For this reason, you will learn about installing UDFs first. If you also have a knowledge of C and want to learn how to write your own functions, you will learn how to do this a little later today.

Preparing `mysqld`

To use UDFs, your operating system must support dynamic loading (which will normally be the case with Unix and Linux).

Your `mysqld` should also have been compiled using `--with-mysqld-ldflags=-rdynamic` as an option to `configure`. So when running `configure`, the options would include (among other options):

```
# ./configure --with-mysqld-ldflags=-rdynamic
```

You may therefore have to recompile `mysqld` to use UDFs (see Day 2, "Installing MySQL," for more information).

Note The typical binary distributions of MySQL are compiled (for speed) with `--with-mysqld-ldflags=-all-static`. They therefore do not support dynamic loading by default.

21

An Overview of Using UDFs

We'll get on to the nitty-gritty of installing UDFs in a moment, but first let's get an overview of what you will achieve with user-definable functions.

You're trying to create a function that you can call with all the convenience of any other MySQL function. You will be able to call your function using, for example, MYFUNC() in your SQL.

To implement a UDF called MYFUNC() requires a C or C++ program containing a set of function calls with names like myfunc() and myfunc_init().

(It's important that the names correspond. The SQL function will usually be referred to in uppercase, although like other functions in SQL it can be called in lowercase too. The C or C++ functions will always be referred to in lowercase.)

Just like other MySQL functions, your user-definable function may return a result that is of type STRING, INTEGER, or REAL.

Simple Functions and Their Definition in C or C++

A "simple" UDF is a function that does not aggregate across rows of a SELECT resultset. It takes only constants or column names as arguments and returns a result based only on those values. It's a function like DATE_FORMAT().

For a simple UDF, the C or C++ program that defines it will have between one and three functions:

- An optional function called myfunc_init(), which checks the arguments that have been passed, allocates memory if need be, and specifies what sort of output the function returns (whether it can be NULL, the maximum length, and so on)

- A mandatory function called myfunc(), which does the actual computation

- An optional function called myfunc_deinit(), which releases any memory allocated by myfunc_init()

Aggregating Functions and Their Definition in C or C++

An aggregating function is a little more complex. In MySQL, an aggregating function always works in the context of a SELECT...GROUP BY query. For example, the SUM() aggregating function sums the values across several rows, returning one result for every "grouped" set of values.

Because of this, when we write an aggregating UDF, a C/C++ function needs to be called to process each row being analyzed.

(For example, in the case of SUM(), it would be adding up the number in the current row to some interim running total.)

Each time the GROUP BY aggregator decides that the end of a group has been reached, it expects that a result row be returned. Therefore, a different routine in the SUM() function (likewise, in an aggregating UDF) needs to be called so that it returns its overall result.

Aggregating functions therefore have some additional C/C++ function calls. In addition to those stated previously for simple functions, an aggregating UDF must have the following:

- A function called myfunc_reset(), which resets the UDF's variables and stores the first argument as the initial value of a new group
- A function called myfunc_add(), which takes subsequent arguments in the group and sums or otherwise processes them, maintaining variables that pertain to the arguments from the group so far

We'll look in more detail at these C/C++ routines in a moment. But before going into this, you should learn about how to make these functions available to MySQL.

Making a Function Available to MySQL

After a function has been written in C or C++, you'll need to tell the MySQL server to load it. MySQL has the CREATE FUNCTION and DROP FUNCTION commands for creating and dropping UDFs.

The syntax for creating a function is as follows:

```
CREATE [AGGREGATE] FUNCTION function_name
RETURNS {STRING|REAL|INTEGER}
SONAME 'shared_object_name'
```

When you run CREATE FUNCTION, it enters details of that function (contained in the binary object given by shared_object_name) into the func table in the mysql database. The optional keyword AGGREGATE tells MySQL that the function is an aggregating one (as opposed to simple), and the RETURNS part specifies the datatype that will be returned when the function is called.

When created like this, a user-defined function persists even if the server is shut down and restarted. It should be considered active and available for use as soon as the command has been run and remains active until the function is dropped.

DROP FUNCTION has the effect of dropping a function:

```
DROP FUNCTION function_name
```

This makes the function immediately inactive, though will not destroy the shared object code.

21

Note

To activate UDFs, you need to have sufficient privileges to perform INSERT and DELETE on the mysql database. Typically, only the root user, or another trusted user, is permitted to make changes like this.

If you have a version of MySQL that is pre-3.23, to make CREATE AGGREGATE FUNCTION work for aggregating functions, you will need to have the column type present on the mysql.func table.

To do this, you need to run the script called mysql_fix_privilege_tables to update them to a newer format. Change to the scripts directory under the source directory—for example, like this (changing the version number to suit your installation):

```
# cd /usr/local/mysql-4.0.2-alpha/scripts
```

Then run the script like this:

```
# ./mysql_fix_privilege_tables
```

You can now describe the func table again:

```
mysql> desc func;
+-------+------------------------------+------+-----+----------+-------+
| Field | Type                         | Null | Key | Default  | Extra |
+-------+------------------------------+------+-----+----------+-------+
| name  | char(64) binary              |      | PRI |          |       |
| ret   | tinyint(1)                   |      |     | 0        |       |
| dl    | char(128)                    |      |     |          |       |
| type  | enum('function','aggregate') |      |     | function |       |
+-------+------------------------------+------+-----+----------+-------+
4 rows in set (0.00 sec)
```

Hands-on: Creating a Simple Function

Now that you have an overview of what needs to be done to create a UDF, let's go step-by-step through the process, with more emphasis on exactly how you will perform such an installation.

You will learn the process using the sample UDFs included in the MySQL distribution. They're in a file called udf-example.cc.

You will

- Compile the C program
- Move it to a place where MySQL can access it
- Tell MySQL to activate its user-defined functions
- Use the functions
- Drop the functions

When you're comfortable with creating UDFs from the examples included, you'll see how to write your own. But first let's go through how to install the sample UDFs.

Compiling the C Program

In this lesson, you will compile the set of sample UDFs included in the MySQL source distribution. You will find all the functions in a single C file called udf_example.cc. You can find this in the MySQL source directory under the subdirectory sql.

To go there, change to the sql subdirectory:

```
$ cd /usr/local/mysql-4.0.2-alpha/sql
```

List what files are there (beginning with "udf"):

```
$ ls udf*
udf_example.cc
```

If you're comfortable reading C, you may want to study the udf_example.cc file. It contains sample code for creating a number of functions:

- metaphon() is a function that takes a string argument and returns the metaphon string (a little like MySQL's SOUNDEX()).
- myfunc_double() returns the average of the ASCII values of the string argument passed to it (it sums up the ASCII values of all the characters and then divides by the number of characters, giving a numeric result).
- myfunc_int() adds up the lengths of all string arguments passed to it and returns the total length as an integer.
- sequence([start]) returns the next integer in sequence, optionally starting from the integer start, or 1 if start is not specified.
- lookup() converts an Internet hostname to its IP address.

21

- `reverse_lookup()` converts an IP address to a hostname.
- `avgcost(`*`qty`*`,`*`price`*`)` is an aggregating function that returns the average cost of a group of quantity and price data.

To compile the shared object containing these functions, you will need to run the compiler on your machine using `make`. The `Makefile` in the `sql` directory will have been produced when you compiled MySQL, and it will cause `make` to run in a way that is appropriate to your system.

First run `make` to produce `udf_example.o`, like this:

```
$ make udf_example.o
```

You're not really interested in creating the `.o` file; you just want to see what parameters `make` likes to be run with.

Here's some sample output, though yours is likely to be a little different:

```
g++ -DMYSQL_SERVER -DDEFAULT_MYSQL_HOME="\"/usr/local/mysql\"" -DDATADIR="\"/us
r/local/mysql/var\""-DSHAREDIR="\"/usr/local/mysql/share/mysql\"" -DHAVE_CONFIG
_H -I../innobase/include -I./../include -I./../regex -I. -I../include -I. -O3 -
DDBUG_OFF -fno-implicit-templates -fno-exceptions -fno-rtti -c udf_example.cc
```

The output, actually just one line, is likely to spill across several lines of your console. If it looks incomprehensible (okay, even ugly), don't worry. Just copy and paste it into an editor. You're going to make some minor changes to it and then paste it back to the console as input.

The changes you'll need to make will be as follows. Change the last few words from this

```
-c udf_example.cc
```

to this

```
-shared udf_example.cc -o my_udfs.so
```

This tells the compiler (in this example, `g++`) to compile `udf_example.cc` and create a shared object called `my_udfs.so`. (You may give the latter a different name if you want.) The `.so` file is the one that MySQL gets its UDFs from.

Now you should run the compiler. Paste the compile command back into the console, with modifications, to make your command line look something like this:

```
$ g++ -DMYSQL_SERVER -DDEFAULT_MYSQL_HOME="\"/usr/local/mysql\"" \
> -DDATADIR="\"/usr/local/mysql/var\"" \
> -DSHAREDIR="\"/usr/local/mysql/share/mysql\"" \
> -DHAVE_CONFIG_H \
> -I../innobase/include \
> -I./../include \
```

```
> -I./../regex \
> -I. -I../include -I. -O3 -DDBUG_OFF \
> -fno-implicit-templates \
> -fno-exceptions \
> -fno-rtti \
> -shared udf_example.cc -o my_udfs.so
```

Put this into the console, and the C program should compile.

> **Note**
>
> If you get errors, you may need to include `-c` on the last line as well as `-o` because some compilers may require this.

If compilation is successful, list the contents of the `sql` directory. You should notice that a file called `my_udfs.so` has been created. If so, you have successfully created the shared object.

Put the Shared Object in the Right Place

When compiled, you will need to move or copy the `.so` file to a location where MySQL can access it. This may be `/usr/lib`, which may well work without further adjustment:

```
$ cp my_udfs.so /usr/lib/
```

Alternatively, you may (like me) prefer to keep it with MySQL's other files, under `/usr/local/mysql`.

For example, you might put your `.so` file in `/usr/local/mysql/lib/mysql`. But if you do this you will need to tell `mysqld` about it by setting its `LD_LIBRARY_PATH` variable. You can set this in `mysql.server` or `mysqld_safe`. Here are some lines that you can add to your `mysql.server` script (which typically resides in `/etc/init.d/`), which will do just this:

```
LD_LIBRARY_PATH=/usr/local/mysql/lib/mysql
export LD_LIBRARY_PATH
```

When `mysql.server` invokes `mysqld_safe` and starts the server, it tells `mysqld` to look in `/usr/local/mysql/lib/mysql` when loading shared objects.

Tell MySQL to Activate the UDF

Now that the shared object is present on the server and in a place where MySQL can read it, you need to tell MySQL to activate the user-defined functions contained within it.

21

You need to tell MySQL the name of the user-definable function, the datatype it returns, and the name of the shared object, like this for one of the sample functions, `metaphon`:

```
mysql> CREATE FUNCTION metaphon RETURNS STRING
    -> SONAME "my_udfs.so";
Query OK, 0 rows affected (0.03 sec)
```

This command creates the function `METAPHON()` and specifies that it returns a string datatype.

> **Caution**
>
> It is important that the datatypes declared in CREATE FUNCTION correspond with their C definitions. If not, the mismatch (and indeed any other errors in the C code) causes mysqld to crash whenever the function is invoked.
>
> For example, if you see unexpected error messages like this:
>
> ```
> ERROR 2006: MySQL server has gone away
> No connection. Trying to reconnect...
> ```
>
> it is likely that mysqld has crashed due to such an error but has been restarted by mysqld_safe.

Here are some more of the `CREATE FUNCTION` commands that you will need to activate the sample functions in `udf_example.cc`:

```
mysql> CREATE FUNCTION myfunc_double RETURNS REAL
    -> SONAME "my_udfs.so";
mysql> CREATE FUNCTION myfunc_int RETURNS INTEGER
    -> SONAME "my_udfs.so";
mysql> CREATE FUNCTION lookup RETURNS STRING
    -> SONAME "my_udfs.so";
```

> **Note**
>
> If you get errors when you try to do CREATE FUNCTION, it may be that you have not moved the .so file to the correct location. In many systems, it will work right away if you move the .so file to /usr/lib. However, you may need to set LD_LIBRARY_PATH to include the path to the directory. See instructions given previously to learn how to do this.
>
> Also note that the lookup and reverse_lookup functions have been compiled only if your operating system has the gethostbyaddr_r function installed.

Use the Functions

Your UDFs should now be installed and available to use just like any normal MySQL function. For example, try out the METAPHON() function, like this:

```
mysql> SELECT METAPHON('hello');
+-------------------+
| METAPHON('hello') |
+-------------------+
| HL                |
+-------------------+
1 row in set (0.09 sec)
```

Try the MYFUNC_DOUBLE(), function like this:

```
mysql> SELECT MYFUNC_DOUBLE('ac');
+---------------------+
| MYFUNC_DOUBLE('ac') |
+---------------------+
|               98.00 |
+---------------------+
1 row in set (0.00 sec)
```

Remove the Functions

Your new functions will remain available even if you stop and restart your MySQL server. However, if you want to deactivate them, you can do so using DROP FUNCTION.

For example, to drop the METAPHON() function, do this:

```
mysql> DROP FUNCTION metaphon;
Query OK, 0 rows affected (0.00 sec)
```

Note   As with other MySQL functions, you can call UDFs in either upper- or lower-case. However, in the C program, convention dictates that they will always be written in lowercase.

Writing Your Own UDFs

By now you should have gathered that UDFs rely on there being a C or C++ program to define them. Although it is straightforward to add the sample UDFs to your MySQL server, you will need some knowledge of at least one of these languages to write your own functions.

21

This section describes the calling procedures for UDFs and explains how to make them operate in the MySQL environment. This section, together with the information contained in Day 13, "Using the C API," is enough to get you coding, provided that you already have a reasonable knowledge of C or C++.

Datatypes and Calling Sequences

As explained previously, a user-defined MySQL function `MYFUNC()` will have a corresponding C function called `myfunc()`. In addition, it may have an optional function called `myfunc_init()` for initialization and argument checking, and optionally `myfunc_deinit()` for cleanup.

An aggregating function such as `avgcost()` also has `avgcost_reset()` and `avgcost_add()`.

The calling sequence for a simple function is like this:

1. `myfunc_init()`, in which the arguments will be checked, error-checking will be performed, and if need be memory allocated.

2. `myfunc()` performs the computation.

3. `myfunc_deinit()` deallocates memory and cleans up.

For an aggregating function, there is a more complex calling sequence, like this:

1. `myfunc_init()` will be called to check the arguments, perform error-checking, and if need be allocate memory.

2. The resultset of the `SELECT` query will be sorted according to the `GROUP BY` clause.

3. `myfunc reset()` will be called to process the first row of a group. Processing will return to this step each time there is a new group in the resultset; any summary variables will be reset here each time.

4. `myfunc add()` will be called to process each subsequent row of the group (but not the first row). Processing will return to this step for each resultset row; `UDF_ARGS` will be added to the internal summary variables.

5. `myfunc()` will be called when the group has been processed entirely and will return the UDF's result.

6. `myfunc deinit()` deallocates memory and cleans up.

The MySQL datatypes passed to and from the C program must correspond according to the following:

- The MySQL `STRING` type corresponds with the C or C++ `char *`.
- The MySQL `INTEGER` type corresponds with C/C++ `long long`.
- The MySQL `REAL` type corresponds with C/C++ `double`.

C Calling Sequences for Simple UDFs

This section describes how you should declare the various C/C++ functions that make up your UDF. For ease of reference, I'm assuming that your function is called MYFUNC().

If your UDF returns a STRING datatype to MySQL, you should define the main myfunc() function as follows:

```
char *myfunc(
    UDF_INIT *initid,
    UDF_ARGS *args,
    char *result,
    unsigned long *length,
    char *is_null,
    char *error);
```

Notice that the arguments initid and args are pointers to UDF_INIT and UDF_ARGS structures, respectively. These are important. You will look in more detail at the UDF_INIT and UDF_ARGS structures in a moment.

For returning results, result points to the result string, and length points to a number that is the length of that string. If your string result is more than 255 bytes, you will need to allocate memory for it using malloc() in myfunc_init(), and free it up again in myfunc_deinit().

is_null() is a flag that indicates a NULL result. You will see this again in myfunc_init() and myfunc_deinit(), and it is cleared or set within each routine.

error is also a flag (not a message) that should be set if an error occurs.

For functions returning an INTEGER datatype, fewer arguments are used. The C type should be long long:

```
long long myfunc(
    UDF_INIT *initid,
    UDF_ARGS *args,
    char *is_null,
    char *error);
```

Functions returning a REAL also take fewer arguments. The C type should be double:

```
double myfunc(
    UDF_INIT *initid,
    UDF_ARGS *args,
    char *is_null,
    char *error);
```

21

Again notice the UDF_INIT and UDF_ARGS structures, but this time with just the is_null and error flags. The value returned from a numeric function is the actual result, unlike a string function, which returns pointers to the result.

The initialization function of the UDF should be declared like this

```
my_bool myfunc_init(
    UDF_INIT *initid,
    UDF_ARGS *args,
    char *message);
```

myfunc_init() should return a 1 if an error occurs (such as because of unsatisfactory arguments being passed to the UDF), or 0 if everything looks okay. In an error situation, your routine should set message to the error message text (a null-terminated string).

The deinitialization function is declared like this

```
void myfunc_deinit(UDF_INIT *initid);
```

Notice that only the UDF_INIT structure is passed, and the routine frees up memory if it has previously been allocated for the function.

Calling Sequences for Aggregating UDFs

As mentioned previously, to create an aggregating function, you need to define the functions myfunc_reset() and myfunc_add(). You need these as well as the ones for simple UDFs, which should be declared in the same way as described just now.

These functions should be declared like this

```
char *myfunc_reset(
    UDF_INIT *initid,
    UDF_ARGS *args,
    char *is_null,
    char *error);
char *myfunc_add(
    UDF_INIT *initid,
    UDF_ARGS *args,
    char *is_null,
    char *error);
```

In aggregating UDFs, the myfunc() function, which in simple UDFs does the meaningful work, will be called only when all rows in the group have been processed. The args pointer passed to it will be meaningless in a group context, so your code in the myfunc() routine should do its processing on the internal summary variables instead.

is_null and error are handled in the same way as in myfunc(). However, whereas is_null is reset for each group (before calling myfunc_reset()), if error is set in any of the routines, it is never reset.

If is_null or error become set any time after running myfunc(), MySQL returns NULL as the UDF result.

The UDF_INIT Structure

You will have noticed that all the C functions described have the initid parameter passed to them. This is in the form of a UDF_INIT structure that communicates initialization information about the UDF between the C functions.

Table 21.1 shows the members of the UDF_INIT structure. Your initialization function myfunc_init() should define values in this structure by setting any number of its members. Alternatively, you may leave them undeclared to take up their default values.

TABLE 21.1   Members of the UDF_INIT Structure

Type	Argument	Usage	Default Value
my_bool	maybe_null	If myfunc() may return NULL, you should set maybe_null to 1 in myfunc_init()	1 if any of the arguments are declared maybe_null.
unsigned int	decimals	The number of digits after the decimal point.	The maximum number of decimals in the arguments passed to the main function
unsigned int	max_length	The maximum length, in characters of the string result.	For string functions, defaults to the length of the longest argument.
			For integer functions, defaults to 21 digits.
			For real functions, the default is 13 plus the number of decimals indicated by initid->decimals.
			(For numeric functions, the length includes sign or decimal point characters.)
			Set this to 64KB or 16MB if you intend to return a blob; no memory is allocated, but if there is a need to temporarily store data, this defines the column type that will be needed.

21

TABLE 21.1 continued

Type	Argument	Usage	Default Value
char	*ptr	You may want to pass other types of information between the functions. For example, functions can use `initid->ptr` to communicate allocated memory between functions. You should allocate memory in `myfunc_init()` as follows: `initid->ptr = allocated_memory;` To use or deallocate memory, refer to `initid->ptr`.	

The UDF_ARGS Structure

The `args` parameter is a pointer to the main data that you will pass among your functions. This data has a UDF_ARGS structure. Table 21.2 lists the members of the UDF_ARGS structure.

TABLE 21.2 Members of the UDF_ARGS Structure

Type	Argument	Usage
unsigned int	arg_count	The number of arguments passed to the UDF. If your UDF should be called with a particular number of arguments, verify this number in `myfunc_init()`.
enum Item_result	*arg_type	`arg_type` points to an array holding the datatype for each argument, with possible values `STRING_RESULT`, `INT_RESULT`, and `REAL_RESULT`. If your UDF should be called with particular datatypes, you should verify these values in `myfunc_init()`.
char	**args	In the context of `myfunc_init()`, `args->args` contains information about the arguments; its values depend on whether a constant or nonconstant argument was passed (in other words, a defined number or string, as opposed to a column name). With a constant value, `args->args[i]` points to the value of the argument, whereas with a nonconstant, the value of `args->args[i]` will be 0.

TABLE 21.1   continued

Type	Argument	Usage
		In the context of `myfunc()`, `args->args` contains the actual arguments passed for the row currently being processed. See the following section on `args->args` for information on how to access this data.
`unsigned long`	`*lengths`	`lengths` points to an array containing the string length of each argument.
		In `myfunc_init()`, this means the maximum string length (which should not be changed).
		In `myfunc()`, it contains the actual lengths of any string arguments in the row currently being processed.

args->args

Within `UDF_ARGS` is the `args->args` array, which contains the actual arguments to be processed. Depending on the type of each argument, your function `myfunc()` refers to them as follows:

- For string arguments (type `STRING_RESULT`), `args->args` represents a string pointer plus its length. (This lets you handle binary data, which may contain nulls, so don't assume that strings will be terminated with a null.) The content of the string is given by `args->args[i]`, and the length is given by `args->lengths[i]`.

- For integer arguments (type `INT_RESULT`), `args->args[i]` represents the `integer` argument itself. However, you must cast it to a `long long` value before processing.

- For arguments of type `REAL_RESULT`, `args->args[i]` represents the `real` argument. However, you must cast `args->args[i]` to a `double` value before processing.

Writing Calling Sequences

The preceding descriptions explain how to set up functions in C or C++. However, this information is targeted at C programmers, who should now have enough information to begin writing their own UDFs.

No examples of writing UDFs are given here; space does not permit the inclusion of several worked examples, which would be helpful. However, refer to the sample UDFs in your MySQL distribution for example code and also to the exercises in this chapter, which also describe the creation of a simple UDF.

21

Summary

In this lesson, you learned the principles of user-definable functions: why you might need them and how to install them.

You saw how to configure your MySQL installation so that it can load user-definable functions. You compiled the sample UDFs included in your MySQL installation, and activated and tested them in the `mysql` console.

You also learned how to write your own UDFs in C or C++, studying the calling sequences that should be used.

Q&A

Q This all sounds complicated, and I don't know much C. Do I really need to learn this?

A In most cases, you can get through life without learning how to create UDFs. However, for reasons of performance or for reducing the complexity of application code, you may sometimes want to perform computations in MySQL rather than in your application. That's why MySQL allows the creation of user-definable functions.

If your application is not speed critical, and you don't need the convenience of embedding new functions within SQL, you can safely avoid UDFs. However, if your application depends on top performance or on running computations within queries, this lesson is worth studying carefully for the new opportunities that it opens up.

Q How do I prepare for UDFs when building the MySQL server from source?

A You should compile MySQL as follows (possibly with additional options to `configure`):

```
# ./configure --with-mysqld-ldflags=-rdynamic
# make
# make install
```

See Day 2 for the full explanation of building MySQL from a source distribution.

Workshop

The exercises are provided to help you solidify your understanding of the material covered today. Try to understand the exercise answers before continuing to tomorrow's lesson.

Quiz

1. True or False: UDFs can be added to a MySQL server that is a standard binary distribution.

2. True or False: If you define a UDF called SOME_FUNC(), a C function within the UDF called some_func_deinit() performs cleanup tasks.

3. True or False: UDFs can be used to create aggregating functions, which calculate values across several rows of a table.

Quiz Answers

1. False. It needs to be compiled with the --with-mysqld-ldflags=-rdynamic option. The standard binary distributions are not compiled with this, so you will need to compile a source distribution with this option to configure.

2. True.

3. True.

Exercises

1. Specify the CREATE FUNCTION and DROP FUNCTION SQL commands for creating and dropping the reverse_lookup and avgcost functions.

2. Write a UDF that returns the cube of a single numeric argument (that is, it returns the argument to the power of 3). It should be called CUBE(). Write the function in C, compile it, install it as a UDF, and test it.

   Hint: Unless you're an experienced C programmer, you may want to use the included udf_example.cc source file as a starting point and pick out the common sections of code required. Then adjust the relevant sections of code for the cube algorithm.

Answers to Exercises

1. Note that avgcost is an aggregating function!

```
mysql> CREATE FUNCTION reverse_lookup
    -> RETURNS STRING SONAME "my_udfs.so";
mysql> CREATE AGGREGATE FUNCTION avgcost
    -> RETURNS REAL SONAME "my_udfs.so";
```

2. You should create a C program called something like myfuncs.cc. A sample program as follows would work:

```
#ifdef STANDARD
#include <stdio.h>
#include <string.h>
#else
#include <my_global.h>
```

21

```
        #include <my_sys.h>
        #endif
        #include <mysql.h>
        #include <m_ctype.h>
        #include <m_string.h>
        // The above lines are recommended
        // as per the samples included with MySQL

        #ifdef HAVE_DLOPEN

        extern "C" {

        my_bool cube_init(
                UDF_INIT *initid,
                UDF_ARGS *args,
                char *message);

        double cube(
            UDF_INIT *initid,
            UDF_ARGS *args,
            char *is_null,
            char *error);

        void cube_deinit(
            UDF_INIT *initid);

        }

        // Initialisation function
        my_bool cube_init(
            UDF_INIT *initid,
            UDF_ARGS *args,
            char *message)
        {
            if (args->arg_count != 1)
            {
                strmov(message,
                    "This function must be passed exactly one argument");
                return 1;
            }
            if (args->arg_count)
                args->arg_type[0]= REAL_RESULT; // Coerce argument to be type real
            return 0;
        }

        // The actual function, in this case cube
        double cube(
            UDF_INIT *initid,
            UDF_ARGS *args,
            char *is_null,
            char *error)
```

```
{
    double val=0;
    if (args->arg_count)
        // The following line casts the argument to type double
        val = *((double*) args->args[0]);
        val = val * val * val;
    return val;
}

// The deinitialization function,
// in this case it doesn't need to do anything
void cube_deinit(UDF_INIT *initid)
{
}

#endif        /* from HAVE_DLOPEN */
```

Then compile your C program, declaring the compiler's name and its options to suit your system as explained previously today; for example:

```
$ g++ -DMYSQL_SERVER -DDEFAULT_MYSQL_HOME="\"/usr/local/mysql\"" \
> -DDATADIR="\"/usr/local/mysql/var\"" \
> -DSHAREDIR="\"/usr/local/mysql/share/mysql\"" \
> -DHAVE_CONFIG_H -I../innobase/include -I./../include \
> -I./../regex -I. -I../include -I. -O3 -DDBUG_OFF \
> -fno-implicit-templates -fno-exceptions -fno-rtti \
> -shared myfuncs.cc -o myfuncs.so
```

Copy your .so file to a location where mysqld can access it:

```
# cp myfuncs.so /usr/local/mysql/lib/mysql/
```

Now go into the mysql console and create the function:

```
mysql> CREATE FUNCTION cube RETURNS REAL SONAME 'myfuncs.so';
```

And test the function (it should work in upper or lower case like any other SQL syntax):

```
mysql> SELECT cube(-2);
+----------+
| cube(-2) |
+----------+
|       -8 |
+----------+
1 row in set (0.00 sec)

mysql> SELECT CUBE(1.5);
+-----------+
| CUBE(1.5) |
+-----------+
|       3.4 |
+-----------+
1 row in set (0.00 sec)
```

21

Appendices

A

B

C

D

APPENDIX **A**

Data Type Reference

MySQL can store numeric, string, and temporal (date and time) data. This appendix serves as a quick reference to the various column types available to you for storing these types of data.

For each column type, the following sections give a brief description, together with the range of values that can be stored, amount of disk storage required, allowable attributes, and any other pertinent information.

For more information about declaring and using column types, and examples, see Day 5, "MySQL Data Types."

Numeric Types

Integer and floating-point numbers are stored using MySQL's numeric column types. This section shows their storage requirements and their allowed value ranges. The ranges of integer types depend on whether they are declared as signed (the default) or unsigned (using the keyword UNSIGNED).

For all numeric column types, you may specify M, and for floating-point types, D as well. M is the display width of the column, and for floating-point types, D is the number of digits after the decimal point. (With the DECIMAL type, M and D are mandatory.)

All integer types can have the attributes UNSIGNED and AUTO_INCREMENT. From MySQL 4.0.2 onward, you can also make floating-point types UNSIGNED. All numeric types can have the attribute ZEROFILL.

TINYINT[(*M*)]

Description: Column to store integer numbers of tiny values

Signed range: -128 to 127 (-2^7 to 2^7-1)

Unsigned range: 0 to 255 (0 to 2^8-1)

Required storage: 1 byte

SMALLINT[(*M*)]

Description: Column to store integer numbers of small values

Signed range: -32768 to 32767 (-2^{15} to $2^{15}-1$)

Unsigned range: 0 to 65535 (0 to $2^{16}-1$)

Required storage: 2 bytes

MEDIUMINT[(*M*)]

Description: Column to store integer numbers of medium values

Signed range: -8388608 to 8388607 (-2^{23} to $2^{23}-1$)

Unsigned range: 0 to 16777215 (0 to $2^{24}-1$)

Required storage: 3 bytes

INT[(*M*)] or INTEGER[(*M*)]

Description: Column to store integer numbers of normal values

Signed range: -2147483648 to 2147483647 (-2^{31} to $2^{31}-1$)

Unsigned range: 0 to 4294967295 (0 to $2^{32}-1$)

Required storage: 4 bytes

BIGINT[(*M*)]

Description: Column to store integer numbers of big values

Signed range: -2^{63} to $2^{63}-1$

Unsigned range: 0 to $2^{64}-1$

Required storage: 8 bytes

FLOAT[(*M*,*D*)]

Description: Column to store floating-point numbers of single precision

Minimum nonzero: $\pm1.175494351E{-}38$

Maximum: $\pm3.402823466E{+}38$

Note: Range is the same for unsigned as for signed (but must be positive).

Required storage: 4 bytes

DOUBLE[(*M*,*D*)]

Description: Column to store floating-point numbers of double precision

Minimum nonzero: $\pm2.2250738585072014E{-}308$

Maximum: $\pm1.7976931348623157E{+}308$

Note: Range is the same for unsigned as for signed (but must be positive).

Required storage: 8 bytes

DECIMAL(*M*,*D*)

Description: Column to store decimals in string format

Range: Depends on *M* and *D* (see Day 5, "MySQL Data Types")

Required storage: *M*+2 bytes

String Types

The string column types can be used to store text or binary data.

CHAR and VARCHAR are for small amounts of storage (up to 255 characters). They can be declared with the optional BINARY attribute, which means that their values are treated as binary strings, and any comparison or sorting is then performed in a case-sensitive way.

The four BLOB (binary large object) types are for larger amounts of storage of binary data (which can include textual data, handled with case sensitivity). The four TEXT types are for larger amounts of textual storage, therefore, where data is not to be treated as binary data, so operations are not case sensitive.

The capacity and number of bytes required for storage are shown in the following sections, where *M* is the declared length of a CHAR or VARCHAR, and *length* is the length of the value stored.

CHAR(*M*)

Description: A fixed-length string column of up to 255 characters

Maximum size: *M* bytes

Required storage: *M* bytes

VARCHAR(*M*)

Description: A variable-length string column of up to 255 characters

Maximum size: *M* bytes

Required storage: *length*+1 bytes

TINYBLOB

Description: A binary (BLOB) column holding data of small size

Maximum size: 2^8-1 bytes

Required storage: *length*+1 bytes

BLOB

Description: A binary (BLOB) column holding data of normal size

Maximum size: 2^{16}-1 bytes

Required storage: *length*+2 bytes

MEDIUMBLOB

Description: A binary (BLOB) column holding data of medium size

Maximum size: 2^{24}-1 bytes

Required storage: *length*+3 bytes

LONGBLOB

Description: A binary (BLOB) column holding data of large size

Maximum size: 2^{32}-1 bytes

Required storage: *length*+4 bytes

TINYTEXT

Description: A text (TEXT) column holding data of small size

Maximum size: 2^8-1 bytes

Required storage: *length*+1 bytes

TEXT

Description: A text (TEXT) column holding data of normal size

Maximum size: 2^{16}-1 bytes

Required storage: *length*+2 bytes

MEDIUMTEXT

Description: A text (TEXT) column holding data of medium size

Maximum size: 2^{24}-1 bytes

Required storage: *length*+3 bytes

LONGTEXT

Description: A text (TEXT) column holding data of large size

Maximum size: 2^{32}-1 bytes

Required storage: *length*+4 bytes

ENUM('value1', 'value2',...)

Description: Can contain exactly one member of an enumerated set of values

Maximum number of values: 65,565

Required storage: 1 byte for up to 255 members, 2 bytes for 256 to 65,535 members

SET('value1', 'value2',...)

Description: Can contain a set (a number) of members of a set of values

Maximum number of values: 64

Required storage: between 1 and 8 bytes depending on number of members

Date and Time Types

This section lists the column types for storing dates and times. No special attributes can be declared for these column types, and only the global attributes (for example, NULL, NOT NULL) are applicable.

DATE

Description: Date in the format *YYYY-MM-DD*

Range: 1000-01-01 to 9999-12-31

Zero value: 0000-00-00

Required storage: 3 bytes

TIME

Description: Time in the format *hh:mm:ss*

Range: -838:59:59 to 838:59:59

Zero value: 00:00:00

Required storage: 3 bytes

DATETIME

Description: Date and time in the format *YYYY-MM-DD hh:mm:ss*

Range: 1000-01-01 00:00:00 to 9999-12-31 23:59:59

Zero value: 0000-00-00 00:00:00

Required storage: 8 bytes

YEAR

Description: Year in the format *YYYY*

Range: 1901 to 2155

Zero value: 0000

Required storage: 1 byte

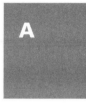

TIMESTAMP (*M*)

Description: Autoset date and time, becoming set to current date and time whenever the row is inserted or updated without a value being written to that column, or when a NULL is written to it. Stores precision to nearest second regardless of display size *M*.

The following list shows TIMESTAMP(*M*) with the display formats for the various values for *M*:

- TIMESTAMP(14) has the format YYYYMMDDhhmmss.
- TIMESTAMP(12) has the format YYYYMMDDhhmm.
- TIMESTAMP(10) has the format YYYYMMDDhh.
- TIMESTAMP(8) has the format YYYYMMDD.
- TIMESTAMP(6) has the format YYYYMM.
- TIMESTAMP(4) has the format YYYY.
- TIMESTAMP(2) has the format YY.

Range: beginning of the year 1970 (19700101000000) to some time in 2037

Zero value: 00000000000000

Required storage: 4 bytes

APPENDIX B

SQL Reference

This appendix details the SQL commands available to you in MySQL 4.0.2.

ALTER [IGNORE] TABLE *table_name action_list*

Description: Changes the structure of an existing table.

Usage: *action_list* can contain any number of actions separated by commas, with keywords whose syntax is listed in Table B.1.

TABLE B.1 Actions Performed by ALTER TABLE

Syntax for Action in action_list	Action Performed
ADD [COLUMN] column_declaration [FIRST | AFTER column_name]	Add a column to the table.
ADD INDEX [index_name] (column_name,...)	Add an index on one or more columns, optionally named but otherwise taking its name from column_name, the first indexed column.
ADD PRIMARY KEY (column_name,...)	Add a primary key.

TABLE B.1 continued

Syntax for Action in action_list	Action Performed
ADD UNIQUE [*index_name*] (*column_name*,...)	Add a unique key on one or more columns, optionally named but otherwise taking its name from *column_name*, the first indexed column.
ADD FULLTEXT [*index_name*] (*column_name*,...)	Add a full-text index on one or more columns, optionally named but otherwise taking its name from *column_name*, the first indexed column.
ADD [CONSTRAINT *symbol*] FOREIGN KEY index_name (column_name,...) [*reference_definition*]	Does nothing; included for compatibility only.
ALTER [COLUMN] *column_name* {SET DEFAULT *literal* | DROP DEFAULT}	Specify new default value for a column or remove old default value.
CHANGE [COLUMN] *column_name* *column_declaration* [FIRST | AFTER *other_column_name*]	Modify declaration of column *column_name* to new name and declaration given by *column_declaration*. Optionally moves column to first position or places it after *other_column_name* if FIRST or AFTER specified.
MODIFY [COLUMN] *column_declaration* [FIRST | AFTER *other_column_name*]	Modify column declaration without renaming declaration given by *column_declaration*. Optionally moves column to first position or places it after *other_column_name* if FIRST or AFTER specified.
DROP [COLUMN] *column_name*	Drop a column and all data contained within it.
DROP PRIMARY KEY	Drop a table's primary key.
DROP INDEX *index_name*	Drop named index from a table.
DISABLE KEYS	Stops MySQL updating non-unique indexes on MyISAM tables (MySQL 4.0 onward).
ENABLE KEYS	Create missing non-unique indexes on MyISAM tables (MySQL 4.0 onward).
RENAME [TO] *new_table_name*	Rename a table.
ORDER BY *column_name*	Sort rows of data on *column_name*. This can improve performance, but rows will not remain sorted after subsequent write operations.
table_options	Change table options. See CREATE TABLE for details.

Description in: Day 6

ANALYZE TABLE *table_name*[,*table_name*...]

Description: Analyzes and stores key distribution for given table or tables, the equivalent of myisamchk -a *table_name*. The stored key distribution is used to help optimization during joins. Returns a resultset table showing the status after running the command.

Limitations: MyISAM and BDB tables

Description in: Day 16

See also: OPTIMIZE TABLE

BACKUP TABLE *table_name*[,*table_name*...] TO '*/backup/directory*'

Description: Copies files containing the information required for rebuilding a table or tables to the backup directory whose path is given by */backup/directory*. Copies the minimum .frm and .MYD files, not the index file. Returns a table resultset with the status after running the command.

Limitations: MyISAM tables

See also: RESTORE TABLE

BEGIN

Description: Begins a transaction out of autocommit mode. A series of statements may follow, the following queries not being committed to the database until a COMMIT is issued (or a SQL command, which automatically ends a transaction).

Limitations: Transaction-safe tables (BDB and InnoDB). With other table types, queries following BEGIN will be committed to the database automatically.

Description in: Day 17

See also: COMMIT, ROLLBACK

CHECK TABLE *table_name*[,*table_name*,...] [*options*]

Description: Checks a table for errors, the equivalent of myisamchk -m *table_name*, and updates the key statistics on the table. Returns a resultset showing the status after running the command.

options can be any number of the following, separated by spaces if more than one is specified:

- QUICK—Does not scan rows for wrong links
- FAST—Only checks tables that have not been closed properly
- CHANGED—Only checks tables that have not been closed properly or that have been changed since the last check
- MEDIUM—Scans rows to verify that deleted links are okay
- EXTENDED—Does a full key lookup for all keys on each row

Limitations: MyISAM and InnoDB tables

Description in: Day 16

See also: REPAIR TABLE

COMMIT

Description: Concludes a transaction made out of autocommit mode (a series of queries following a BEGIN) and writes changes to the database on disk.

The following commands effectively do a COMMIT by ending a transaction automatically: ALTER TABLE, BEGIN, CREATE INDEX, DROP DATABASE, DROP TABLE, RENAME TABLE, and TRUNCATE.

Limitations: Transaction-safe tables (BDB and InnoDB). With other table types, queries following BEGIN will be committed to the database automatically.

Description in: Day 17

See also: BEGIN, ROLLBACK

CREATE DATABASE [IF NOT EXISTS] *database_name*

Description: Creates a database with the name *database_name*. Specifying IF NOT EXISTS suppresses an error if a database already exists with that name.

Description in: Day 6

See also: DROP DATABASE

CREATE [AGGREGATE] FUNCTION *function_name*

RETURNS {STRING|REAL|INTEGER} SONAME *shared_library_name*

Description: Creates a new user-defined function (UDF) that may be called as *function_name*() in the same way as MySQL's built-in functions.

The AGGREGATE option (new in version 3.23) specifies that the function will be an aggregating function (such as COUNT()).

Functions must be written in C or C++. *shared_library_name* is the name of the compiled .so file, residing in a directory searched by ld.

Limitations: Requires user to have insert privileges for the mysql database. MySQL must have been compiled dynamically, and the operating system must support dynamic loading.

Description in: Day 21

See also: DROP FUNCTION

CREATE [UNIQUE|FULLTEXT] INDEX *index_name*

ON *table_name* (*column_list*)

Description: Creates an index called *index_name* on the column or columns given by *column_list* (names of columns are comma-separated if more than one) of the table *table_name*.

UNIQUE option specifies a unique index. FULLTEXT option specifies a full-text index that will help a SELECT...WHERE MATCH...AGAINST query. If neither UNIQUE or FULLTEXT are specified, the index will be non-unique.

Synonymous with ALTER TABLE...ADD INDEX.

Limitations: FULLTEXT option works only on VARCHAR and TEXT columns of MyISAM tables, and only in versions 3.23.23 and later.

Description in: Day 9

See also: ALTER TABLE, DROP INDEX

B

CREATE [TEMPORARY] TABLE [IF NOT EXISTS] *table_name* [(*create_definition*,...)] [*table_options*] [*select_statement*]

Description: Creates a table called *table_name*. The table name can be specified as *database_name.table_name* to create a table in a database not currently selected.

TEMPORARY option creates a table that will be dropped automatically when the database connection closes (version 3.23 and later).

IF NOT EXISTS option suppresses the error that will be returned if you try to create a table when another table with that name currently exists (version 3.23 and later).

The *create_definition* for each column can contain the following for defining a column:

- *column_name column_type* [NOT NULL|NULL] [DEFAULT *default_value*] [AUTO_INCREMENT] [PRIMARY KEY] [*reference_definition*]

and any of the following for defining an index on a column:

- PRIMARY KEY (*column_list*)
- {INDEX|KEY} [*index_name*] (*column_list*)
- UNIQUE [*index_name*] (*column_list*)
- FULLTEXT [*index_name*] (*column_list*)
- [CONSTRAINT symbol] FOREIGN KEY *index_name* (*column_list*) [*reference_definition*]
- CHECK (*expression*)

For each column definition

- *column_type* can be any valid column type as detailed in Appendix A, "Data Type Reference."
- If neither NULL nor NOT NULL is specified, behavior will be as if NULL had been specified.
- If DEFAULT is specified, whenever an insert occurs, *default_value* will be inserted unless another value is specified.
- If DEFAULT is not specified, on nullable columns, MySQL will apply a default value of NULL, and on NOT NULL defined columns will apply a default of 0 for numeric

types, the current date and time on TIMESTAMP columns, the zero value for other temporal columns, and the empty string for string types (apart from ENUM, which will default to the first member).

- AUTO_INCREMENT on an integer column will cause the previous largest value plus one to be inserted whenever an insert occurs, provided that that column's value is not set, or NULL or 0 is inserted into it; a table can have only one AUTO_INCREMENT column, and it must be an index.

For index definitions, *column_list* is one or more column names (comma-separated if more than one). The first column name will be used as the index name if *index_name* is not specified.

PRIMARY KEY specifies a primary key (unique and with no values set to NULL). INDEX and KEY are synonymous, creating a non-unique index. UNIQUE specifies a unique index, and on versions 3.23.23 and later, and with MyISAM tables, you can use FULLTEXT to specify a full-text index.

The *reference_definition*, FOREIGN KEY, and CHECK do nothing and are included for compatibility of SQL with other systems.

table_options allow you to specify a number of options for the table. This can include the table type, specified as TYPE=*table_type*, where *table_type* is one of

- ISAM—The original type of MySQL table
- MyISAM—The default, the newer storage type replacing ISAM
- MERGE or the synonym MRG_MERGE—A collection of MyISAM tables treated as one
- BDB—The Berkeley transaction-safe table type with page locking
- InnoDB—The transaction-safe table type with row locking
- HEAP—A table stored only in memory

Other *table_options* can include the following:

- AUTO_INCREMENT=*value*—Sets the starting value of the AUTO_INCREMENT column (MyISAM tables only)
- AVG_ROW_LENGTH=*value*—Sets the approximate length of a table row on tables with variable-sized columns and of large size (rarely used)
- CHECKSUM={0|1}—Set to 1 causes MySQL to maintain a checksum on the data in all rows, making it easier to spot corrupted tables but adding a small performance overhead
- COMMENT="*comment_text*"—Specifies a comment for the table, up to 60 characters long

- `MAX_ROWS=value`—Sets the maximum number of rows allowed to be stored in a table (may help performance)
- `MIN_ROWS=value`—Sets the minimum number of rows you expect to store in a table (may help performance)
- `PACK_KEYS={0|1|DEFAULT}`—If set to 1 (`MyISAM` and `ISAM` tables only), makes indexes smaller and faster but slows down updates; if set to `DEFAULT` (versions 4.0 and later), causes only long `CHAR` and `VARCHAR` column indexes to be packed
- `PASSWORD="password"`—Encrypts the `.frm` file with a password (does nothing on standard MySQL versions)
- `DELAY_KEY_WRITE={0|1}`—If set to 1, delays the updating of keys until the table is not in use (`MyISAM` tables only)
- `ROW_FORMAT={DEFAULT|DYNAMIC|FIXED|COMPRESSED}`—Defines how rows should be stored (`MyISAM` tables only)
- `RAID_TYPE=STRIPED`—Helps get around the size limitation imposed by the operating system (typically 2GB or 4GB) for `MyISAM` data files by splitting up the data file into chunks
- `UNION=(table_name[,table_name...])`—Works on a `MERGE` table to combine several other tables into one
- `INSERT_METHOD={NO|FIRST|LAST}`—Must be specified on a `MERGE` table if you intend to insert data into it, to define how inserts should occur
- `DATA DIRECTORY="/path/to/directory"`—Specifies where data files should be stored in the file system (version 4.0 and later, with `MyISAM` tables only)
- `INDEX DIRECTORY="/path/to/directory"`—Specifies where index files should be stored in the file system (version 4.0 and later, with `MyISAM` tables only)

By using a *select_statement*, the table will be created and populated using the resultset from a `SELECT` query (the resulting columns and data). The new table will have any columns and indexes specified in the *create_definition* list, followed by any columns created as a result of the `SELECT`. Without a *create_definition*, only the columns of the `SELECT` resultset will be created in the new table.

Description in: Day 6

See also: ALTER TABLE, DROP TABLE, DESCRIBE, SELECT

CROSS JOIN

Syntax:

```
SELECT...FROM table_reference1
  CROSS JOIN table_reference2 join_condition
```

Description: Performs a cross join as part of a SELECT statement. In a cross join, every row of *table_reference1* is crossed with every row of *table_reference2*.

Description in: Day 9

See also: INNER JOIN

DELETE

Syntax:

```
DELETE [LOW_PRIORITY|QUICK] FROM table_name
  [WHERE where_definition]
  [ORDER BY column_list]
  [LIMIT num_rows]
```

Description: Deletes rows of data from *table_name* where any conditions given by WHERE *where_definition* are met. Without *where_definition*, all rows are deleted.

LOW_PRIORITY can be used to delay the action until no other clients are reading from the table.

QUICK can speed up deletes in some circumstances because the index leaves will not be merged during the delete.

LIMIT can be used to limit the number of rows deleted to *num_rows*. ORDER BY may be used with LIMIT to sort on a column or columns given by *column_list* before deleting the first *num_rows* in the sort order.

Multitable syntax (from MySQL 4.0):

```
DELETE [LOW_PRIORITY|QUICK]
  table_name1 [, table_name2...]
  FROM table_references
  [WHERE where_definition]
```

or the equivalent:

```
DELETE [LOW_PRIORITY|QUICK]
  FROM table_name1 [, table_name2...]
  USING table_references
  [WHERE where_definition]
```

In these forms, DELETE performs deletion of rows from tables *table_name1*, *table_name2*, and any others in the first list of tables.

Rows are deleted where the *where_definition* is met. However, the *where_definition* may refer to columns in tables from which no deletion is to occur. The full list of tables referred to is given by *table_references*.

Description in: Day 8

DESCRIBE *table_name* [*column_name*]

Description: Returns information about all the columns in a given table. If *column_name* is specified, information is provided about that column only.

Description in: Day 8

See also: SHOW COLUMNS

DESC

Description: Synonymous with DESCRIBE.

Description in: Day 8

See also: DESCRIBE

DROP DATABASE [IF EXISTS] *database_name*

Description: Drops (deletes) a database with the name *database_name*. Specifying IF EXISTS suppresses an error if a database with that name does not exist.

Description in: Day 6

See also: CREATE DATABASE

DROP FUNCTION *function_name*

Description: Drops the user-defined function (UDF) *function_name*(), created using CREATE FUNCTION.

Limitations: Requires user to have delete privileges for the mysql database.

Description in: Day 21

See also: CREATE FUNCTION

DROP INDEX *index_name* ON *table_name*

Description: Drops the index called *index_name* from *table_name*.

Synonymous with ALTER TABLE...DROP INDEX

Description in: Day 9

See also: ALTER TABLE, CREATE INDEX

DROP TABLE [IF EXISTS] *table_name*[,*table_name*...]

Description: Drops the table (or tables) specified by *table_name*, deleting all data within it.

IF EXISTS can be specified to suppress an error message if a table with the name specified does not exist.

Description in: Day 6

See also: CREATE TABLE, DROP DATABASE

EXPLAIN SELECT *select_statement*

Description: Provides the query plan for a SELECT. MySQL shows how it will join any tables and in which order.

This can enable you to see whether the query optimizer will join the tables in the optimal order. You can override this order using a SELECT with a STRAIGHT_JOIN clause.

Description in: Day 18

See also: SELECT and the STRAIGHT_JOIN clause

EXPLAIN *table_name*

Description: Synonymous with DESCRIBE.

Description in: Day 8

See also: DESCRIBE

FLUSH *flush_option*[,*flush_option*...]

Description: Clears the various internal caches used by MySQL.

flush_option can be any of the following:

- HOSTS—Clears the host cache tables.
- LOGS—Closes and reopens all logs.
- PRIVILEGES—Reloads the grant tables.
- TABLES—Closes all tables, even those in use, saving them to disk.
- TABLE *table_name* and TABLES *table_name1,table_name2*...—Closes only the given tables, saving them to disk.
- TABLES WITH READ LOCK—Closes all open tables and places a read lock on all tables in all databases; tables remain locked until you issue an UNLOCK TABLES; can be useful for taking a snapshot, such as for backup purposes.
- STATUS—Resets most system status variables to zero.

The equivalent of mysqladmin flush-*option*.

Description in: Day 15

GRANT

Syntax:

```
GRANT privileges [(column_list)] [,privileges [(column_list)]...]
  ON database_name.table_name
  TO username@hostname [IDENTIFIED BY 'password']
  [REQUIRE [SSL | X509]
    [CIPHER cipher [AND]]
    [ISSUER issuer [AND]]
    [SUBJECT subject]]
  [WITH GRANT OPTION |
    MAX_QUERIES_PER_HOUR num |
    MAX_UPDATES_PER_HOUR num |
    MAX_CONNECTIONS_PER_HOUR num ]
```

Description: Grants user privileges.

privileges may be given by any of ALL PRIVILEGES (or its synonym ALL), ALTER, CREATE, CREATE TEMPORARY TABLES, DELETE, DROP, EXECUTE, FILE, INDEX, INSERT, LOCK TABLES, PROCESS, REFERENCES, RELOAD, REPLICATION CLIENT, REPLICATION SLAVE, SELECT, SHOW DATABASES, SHUTDOWN, SUPER, UPDATE, and USAGE.

database_name and *table_name* may be specified, or you may give wildcards, such as *database_name*.* (all tables in a given database), or *.* or its equivalent * (meaning all databases and all tables on the server).

The user is specified along with the hostname from which he may connect with these privileges, with *username@hostname*.

The optional IDENTIFIED BY '*password*' can be used to create a password for that user, which will be automatically encrypted. Specifying it for an existing user will change that user's password.

The REQUIRE, CIPHER, ISSUER, and SUBJECT keywords can be used to require a secure connection to MySQL.

Specifying WITH GRANT OPTION gives the user the ability to grant to other users any privileges that he has himself.

Speficying MAX QUERIES... will limit the number of queries, updates, and/or connections that can be made by that user per hour.

Description in: Day 14

See also: REVOKE, SHOW GRANTS

HANDLER

Syntax:

```
HANDLER table_name OPEN [AS alias_name]

HANDLER table_name READ index_name {= | >= | <= | <} (value1, value2,...)
  [WHERE...] [LIMIT num_rows]

HANDLER table_name READ index_name {FIRST | NEXT | PREV | LAST}
  [WHERE...] [LIMIT num_rows]

HANDLER table_name READ {FIRST | NEXT }
  [WHERE...] [LIMIT num_rows]

HANDLER table_name CLOSE
```

Description: Runs a query through the table interface directly without using the query optimizer. It is a low-level command compared with SELECT.

The first form, using keyword OPEN, opens a table so that it may be read by the following READ commands. The table will not be shared until the HANDLER...CLOSE command is issued or the thread dies.

The first form of HANDLER...READ fetches one row (or num_rows if there is a LIMIT clause) where the index index_name compares as specified with value1 and the WHERE condition is met. An index may incorporate several columns, so a list of values may be specified, starting from the leftmost column of the index.

The second form of HANDLER...READ fetches one row (or num_rows if there is a LIMIT clause) where the WHERE condition is met, in index order.

The third form of HANDLER...READ fetches one row (or num_rows if there is a LIMIT clause) where the WHERE condition is met, in the order of the rows in the table.

See also: SELECT

INNER JOIN

Syntax:

```
SELECT...FROM table_reference1
  INNER JOIN table_reference2 join_condition
```

Description: Performs an inner join as part of a SELECT statement. An inner join is the default type of join, in which rows of table_reference1 are crossed with rows of table_reference2 where join_condition is met.

table_reference is either a table name, or uses an alias to that table, in the format table_name AS alias_name.

join_reference defines the relationship used in the join and is either ON *conditional_expression* or USING (*column_list*).

Description in: Day 9

See also: CROSS JOIN, INNER JOIN, LEFT JOIN, NATURAL JOIN

INSERT

Syntax:

```
INSERT [LOW PRIORITY | DELAYED] [IGNORE]
  [INTO] table_name
  SET column_name1=expression1, column_name2=expression2,...
```

or

```
INSERT [LOW PRIORITY | DELAYED] [IGNORE]
  [INTO] table_name [(column_name,...)]
  VALUES (expression,...),(...)...
```

or

```
INSERT [LOW PRIORITY | DELAYED] [IGNORE]
  [INTO] table_name [(column_name,...)]
  SELECT...
```

Description: Adds new rows of data to an existing table given by *table_name*.

INSERT can take a number of forms as shown previously. In the first form using SET, each column is named together with the value *expression* to which it will be set, or (in MySQL 4.0.3 and later) *expression* may be replaced by the keyword DEFAULT to set a column to its default value.

The second form takes the VALUES keyword with a list of values. The values in the list must correspond with the columns in the target table: There must be the same number of them, and their types should correspond or data conversion will occur. Again, *expression* may be any expression, or DEFAULT in 4.0.3 or later.

The third form performs a SELECT and inserts data from the resultset into the table. As with the VALUES form, the resultset's column types and the number of its columns should correspond with those of the target table.

By specifying LOW_PRIORITY, the insert will not take place until no other clients are reading from the table.

Using the DELAYED option means that the client will get an instant response that the insert has been performed, but the data will be inserted only after the table is not in use by another thread.

IGNORE causes an insert with many rows to ignore any rows that would duplicate an existing primary or unique key. Without IGNORE, the insert will abort if any row tries to duplicate such a key.

Whether INTO is specified has no effect on the action of INSERT.

The action of an INSERT can be ascertained using mysql_affected_rows(), which returns the number of rows inserted.

Description in: Day 7

See also: REPLACE

KILL *thread_id*

Description: Kills the thread identified by *thread_id*. (A thread represents one MySQL connection and is not the same as a Unix thread.)

Works the same as mysqladmin kill *thread_id*.

Description in: Day 15

See also: SHOW PROCESSLIST

LEFT JOIN

Syntax:
```
SELECT...FROM table_reference1
  LEFT JOIN table_reference2 join_condition
```

Description: Performs a left join as part of a SELECT statement. A left join is a join in which all rows in the left table *table_reference1* are returned (subject to any WHERE condition); wherever these rows match with rows of *table_reference2* through a *join_condition*, values from the right table appear in the resultset, or NULL otherwise.

table_reference either is a table name or uses an alias to that table, in the format *table_name* AS *alias_name*.

join_condition defines the relationship used in the join and is either ON *conditional_expression* or USING (*column_list*).

Description in: Day 9

See also: CROSS JOIN, INNER JOIN, LEFT JOIN, NATURAL LEFT JOIN, RIGHT JOIN

LEFT OUTER JOIN

Description: Synonymous with LEFT JOIN and included only for compatibility with ODBC.

Description in: Day 9

See also: LEFT JOIN

LOAD DATA INFILE

Syntax:

```
LOAD DATA [LOW_PRIORITY | CONCURRENT] [LOCAL]
  INFILE 'filename'
  [REPLACE | IGNORE]
  INTO TABLE table_name
  [FIELDS [TERMINATED BY 'char']
    [[OPTIONALLY] ENCLOSED BY 'char']
    [ESCAPED BY 'char' ]]
  [LINES TERMINATED BY 'char']
  [IGNORE num LINES]
  [(column_list)]
```

Description: Reads the text file given by *filename* and imports data into the table given by *table_name*. Works the same as mysqlimport.

By specifying LOW_PRIORITY, execution waits until no other clients are reading from the table. By specifying CONCURRENT with a MyISAM table, other clients can read from the table while LOAD DATA INFILE is executing.

LOCAL means that a local file on the client, rather than the server, will be used for reading.

The REPLACE and IGNORE keywords cause rows with duplicate primary or unique keys to be replaced by those in the new file, or ignored, respectively.

The optional FIELDS keyword can be followed by a number of keywords:

- TERMINATED BY—Specifies the character used to separate the fields (default \t).
- ENCLOSED BY—The characters enclosing each field (default nothing); if you specify OPTIONALLY ENCLOSED BY, the character is expected to enclose CHAR and VARCHAR fields only.
- ESCAPED BY—Specifies the escape character for special characters (default \).
- LINES TERMINATED BY—Specifies the termination of each row (default \n).

The IGNORE *num* LINES causes the first *num* lines at the start of the file to be skipped.

To load only some of a table's columns, specify column_list, a list of column names separated by commas. Data in the file that corresponds with columns not listed will be ignored.

Description in: Day 7

LOCK TABLES

```
LOCK TABLES table_name [AS alias_name] {READ | [LOW_PRIORITY] WRITE}
  [, table_name [AS alias_name] {READ | [LOW_PRIORITY] WRITE} ...]
```

Description: Obtains a lock on a table or tables given by `table_name`, for use by the current thread.

LOCK TABLES may have to wait for other threads to finish before locks on all tables are obtained, and MySQL operates a queuing system to manage the granting of READ and WRITE locks. When using this statement, you must lock all tables that will be used by the subsequent queries. Locks are released when the thread finishes, when another LOCK TABLES is issued, or when an UNLOCK TABLES is issued.

If a thread obtains a READ lock, that thread and all other threads can perform only read operations from those tables.

If a thread obtains a WRITE lock, it becomes the only thread with any access to those tables. It can read and write, but no other threads can access the tables.

Normally, MySQL grants a lock to a thread in the READ queue only when no threads are waiting to obtain a WRITE lock (thus giving WRITE locks a higher priority). LOW_PRIORITY WRITE makes the queuing system behave the opposite way, so that a WRITE lock has to wait until all pending READ locks are cleared from the queues before the WRITE lock is granted.

Description in: Day 17

See also: UNLOCK TABLES, SELECT...HIGH PRIORITY

NATURAL JOIN

Syntax:

```
SELECT...FROM table_reference1
  NATURAL JOIN table_reference2
```

Description: Performs an inner join as part of a SELECT statement, crossing rows of `table_reference1` with rows of `table_reference2` with matching values, in all columns where the column names are identical in both tables. (Therefore, this is the same as an INNER JOIN with a USING clause that lists all columns that exist in both tables.)

`table_reference` is either a table name, or uses an alias to that table, in the format `table_name` AS `alias_name`.

Description in: Day 9

See also: INNER JOIN, NATURAL LEFT JOIN

NATURAL LEFT JOIN

Syntax:

```
SELECT...FROM table_reference1
  NATURAL LEFT JOIN table_reference2
```

Description: Performs a left join as part of a SELECT statement, crossing rows of *table_reference1* with rows of *table_reference2*, in all columns where the column names are identical in both tables. (Therefore, this is the same as a LEFT JOIN with a USING clause that lists all columns that exist in both tables.)

table_reference either is a table name or uses an alias to that table, in the format *table_name* AS *alias_name*.

Description in: Day 9

See also: LEFT JOIN, NATURAL JOIN

NATURAL LEFT OUTER JOIN

Description: Synonymous with NATURAL LEFT JOIN.

Description in: Day 9

See also: NATURAL LEFT JOIN

NATURAL RIGHT JOIN

Description: Performs a natural right join as part of a SELECT statement. Analogous to NATURAL LEFT JOIN, which should be used instead, to maintain compatibility with other databases.

Description in: Day 9

See also: RIGHT JOIN, NATURAL LEFT JOIN

NATURAL RIGHT OUTER JOIN

Description: Synonymous with NATURAL RIGHT JOIN

See also: NATURAL RIGHT JOIN

OPTIMIZE TABLE *table_name*[,*table_name*...]

Description: Defragments the data file for a table or tables.

Running this command recovers space taken up by deleted records. It should be run when many rows have been deleted, or when many changes have been made to tables with variable-length columns.

This command works the same as `myisamchk --quick --check-only-changed --sort-index --analyze` on `MyISAM` tables.

Limitations: `MyISAM` and `BDB` tables. For `BDB` tables `OPTIMIZE TABLE` is the same as `ANALYZE TABLE`.

Description in: Day 16

See also: `ANALYZE TABLE`

B

RENAME TABLE *table_name* TO *new_table_name*

[, *table_name2* TO *new_table_name2* ...]

Description: Renames a table from *table_name* to *new_table_name*.

When multiple tables are being renamed in the same statement, they are read from left to right. It is possible to swap the names of two tables by renaming the first to a temporary name, renaming that to the first table's eventual name after the second table has been renamed.

Description in: Day 6

See also: `ALTER TABLE`

REPAIR TABLE *table_name*[,*table_name*,...]
[*options*]

Description: Repairs a possibly corrupted table, the equivalent of `myisamchk -r` *table_name*. Returns a resultset table showing the status after running the command.

This command is rarely used, except when database corruption has occurred, when it should manage to recover corrupted data.

options can be any number of the following, separated by spaces if more than one is specified:

- `QUICK`—Performs a repair of the index tree only
- `EXTENDED`—Creates the index row by row
- `USE_FRM`—Re-creates the index if it is missing or badly corrupted (MySQL 4.0.2 onward)

Limitations: `MyISAM` tables

Description in: Day 16

See also: `CHECK TABLE`

REPLACE

Syntax:

```
REPLACE [LOW PRIORITY | DELAYED]
  [INTO] table_name
  SET column_name1=expression1, column_name2=expression2,...
```

or

```
REPLACE [LOW PRIORITY | DELAYED]
  [INTO] table_name [(column_name,...)]
  VALUES (expression,...),(...)...
```

or

```
REPLACE [LOW PRIORITY | DELAYED]
  [INTO] table_name [(column_name,...)]
  SELECT...
```

Description: Adds new rows of data to an existing table given by *table_name*. Works like INSERT, but where it tries to insert a row with the same primary or unique key as an existing row, the old row is replaced by the new.

REPLACE can take a number of forms as shown previously. In the first form using SET, each column is named together with the value to which it is to be set.

The second form takes the VALUES keyword with a list of values. The values in the list must correspond with the columns in the target table: There must be the same number of them, and their types should correspond or data conversion will occur.

The third form performs a SELECT and inserts data from the resultset into the table. As with the VALUES form, the resultset's column types and the number of its columns should correspond with those of the target table.

By specifying LOW_PRIORITY, the insert will not take place until no other clients are reading from the table.

Using the DELAYED option means that the client will get an instant response that the insert has been performed, but the data will be inserted only after the table is not in use by another thread.

Whether INTO is specified has no effect on the action of REPLACE.

The action of a REPLACE can be ascertained using mysql_affected_rows(). Where a row of data has been replaced rather than inserted (effectively an old row deleted and a new one inserted), mysql_affected_rows() returns 2, whereas it returns 1 for a pure insert.

Description in: Day 7

See also: INSERT

RESTORE TABLE *table_name*[,*table_name...*]
FROM '*/backup/directory*'

Description: Restores a table or tables from the given backup directory whose path is given by */backup/directory*. Rebuilds any index files. Does not overwrite an existing table. Returns a table resultset with the status after running the command.

Limitations: MyISAM tables

See also: BACKUP TABLE

REVOKE *privileges* [(*column_list*)]

[,*privileges* [(*column_list*)]...]

ON {*database_name.table_name*}

FROM *username@hostname*

Description: Removes user privileges.

The parameters that may be passed to REVOKE (the privileges, columns, database, and table names, and the user- and hostnames) work in the same way as the parameters for GRANT. See GRANT for a description.

Description in: Day 14

See also: GRANT, SHOW GRANTS

RIGHT JOIN

Description: Performs a right join as part of a SELECT statement. This is analogous to LEFT JOIN, which should be used instead to maintain compatibility with other databases.

Description in: Day 9

See also: LEFT JOIN

RIGHT OUTER JOIN

Description: Synonymous with RIGHT JOIN.

Description in: Day 9

See also: RIGHT JOIN

B

ROLLBACK

Description: Concludes a transaction made out of autocommit mode (a series of queries following a BEGIN) and discards any changes without writing to the database on disk.

Limitations: Transaction-safe tables (BDB and InnoDB). With other table types, queries following BEGIN will be committed to the database automatically.

Description in: Day 17

See also: BEGIN, COMMIT

SELECT

Syntax:

```
SELECT [STRAIGHT_JOIN] [SQL_SMALL_RESULT] [SQL_BIG_RESULT] [SQL_BUFFER_RESULT]
  [HIGH_PRIORITY]
  [DISTINCT]
select_expression,...
[INTO {OUTFILE | DUMPFILE} '/path/to/filename' export_options]
[FROM table_references
  [WHERE where_definition]
  [GROUP BY {column_name | column_alias | column_position | formula}
    [ASC | DESC], ...]
  [HAVING where_definition]
  [ORDER BY {column_name | column_alias | column_position | formula}
    [ASC | DESC], ...]
  [LIMIT [offset,] num_rows]
  [PROCEDURE procedure_name]
```

Description: Runs a query on one or more tables and returns a resultset table populated with the rows of data retrieved.

select_expression specifies the columns to be retrieved, and *table_references* is a list of table names (comma-separated if more than one, and optionally with alias names and/or JOINs) in which those columns reside. *where_definition* specifies the conditions for inclusion of rows.

The following options can also be used:

- STRAIGHT_JOIN—When used with a JOIN, forces the query optimizer to join the tables in the order they are named in *table_references*.
- SQL_SMALL_RESULT—Can help the query optimizer when using DISTINCT and GROUP BY if you know that the resultset will be small (shouldn't be needed after MySQL version 3.23).
- SQL_BIG_RESULT—Can help the query optimizer when using DISTINCT and GROUP BY if you know that the resultset will have many rows.

- SQL_BUFFER_RESULT—Forces the resultset to be put into a temporary table, helping to free all table locks quickly.

- HIGH_PRIORITY—Lets the SELECT execute when the table is locked with a READ lock by another thread, and even if there is a WRITE lock waiting in the queue.

- DISTINCT—Returns only unique rows in the resultset, so duplicate rows will be eliminated from the resultset.

- INTO OUTFILE—Causes the resultset to be written to a file given by /path/to/filename (which must not exist already), the opposite of LOAD DATA INFILE; INTO DUMPFILE does much the same but inserts no field or row termination, thus creating a single line of data.

- GROUP BY and ORDER BY—Cause the resultset to be sorted by the column or columns specified, either by the names of the columns, by their aliases, or by their ordinal positions in the resultset. By default, the sort order is ASC (ascending), but DESC can be specified to reverse this. GROUP BY specifies that the resultset will be aggregated by the columns specified, and aggregating functions should be applied to columns not mentioned in the GROUP BY clause.

- HAVING—Can be used to apply a condition that rows must satisfy once in the resultset; this is the last thing to be processed before the resultset is returned to the client. Conditions should normally be placed in the WHERE clause where their processing can be optimized, but HAVING can be used where this is not possible.

- LIMIT *num_rows*—Limits the number of rows that can be returned in the resultset; *offset* can be used to specify the number of the first row to return, counting from 0.

- PROCEDURE—Can be used to specify a procedure written in C++ to which the resultset will be sent before being returned to the user.

Description in: Day 8

See also: EXPLAIN, LOCK TABLES, LOAD DATA INFILE

SET [OPTION] *option=value,...*

Description: Sets options that govern the operation of the client or the server. Unless specified, options take effect immediately; however, the next time the client is restarted, they go back to either the default values, or the values in the various config files (such as /etc/my.cnf), which will override the defaults.

The client options only live until the thread exits.

The keyword OPTION has no effect. The possible syntax for *option=value* is given in Table B.2.

TABLE B.2 Options for SET SQL_VALUE_OPTION

Syntax for *option=value*	Action Performed
AUTOCOMMIT={0|1}	Turns autocommit mode on (1) or off (0). If set to 0, all updates will require a COMMIT or ROLLBACK to tell MySQL to accept or revoke the transaction.
CHARACTER SET {*charset_name*|DEFAULT}	Specifies the character set mapping that will be used for all string data going to and from the client. Currently only cp1251_koi8 is available, but others can be added.
	Note: In the syntax for this option, no = (equals) is required.
INSERT_ID=*value*	Specifies the next integer value to be used for an AUTO_INCREMENT column in the next INSERT or ALTER TABLE operation.
LAST_INSERT_ID=*value*	Sets the value that will be returned by the LAST_INSERT_ID().
	Note: Seldom used, except in the update log.
SQL_AUTO_IS_NULL={0|1}	When set to 1, a query (as used in some ODBC programs) can use ...WHERE *auto_inc_col* IS NULL to retrieve the last row inserted into a table with an AUTO_INCREMENT column.
	Default: 1
SQL_BIG_SELECTS={0|1}	Allows MySQL to run a SELECT query that it anticipates will return a big resultset (more rows than the system variable max_join_size). If set to 0, it will abort if a big resultset is expected.
	Default: 1
SQL_MAX_JOIN_SIZE={*value*|DEFAULT}	Sets the maximum_join_size allowed for this client, and sets SQL_BIG_SELECTS to 0. When set, a SELECT query will abort if a big resultset is expected.
	Default: According to MySQL global variables
SQL_BIG_TABLES={0|1}	Tells MySQL to store temporary tables on disk rather than in memory (the default). This is slower but allows larger temporary tables to be handled, avoiding an error that may arise from a SELECT that uses a large temporary table.
	Default: 0

TABLE B.2   continued

Syntax for *option=value*	Action Performed
SQL_BUFFER_RESULT={0|1}	Forces MySQL to create a temporary table for the resultset of a SELECT. This frees table locks as soon as possible for the benefit of other threads.
	Default: 0
SQL_LOG_OFF={0|1}	When set to 1, prevents entries from being written to the standard log for this client. Client requires process privilege to run this.
	Default: According to MySQL global variables
SQL_LOG_UPDATE={0|1}	When set to 0, prevents entries from being written to the update log for this client. Client requires process privilege to run this.
	Default: According to MySQL global variables
SQL_LOW_PRIORITY_UPDATES={0|1}	When set to 1, all INSERT, UPDATE, DELETE, and LOCK TABLE WRITE queries will be treated as low priority. They will wait until no SELECT or LOCK TABLE READ is using the table.
	Default: 0
SQL_QUOTE_SHOW_CREATE={0|1}	Causes quotes (') to be placed around column and table names when running SHOW CREATE TABLE.
	Default: 1
SQL_SAFE_UPDATES={0|1}	Helps prevent accidental deletion or updating of all rows in a table. When set to 1, any update command must be issued with a WHERE clause on an index or with a LIMIT clause; otherwise, it will abort.
	Default: 0
SQL_SELECT_LIMIT={*value*|DEFAULT}	When set to an integer *value*, all SELECT queries will be run as if a LIMIT *value* clause were added to them, although any actual LIMIT clause will override the value set here.
	Default: DEFAULT, meaning unlimited
PASSWORD [FOR *username@hostname*] =PASSWORD("*password*")	Sets the password for a given user. Defaults to the current user if another user is not specified.
	Note: Value is maintained when current thread exits.
TIMESTAMP={*unix_timestamp*|DEFAULT}	Sets the date and time for this client. NOW() (and its equivalents) will be fixed at the time specified.
	Note: Mostly used when restoring from an update log.

B

SHOW *keyword parameters*

Description: Provides information in a resultset, based on the *keyword* and *parameters* provided.

Options are as follows:

- SHOW COLUMNS FROM *table_name*—Provides information on the columns of a table.
- SHOW DATABASES [LIKE *'wildcard'*]—Lists the databases on the MySQL server.
- SHOW [OPEN] TABLES [FROM *database_name*] [LIKE *'wildcard'*]—Lists tables on the MySQL server, those currently open in the table cache.
- SHOW [FULL] COLUMNS FROM *table_name* [FROM *database_name*] [LIKE *'wildcard'*]—Lists columns in a given table; specifying FULL displays the privileges you have on each column.
- SHOW {INDEX|KEYS} FROM *table_name* [FROM *database_name*]—Lists all the indexes in a given table; KEYS and INDEX are synonymous.
- SHOW TABLE STATUS [FROM *database_name*] [LIKE *'wildcard'*]—Provides detailed information on the status of a table and how it has recently been used.
- SHOW STATUS [LIKE *'wildcard'*]—Displays detailed information about the status of the MySQL server.
- SHOW VARIABLES [LIKE *'wildcard'*]—Lists the MySQL system variables.
- SHOW LOGS—Shows information about MySQL's log files.
- SHOW [FULL] PROCESSLIST—Lists the threads currently running; without the FULL option, only the first 100 characters of each line are shown.
- SHOW GRANTS FOR *username@hostname*—Displays the grants for a given user.
- SHOW CREATE TABLE *table_name*—Displays the CREATE TABLE statement that creates a given table.
- SHOW MASTER STATUS, SHOW MASTER LOGS, and SHOW SLAVE STATUS—Have to do with replication and display the status of the master and slave databases.

Where the preceding commands allow you to optionally specify FROM *database_name*, you can run SHOW on a database other than the one currently selected.

Where the preceding commands allow you to optionally specify LIKE *'wildcard'*, you can limit SHOW to entities that have names like *wildcard*, in which you can use the % character for wildcard text matching.

See also: DESCRIBE

TRUNCATE TABLE *table_name*

Description: Does the same as COMMIT, DELETE FROM *table_name* but is faster.

See also: DELETE

UNION

Syntax:

```
SELECT...
  UNION [ALL]
  SELECT
    [UNION
    SELECT ...]
```

Description: Combines the resultsets of several SELECT queries into a single resultset.

Without ALL specified, the rows of the final resultset will be unique (like a SELECT DISTINCT). With ALL, the rows from all the SELECT statements will be included.

Limitations: Version 4.0.0 and later. Only the last SELECT can have INTO OUTFILE or ORDER BY.

Description in: Day 8

See also: SELECT

UNLOCK TABLES

Description: Releases any table locks held by the current thread.

Description in: Day 17

See also: LOCK TABLES

UPDATE

Syntax:

```
UPDATE [LOW PRIORITY] [IGNORE] table_name
  SET column_name1=expression1, column_name2=expression2,...
  [WHERE where_definition]
  [LIMIT num]
```

Description: Modifies the values held in existing rows in a table.

The SET portion defines the new values for the named columns, which will be updated to *expression* where the rows match the *where_definition*.

B

By specifying LOW_PRIORITY, the update does not take place until no other clients are reading from the table.

Using IGNORE, the statement keeps processing even if a modification occurs that tries to infringe a primary or unique key.

Specifying LIMIT restricts the maximum number of rows that may be affected by the update to *num*.

Description in: Day 7

See also: INSERT, DELETE

USE *database_name*

Description: Instructs MySQL to use the database given by *database_name* as the default database for subsequent queries. Remains current until the thread finishes or another USE is issued.

APPENDIX C

Function and Operator Reference

This appendix details the SQL functions available to you in MySQL 4.0.2.

&, Bitwise AND

Description: Bitwise AND operator.

Example:

- 4 & 1 returns 0.

&&, Logical AND

Description: Logical AND operator, and synonymous with AND. Returns 0 if either argument is 0 or NULL; otherwise 1.

See also: AND

|, Bitwise OR

Description: Bitwise OR operator.

Example:

- 4 | 1 returns 5.

||, Logical OR

Description: Logical OR operator, and synonymous with OR. Returns 1 if either argument is not 0 and not NULL; otherwise 0.

Examples:

- 'a' OR 1 returns 1.
- 'a' || 0 returns 0.

See also: OR

$x<<n$, Bitwise Left-Shift

Description: Bitwise left-shift operator. Shifts x, a 64-bit (BIGINT) number, n bits to the left.

Example:

- 8 << 2 returns 32.

See also: >>

$x>>n$, Bitwise Right-Shift

Description: Bitwise right-shift operator. Shifts x, a 64-bit (BIGINT) number, n bits to the right.

Example:

- 8 >> 2 returns 2.

See also: <<

~, Bitwise Inversion

Description: Inverts all bits of 64-bit (BIGINT) number.

Example:

- 15 & ~2 returns 13.

!, Not

Description: Logical NOT operator, and synonymous with NOT. Returns 1 if argument is 0; otherwise 0. But ! NULL and NOT NULL return NULL.

See also: NOT

+, Addition

Description: Addition operator.

Example:

- 4 + 2 returns 6.

In version 3.23 onward, synonymous with ADDDATE() when used with dates, when used in the following format:

INTERVAL *expression type* + *date*

See also: ADDDATE()

-, Subtraction

Description: In version 3.23 onward, synonymous with ADDDATE() when used with dates, when used in the following format:

date - INTERVAL *expression type*

See also: SUBDATE()

*, Multiplication

Description: Multiplication operator.

Example:

- 4 * 2 returns 8.

/, Division

Description: Division operator. Division by zero returns a NULL result.

Examples:

- 8 / 2 returns 4.
- 8 / 0 returns NULL.

%, Modulo

Description: Synonymous with MOD.

Example:

- 8 % 7 returns 1.

See also: MOD

-, Unary Minus

Description: Changes the sign of an argument.

Example:

- -4 returns -4.

=, Equals

Description: Equals operator.

Examples:

- 4 = 2 returns 0.
- 4 = NULL returns NULL.

<=>, NULL-Safe Equals

Description: NULL-safe equals operator.

Examples:

- 4 <=> 2 returns 0.
- 4 <=> NULL returns 0.

<>, Not Equal To

Description: Not equal to operator. != is synonymous.

Examples:

- 4 <> 2 returns 1.
- 4 != NULL returns NULL.

>, Greater Than

Description: Greater than operator.

Example:

- 4 > 2 returns 1.

>=, Greater Than or Equal To

Description: Greater than or equal to operator.

Example:

- 4 >= 2 returns 1.

<, Less Than

Description: Less than operator.

Example:

- 4 < 2 returns 0.

<=, Less Than or Equal To

Description: Less than or equal to operator.

Example:

- 4 <= 2 returns 0.

ABS(x)

Description: Returns the absolute value of x (in other words, makes x non-negative).

Example:

- ABS(-1.5) returns 1.5.

See also: ROUND()

ACOS(x)

Description: Returns the arc cosine of x (the value, in radians, of which x is the cosine). x must be in the range -1 to 1, or a NULL will be returned.

Example:

- ACOS(-1) returns 3.141593.

See also: COS()

ADDDATE(*date*,INTERVAL *expression type*)

Description: Returns the date that results from adding an interval *expression* to *date* (a DATE or DATETIME type), where the interval is of *type* as shown in Table C.1.

If *date* is of type DATE and *type* contains only year, month, and day calculations, a date will result; if *date* is of type DATETIME or *type* includes hour, minute, or second calculations, a date and time will result.

ADDDATE() is synonymous with DATE_ADD() and +.

TABLE C.1 Values for *expression* and *type* When Adding and Subtracting Time Using ADDDATE(), SUBDATE(), and Synonymous Functions

Value of *type*	Format for *expression*
SECOND	*ss*
MINUTE	*mm*
HOUR	*hh*
DAY	*DD*
MONTH	*MM*
YEAR	*YY*
MINUTE_SECOND	"*mm:ss*"
HOUR_MINUTE	"*hh:mm:ss*"
DAY_HOUR	"*DD hh*"
YEAR_MONTH	"*YY-MM*"
HOUR_SECOND	"*hh:mm:ss*"
DAY_MINUTE	"*DD hh:mm*"
DAY_SECOND	"*DD hh:mm:ss*"

Examples:

- ADDDATE('2002-01-05',INTERVAL 3 DAY) returns 2002-01-08.
- ADDDATE('2002-01-05 12:00:00',INTERVAL 3 DAY) returns 2002-01-08 12:00:00.
- ADDDATE('00-02-07 09:00:00',INTERVAL 36 HOUR) returns 2000-02-08 21:00:00.
- ADDDATE('1964-12-01',INTERVAL "37 6" YEAR_MONTH) returns 2002-06-01.

See also: DATE_ADD(), SUBDATE()

AES_DECRYPT(*string,key*)

Description: Decrypts a given encrypted `string` that has been encrypted using `password` using AES (Advanced Encryption Standard).

See also: AES_ENCRYPT()

AES_ENCRYPT(*encrypted_string,key*)

Description: Encrypts a given `string` that has been encrypted using `password` using AES (Advanced Encryption Standard).

The most cryptographically secure encryption/decryption algorithm available in MySQL, it uses a 128-bit key length.

Example:

- `AES_ENCRYPT('message', 'the key')` returns a binary string.

See also: AES_DECRYPT(), ENCODE(), ENCRYPT()

AND, Logical

Description: Synonymous with &&.

See also: &&

ASCII(*string*)

Description: Returns the ASCII code of the leftmost character of `string`.

Examples:

- `ASCII('1')` returns 49.
- `ASCII(1)` returns 49.
- `ASCII('abc')` returns 97.

See also: ORD(), CHAR()

ASIN(*x*)

Description: Returns the arc sine of *x* (the value, in radians, of which *x* is the sine). *x* must be in the range -1 to 1, or a NULL will be returned.

Example:

- `ASIN(-1)` returns -1.570796.

See also: SIN()

ATAN(*x*)

Description: Returns the arc tangent of *x* (the value, in radians, of which *x* is the tangent)

Example:

- ATAN(1) returns 0.785398.

See also: TAN()

ATAN(*x*,*y*)

Description: Returns the arc tangent of *x* and *y*.

The signs of both arguments are used to determine the quadrant of the result, but otherwise is similar to the arc tangent of *y*/*x*.

Examples:

- ATAN(-2,2) returns -0.785398.
- ATAN(2,-2) returns 2.356194.

See also: TAN()

ATAN2(*x*,*y*)

Description: Synonymous with ATAN(x,y).

See also: ATAN(x,y)

AVG(*expression*)

Description: Returns the average value of *expression*. Generally used with GROUP BY clause, but otherwise will operate on all rows returned.

Example:

```
SELECT city_name, AVG(temperature)
  FROM weather
  GROUP BY city_name
```

returns the average temperature recorded for each city in the weather table.

BENCHMARK(*count*,*expression*)

Description: Executes *expression* the number of times specified by *count*.

BENCHMARK() always returns 0. However, if this command is run from the mysql monitor client, mysql displays the elapsed time in seconds.

This is a way of measuring the time taken to execute a command. However, because elapsed time, not CPU time, is measured by mysql, the load on the server from other clients should be taken into account to get a meaningful result.

Example (in mysql monitor):

```
mysql> SELECT BENCHMARK(1000000000,"SELECT * FROM products ORDER BY price");
+-------------------------------------------------------------+
| BENCHMARK(1000000000,"SELECT * FROM products ORDER BY price") |
+-------------------------------------------------------------+
|                                                           0 |
+-------------------------------------------------------------+
1 row in set (28.42 sec)
```

indicates that the SELECT executes, on average, in $28.42/1000000000 = 2.842 \times 10^{-8}$ seconds.

expression BETWEEN *min* AND *max*

Description: Returns 1 if *expression* is greater than or equal to *min* and less than or equal to *max*; 0 otherwise.

The comparison is performed according to the following rules:

- If *expression* is a TIMESTAMP, DATE, or DATETIME column, *min* and *max* are interpreted as the same datatype if they are constants.
- If *expression* is a string that is not case-sensitive, the comparison is done in a way that is not case-sensitive.
- If *expression* is a string that is case-sensitive, the comparison is done in a case-sensitive way.
- If *expression* is evaluated to be an integer, an integer comparison is done.
- Otherwise, a floating-point comparison is done.

Examples:

- 10 BETWEEN 12 AND 20 returns 0.
- 10 BETWEEN '10' AND '20' returns 1.
- 'a' BETWEEN 'X' AND 'z' returns 0.
- BINARY 'a' BETWEEN 'X' AND 'z' returns 1.
- 'a' BETWEEN BINARY 'X' AND 'z' returns 0.

See also: GREATEST(), LEAST()

BIN(*n*)

Description: Returns a binary representation of BIGINT number *n*.

A string value is returned. Returns NULL if *n* is NULL.

Example:

- BIN(7) returns 111.

See also: CONV()

BINARY

Description: Causes the string following the word BINARY to be typecast as a binary string.

Its typical use is to force a case-sensitive comparison, even though the string is not already binary data or a BLOB column type. Was introduced in version 3.23.0.

Examples:

- SELECT 'A'='a' returns 1.
- SELECT BINARY 'A'='a' returns 0.

BIT_AND(*expression*)

Description: Returns the bitwise AND of all bits in *expression*. Generally used with GROUP BY clause, but otherwise operates on all rows returned.

Performed with 64-bit (BIGINT) precision.

Example:

```
SELECT BIT_AND(some_flag)
  FROM table
```

See also: BIT_OR()

BIT_COUNT(*expression*)

Description: Returns the number of bits that are set to 1 in *expression*.

Example:

- BIT_COUNT(7) returns 3.

BIT_OR(*expression*)

Description: Returns the bitwise OR of all bits in *expression*. Generally used with GROUP BY clause, but otherwise operates on all rows returned.

Performed with 64-bit (`BIGINT`) precision.

Example:

```
SELECT BIT_OR(some_flag)
  FROM table
```

See also: `BIT_AND()`

CASE

There are two forms of syntax:

```
CASE expression
  WHEN compare_expr1 THEN result1
  [WHEN compare_expr2 THEN result2...]
  [ELSE other_result]
  END

CASE
  WHEN [condition1] THEN result1
  [WHEN [condition2] THEN result2...]
  [ELSE other_result]
  END
```

Description: The first version compares *expression* with each value for *compare_expr* and returns *result* when there is a match. If none matches, it returns *other_result* if there is an `ELSE`, or `NULL` otherwise.

The second version evaluates each *condition* until it finds one that is true and returns the accompanying *result*. If none is true, it returns *other_result* if there is an `ELSE`, or `NULL` otherwise.

Examples:

```
SELECT CASE 1
  WHEN 0 THEN 'zero'
  WHEN 1 THEN 'one'
  WHEN 2 THEN 'two'
  ELSE 'no match'
  END
```

returns one.

```
SELECT CASE 5
  WHEN 0 THEN 'zero'
  WHEN 1 THEN 'one'
  WHEN 2 THEN 'two'
  ELSE 'no match'
  END
```

returns no match.

```
SELECT CASE 5
  WHEN 0 THEN 'zero'
  WHEN 1 THEN 'one'
  WHEN 2 THEN 'two'
  END
```

returns NULL.

```
SELECT CASE
WHEN 'B'='a' THEN 'a'
WHEN 'B'='b' THEN 'b'
WHEN 'B'='c' THEN 'c'
ELSE 'no match'
END
```

returns b.

See also: IF()

CEILING(*x*)

Description: Returns the smallest integer value (as a BIGINT) that is greater than or equal to *x*.

Examples:

- CEILING (7.5) returns 8.
- CEILING(-7.5) returns -7.

See also: FLOOR(), ROUND()

CHAR(*n1*[,*n2*...])

Description: Returns a character representation of the ASCII codes given by values of *n*.

Interprets the arguments as integers and skips NULL values.

Example:

- CHAR(83,113,76) returns SqL.

See also: ASCII()

CHAR_LENGTH(*string*)

Description: Synonymous with LENGTH().

See also: LENGTH()

CHARACTER_LENGTH(*string*)

Description: Synonymous with LENGTH().

See also: LENGTH()

COALESCE(value[,...])

Description: Returns the first non-NULL value in a list of one or more values, or NULL if they are all NULL.

Example:

- COALESCE(NULL,0,2) returns 0.

CONCAT(*string1*[,*string2*,...])

Description: Concatenates all strings together in the order specified and returns the resulting string.

Numeric arguments are converted to strings. Any NULL string causes a NULL to be returned.

Examples:

- CONCAT('a','B','z') returns aBz.
- CONCAT('a',5,7.5) returns a57.5.
- CONCAT('a',NULL) returns NULL.

CONCAT_WS(*separator*,*string1*[,*string2*,...])

Description: Concatenates all strings together in the order specified, with separator given by *separator*, and returns the resulting string.

Numeric arguments are converted to strings. Any NULL string is skipped. A NULL separator causes a NULL to be returned.

Examples:

- CONCAT_WS('+','a','2','z') returns a+2+z.
- CONCAT_WS('/',14,5,2000) returns 14/5/2000.
- CONCAT_WS(NULL,'a','b') returns NULL.

C

CONNECTION_ID()

Description: Returns the connection (thread) ID for the connection.

Example:

- CONNECTION_ID() returns 33.

See also: DATABASE(), USER(), VERSION()

CONV(n,base1,base2)

Description: Returns the result of converting number n from base base1 to base base2.

base1 and base2 should be integers between 2 and 36. x is treated as a BIGINT but may be specified as a string (which may be required for bases above base-10, in which characters A through Z, or equally a through z, may be used).

Returns a string result. Returns a NULL if any argument is NULL. Returns 0 if n is not legal in base1.

Examples:

- CONV(1001,2,10) returns 9.
- CONV('FF',16,10) returns 255.
- CONV('abc',16,10) returns 2748.
- CONV(16,10,8) returns 20.
- CONV('abc',16,10) returns 2748.
- CONV(10101010,2,16) returns AA.

See also: BIN(), HEX(), OCT()

COS(x)

Description: Returns the cosine of x, where x is in radians.

Example:

- COS(3.1415) returns -1.000000.

See also: SIN(), TAN()

COT(*x*)

Description: Returns the cotangent of *x*.

Example:

- COT(PI()/2) returns `0.00000000`.

See also: TAN()

COUNT(*expression*)

Description: Returns the number of rows retrieved in a SELECT statement where values of *expression* are not NULL. Generally used with GROUP BY clause.

Note that COUNT(*) returns the number of rows retrieved by a query, even if their values are NULL.

Examples:

```
SELECT city_name, COUNT(temperature)
  FROM weather
  GROUP BY city_name
```

returns the number of temperatures recorded, grouped by city name.

```
SELECT COUNT(*)
  FROM weather
```

returns the total number of rows in table weather.

See also: COUNT(DISTINCT)

COUNT(DISTINCT *expression*[,*expression*...])

Description: Returns the number of rows retrieved in a SELECT statement where values of *expression* are distinct and not NULL. Generally used with GROUP BY clause.

Examples:

```
SELECT COUNT(DISTINCT city_name)
  FROM weather
```

returns the total number of different cities named.

```
SELECT city_name, COUNT(DISTINCT temperature)
  FROM weather
  GROUP BY city_name
```

returns the number of different temperatures recorded, for each city.

See also: COUNT()

CURDATE()

Description: Returns the current date in the format YYYY-MM-DD or YYYYMMDD.

Examples:

- CURDATE() returns 2002-04-23.
- CURDATE()+0 returns 20020423.

See also: CURRENT_DATE(), CURTIME()

CURRENT_DATE

Description: Synonymous with CURDATE().

See also: CURDATE()

CURRENT_TIME

Description: Synonymous with CURTIME().

See also: CURTIME()

CURRENT_TIMESTAMP

Description: Synonymous with NOW().

See also: NOW()

CURTIME()

Description: Returns the current time in the format hh:mm:ss or hhmmss.

Examples:

- CURTIME() returns 17:12:10.
- CURTIME()+0 returns 171210.

See also: CURRENT_TIME(), CURDATE()

DATABASE()

Description: Returns the current database name.

Example:

- DATABASE() returns cms.

DATE_ADD(*date*,INTERVAL *expression type*)

Description: Synonymous with ADDDATE().

See also: ADDDATE()

DATE_FORMAT(*date*,*format*)

Description: Returns a *date* (a DATE or DATETIME type), in a format specified by *format* as shown in Table C.2.

TABLE C.2 Display Formats for DATE_FORMAT() and TIME_FORMAT() Functions

Parameter Within *Format*	Output Format	Example
%a	Weekday name, abbreviated	Sun, Mon
%b	Month name, abbreviated	Jan
%c	Month without leading 0	1, 2...12
%D	Day of month, suffixed	1st, 2nd
%d	Day of month with leading 0	01, 02
%e	Day of month without leading 0	1, 2
%h or %I	Hour with leading 0 (12h)	01, 02...12
%H	Hour with leading 0 (24h)	00, 01...23
%i	Minutes	00, 01...59
%j	Day of year with leading 0's	001, 002...366
%k	Hour without leading 0 (24h)	0, 1...23
%l	Hour without leading 0 (12h)	1, 2...12
%M	Month name	January
%m	Month with leading 0	01
%P	AM or PM	AM, PM
%r	12-hour time	10:30:21 PM
%S or %s	Seconds	00, 01...59
%T	24-hour time	22:30:21
%U	Week number in the year*	01, 02...52
%u	Week number in the year**	01, 02...52
%X and %V	Year and week number*	2001 52
%x and %v	Year and week number**	2001 52
%W	Weekday name	Sunday, Monday
%w	Weekday number*	0, 1...6

TABLE C.2   continued

Parameter Within Format	Output Format	Example
%y	Numeric year, 2-digit	02
%Y	Numeric year, 4-digit	2002
%%	Literal % symbol	%

* in which Sunday is the first day of the week (day 0)

** in which Monday is the first day of the week

Examples:

- DATE_FORMAT('2002-01-05','%W %D %M %Y') returns Saturday 5th January 2002.
- DATE_FORMAT('2002-01-05 16:20:00','%D %M %Y at %r') returns 5th January 2002 at 04:20:00 PM.

See also: TIME_FORMAT()

DATE_SUB(*date*,INTERVAL *expression type*)

Description: Synonymous with SUBDATE().

See also: SUBDATE(), ADDDATE()

DAYNAME()

Description: Returns the day of the month for *date* (a date, or date and time) in the range 1 to 31.

Examples:

- DAYNAME('2002-01-05') returns Saturday.
- DAYNAME('1999-12-31 23:59:59') returns Friday.

See also: DAYOFMONTH()

DAYOFMONTH(*date*)

Description: Returns the day of the month for *date* (a date, or date and time) in the range 1 to 31.

Examples:

- DAYOFMONTH('2002-01-05') returns 5.
- DAYOFMONTH('2002-01-05 23:00:00') returns 5.

See also: DAYNAME()

DAYOFWEEK(*date*)

Description: Returns the weekday index of *date* (a date, or date and time) in the range 1 to 7, where 1=Sunday, 2=Monday, and so on, as per the ODBC standard.

Examples:

- DAYOFWEEK('2000-01-01') returns 7 (Saturday).
- DAYOFWEEK('2000-01-01 08:00:00') returns 7 (Saturday).

See also: WEEKDAY()

DAYOFYEAR()

Description: Returns the day of the year for *date* (a date, or date and time) in the range 1 to 366.

Examples:

- DAYOFYEAR('2002-01-05') returns 5.
- DAYOFYEAR('1999-12-31 23:59:59') returns 365.

See also: DAYNAME(), DAYOFMONTH()

DECODE(*encoded_string*,*password*)

Description: Decodes a binary *encoded_string* using *password* as the password, returning the decoded result.

The binary string will normally have been created using ENCODE().

Example:

- DECODE(ENCODE('My secret','my_pass'),'my_pass') returns My secret.

See also: ENCODE()

DEGREES(*x*)

Description: Returns the value of *x* in radians, converted to degrees.

Example:

- DEGREES(PI()) returns 180.

See also: RADIANS()

DES_DECRYPT(*encrypted_string* [, *key_string*])

Description: Decodes an `encrypted_string` that has been encrypted with `DES_ENCRYPT()`.

See also: `DES_ENCRYPT()`

DES_ENCRYPT(*string* [, (*key_number* | *key_string*)])

Description: Using the DES algorithm, encrypts the given `string` using the optional key given by `key_number` or `key_string`.

Can be used only when MySQL is compiled with support for SSL connections. Introduced in MySQL 4.0.1.

See also: `DES_DECRYPT()`

ELT(*n*,*string1*[,*string2*,*string3*...])

Description: Returns `string1` if *n*=1, `string2` if *n*=2, and so on. If *n* is greater than the number of strings, or less than 1, returns `NULL`.

Example:

- `ELT(3,'John','William','Smith')` returns `Smith`.

See also: `FIELD()`.

ENCODE(*string*,*password*)

Description: Encodes `string` using `password` as the password, returning the encoded result.

The result can be decoded using `DECODE()`. The result is in binary and has the same length as that of `string`, so if saving the result, a `BLOB` column type of suitable length should be used.

Examples:

- `ENCODE('My secret message','my_pass')` returns a binary string (unprintable).

See also: `AES_ENCRYPT()`, `DECODE()`, `ENCRYPT()`, `MD5()`, `PASSWORD()`

ENCRYPT(*string*[,*salt*])

Description: Encrypts `string` using the Unix `crypt()` function, returning the encrypted result.

If *salt* is omitted, a random salt is used, so that the result is different every time. If *salt* is specified, the result of encrypting *string* will always be the same with that *salt*.

On systems without crypt() available, ENCRYPT() returns NULL. On most systems, only the first eight characters of *string* are used for encryption; the rest are ignored.

Examples:

- ENCRYPT('My secret message') returns FOXv7kZdrHGkw.
- ENCRYPT('My secret message','xx') returns xxgNrzQDHDL/g.

See also: AES_ENCRYPT(), ENCODE(), MD5(), PASSWORD()

EXP(*x*)

Description: Returns *e* to the power of *x*, where *e* is the base of natural logarithms.

Examples:

- EXP(2) returns 7.389056.
- EXP(-2) returns 0.135335.

See also: LOG(), LOG10(), POWER()

EXPORT_SET(*bits,on_str,off_str*[,*separator*][,*num_bits*])

Description: Converts the bit pattern of *bits* from 1's and 0's to strings given by *on_str* and *off_str*, returning a string set (a list of strings separated by commas).

If *separator* is specified, the result is a string set with items separated by that separator rather than a comma (,).

If *num_bits* is specified, that number of items will be returned in the string set, or 64 items if not specified, padding out to the right after the bits governed by *bits*.

Note that the first item of the string set returned corresponds with the least significant bit of *bits*, and so on.

Examples:

- EXPORT_SET(7,'A','a',',',3) returns A,A,A.
- EXPORT_SET(4,'On','Off','-',3) returns Off-Off-On.
- EXPORT_SET(4,'On','Off','-',4) returns Off-Off-On-Off.

See also: FIND_IN_SET(), MAKE_SET()

EXTRACT(*type* FROM *date*)

Description: Extracts the given type (YEAR, HOUR, and so on) from *date* (a date, or date and time). The formatting principles are the same as for ADDDATE(), and possible values for *type* are as shown previously in Table C.1.

Examples:

- EXTRACT(YEAR_MONTH FROM '2002-06-01') returns 200206.
- EXTRACT(HOUR_MINUTE FROM '2002-06-01 09:30:00') returns 930.

See also: ADDDATE()

FIELD(*string*,*string1*[,*string2*,*string3*...])

Description: Returns 1 if *string*=*string1*, 2 if *string*=*string2*, and so on. If there is no match, returns 0.

Examples:

- FIELD('Smith','John','William','Smith') returns 3.
- FIELD('Zoe','John','William','Smith') returns 0.

See also: ELT()

FIND_IN_SET(*string*,*string_set*)

Description: If *string_set* is a string consisting of a set of comma-separated values, function returns a 1 if *string* matches the first item in the set, 2 for the second, and so on.

Works most efficiently if *string_set* is a column of type SET because it then uses bit arithmetic. Returns 0 if *string* is not found in *string_set* or *string_set* is the empty string, or NULL if either argument is NULL. Note that *string* may not contain a comma (,).

Example:

- FIND_IN_SET('c','a,b,c,d,e') returns 3.

See also: EXPORT_SET(), MAKE_SET()

FLOOR(*x*)

Description: Returns the largest integer value (as a `BIGINT`) that is less than or equal to *x*.

Examples:

- `FLOOR(7.5)` returns 7.
- `FLOOR(-7.5)` returns -8.

See also: `CEILING()`, `ROUND()`

FORMAT(*x,d*)

Description: Returns the number *x* formatted with commas and rounded to *d* decimal places.

Examples:

- `FORMAT(12345.678,2)` returns 12,345.68.
- `FORMAT(12345.678,0)` returns 12,346.

See also: `ROUND()`, `TRUNCATE()`

FROM_DAYS(*num*)

Description: Returns the date obtained by adding *num* days to the year 1 A.D.

This function is intended to be used only on dates after 1582, when the Gregorian calendar was introduced.

Example:

- `FROM_DAYS(1000000)` returns the millionth day, 2737-11-28.

See also: `TO_DAYS()`

FROM_UNIXTIME(*unix_timestamp*[*,format*])

Description: Returns the date and time of *unix_timestamp*, which specifies the number of seconds since 1 January 1970 at 00:00:00 GMT. Formatting options are the same as for `DATE_FORMAT()` and are as shown previously in Table C.2.

Examples:

- `FROM_UNIXTIME(1000000000)` returns 2001-09-09 01:46:40.
- `FROM_UNIXTIME(1000000000)+0` returns 20010909014640.
- `FROM_UNIXTIME(1000000000,'%W at %r')` returns Sunday at 01:46:40 AM.

See also: `NOW()`, `UNIX_TIMESTAMP()`

GET_LOCK(*string*,*timeout*)

Description: Attempts to gain an advisory lock with the name given by *string*, with a timeout given in seconds by *timeout*. Returns 1 if attempt is successful, 0 if a timeout occurs, or NULL if an error occurs.

GET_LOCK() is meant for use in conjunction with RELEASE_LOCK() to perform advisory or cooperative locking (that is, applications must cooperate with each other). Importantly, these functions do not perform table or row locking, such as the LOCK TABLES command does. They are intended for use in applications that cooperate by using an agreed-on lock name.

A lock is released when the thread finishes, another GET_LOCK() is issued, or a RELEASE_LOCK() is issued.

To see whether a lock is in place without waiting, GET_LOCK(*string*,0) may be used. This obtains the lock if it is not currently in force, so may have to be released using RELEASE_LOCK(*string*) if appropriate.

Example (commands run in sequence):

- GET_LOCK("my_lock",5) by thread 1 returns 1 (lock obtained successfully).
- GET_LOCK("my_lock",0) by thread 2 returns 0 immediately (unable to obtain lock at this time).
- RELEASE_LOCK("my_lock") by thread 1 returns 1 (lock released successfully).
- GET_LOCK("my_lock",0) by thread 2 returns 0 immediately (lock obtained successfully).

See also: RELEASE_LOCK(), LOCK TABLES (see Appendix B, "SQL Reference")

GREATEST(*x1*,*x2*[,...])

Description: Returns the greatest of a list of at least two values.

The rules for comparison are as follows:

- If all arguments are integers or function is used in an integer context, arguments are compared as integers.
- If all arguments are floating-point or function is used in a floating-point context, arguments are compared as floating-point values.
- If any argument is a case-sensitive (binary) string, the arguments are compared as strings in a case-sensitive way; otherwise, the arguments are compared as strings in a way that is not case-sensitive.

Examples:

- `GREATEST(32,1)` returns 32.
- `GREATEST(32,1)+0.00` returns 32.00.
- `GREATEST(-32,-1)` returns -1.
- `GREATEST(BINARY "x","Y")` returns x.
- `GREATEST("x","Y")` returns Y.

See also: `LEAST()`, `MAX()`

HEX(*n*)

Description: Returns a hexadecimal representation of `BIGINT` number *n*.

A string value is returned. Returns `NULL` if *n* is `NULL`.

Example:

- `HEX(1000)` returns 3E8.

See also: `CONV()`

HOUR(*time*)

Description: Returns the hour of *time* (a time, or date and time) in the range 0 to 23.

Example:

- `HOUR('23:15:00')` returns 23.

See also: `MINUTE()`, `SECOND()`

IF(*test_expression*,*expression_true*,*expression_false*)

Description: Returns *expression_true* if *test_expression* is `TRUE`, or *expression_false* otherwise.

expression_test is interpreted as an integer. `IF()` returns a datatype according to the following:

- If *expression_true* or *expression_false* returns a string, the result will be a string.
- If *expression_true* or *expression_false* returns a floating-point number, the result will be a floating-point number.
- If *expression_true* or *expression_false* returns an integer, the result will be an integer.

Examples:

- IF(5>3,'more','not more'); returns more.
- IF(2>3,'more',0) returns 0 (as a string).
- IF(2>3,1,0) returns 0 (as a numeric).

Note that

- IF(0.2,'nonzero','zero') returns zero (because 0.2 is converted to an integer, becoming 0).
- IF(0.2<>0,'nonzero','zero') returns nonzero (because 0.2 is compared with zero as a floating-point number, before the result is converted to an integer).

See also: CASE()

IFNULL(*expression1*,*expression2*)

Description: Returns *expression1* if it is not NULL; otherwise, returns *expression2*.

Returns a string or numeric value according to the context in which it is used.

Examples:

- IFNULL(NULL,1) returns 1.
- IFNULL('x',1) returns x.

See also: NULLIF()

expression IN (*value*[,...])

Description: Returns 1 if expression is any of the values in the list of one or more values; 0 otherwise.

The comparison is done according to the datatype of *expression*. If a case-sensitive expression, the comparison is done in a case-sensitive way.

Examples:

- 5 IN (43, 5, 12) returns 1.
- 'a' IN ('A', 'B', 'C') returns 1.
- BINARY 'a' IN ('A', 'B', 'C') returns 0.

INET_ATON(*expression*)

Description: Returns an integer representing the dotted decimal network address given by *expression*. May be a 4- or 8-byte address.

Example:

- INET_ATON("213.234.21.67") returns 3588887875.

The example is calculated as $213*255^3+234*255^2+21*255+67$.

See also: INET_NTOA()

INET_NTOA(*expression*)

Description: Returns a dotted decimal network address (4- or 8-byte) calculated from the integer given by *expression*.

Example:

- INET_NTOA(3588887875) returns 213.234.21.67.

See also: INET_ATON()

INSERT(*string,position,length,substr*)

Description: Within *string*, goes to *position* characters from the left and replaces *length* characters with string *substr*.

Example:

- INSERT('John Smith',6,3,'Browne') returns John Browneth.

See also: INSTR(), LOCATE()

INSTR(*string,substr*)

Description: Returns the character position of the first occurrence of *substr* within *string*, or 0 if it does not occur.

Works the same as LOCATE() with only two arguments, but with the arguments reversed.

Examples:

- INSTR('Harold Jacobs','a') returns 2.
- INSTR('Harold Jacobs','JACOBS') returns 8.
- INSTR('Harold Jacobs',BINARY 'JACOBS') returns 0.

See also: LOCATE()

INTERVAL(*x,n0,n1[,n2,...]*)

Description: Returns 0 if x is less than $n0$, 1 if x is less than $n1$, 2 if x is less than $n2$, and so on. Returns the last n value if x is greater than all of them.

It is required that $n0<n1<n2<\ldots$. All the arguments are treated as integers.

Examples:

- `INTERVAL(1,0,1,2)` returns 2.
- `INTERVAL(-1,0,1,2)` returns 0.
- `INTERVAL(10,1,3,5)` returns 3.

expression IS NOT NULL

Description: Tests whether preceding *expression* is not NULL, returning TRUE if it is not NULL, or FALSE otherwise.

Examples:

- `'abc' IS NOT NULL` returns 1.
- `NULL IS NOT NULL` returns 0.

See also: IS NULL

expression IS NULL

Description: Tests whether preceding *expression* is NULL, returning TRUE if it is, or FALSE otherwise

Examples:

- `'abc' IS NULL` returns 0.
- `NULL IS NULL` returns 1.

See also: IS NOT NULL

ISNULL(*expression*)

Description: Returns 1 if *expression* is NULL; 0 otherwise.

Examples:

- `ISNULL(1)` returns 0.
- `ISNULL(0)` returns 0.
- `ISNULL('')` returns 0.
- `ISNULL(NULL)` returns 1.
- `ISNULL(1/0)` returns 1.

See also: IS NULL, IS NOT NULL

LAST_INSERT_ID([*expression*])

Description: Returns the last value generated automatically in an AUTO_INCREMENT column as the result of an INSERT.

Returns the last value generated by the same thread, not a value generated by another thread. Returns 0 if no value has been generated.

Note that if an insert created several new rows, LAST_INSERT_ID() returns the value from the first row inserted (not the last).

Examples:

* LAST_INSERT_ID() returns 1000023.

LAST_INSERT_ID() can be used with an optional *expression*: this version is intended for use with an UPDATE statement, which can produce sequences without the need for storing the ID in an application.

Example:

```
UPDATE some_table
  SET some_id=LAST_INSERT_ID(some_id+1)
```

LCASE(*string*)

Description: Returns *string* with all characters converted to lowercase.

The current character set mapping will be used, the default being ISO-88859-1 Latin1.

Example:

* LCASE('AbCdE') returns abcde.

See also: LOWER(), UCASE()

LEAST(*x1*,*x2*[,...])

Description: Returns the lowest of a list of at least two values.

The rules for comparison are the same as for GREATEST().

Examples:

* LEAST(32,1) returns 1.
* LEAST(-32,-1) returns -32.
* LEAST(BINARY "x","Y") returns Y.
* LEAST("x","Y") returns x.

See also: GREATEST(), MIN()

LEFT(*string*,*length*)

Description: Returns the left-most *length* characters of *string*.

Examples:

- LEFT('abcde',3) returns abc.
- LEFT('abcde',10) returns abcde.

See also: RIGHT(), SUBSTRING()

LENGTH(*string*)

Description: Returns the character length of *string*.

Example:

- LENGTH('some text') returns 9.

string LIKE *pattern* [ESCAPE *escape_character*]

Description: Looks for *pattern* within *string*, performing a pattern-match comparison using SQL simple regular expressions, returning TRUE if a match is obtained or FALSE if not.

pattern may contain wildcard characters:

- %—For matching any number of characters of *string*, including none
- _ (underscore)—For matching exactly one character

To match on the % and _ characters themselves, they will need to be preceded by an escape character. This is \ by default, unless otherwise specified by *escape_character*.

Examples:

- 'Jonathan' LIKE 'Jon%' returns 1.
- 'Jonathan' LIKE 'JON%' returns 1.
- 'Jonathan' LIKE BINARY 'JON%' returns 0.
- 'Jonathan' LIKE 'J%n' returns 1.
- 'Jonathan' LIKE 'Jo%nathan' returns 1.
- 'John Smith' LIKE '% S_%' returns 1.
- 'John Smith' LIKE '% S_' returns 0.
- 100 LIKE '1__' returns 1.

- 'J_Smith' LIKE 'J_%' returns 1.
- 'J_Smith' LIKE 'J#_%' ESCAPE '#' returns 1.

See also: RLIKE

LOAD_FILE(*filename*)

Description: Opens a file on the server whose full path and name are given by *filename* and returns the contents as a string. The MySQL user must have File_priv privilege; the file must be globally readable and must be no larger than the max_allowed_packet MySQL system variable.

Returns NULL if any of the preceding requirements are not met.

For versions of MySQL prior to 3.23, see the MySQL Technical Reference for details of how this function works in older versions.

Example:

```
INSERT INTO mytable
SET mydata=LOAD_FILE('/home/tonyb/mystuff.txt')
```

opens the file mystuff.txt and inserts its contents into the column mydata in table mytable.

LOCATE(*substr*,*string*[,*position*])

Description: Without *position*, returns the character position of the first occurrence of *substr* within *string*, or 0 if it does not occur.

With *position*, returns the first occurrence of *substr* at or after that number of characters from the start of *string*.

Examples:

- LOCATE('a','Harold Jacobs') returns 2.
- LOCATE('JACOBS','Harold Jacobs') returns 8.
- LOCATE(BINARY 'JACOBS','Harold Jacobs') returns 0.
- LOCATE('a','Harold Jacobs',6) returns 9.

See also: INSTR(), POSITION()

LOG()

Description: Returns the natural logarithm of *x* (base *e*).

Examples:

- LOG(7.389056) returns 2.000000.
- LOG(-2) returns NULL.

See also: EXP(), LOG10(), POWER()

LOG10(*x*)

Description: Returns the base-10 logarithm of *x*.

Examples:

- LOG10(100) returns 2.000000.
- LOG10(-100) returns NULL.

See also: EXP(), LOG(), POWER()

LOWER()

Description: Synonymous with LCASE().

See also: LCASE()

LPAD(*string*,*length*,*padding*)

Description: Returns *string* with its length increased to *length* characters by padding out to the left with *padding*.

If *string* is longer than *length*, it will be shortened to that length.

Examples:

- LPAD('Tony',5,'*') returns *Tony.
- LPAD('Tony',2,'*') returns To.
- LPAD('Tony',20,'* ') returns * * * * * * * * Tony.

See also: RPAD()

LTRIM(*string*)

Description: Returns *string* with spaces at the left-hand end of the string removed.

Example:

- LTRIM('   abc') returns abc.

See also: RTRIM(), TRIM()

MAKE_SET(*bits*,*string1*[,*string2*...])

Description: Returns a string set (a string consisting of a set of comma-separated values), composed of *string1*, *string2*, and so on, according to the bits that are set to 1 in the binary representation of *bits*.

Note that *string1* corresponds with bit 0 of *bits* (the least significant). Any NULL strings are ignored.

Examples:

- MAKE_SET(1,'John','William','Smith') returns John.
- MAKE_SET(2,'John','William','Smith') returns William.
- MAKE_SET(4+1,'John','William','Smith') returns John,Smith.
- MAKE_SET(15,'John','W',NULL,'Smith') returns John,W,Smith.

See also: EXPORT_SET(), FIND_IN_SET()

MASTER_POS_WAIT(*log_name*,*log_pos*)

Description: Intended for control of master-slave synchronization during replication. Makes replication wait until the slave reaches the specified position *log_pos* in master log *log_name*, returning the number of log events the slave had to wait before reaching the specified position, or NULL in case of error.

MATCH (*column1*[,*column2*,...] AGAINST (*string*)

Description: Performs a full-text search on a column or columns for the text given by *string*, returning a floating-point measure of similarity, or 0 for no match.

A FULLTEXT index must exist on the columns being searched.

Introduced in version 3.23.23.

See also: Day 8, "Querying Data," for full description and examples.

MAX(*expression*)

Description: Returns the maximum value of *expression*. Generally used with GROUP BY clause, but otherwise operates on all rows returned.

May take a string argument, returning the maximum string value.

Example:

```
SELECT city_name, MAX(temperature)
  FROM weather
  GROUP BY city_name
```

See also: MIN()

MD5(*string*)

Description: Returns the MD5 checksum of *string*. The returned value is a 32-character hexadecimal.

Example:

- MD5("Special message") returns e917d9b9d5d1904f8628b6f265d857e1.

See also: ENCODE(), ENCRYPT(), PASSWORD(), SHA()

MID(*string,position,length*)

Description: Synonymous with SUBSTRING() with *length* specified.

See also: SUBSTRING()

MIN(expression)

Description: Returns the minimum value of *expression*. Generally used with GROUP BY clause, but otherwise operates on all rows returned.

May take a string argument, returning the maximum string value.

Example:

```
SELECT city_name, MIN(temperature)
  FROM weather
  GROUP BY city_name
```

See also: MAX()

MINUTE(*time*)

Description: Returns the minute of *time* (a time, or date and time) in the range 0 to 59.

Example:

- MINUTE('23:15:00') returns 15.

See also: HOUR(), SECOND()

MOD(*n*,*m*)

Description: Returns the remainder of *n* divided by *m*.

Example:

- MOD(8,5) returns 3.

See also: %

MONTH()

Description: Returns the month of the year for *date* (a date, or date and time) in the range 1 to 12.

Examples:

- MONTH('2002-01-05') returns 1.
- MONTH('1999-12-31 23:59:59') returns 12.

See also: MONTHNAME()

MONTHNAME()

Description: Returns the name of the month for *date* (a date, or date and time).

Examples:

- MONTHNAME('2002-01-05') returns January.
- MONTHNAME('1999-12-31 23:59:59') returns December.

See also: MONTH()

NOT IN

Description: Same as NOT(*expression* IN (*value*[,...])).

See also: IN

string NOT LIKE *pattern* [ESCAPE *escape_character*]

Description: Same as NOT(*string* LIKE *pattern* [ESCAPE '*escape_character*']).

See also: LIKE

string NOT REGEXP *pattern*

Description: Same as NOT(*string* REGEXP *pattern*).

See also: REGEXP

string NOT RLIKE *pattern*

Description: Same as NOT(*string* RLIKE *pattern*).

See also: REGEXP

NOT

Description: Synonymous with !, logical NOT.

See also: !

NOW()

Description: Returns the current date and time in the format YYYY-MM-DD hh:mm:ss or YYYYMMDDhhmmss.

Examples:

- NOW() returns 2002-04-23 17:13:50.
- NOW()+0 returns 20020423171350.

See also: CURDATE(), CURTIME()

NULLIF(*expression1*,*expression2*)

Description: Returns NULL if *expression1*=*expression2*; otherwise, returns *expression1*.

Returns a string or numeric value according to the datatype of *expression1*. If either *expression* is case-sensitive, a string comparison is done in a case-sensitive way.

Examples:

- NULLIF(2,2) returns NULL.
- NULLIF(1,2) returns 1.

- NULLIF('a','A') returns NULL.
- NULLIF(BINARY 'a','A') returns a.

See also: IFNULL()

OCT(*n*)

Description: Returns an octal representation of BIGINT number *n*.

A string value is returned. Returns NULL if *n* is NULL.

Example:

- OCT(10) returns 12.

See also: CONV()

OCTET_LENGTH(*string*)

Description: Synonymous with LENGTH().

See also: LENGTH()

OR

Description: Synonymous with ||, logical OR.

See also: ||

ORD()

Description: If the leftmost character of *string* is a multibyte character, returns the code of that character, calculated as

```
((first byte ASCII code)*256) + (second byte ASCII code))
 ➥[*256 + (third byte ASCII code)...]
```

If the leftmost character of *string* is not a multibyte character, it returns the ASCII code in the same way as ASCII().

Example:

- ORD('abc') returns 97.

See also: ASCII()

PASSWORD(*string*)

Description: Encrypts *string* as a MySQL password, returning the encrypted result.

The encryption method is that used in the MySQL user grant table and is not reversible.

Example:

- PASSWORD('mySecret') returns 6870d782135294c9.

See also: ENCODE(), ENCRYPT(), MD5()

PERIOD_ADD(*period*,*months*)

Description: Returns a year and month in the format YYYYMM, resulting from the addition of *months* to *period* (in the format YYYYMM or YYMM).

Examples:

- PERIOD_ADD(200212,1) returns 200301.
- PERIOD_ADD(212,1) returns 200301.

See also: PERIOD_DIFF()

PERIOD_DIFF(*period1*,*period2*)

Description: Returns the number of months between *period1* and *period2* (both in the format YYYYMM or YYMM). The result will be positive if *period1* is later than *period2*.

Examples:

- PERIOD_DIFF(200212,200301) returns -1.
- PERIOD_DIFF(0302,0212) returns 2.

See also: PERIOD_ADD()

PI()

Description: Returns the value of π.

Returns five decimal places by default. MySQL uses double precision internally, so add zeros as shown in the following examples to display up to 18 decimal places.

Examples:

- PI() returns 3.141593.
- PI()+0.000000000000000000 returns 3.141592653589793116.

POSITION(*substr* IN *string*)

Description: Synonymous with LOCATE().

See also: LOCATE()

POW()

Description: Synonymous with POWER().

See also: POWER()

POWER(*x*,*y*)

Description: Returns *x* raised to the power of *y*.

Examples:

- POWER(10,2) returns 100.000000.
- POWER(2,10) returns 1024.000000.
- POWER(2,-3) returns 0.125000.
- POWER(-2,-3) returns -0.125000.

See also: EXP(), LOG(), LOG10()

QUARTER()

Description: Returns the quarter of the year for *date* (a date, or date and time) in the range 1 to 4.

Examples:

- QUARTER('2002-01-05') returns 1.
- QUARTER('1999-12-31 23:59:59') returns 4.

See also: MONTH()

RADIANS(*x*)

Description: Returns the value of *x* in degrees, converted to radians.

Example:

- RADIANS(180) returns 3.1415926535898.

See also: DEGREES()

RAND([n])

Description: Returns a random number, of floating-point type, between 0 and 1. Where *n* is specified, it is used as a seed value.

Examples:

- `RAND()` used once returns `0.08963118688169`.
- `RAND()` used again returns `0.77209187464052`.
- `RAND(2)` returns `0.65558664654902` every time (on a given system).

string REGEXP *pattern*

Description: Looks for *pattern* within *string*, performing a pattern-match comparison using extended regular expressions, returning `TRUE` if a match is obtained or `FALSE` if not.

Note that any \ that you use as an escape character within *pattern* must be doubled—that is, you must use \\.

Examples:

- `'Smith' RLIKE '^sm'` returns 1.
- `'Smith' RLIKE BINARY '^sm'` returns 0.
- `'Smith' RLIKE '[0-9]$'` returns 0.
- `'Smith45' RLIKE '[0-9]$'` returns 1.
- `'Line1\nLine2' RLIKE '\\n'` returns 1.

See also: `LIKE`, and Day 10, "Operators and Functions in MySQL," for more about regular expressions

RELEASE_LOCK(*string*)

Description: Releases an advisory lock named *string*. Used in conjunction with `GET_LOCK()`. Returns 1 if lock is released successfully, 0 if lock is held by a different thread (a thread can only release its own locks), or `NULL` if no lock exists with the name *string*.

See also: `GET_LOCK()` for full explanation and examples

REPEAT(*string*,*count*)

Description: Returns *string* repeated *count* times.

Example:

- `REPEAT('Me',5)` returns MeMeMeMeMe.

REPLACE(*string*,*from_string*,*to_string*)

Description: Replaces all occurrences of *from_string* with *to_string* within *string*, and returns the result.

Examples:

- REPLACE('John Smith',' ','') returns JohnSmith.
- REPLACE('HTTP://mysite.com','HTTP','http') returns http://mysite.com.

REVERSE(*string*)

Description: Returns *string* with its characters in reverse order.

Example:

- REVERSE('John Smith') returns htimS nhoJ.

RIGHT(*string*,*length*)

Description: Returns the rightmost *length* characters of *string*.

Examples:

- RIGHT('abcde',3) returns cde.
- RIGHT('abcde',10) returns abcde.

See also: LEFT(), SUBSTRING()

string RLIKE *pattern*

Description: Synonymous with REGEXP.

See also: REGEXP

ROUND(*x*)

Description: Returns *x* rounded to the nearest integer.

Examples:

- ROUND(7.4) returns 7.
- ROUND(7.5) returns 8.
- ROUND(-7.4) returns -7.
- ROUND(-7.5) returns -8.

See also: CEILING (), FORMAT(), FLOOR()

C

ROUND(*x*,*d*)

Description: Returns *x* rounded to *d* decimal places.

Examples:

- ROUND(7.49999,1) returns 7.5.
- ROUND(7.5123567,2) returns 7.51.
- ROUND(-7.49999,3) returns -7.500.
- ROUND(-7.49999,0) returns -7.

See also: CEILING (), FLOOR(), TRUNCATE()

RPAD()

Description: Returns *string* with its length increased to *length* characters by padding out to the right with *padding*.

If *string* is longer than *length*, it will be shortened to that length.

Examples:

- RPAD('Tony',5,'*') returns Tony*.
- RPAD('Tony',2,'*') returns To.
- RPAD('Tony',20,'* ') returns Tony* * * * * * * *.

See also: LPAD()

RTRIM()

Description: Returns *string* with spaces at the right-hand end of the string removed.

Example:

- RTRIM('abc   ') returns abc.

See also: LTRIM(), TRIM()

SEC_TO_TIME(*seconds*)

Description: Returns the time that is the given number of *seconds* since the beginning of the day.

Example:

- SEC_TO_TIME(3600) returns 01:00:00.

See also: TIME_TO_SEC()

SECOND()

Description: Returns the second of *time* (a time, or date and time) in the range 0 to 59.

Example:

- SECOND('23:15:00') returns 0.

See also: HOUR(), MINUTE()

SESSION_USER()

Description: Synonymous with USER().

See also: USER()

SHA(*string*)

Description: Returns an SHA1 (Secure Hash Algorithm) 160-bit checksum for the given *string*. Similar to MD5(), but cryptographically more secure. Introduced in MySQL 4.0.2.

Example:

- SHA('secret message') returns '4dea808c5b4e74af6f70fa10cec96d5f98e143e8'.

See also: MD5()

SIGN(*x*)

Description: Returns the sign of *x*: -1 for negative, 1 for positive, 0 for zero.

SIN()

Description: Returns the sine of *x*, where *x* is in radians.

Examples:

- SIN(3.1) returns 0.041581.
- SIN(PI()) returns 0.000000.

See also: COS(), TAN()

SOUNDEX(*string*)

Description: Returns a soundex value for *string*.

Although a standard soundex string is four characters long, SOUNDEX() can return a string of any length. Nonalphanumeric characters in *string* are ignored, and international characters outside A–Z are treated as vowels.

Examples:

- SOUNDEX('Dave') returns D100.
- SOUNDEX('David') returns D130.
- SOUNDEX('Davidson') returns D1325.

SPACE(*length*)

Description: Returns a string of spaces, of length given by length.

Example:

- SPACE(5) returns five spaces, "   " (without the quotes).

See also: REPEAT()

SQRT(*x*)

Description: Returns the (non-negative) square root of *x*.

Examples:

- SQRT(10) returns 3.162278.
- SQRT(100) returns 10.000000.
- SQRT(-100) returns NULL.

See also: POWER()

STD(*expression*)

Description: Returns the standard deviation of *expression*. Generally used with GROUP BY clause, but otherwise operates on all rows returned.

Example:

```
SELECT city_name, STD(temperature)
  FROM weather
  GROUP BY city_name
```

returns the standard deviation of temperatures recorded for each city in table weather.

STDDEV()

Description: Synonymous with STD().

See also: STD()

STRCMP(*string1*,*string2*)

Description: Compares *string1* with *string2* and returns the following:

- 0 if the strings are the same
- 1 if *string1* is greater than *string2*
- -1 if *string1* is less than *string2*

Examples:

- STRCMP('x','x') returns 0.
- STRCMP('x','Y') returns -1.
- STRCMP(BINARY 'x','Y') returns 1.

See also: LEAST(), GREATEST()

SUBDATE(*date*,INTERVAL *expression type*)

Description: Returns the date that results from subtracting an interval *expression* from *date* (a DATE or DATETIME type), where the interval is of *type*. The formatting principles are the same as for ADDDATE(), and expected formats for *expression* are as shown previously in Table C.1.

SUBDATE() is synonymous with DATE_SUB() and -.

Examples:

- SUBDATE('2002-01-05',INTERVAL 3 DAY) returns 2002-01-02.
- SUBDATE('2002-01-05 12:00:00',INTERVAL 3 DAY) returns 2002-01-02 12:00:00.
- SUBDATE('00-02-07 09:00:00',INTERVAL 36 HOUR) returns 2000-02-05 21:00:00.
- SUBDATE('2002-06-01',INTERVAL "37 6" YEAR_MONTH) returns 1964-12-01.

See also: DATE_SUB(), ADDDATE()

SUBSTRING(*string*,*delimiter*,*count*)

Syntax:

SUBSTRING(*string*,*position*[,*length*])

SUBSTRING(*string* FROM *position*[FOR *length*])

Description: Returns the portion of *string* starting at *position* characters from the left. If *length* is specified, no more than *length* characters will be returned.

Examples:

- `SUBSTRING('Howard Jacobs' FROM 4)` returns ard Jacobs.
- `SUBSTRING('Howard Jacobs' FROM 4 FOR 2)` returns ar.
- `SUBSTRING('Howard Jacobs',4,2)` returns ar.

See also: `LEFT()`, `MID()`, `RIGHT()`, `SUBSTRING_INDEX()`

SUBSTRING_INDEX(*string*,*delimiter*,*count*)

Description: If *count* is positive, returns the portion of *string* to the left of occurrence number *count* of *delimiter*.

If *count* is negative, returns the portion of *string* to the right of occurrence number *count* of *delimiter* starting from the right.

Examples:

- `SUBSTRING_INDEX('www.mysite.com','.',1)` returns www.
- `SUBSTRING_INDEX('www.mysite.com','.',-1)` returns com.

See also: `SUBSTRING()`

SUM(*expression*)

Description: Returns the sum of *expression*. Generally used with `GROUP BY` clause, but otherwise operates on all rows returned.

If the set has no rows, it returns `NULL`.

Example:

```
SELECT city_name, SUM(temperature)
  FROM weather
  GROUP BY city_name
```

returns the minimum temperature recorded for each city in table `weather`.

SYSDATE()

Description: Synonymous with `NOW()`.

See also: `NOW()`

SYSTEM_USER()

Description: Synonymous with USER().

See also: USER()

TAN()

Description: Returns the tangent of x, where x is in radians.

Examples:

- TAN(0) returns 0.000000.
- TAN(PI()/2) returns 16331778728383844.000000.
- TAN(PI()/4) returns 1.000000.

See also: COS(), SIN()

TIME_FORMAT(*time*)

Description: Returns a *time* in a format specified by *format*. Formatting options are the same as for DATE_FORMAT() and are as shown previously in Table C.2.

TIME_FORMAT() can handle only format specifiers for hours, minutes, and seconds, or NULL or 0 will be returned.

Examples:

- TIME_FORMAT('2002-01-05 16:20:00','%r') returns 04:20:00 PM.
- TIME_FORMAT('16:20:00','At %r') returns At 04:20:00 PM.

See also: DATE_FORMAT()

TIME_TO_SEC(*time*)

Description: Returns the number of seconds since the beginning of the day for a given *time* (a time, or date and time).

Example:

- TIME_TO_SEC('15:00:00') returns 54000.

See also: SEC_TO_TIME()

C

TO_DAYS(*date*)

Description: Returns the day number (number of days since the year 1 A.D.) of *date*.

This function is only intended to be used on dates after 1582, when the Gregorian calendar was introduced.

Example:

- TO_DAYS('2001-01-01') returns 730851.

See also: FROM_DAYS()

TRIM([[LEADING|TRAILING|BOTH] [*substring*] FROM] *string*)

Description: Returns *string* with any leading or trailing occurrences of *substring* removed, according to whether LEADING or TRAILING is specified.

If neither LEADING nor TRAILING is specified, BOTH will be assumed, which will remove occurrences of *substring* from both ends of *string*.

If *substring* is not specified, spaces will be assumed.

Examples:

- TRIM(LEADING 'www.' FROM 'www.mysite.com') returns mysite.com.
- TRIM(LEADING 'w' FROM 'www.mysite.com') returns .mysite.com.
- TRIM('m' FROM 'mysite.com') returns ysite.co.
- TRIM(' mysite.com ') returns mysite.com.

See also: LTRIM(), RTRIM()

TRUNCATE(*x*,*d*)

Description: Returns the value of *x* truncated to *d* decimal places.

Examples:

- TRUNCATE(2.26,1) returns 2.2.

But beware:

- TRUNCATE(2.26,2) returns 2.25 because non-integer numbers are normally stored as double precision values.
- TRUNCATE(2.26,4) returns 2.2599.

See also: ROUND(), FORMAT()

UCASE(*string*)

Description: Returns *string* with all characters converted to uppercase.

The current character set mapping will be used, the default being ISO-88859-1 Latin1.

Example:

- UCASE('AbCdE') returns ABCDE.

See also: LCASE(), UPPER()

UNIX_TIMESTAMP([*date*])

Description: Returns the number of seconds since 1 January 1970 at 00:00:00 GMT, of *date* (a DATE or DATETIME type). If *date* is omitted, the current date and time are used.

Examples:

- UNIX_TIMESTAMP('2002-01-05') returns 1010188800.
- UNIX_TIMESTAMP() returns 1019582548.

See also: NOW(), FROM_UNIXTIME()

UPPER(*string*)

Description: Synonymous with UCASE().

See also: UCASE()

USER()

Description: Returns the current MySQL username.

Example:

- USER() returns tonyb@localhost.

See also: SYSTEM_USER(), SESSION_USER()

VERSION()

Description: Returns the MySQL server version.

Example:

- VERSION() returns 4.0.1-alpha-log.

See also: CONNECTION_ID(), DATABASE(), USER()

WEEK(*date*[,*first*])

Description: Returns the week of the year of *date* (a date, or date and time) in the range 0 to 53. Without *first* specified, Sunday is taken as the first day of the week (day 0). With *first* set to 0, the first day is taken as Sunday, or if set to 1, the first day is taken as Monday.

Examples:

- DAYNAME('2002-01-01') returns Tuesday.
- WEEK('2002-01-01') returns 0.
- WEEK('2002-01-01',0) returns 0.
- WEEK('2002-01-06',0) returns 1.
- WEEK('2002-01-01',1) returns 1.

Note that from MySQL 4 onward, WEEK() was changed to return the week number according to the US calendar; if a week started in the previous year, WEEK(*date*,0) returns 0.

See also: YEARWEEK()

WEEKDAY(*date*)

Description: Returns the weekday index of *date* (a date, or date and time) in the range 0 to 6, where 0=Monday, 1=Tuesday, and so on.

Examples:

- WEEKDAY('2000-01-01') returns 5 (Saturday).
- WEEKDAY('2000-01-01 08:00:00') returns 5 (Saturday).

See also: DAYOFWEEK()

YEAR(*date*)

Description: Returns the year of *date* (a date, or date and time) in the range 1000 to 9999.

Example:

- YEAR('2000-01-01') returns 2000.

See also: YEARWEEK()

YEARWEEK(*date*[,*first*])

Description: Returns the year and week of *date* (a date, or date and time). The optional argument first can be used to specify the first day of the week, working in the same way as the argument in WEEK().

Examples:

- YEARWEEK('2001-02-01') returns 200104.
- YEARWEEK('2002-01-01',1) returns 200201.

See also: YEAR(), WEEK()

C

APPENDIX D

The PHP API

This appendix covers the PHP API functions for MySQL, for PHP version 4.2.2 and later.

Functions that are now deprecated are noted as such, and a small number that are not present after version 3 are not shown.

mysql_affected_rows([*link_identifier*])

Description: Returns (as an integer) the number of rows affected in the last MySQL operation that modified data (such as an INSERT, UPDATE, or DELETE).

If *link_identifier* is specified (referring to a database connection), it refers to a query made with that database connection. If not specified, it refers to the last link opened with a mysql_connect().

Notes:

- If an UPDATE is performed by the query, and it matches rows (therefore writing data) but without actually changing values in those rows, these rows are not counted in the value returned by mysql_affected_rows(); only those rows where data is actually changed are counted.
- The function returns -1 if an error occurs in the query.

- It returns 0 if the query was a DELETE with no WHERE clause, resulting in all rows of a table being deleted.
- If used with transactions, the function must be called before the COMMIT.

Example:

```
mysql_query("DELETE FROM some_table WHERE id = 101");
$aff = mysql_affected_rows();
```

See also: mysql_connect(), mysql_num_rows()

mysql_close([*link_identifier*])

Description: Closes the connection to the MySQL server.

If *link_identifier* is not specified, the current active connection is assumed. Returns TRUE on success; FALSE otherwise.

Note: It is not normally necessary to call mysql_close() because terminating the thread normally closes the connection (unless opened using mysql_pconnect(), whose connections will not be closed with mysql_close()).

See also: mysql_connect(), mysql_pconnect()

mysql_connect([*server*[,*username*[,*password*[, *new_link*]]]])

Description: Opens a connection to a MySQL server. Returns a resource identifier (referred to as *link_identifier* in this appendix) if a connection is made successfully, or FALSE otherwise.

server can be specified (optionally including :*port* for a port number, and optionally :*/path/to/socket* to give the path to a Unix socket), defaulting to localhost:3306 if not specified.

username can be specified, defaulting to the Unix user running the database server process if not given.

password can be specified, defaulting to the empty password if not given.

new_link was introduced in PHP 4.2.0. Normally, if there is a second call to mysql_ connect() within the same parameters, the first-established link will be used again. However, if *new_link* is set to TRUE, it forces a new link to be created each time.

A connection can be closed using mysql_close() or when execution of the script finishes.

Note that if the connection fails to be made, FALSE is returned and an error message is generated. This error message can be suppressed by prefixing the function with a @.

Example:

```
$link_id = @mysql_connect ("localhost", "the_user", "my_password");
if ($link_id) {
    echo "Link id is $link_id<BR>\n";
} else {
    echo "Failed to connect<BR>\n";
}
```

See also: mysql_close(), mysql_select_db(), mysql_pconnect()

mysql_create_db(*database_name*[,*link_identifier*])

Description: Creates a MySQL database with a name given by *database_name*, returning TRUE on success; FALSE otherwise.

Note: Deprecated, so its use is not recommended. mysql_query() should be used instead with a CREATE DATABASE SQL command.

See also: mysql_query()

mysql_data_seek(*result*,*row_number*)

Description: Moves the internal result pointer *result* within a resultset, to the row given by *row_number*.

Can be used in conjunction with mysql_query() and mysql_fetch_row() to run a query and then move forward and backward within the resultset. After calling mysql_data_seek() to go to a specific row number, the following call to mysql_fetch_row() retrieves that row.

See also: mysql_fetch_row()

mysql_db_name(*result*,*offset*[,*field*])

Description: Returns the database name of a field in a result.

After calling mysql_list_dbs(), which returns a resource identifier given by *result*, mysql_db_name() returns the name of the table indexed by *offset*.

See also: mysql_list_dbs()

mysql_db_query(*database_name*,*query*[, *link_identifier*][,*result mode*])

Description: Selects a MySQL database and sends a query to it in the same way as mysql_query().

D

Note: Deprecated as of PHP 4.0.6, so its use is not recommended. `mysql_select_db()` and `mysql_query()` should be used instead.

See also: `mysql_query()`, `mysql_select_db()`

mysql_drop_db(*database_name*[,*link_identifier*])

Description: Drops (deletes) a MySQL database whose name is given by *database_name*, returning TRUE on success; FALSE otherwise.

Note: Deprecated, so its use is not recommended. `mysql_query()` should be used instead with a DROP DATABASE SQL command.

See also: `mysql_query()`

mysql_errno([*link_identifier*])

Description: Returns the error message number from the previous MySQL operation, or 0 if no error occurred.

See also: `mysql_error()`

mysql_error([*link_identifier*])

Description: Returns the error message text from the previous MySQL operation, or the empty string if no error occurred.

Example:

```
if ($result = mysql_query ("select * from bad_table")) {
    # query worked okay, keep going
} else {
    echo "A database error occurred!<BR>\n";
    echo mysql_error() ." (error no. ". mysql_errno() .")<BR>\n";
    exit;
}
```

See also: `mysql_errno()`

mysql_escape_string(*raw_string*)

Description: Escapes special characters in a string given by *raw_string* for use in a SQL statement.

Returns the escaped string with special characters escaped; safe to be passed on to `mysql_query()`.

Unlike `mysql_real_escape_string()`, does not take into account the current character set of the connection.

See also: `addslashes()`, `mysql_real_escape_string()`

mysql_fetch_array(*result*)

Description: Fetches one row of data from the resultset associated with the identifier *result*, returning a numeric array, an associative array, or both.

Each call to mysql_fetch_array() fetches the next row of data from the resultset. When there are no more rows, it returns FALSE.

```
while ($row = mysql_fetch_array ($result)) {
    echo "$row[lastname], $row[firstname], $row[2]<BR>\n";
}
```

See also: mysql_fetch_row(), mysql_fetch_object()

mysql_fetch_assoc(*result*)

Description: Fetches a result row as an associative array.

Works the same way as mysql_fetch_array() but does not allow access to the result as a numeric array.

Note: mysql_fetch_array() is far more useful.

See also: mysql_fetch_array()

mysql_fetch_field(*result*,[*offset*])

Description: Gets column information from a result given by *result* and returns as an object.

Returns information about the fields in a query result. The integer *offset* is used to specify the field, but if not specified, information is returned about the next field that has not already been reported on by mysql_fetch_field().

The object returned has the following properties:

- name—The column name
- table—The name of the table to which the column belongs
- not_null—Set to 1 if the column is NOT NULL
- primary_key—Set to 1 if the column is the primary key
- unique_key—Set to 1 if the column is a unique key
- multiple_key—Set to 1 if the column is a non-unique key
- numeric—Set to 1 if the column is a numeric type
- blob—Set to 1 if the column is of type BLOB
- max_length—The column's maximum length
- type—The type of the column

D

- unsigned—Set to 1 if the column is unsigned
- zerofill—Set to 1 if the column has the ZEROFILL attribute

Example:

```
$result = mysql_query ("select * from subscribers");
while ($data = mysql_fetch_field ($result)) {
    echo "$data->name, $data->type $data->max_length<BR>\n";
}
```

mysql_fetch_lengths(*result*)

Description: Returns an array representing the lengths of the data in the fields of the last row fetched by mysql_fetch_array(), mysql_fetch_row(), or mysql_fetch_object().

Example:

```
$result = mysql_query ("select name from products");
while ($row = mysql_fetch_array ($result)) {
    $leng = mysql_fetch_lengths ($result);
    echo "Length of $row[0] is $leng[0]<BR>\n";
}
```

mysql_fetch_object(*result*)

Description: Fetches one row of data from the resultset associated with the identifier *result* as an object.

Each call to mysql_fetch_object() fetches the next row of data from the resultset as an object, making the data accessible by their column names but not numerically. When there are no more rows, it returns FALSE.

Example:

```
while ($row = mysql_fetch_object ($result)) {
    echo "$row->lastname, $row->firstname, $row->date_of_birth<BR>\n";
}
```

See also: mysql_fetch_array(), mysql_fetch_row()

mysql_fetch_row(*result*)

Description: Fetches one row of data from the resultset associated with the identifier *result*, returning a numerical array.

Each call to mysql_fetch_row() fetches the next row of data from the resultset. When there are no more rows, it returns FALSE.

Example:

```
while ($row = mysql_fetch_row ($result)) {
    echo "$row[0], $row[1], $row[2]<BR>\n";
}
```

See also: mysql_fetch_array(), mysql_fetch_object()

mysql_field_flags(*result*,*offset*)

Description: Returns the flags associated with a specified field in a result.

After calling mysql_list_fields(), mysql_query(), or another function that returns a resource identifier given by *result*, mysql_field_flags() returns the flags of a given field indexed by *offset*. Flags are returned as a string of text separated by spaces, including any of the following: auto_increment, not_null, primary_key, unique_key, multiple_key, blob, unsigned, zerofill, binary, enum, timestamp, or according to the version of MySQL in use.

Example:

```
$result = mysql_list_fields ("cms", "subscribers");
$flags = mysql_field_flags ($result, 0);  // offset of 0 means the first column
$flags_array = explode (" ", $flags);
while (list ($k,$flag) = each ($flags_array)) {
    echo "$flag<BR>\n";
}
```

See also: mysql_field_len(), mysql_field_name(), mysql_field_type(), mysql_list_fields()

mysql_field_len(*result*,*offset*)

Description: Returns the length of a specified field in a result.

After calling mysql_list_fields(), mysql_query(), or another function that returns a resource identifier given by *result*, mysql_field_len() returns the length of a given field indexed by *offset*.

Example:

```
$result = mysql_list_fields ("cms", "subscribers");
$length = mysql_field_len ($result, 0);  // offset of 0 means the first column
echo "$length<BR>\n";
```

See also: mysql_field_flags(), mysql_field_name(), mysql_field_type(), mysql_list_fields()

D

mysql_field_name(*result*,*offset*)

Description: Returns the name of a specified field in a result.

After calling mysql_list_fields(), mysql_query(), or another function that returns a resource identifier given by *result*, mysql_field_name() returns the name of a given field indexed by *offset*.

Example:

```
$result = mysql_list_fields ("cms", "subscribers");
$name = mysql_field_name ($result, 0);  // offset of 0 means the first column
echo "$name<BR>\n";
```

See also: mysql_field_flags(), mysql_field_len(), mysql_field_type(), mysql_list_fields()

mysql_field_seek(*result*,*offset*)

Description: Sets result pointer *result* to a specified field *offset*.

See also: mysql_fetch_field()

mysql_field_table(*result*,*offset*)

Description: Returns the name of the table a field is in, where *result* is a pointer to the resultset of a query, and *offset* is the index of the field in the resultset starting from 0.

mysql_field_type(*result*,*offset*)

Description: Returns the type of a specified field in a result.

After calling mysql_list_fields(), mysql_query(), or another function that returns a resource identifier given by *result*, mysql_field_name() returns the type of a given field indexed by *offset*, being one of int, string, real, blob, and so on.

Example:

```
$result = mysql_list_fields ("cms", "subscribers");
$name = mysql_field_type ($result, 2);  // offset of 2 means the third column
echo "$name<BR>\n";
```

See also: mysql_field_flags(), mysql_field_len(), mysql_field_name(), mysql_list_fields()

mysql_free_result(*result*)

Description: Frees all memory in use by the result pointer *result*.

Note: It is not necessary to call `mysql_free_result()` unless queries return large result-sets and occupy a large amount of memory. Result memory is automatically freed up when the script finishes executing.

Returns TRUE on success; FALSE otherwise.

mysql_get_client_info()

Description: Returns the version of the `mysql` client library.

Example:

```
echo mysql_get_client_info();
```

returns `4.0.1` (or whatever your client version is).

See also: `mysql_get_host_info()`, `mysql_get_proto_info()`, `mysql_get_server_info()`

mysql_get_host_info([link_identifier])

Description: Returns a string that specifies the hostname and the type of connection in use with the connection given by `link_identifier`.

If `link_identifier` is not specified, the last opened connection is assumed.

Example:

```
echo mysql_get_host_info();
```

returns `Localhost via UNIX socket`.

See also: `mysql_get_client_info()`, `mysql_get_proto_info()`, `mysql_get_server_info()`

mysql_get_proto_info([link_identifier])

Description: Returns an integer with the protocol version in use with the connection given by `link_identifier`.

If `link_identifier` is not specified, the last opened connection is assumed.

Example:

```
echo mysql_get_proto_info();
```

returns `10`.

See also: `mysql_get_client_info()`, `mysql_get_host_info()`, `mysql_get_server_info()`

mysql_get_server_info([*link_identifier*])

Description: Returns a string that specifies the version of the MySQL server used, with the connection given by *link_identifier*.

If *link_identifier* is not specified, the last opened connection is assumed.

Example:

```
echo mysql_get_server_info();
```

returns 4.0.1-alpha-log.

See also: mysql_get_client_info(), mysql_get_host_info(), mysql_get_proto_info()

mysql_insert_id([*link_identifier*])

Description: Returns the ID generated in an AUTO_INCREMENT column from the previous INSERT operation.

If *link_identifier* is not specified, the current active connection is assumed.

Returns 0 if the previous query did not generate an AUTO_INCREMENT value, so you should save any value from mysql_insert_id() immediately after the INSERT query and before any other query.

Note: If the AUTO_INCREMENT column type is BIGINT, the returned value will not be correct. You should then use the LAST_INSERT_ID() SQL function instead.

Example:

```
mysql_query ("INSERT INTO invoices SET date=$some_date, price=$p");
echo "Invoice number is: ".mysql_insert_id ()."<BR>\n";
```

See also: mysql_affected_rows(), mysql_query()

mysql_list_dbs([*link_identifier*])

Description: List databases available on a MySQL server.

Retrieves information about databases on the current server (or that are associated with *link_identifier* if given) and returns a result pointer. This pointer (denoted in this appendix by *result*) can then be passed to other functions that use *result* (such as mysql_db_name()) to return information on database names.

See also: mysql_db_name()

mysql_list_fields(*database_name*,*table_name*[, *link_identifier*])

Description: Lists MySQL columns in a given table.

Retrieves information about table *table_name* in database *database_name* and returns a result pointer. This pointer (denoted in this appendix by *result*) can then be passed to other functions to extract information on column names, lengths, types, and flags.

```
$f = mysql_list_fields ("some_db", "some_table");
```

See also: mysql_field_flags(), mysql_field_len(), mysql_field_name(), mysql_field_type()

mysql_list_tables(*database_name*,[,*link_identifier*])

Description: Lists tables in a MySQL database.

Retrieves information about database *database_name* and returns a result pointer. This pointer (denoted in this appendix by *result*) can then be passed to mysql_tablename(), which returns information on table names.

Example:

```
$result = mysql_list_tables ("products_db");
while ($row = mysql_fetch_row ($result)) {
    echo "$row[0]<BR>\n";
}
```

See also: mysql_field_flags(), mysql_field_len(), mysql_field_name(), mysql_field_type()

mysql_num_fields(*result*)

Description: Returns the number of fields in a resultset given by *result*.

See also: mysql_fetch_field(), mysql_num_rows()

mysql_num_rows(*result*)

Description: Returns (as an integer) the number of rows resulting from a query that retrieved data (such as a SELECT).

result must be specified, referring to a resource identifier returned from a mysql_query() or similar.

Example:

```
$result = mysql_query("SELECT * FROM some_table WHERE some_value > 10");
$num_rows = mysql_num_rows($result);
```

See also: mysql_affected_rows()

D

mysql_pconnect([*server*[,*username*[,*password*]]])

Description: Opens a persistent connection to a MySQL server. Returns a resource identifier (referred to as *link_identifier* in this appendix) if a connection is made successfully, or FALSE otherwise.

server can be specified (optionally including :*port* for a port number, and optionally :*/path/to/socket* to give the path to a Unix socket), defaulting to localhost:3306 if not specified.

username can be specified, defaulting to the Unix user running the database server process if not given.

password can be specified, defaulting to the empty password if not given.

A persistent connection is held open even if mysql_close() is encountered or execution of the script finishes. The next time a script tries to do a mysql_pconnect() using the same connection parameters, if it can find an existing link with these parameters, that link will be used again.

Note that if the connection fails to be made, FALSE is returned and an error message is generated. This error message can be suppressed by prefixing the function with a @.

Example:

```
$link_id = @mysql_pconnect ("localhost", "the_user", "my_password");
if ($link_id) {
    echo "Link id is $link_id<BR>\n";
} else {
    echo "Failed to connect<BR>\n";
}
```

See also: mysql_select_db(), mysql_connect()

mysql_query(*query*[,*link_identifier*][,*result_mode*])

Description: Sends a query to the currently selected MySQL database on the MySQL server specified by *link_identifier*. If *link_identifier* is not specified, the last opened database connection is used.

The string *query* must be specified (without a semicolon at the end, as might be used with the mysql client program).

result_mode may optionally be specified, as either MYSQL_STORE_RESULT or MYSQL_USE_RESULT. Unspecified (the most commonly used form), it defaults to MYSQL_STORE_RESULT, which buffers the result on the client.

For queries that return a resultset (SELECT, SHOW, DESCRIBE, and so on), mysql_query() returns a resource identifier (called *result* in this appendix) if the query executes correctly (even if there is nothing in the resultset), or FALSE if there is an error. After calling mysql_query() and getting a valid result, *result* is usually passed to mysql_fetch_array() to process the resultset.

For queries that return no resultset (INSERT, UPDATE, and so on), mysql_query() returns TRUE if the query executes correctly (even if no data is modified), or FALSE if there is an error.

Examples:

```
// Example of bad query
if (!$result = mysql_query("SELECT nonsense FROM no_table WHERE 1")) {
    // this query fails
    print "An error occurred: \n".mysql_error()."\n";
}

// Example of query which returns a result set
$sql = "SELECT * FROM some_table";
if ($result = mysql_query($sql)) {
    // this query succeeds and produces a result set
    while ($row = mysql_fetch_array($result) {
        // process result set...
    }
} else {
    print "An error occurred in $sql: \n".mysql_error()."\n";
}

// Example of query which returns no result set
$sql = "DELETE FROM some_table WHERE id=101";
if (mysql_query($sql)) {
    // this query succeeds but produces no result set
    $aff = mysql_affected_rows();
    print $aff." rows deleted.\n";
} else {
    print "An error occurred in $sql: \n".mysql_error()."\n";
}
```

See also: mysql_affected_rows(), mysql_fetch_array(), mysql_num_rows()

mysql_real_escape_string(*raw_string*[, *link_identifier*])

Description: Escapes special characters in a string given by *raw_string* for use in a SQL statement.

Returns the escaped string with special characters escaped; safe to be passed on to mysql_query(). Takes into account the current character set of the connection (either the current active connection, or that given by *link_identifier*).

See also: addslashes(), mysql_escape_string()

mysql_result(*result*,*row_offset*[,*field*])

Description: Returns the contents of one cell of a result given by *result*, whose row in the resultset is given by the integer *row_offset*.

field can be used to specify the numeric offset of the field, the name of the field, the aliased name (which should be used if that column has been aliased), or the dotted name of the field (*table_name.field_name*).

Note: Although `mysql_result()` is efficient if you need to retrieve only one cell from a resultset, repeated calls to `mysql_result()` are not as efficient as using `mysql_fetch_array()`, `mysql_fetch_row()`, and `mysql_fetch_object()`.

See also: `mysql_fetch_array()`, `mysql_fetch_row()`, `mysql_fetch_object()`

mysql_select_db(*database_name*[,*link_identifier*])

Description: Selects a MySQL database.

`mysql_select_db()` sets *database_name* as the current active database to associate with *link_identifier*. If *link_identifier* is not given, it assumes the last opened MySQL connection.

Returns TRUE on success, or FALSE otherwise.

Example:

```
if (mysql_select_db ("products_db")) {
    echo "Connected to products!<BR>\n";
}
```

mysql_tablename(*result*,*offset*)

Description: Returns the table name of a field in a result.

After calling `mysql_list_tables()`, which returns a resource identifier given by *result*, `mysql_tablename()` returns the name of the table indexed by *offset*.

Example:

```
$result = mysql_list_tables ("products_db");
for ($i = 0; $i < mysql_num_rows ($result); $i++) {
    echo mysql_tablename ($result, $i)."<BR>\n";
}
```

See also: `mysql_list_tables()`

mysql_unbuffered_query(*query*[,*link_identifier*] [,*result_mode*])

Description: Sends a query to the currently selected MySQL database on the MySQL server specified by *link_identifier*, without fetching and buffering the resultset rows automatically. If *link_identifier* is not specified, the last opened database connection is used.

result_mode may optionally be specified, as either MYSQL_USE_RESULT or MYSQL_STORE_RESULT. Unspecified (the most commonly used form), it defaults to MYSQL_USE_RESULT, which does not buffer the result on the client. This default behavior is the opposite of mysql_query().

By not buffering on the client, memory is saved. However, you have to fetch all result rows before a second query can be issued, and you cannot use functions that work on the entire resultset, such as mysql_num_rows().

In other ways, mysql_unbuffered_query() works like mysql_query(), which you should see for examples.

See also: mysql_query()

D

INDEX

Symbols

+ (addition) operator, 179, 493

= (assignment) operator, 212

* (asterisk)
  search modifier, 147
  wildcard, 129

& (bitwise AND) operator, 185, 491

~ (bitwise inversion) operator, 492

<< (bitwise left-shift) operator, 185, 492

| (bitwise OR) operator, 185, 492

>> (bitwise right-shift) operator, 185, 492

^ (caret), 183

/ (division) operator, 179, 493

$ (dollar sign), 183, 209

" (double quotes), 147, 208

= (equals) operator, 177, 494

> (greater than) operator, 495

> (greater than) search modifier, 147

>= (greater than or equal to) operator, 178, 495

- (hyphen) search modifier, 147

< (less than) operator, 178, 495

<= (less than or equal to) operator, 177-178, 495

< (less than) search modifier, 147

&& (logical AND) operator, 181, 491

|| (logical OR) operator, 181, 492

% (modulo) operator, 180, 494

* (multiplication) operator, 179, 493

! (NOT) operator, 180, 493

<> (not equal) operator, 494

<=> (NULL-safe equals) operator, 177, 494

% (percent sign) wildcard, 181

+ (plus sign) search modifier, 147

-? (question mark) option
  myisamchk, 346
  mysqlimport, 119

() search modifier, 147

; (semicolon), 92

' (single quotes, 208

- (subtraction) operator, 180, 493

A